Henrikke Baumann &

The Hitch Hiker's Guide to LCA

An orientation in life cycle assessment
methodology and application

Studentlitteratur

Illustrations in Chapter 13 by Anna Kellström

 Copying prohibited

The papers and inks used in this product are eco-friendly.

Art. No 31027
ISBN 978-91-44-02364-9
Edition 1:7

© The authors and Studentlitteratur 2004
www.studentlitteratur.se
Studentlitteratur AB, Lund

Cover design by Henry Sivula

Printed by Holmbergs i Malmö AB, Sweden 2012

Contents

Part 3
LCA applications

6

Excerpt from *The Hitch Hiker's Guide to the Galaxy* by Douglas Adams

Chapter 27

...

There was a moment's expectant pause whilst panels slowly came to life on the front of the console. Lights flashed on and off experimentally and settled down into a businesslike pattern. A soft low hum came from the communication channel.

'Good-morning,' said Deep Thought at last.

'Er... Good-morning, O Deep Thought,' said Loonquawl nervously, 'do you have... er, that is...'

'An answer for you?' interrupted Deep Thought majestically. 'Yes. I have.'

The two men shivered with expectancy. Their waiting had not been in vain.

'There really is one?' breathed Phouchg.

'There really is one,' confirmed Deep Thought.

'To Everything? To the great Question of Life, the Universe and Everything?'

'Yes.'

Both of the men had been trained for this moment, their lives had been in preparation for it, they had been selected at birth as those who would witness the answer, but even so they found themselves gasping and squirming like excited children.

'And you're ready to give it to us?' urged Loonquawl.

'I am.'

'Now?'

'Now,' said Deep Thought.

They both licked their dry lips.

'Though I don't think,' added Deep Thought, 'that you're going to like it.'

'Doesn't matter,' said Phouchg. 'We must know it! Now!'

'Now?' inquired Deep Thought.

'Yes! Now...'

'All right,' said the computer and settled into silence again. The two men fidgeted. The tension was unbearable.

'You're really not going to like it,' observed Deep Thought.

'Tell us!'

'All right,' said Deep Thought. 'The Answer to the Great Question...'

'Yes...!'

'Of Life, the Universe and Everything...' said Deep Thought.

'Yes...!'

'Is...'

'Yes...!!!...?'

'Forty-two,' said Deep Thought, with infinite majesty and calm.

Chapter 28

It was a long long time before anyone spoke.

Out of the corner of his eye Phouchg could see the sea of tense expectant faces down in the square outside.

'We're going to get lynched aren't we?' he whispered.

'It was a tough assessment,' said Deep Thought mildly.

'Forty-two!' yelled Loonquawl. 'Is that all you've got to show for seven and a half million years' work?'

'I checked it very thoroughly,' said the computer, 'and that quite definitely is the answer. I think the problem, to be quite honest with you, is that you've never actually known what the question is.'

...

Foreword

The environmental life cycle of a product consists of all the stages from raw material extraction to its waste management. Life cycle assessment, then, is the assessment of the environmental impact of a product across its life cycle. The holistic environmental perspective that LCA provides on products has made it a central concept for both environmental management in industry and environmental policy-making in public government. The holistic perspective is also an ambitious one and as such it puts taxing requirements on the methodology for describing, comparing and evaluating complex product chains with diverse environmental impacts. Without a clear life cycle logic, one may end up in the same predicament as the characters portrayed in the quoted passage from Douglas Adams' book.

Replace Deep Thought with an LCA software/analyst and replace Loonquawl and Phouchg with two commissioners of an LCA study. The text then describes a not unusual situation, which has been the object for jokes for a long time in the LCA community. The joke, unfortunately, is well grounded in reality. Many an expectant LCA commissioner have enthusiastically hoped for a simple answer to their environmental dilemmas, only to become disappointed when obtaining answers with little meaning to them. Unless their dilemmas are better expressed, i.e. as well defined questions, answers will remain as obscure as "42".

So, when deciding to write a textbook, we wanted to give a basis for developing the ability to pose questions and the capability to answer them. In LCA language, this means the ability to make methodological choices that are relevant with respect to the goal of an LCA study. Knowledge of the broad repertoire of methodological alternatives and their different consequences will give a key to interpreting what "42" actually stands for.

The title to our textbook, then, came by itself, as a paraphrase on Douglas Adams' famous story.

The book is organised in three parts covering *LCA methodology*, *LCA applications* and *exercises* on LCA. Two introductory chapters give a general overview of the LCA concept and its historical development. After that, LCA methodology is described in detail in chapters 3 to 8. Different fields for LCA application are covered in chapters 9 to 13. Each chapter covers a different area of industrial activity, e.g. product development, marketing, production and waste management. Each type of activity has its own set of issues and problems and consequently its special requirements on LCA methodology, albeit they all share the logic of the cradle-to-grave perspective.

Since the aim of the book is to teach the execution of LCA, there are also a number of *exercises*, both smaller and larger ones. The smaller ones (exercises A to G) train different aspects of LCA methodology and prepare for the larger ones, ten complete LCA exercise projects (H1 to H10). From our experience of teaching LCA, we have seen that learning by doing is an effective way towards becoming able to independently carry out LCA studies. The exercise projects are complete projects, based on real LCA studies, with all the necessary data provided, but small enough so that they can be calculated by hand and with the help of simple spreadsheet software. This allows for full control over modelling, methodological choices and data. Data is somewhat dated but this has little importance from the point of view of learning to execute LCA.

It is important to point out that this book is a *textbook* intended for the LCA beginner, and not a research review for advanced LCA researchers, nor a rule-describing manual. There are already a number of LCA manuals and even a set of guidelines in the form of an international LCA standard. The descriptions of LCA methodology in these are often detailed and rule-oriented. Unfortunately for the LCA beginner, they are also too general in character. It is implicitly assumed that the reader has knowledge of what guides and defines methodological choices in practical LCA application. The publication of an LCA standard evidences that LCA methodology has reached certain maturity and stability even if research concerning LCA is diverse and still growing. Hovever, our aim has not been to give a complete account of all past and on-going research that

10

have shaped the present state of LCA methodology. Instead, the main focus of the text is to convey an LCA logic and present the principles of methodological alternatives and different applications. With regard to the state of research, the ambition of the book is to present the main line of arguments and trends in LCA development. Moreover, in line with the above, general life cycle inventory and impact assessment data listed in the appendices are selected for the purpose of the exercises. For complete lists, it is advisable to turn to the original sources.

Many find the LCA methodology somewhat complicated, but this is more a case of LCA reflecting the complexities of our world. LCA is very good at that. However, in the systematic study that discovers and "untangles" such complexities lies a deep satisfaction. We hope that this book will convey a joy of discovery propelled by the unfolding of an LCA logic, rather than the dogmatism of rules. We wish all students good luck and bon voyage in their explorations of the environmental dimension of 'life, the universe and everything' with LCA as their vehicle. You will see that there is much more than "42" to it.

Göteborg, September 2003

Henrikke Baumann & Anne-Marie Tillman

List of abbreviations

ADI	Acceptable daily intake
AP	Acidification potential
BAT	Best available technology
BOD	Biological oxygen demand
BUS	Bundesamt für Umweltschutz, Switzerland
BUWAL	Bundesamt für Umwelt, Wald und Landschaft, Switzerland
CFC	Chloro-fluoro carbon, also known as freon
CH_4	Methane
CML	Centre of Environmental Science, Leiden University, the Netherlands
CO	Carbon monoxide
CO_2	Carbon dioxide
COD	Chemical oxygen demand
CPM	Centre for Environmental Assessment of Product and Material Systems, Chalmers University of Technology, Sweden
DfE	Design for Environment
EDIP	Environmental Design of Industrial Products
EEA	European Environmental Agency
ELU	Environmental load unit
EPD	Environmental product declaration
EPS	Environmental Priority Strategies in product design
ET	Environmental Theme
ETH	Swiss Federal Institute of Technology
GEN	Global Eco-labelling Network
GIS	Geographical Information System
GWP	Global warming potential
HC	Hydrocarbon
HCl	Hydrogen chloride, hydrochloric acid

HTP	Human toxicity potential
IEA	International Energy Agency
IFP	Swedish Institute for Fibres and Polymers
IPCC	Intergovernmental Panel on Climate Change
IPP	EU directive on Integrated Product Policy
IPPC	EU directive on Intergrated Pollution Prevention and Control
ISO	International Organization for Standardization
ISO/TR	International Organization for Standardization/ Technical Requirements
ISO/TS	International Organization for Standardization/ Technical Specification
LCA	Life cycle assessment
LCI	Life cycle inventory
LCIA	Life cycle impact assessment
LCM	Life cycle management
LGUT	Landis & Gyr Utilities
MCDA	Multi-criteria decision analysis
MIPS	Material intensity per service unit
MRI	Midwest Research Institute
MSR	Miljöstyrningsrådet, Swedish Environmental Management Council
NMVOC	Non-methane volatile organic carbon
NO_x	Nitrogen oxides, i.e. NO and NO_2
NPK	Nitrogen – phosphorus – potassium fertiliser
NTM	Nätverket för transporter och miljö, the Swedish Network for Transport and the Environment
ODP	Ozone depletion potential
OECD	Organisation for Economic Co-operation and Development
PAH	Polyaromatic hydrocarbons
PDI	Predicted daily intake
PE	Polyethylene
PEC	Predicted environmental concentration
PET	Polyethylene terephtalate
PNEC	Predicted no-effect concentration
POCP	Photo-oxidant creation potential
PS	Polystyrene
PSR	Product specific rule

14

PVC	Polyvinyl chloride
REPA	Resource and environmental profile analysis
SETAC	Society of Environmental Toxicology and Chemistry
SETAC-WIA2	Society of Environmental Toxicology and Chemistry, 2nd working group on impact assessment
SO_2	Sulphur dioxide
SPI	Sustainable process index
SPOLD	Society for the Promotion of Life Cycle Development
Tot-N	Total nitrogen
Tot-P	Total phosporus
UCPTE	Union pour la co-ordination de la production et du transport de l'électricité
UNEP	United Nations Environmental Programme
US-EPA	Environmental Protection Agency of the United States
VOC	Volatile organic carbons
WBCSD	World Business Council for Sustainable Development
WICE	World Industry Council for the Environment, International Chamber of Commerce
WMO	World Meteorological Organisation

Part 1
Introduction to LCA

The LCA concept is presented in the first two chapters. Chapter 1 gives a rudimentary description of LCA methodology. Chapter 2 describes the historical development of the LCA concept. Chapter 2 also presents an overview of the use of LCA, both concerning different fields of application and in relation to other environmental tools.

1 LCA in a nutshell

The environmental challenge of turning the consumer society in a more sustainable direction is tremendous. In this context, life cycle assessment (LCA) has been brought forward as an important and comprehensive method for analysis of the environmental impact of products and services. In an LCA study, the whole industrial system involved in the production, use and waste management of a product or service is described. It would be daunting to launch straight into the detailed description of such an ambitious method as LCA. Instead, the basic characteristics of LCA will be presented in this introduction to the method. The rest of the book enters more deeply into different parts of LCA methodology and different types of LCA applications.

1.1 What is LCA?

What is LCA? The three letters stand for *Life Cycle Assessment*, but what does it mean? The concept of a product life cycle can be understood intuitively. It means that a product is followed from its "cradle" where raw materials are extracted from natural resources through production and use to its "grave", the disposal. In environmental life cycle assessment, natural resource use and pollutant emission are described in quantitative terms as shown in the left part of figure 1.1. However, LCA is more than that. It can also be described as a whole procedure for how such studies are done and interpreted, as illustrated in the right part of figure 1.1. First, the product to study and the purpose of the LCA are specified in the goal and scope definition. Inventory analysis implies the construction of the life cycle model and calculation of the emissions pro-

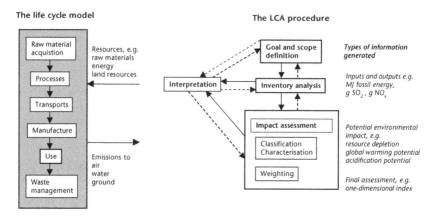

Figure 1.1 *The life cycle model and the LCA procedure. In the <u>model</u>, boxes indicate physical processes and arrows flows of energy and matter whereas in the <u>procedure</u> the boxes indicate procedural steps and the arrows the order in which these are performed. Broken arrows indicate possible iterations.*

duced and the resources used during the life cycle. In the impact assessment phase, the emissions and resources are related to various environmental problems through the act of classification and characterisation. Finally, the different environmental impacts related to the life cycle may be put on the same scale through weighting.

Before we give a basic description of LCA modelling and LCA procedure, let us first look into what LCA can be used for.

What is LCA good for?

It takes a lot of effort to do an LCA study, exploring large industrial systems, collecting and analysing a lot of environmental information. In practice, this can seem to be an overwhelming task and one may wonder why one should bother with it.

One of the reasons for undertaking an LCA study is that there are growing concerns about a variety of environmental issues as expressed by public opinion, political bodies and industry. Environmental concern may be related to the long-term resource base of human societies or may be more health related or it may be a concern for the natural environment as such. Whatever the reasons for people's environmental concerns, they result in actions, e.g. regulation, environmental adaptation of industry, change of personal lifestyle, etc. But how can we know which course of action is more "environmentally friendly" and which is less? Clearly we need assessment tools as well as structured ways to think about the environment. LCA is one such assessment tool, useful for the environmental assessment of *products*.

The strength of LCA is that it studies a whole product system. This enables us to avoid the sub-optimisation that may be the result if only a few processes are focused on. The results are related to the function of a product, which allows comparisons between alternatives. It is an engineering tool in the sense that technical systems and potential changes in them are studied. At the same time, the tool is multi-disciplinary in the sense that also impacts on the natural environment and even people's relations to such impacts are modelled.

Since a whole life cycle is studied, LCA is not site specific. Thus, environmental impact cannot be modelled at a very detailed level. Economical and social aspects are not included in LCA other than when used as a basis for weighting. Risk is another matter not dealt with in LCA.

There is an international standard for LCA that lists the following applications: identification of improvement possibilities, decision making, choice of environmental performance indicators and market claims (ISO 14040 1997). Another important application of LCA is that of learning, e.g. exploring the environmental properties of the product system studied and learning about the relationships of the production system (Baumann 1998). All these applications aim at change or improvement, some in more direct ways (decision making), some in more indirect ways through influencing market behaviour or through identifying improvement possibilities. Applications of LCA are summarised and categorised in table 1.1.

Table 1.1 LCA applications.

Decision making, e.g.	product design and development process design and development purchasing support for regulatory measures and policy instruments
Learning/exploration, e.g.	characterisation of production systems identification of improvement possibilities selection of environmental performance indicators
Communication, e.g.	LCA-based eco-labelling environmental product declarations benchmarking

The international standards for LCA and other LCA guidelines

As already mentioned, there is a series of international standards for LCA, ISO 14040–14043, which was issued from 1997 onwards. In the umbrella document, ISO 14040 (1997), LCA is defined through the procedure for performing an LCA.

> "LCA is a technique for assessing the environmental aspects and potential impacts associated with a product by:
>
> - compiling an inventory of relevant inputs and outputs of a product system;
> - evaluating the potential environmental impacts associated with those inputs and outputs;
> - interpreting the results of the inventory analysis and impact assessment phases in relation to the objectives of the study."

In addition it is stated that LCA describes environmental aspects and potential impacts throughout a product's *life cycle*, i.e. raw material acquisition, production, use and disposal. Resource use, human health and ecological consequences are the three general impact categories to be considered (ISO 14040 1997). In LCA the concept *product* refers not only to material products but also to services.

There are also a number of more practical guidelines on how to conduct an LCA such as the SETAC Code of Practice (SETAC 1993) and guidelines for environmental LCA from the Netherlands (CML/ NOH 1992), the Nordic countries (Nord 1995), Denmark (EDIP 1997) and the US (US-EPA 1993). Most of the guidelines were written before the standard was issued and they made important contributions to the development of the standard. The Dutch guidelines have been up-dated to an operational guide to the ISO standards (CML 2002). The guidelines are more detailed in their recommendations than the standard and most of them include data for impact assessment. Some of them explicitly support LCA for a specific purpose. For example, the Danish EDIP method (EDIP 1997) was designed for product development purposes and the Nordic Guidelines are guidelines on how to perform a "key issue identification" LCA (Nord 1995).

Terminology differs a bit between the guidelines since most of them were written before or in parallel with the standard. Neither do the manuals nor the standard always make a clear distinction between the procedure for doing an LCA (sequence of activities, parties involved, etc.), modelling requirements (e.g. system boundaries), and reporting requirements (e.g. transparency). A quick comparison of the different LCA documents can be quite confusing unless one is well versed in LCA terminology and has followed the scientific debate on LCA methodology over the years.

1.2 LCA methodology in short

In this section we briefly look into what is included in the main phases of the LCA procedure: the goal and scope definition, inventory analysis and impact assessment. These brief presentations are intended to give an overview. Chapters 3 to 8 give more detailed descriptions of LCA methodology.

Two LCA case studies will be used as examples. One of them is a study carried out by Akzo Nobel Surface Chemistry on two detergents (Arvidsson 1995). The other is a packaging study conducted on behalf of the Swedish Ministry of Environment (Tillman et al. 1991). There will be no discussion of these results in this chapter, but we will return to the examples in chapter 6 on interpretation. In the last part of this chapter we will look into some crucial aspects of

LCA methodology, aspects that a reader of an LCA should be aware of and ready to ask questions about so as not to misinterpret the meaning of the results of an LCA.

Goal and scope definition

In the goal and scope definition the product to be studied and the purpose of the study are decided on. According to the ISO standard (ISO 14040 1997) the goal definition includes stating the intended application of the study, the reason for carrying it out and to whom the results are intended to be communicated. The standard stresses that the goal and scope of an LCA study must be clearly defined and consistent with the intended application.

When an LCA study is initiated the purpose is often formulated very vaguely and generally. Initially it may be expressed as "We want to do an LCA on our product" or "We want to show the environmental advantages of this product". Before an LCA can be performed, the problem formulation needs to be specified more clearly than that. Examples of such more specific questions are: "Which are the main environmental problems in this product's life cycle?" or "Of these three options, which is the environmentally preferred modification to this process?"

In our example detergent study (Arvidsson 1995) the specified purpose was

1 to perform an inventory of all ingredients in two different detergents,
2 to compare two different detergent formulations with respect to environmental impact and
3 to identify the activities in the life cycle making the largest contributions to the total environmental impact.

In the remaining parts of the goal and scope definition, the *context* of the study is defined, for example to whom and how the results are to be communicated. *Specifications of the modelling* to be performed are also made and the *project is planned.*

One example of such modelling specification is the choice of functional unit. LCA relates environmental impact to a product or

© The authors and Studentlitteratur

rather to the function of a product system. Thus, there is a need to express the function in quantitative terms, as a functional unit. Examples of functional units are

- Beverage packaging   litres of packaged drink
- Decoration material (paint, flooring,
  etc.) $m^2 \times$ year
- Passenger transportation   person $\times$ km

In the detergent study, 100 kg of clean laundry was used as a functional unit. It was assumed that the two detergents were equivalent concerning function, that is, cleaning efficiency. However, some of the comparisons were made on the basis of 1 kg of detergent since the same dosage was recommended for the two compared products.

Many other choices related to the modelling are made during the goal and scope definition. They are listed in the following and further described in section 1.4 and chapter 3.

- System boundaries, such as which processes to include. The choices of what to study are made during goal and scope definition and govern the system boundaries of the flow model constructed in the subsequent inventory analysis.
- Types of environmental impacts being considered. There is a more or less default list of impacts which are considered in most LCAs, including for example resource use, global warming, acidification and eutrophication, but sometimes LCAs are limited to covering only certain impacts. The chosen impacts determine the parameters for which data will be collected during inventory analysis.
- Level of detail in the study and thus the requirements on the data (e.g. whether to use site specific data or data describing an average over a number of production sites).

Inventory analysis

Inventory analysis means to build a systems model according to the requirements of the goal and scope definition. The systems model is a flow model of a technical system with certain types of system boundaries ("cradle-to-grave") as shown in figure 1.1. The result is an *incomplete* mass and energy balance for the system. It is incomplete in the sense that only the environmentally *relevant* flows are considered, which more or less include use of scarce resources and emissions of substances considered harmful. Environmentally indifferent flows such as water vapour emissions from combustion and industrial surplus heat are disregarded.

Activities of the life cycle inventory analysis (LCI) are described briefly in the following and in more detail in chapter 4. They include the following:

1 Construction of the flow model according to the system boundaries decided on in the goal and scope definition. The flow model is usually documented as a flowchart that shows the activities included in the analysed system (production, processes, transports, use and waste management) and the flows between these activities. Figure 1.2 shows an example of such a flowchart taken from the detergent LCA (Arvidsson 1995).

2 Data collection for all the activities (processes and transports) in the product system. The collected data include inputs and outputs of all activities such as

   • raw materials, including energy carriers,
   • products and
   • solid waste and emissions to air and water.

3 Calculation of the amount of resource use and pollutant emission of the system in relation to the functional unit. Table 1.2 shows results from the example detergent LCA (Arvidsson 1995) to give an idea of the type of parameters used in a life cycle inventory. The number of parameters was even larger in the original study and only a selection is shown here.

Inventory results are often presented as bar charts and other types of graphic presentation. You will find examples of different ways to present LCA results in chapter 6.

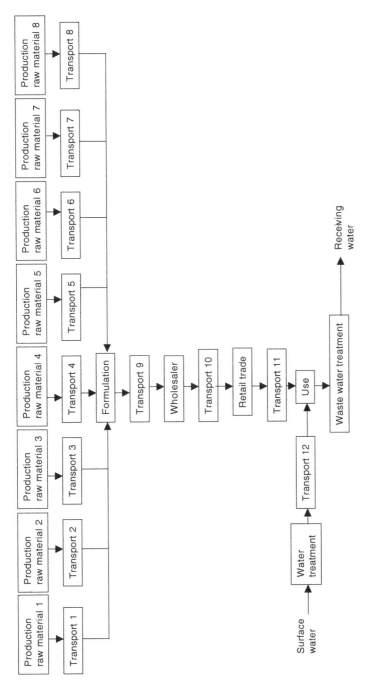

Figure 1.2 Flowchart for the life cycle of a detergent (Arvidsson 1995). This is a simplified flowchart–a much more detailed one was used when the study was conducted.

	Detergent 1	Detergent 2	Unit
Energy consumption			
Fossil	11.6	9.7	MJ
Electricity	4.4	3.3	MJ
Inherent	3.6	2.8	MJ
Renewable	1.0	0.6	MJ
Resource use			
Oil	0.36	0.29	kg
P	33	44	g
S	0.6	0.3	g
Al	0.048	0.04	g
Emissions to air			
CO_2	1.5	1.4	kg
Particles	24.5	30.4	g
NO_x	5.3	4.4	g
Ashes	5.2	5.4	g
Fluorides	3.8	5.1	g
SO_2	3.8	2.9	g
HC	2.4	1.5	g
CO	0.9	1.0	g
NH_3	0.9	1.0	g
CH_4	0.4	0.6	g
HAc	0.2	0.001	g
Acetaldehyde	0.0043	0.0043	g
Ethylene oxide	0.0024	0.0031	g
Hg	1.9×10^{-6}	1.2×10^{-5}	g
HCFC	3.1×10^{-7}	5.6×10^{-7}	g
Emissions to water			
Gypsum	370	500	g
TSS	6.3	5.0	g
Fluorides	5.7	7.6	g
COD	4.1	1.2	g
TDS	0.3	0.2	g
Tot-N	0.3	0.2	g
SO_4	0.2	0.3	g
DSS	0.2	0.2	g
BOD	0.3	0.2	g
H_2SO_4	0.1	0.2	g
Oil	0.014	0.014	g
Heavy metals	0.022	0.03	g
MCA	0.011	0.006	g
HC	0.0018	0.0020	g
Tot-P	0.0010	0.0010	g
DSO	3.0×10^{-4}	–	g
Phenol	5.4×10^{-5}	5.6×10^{-5}	g
Waste			
Solid, unspecified	530	520	g
Organic	8.9	1.7	g
Mineral	0.5	0.5	g
Radioactive	0.043	0.035	g

Table 1.2 Inventory analysis results from a comparative study of two detergents (Arvidsson 1995). Results are given per functional unit (1 kg of detergent). They represent a cradle-to-gate system, which means that all the activities in figure 1.2 are included, except product use and waste water treatment. It should be noted that the data underlying these results were collected during 1994 and may have changed considerably since then.

Inventory analysis may seem very straightforward but usually it is complicated by the fact that many technical processes produce more than one product. The environmental load of such processes may be *allocated*, i.e. *partitioned* between its different products. There are also other ways to deal with multiple functions. Allocations complicate life cycle inventories considerably. We will discuss allocation and related matters further in this chapter in section 1.4 and in more detail in chapter 4.

Impact assessment

Life Cycle Impact Assessment (LCIA) aims to describe, or at least to indicate, the impacts of the environmental loads quantified in the inventory analysis. One purpose of the LCIA is thus to turn the inventory results into more environmentally relevant information, i.e. information on impacts on the environment rather than just information on emissions and resource use. Another purpose, per- · haps less often stated, is to aggregate the information from the LCI in fewer parameters as indicated in figure 1.3.

The first step – *classification* – simply means sorting the inventory parameters according to the type of environmental impact they contribute to. In the next step – *characterisation* – the relative contributions of the emissions and resource consumptions to each type of environmental impact are calculated. For example, all emissions of greenhouse gases may be aggregated into one indicator for global warming and all acidifying emissions into one indicator for acidification. Such calculations are based on scientific models of cause-effect chains in the natural systems. However, the cause-effect models used in LCIA are sometimes very simplified. This is further described and discussed in chapter 5.

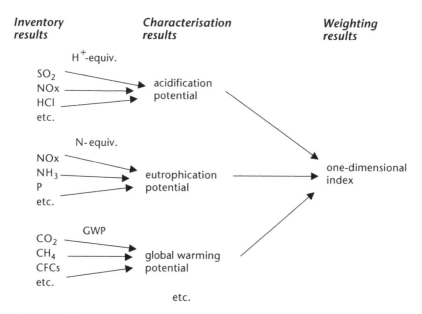

Figure 1.3 Illustration of the stepwise aggregation of information in LCA.

In spite of uncertainties and other limitations of characterisation, the numerous result parameters of an LCA may be aggregated into a limited number of impact categories. Sometimes these results need to be interpreted and aggregated even further. This can be done in different ways, for instance with formalised and quantitative weighting procedures or through using expert panels or with qualitative, verbal argumentation, to name a few. In no case can this be done based solely on natural science but values must be introduced. Such a weighting method can be described as a "yardstick" with which all environmental problems are measured. Such "yardsticks" are based on values and preferences concerning environmental issues expressed by people. For example, political environmental goals may be used to create a weighting system. There are several other options, as further discussed in chapter 5.

Life cycle impact assessment is thus a stepwise aggregation of the information given by the inventory results as illustrated in figure 1.3. Classification and characterisation are compulsory in LCA according to the standard (ISO 14042 2000) whereas weighting is

30

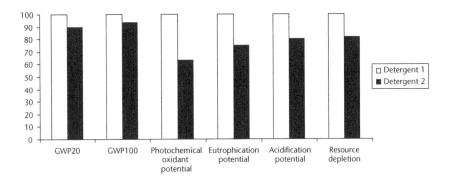

Figure 1.4 Example of characterisation results from a comparative study of two detergents (Arvidsson 1995). The results from this particular study were presented as relative values. Not all possible impact categories were evaluated.

optional. If no impact assessment is performed, but only an inventory, the study is referred to as an LCI (life cycle inventory analysis).

Classification results for the detergent study are shown in figure 1.4 (Arvidsson 1995). As the study was a comparative one, the results are presented as relative values, i.e. the highest score for each category is given the value 100.

1.3 LCA and environmental systems analysis

LCA belongs to a whole family of environmental assessment tools, some more focused on physical metrics such as Environmental Impact Assessment (EIA), Ecological Risk Assessment (ERA) and Material Flow Analysis (MFA) and others more focused on economic metrics such as Cost-Benefit Analysis (CBA). Together they are often called environmental systems analysis tools. In the following we will discuss how LCA relates to environmental systems analysis in general.

Figure 1.5 shows a general framework for environmental systems analysis depicting the social system, the technical system and the natural system and the relationships between them. As we will see, LCA methodology fits well within this framework.

Technical systems are the kind of systems focused on in LCA and they are modelled in the inventory analysis. However, technical systems do not exist in isolation. They exist to supply people, i.e. social systems, with products and services and they are also managed and controlled by social systems. Thus, information about technical systems generated by LCA studies must be meaningful to the people and organisations controlling them, and sometimes also to other stakeholders.

Technical systems use resources from natural systems and they release pollutants and wastes to the natural systems, which causes changes in them. Such changes are modelled in the characterisation. To what extent changes in natural systems are interpreted as environmental problems is a matter for social systems to decide, which means that weighting methods are models reflecting people's values and preferences regarding the environment.

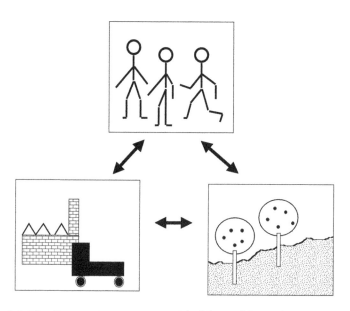

Figure 1.5 The three systems represented in LCA and in environmental systems analysis in general.

Since LCA models all three systems, it needs to be multi-disciplinary. Inventory analysis requires engineering skills, whereas impact assessment relies on natural science. Even social sciences must be involved, for instance in understanding the context in which LCA is used and to perform weighting.

1.4 Pay attention to ...

There are a number of issues the reader of an LCA should bear in mind in order to interpret the information correctly and to be critical. First of all, there is no such thing as stand-alone LCA results, only LCA results in relation to a goal definition with a specific purpose. An LCA tries to answer certain questions, and methodology is chosen to answer the questions posed. Other choices of methodology lead to other numerical results and usually mean that answers are given to other questions. As a reader one should be aware that such choices may be more or less appropriately made. The four most critical choices of methodology, *definition of functional unit, system boundaries and allocation procedure, type of data used* and *impact assessment* are presented in this section.

Functional unit

To critically check the functional unit is always useful. What is the functional unit that the results of the study are related to? Is it a relevant one? Does it allow fair comparison? It is worth noticing that in a comparative study, the compared products are seldom exactly identical. They may not be of equal quality or one of the products may have additional functions. This complicates the definition of the functional unit, especially when the differences are difficult to capture in numbers.

Consider for example a study where wood and concrete floor constructions are compared. The functional unit may be based on the load bearing capacity of the constructions. However, there are more functions than load bearing to a floor construction, such as noise reduction and fire protection. In a comparative study, differences in these properties may either be tolerated (and hopefully remembered when the results are interpreted) or the compared constructions may be made functionally equal through complementing the wood construction with insulating materials. The latter option is preferable from an LCA point of view. However, it may lead to technically unreasonable assumptions and a compromise may have to be made.

It should be remembered that the functional unit does not relate to production or consumption volumes, only to product function. This means that mainstream LCA methodology does not allow for analysis of consequences of changes in production or consumption volume. In the future, this may change since research is being done both on merging LCA with national production statistics and on dynamic LCA modelling.

System boundaries and allocation

Inventory analysis is complicated by life cycles of different products being connected to each other, since an LCA focuses on a single product at a time. This raises several issues about the system boundaries for an LCA study. A particular problem is related to the fact that more than one product is often produced in a process. The same type of problem arises when many different products are collectively treated in the same waste treatment process. When products are recycled, even the same material is used consecutively in different products. This particular problem is called an *allocation problem*, i.e. how to relate or ascribe the environmental loads of shared processes to the products delivered. Most LCA guidelines, including the ISO standard (ISO 14041 1998), address the allocation problem through recommending an *allocation procedure*. It is usually expressed in terms of "If you are able to deal with the allocation problem in such and such manner, do so. If not, use this alternative manner". *Allocation*, as such, is defined as "partitioning the input or output flows of a process to the product system under study" (ISO 14040 1997).

Having defined the allocation problem and terminology, let us discuss allocation in relation to an example. The example is a study of packaging commissioned by national authorities wanting sup-

34   © The authors and Studentlitteratur

port for regulations on treatment of packaging waste (Tillman et al. 1991). The goal definition may be phrased as follows: What are the environmental differences between the following alternative treatments of packaging waste:

- Landfilling
- Incineration with heat recovery
- Material recycling
- Reuse

The life cycles of the packaging materials were modelled as in figure 1.6.

The most critical allocation problem in the packaging study was the incineration process. Incineration has two functions: it does away with the waste and at the same time it delivers heat for a district heating system. The problem was worded as: How should the emissions from the incineration plant be allocated between the two functions? It was solved through what is now called *system expansion*, as illustrated in figure 1.7. The packaging material system was

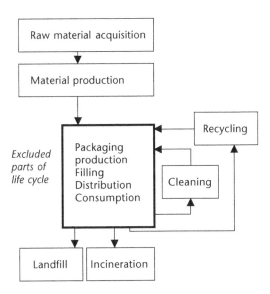

Figure 1.6 Principle flowchart of packaging materials. Transports are omitted to simplify the flowchart.

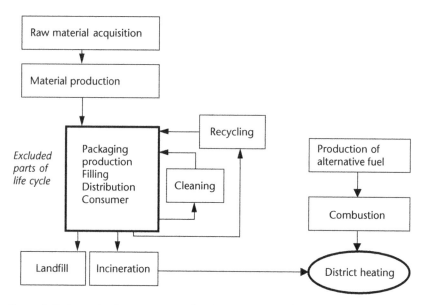

Figure 1.7 Example of system expansion in an LCA of packaging materials.

credited with the environmental load that would have occurred had the same amount of heat been produced by an alternative fuel.

An alternative way of dealing with the allocation problem would have been to "simply" partition the emissions from the incineration process between its two functions, waste treatment and heat production. This would have given very different numerical results. Actually, partitioning was the way many other allocation problems in the life cycles of the packaging materials were dealt with, for example the oil refinery processes that were part of the life cycles of plastic materials. System expansion was applied to the incineration process since whether or not to incinerate was at the core of the investigation.

The topic of the study, comparison of alternative waste treatment options, led to another choice concerning system boundaries. As indicated in figures 1.6 and 1.7, production of the actual packaging from the material and filling, distribution and consumption of its contents were excluded from the system studied. The reason was that these processes would be the same irrespective of whether the packaging was produced from new or recycled material.

The choices concerning system boundaries and the way to deal with allocation problems were guided by the goal definition. Since the study was change-oriented, it was designed to answer the question: "What would happen if … recycling/reuse is increased?" Since some parts of the life cycle (packaging production, filling, distribution and consumption) would not be affected by changed recycling/reuse rates, they were excluded and since some processes outside the life cycles of the packaging materials would be affected (district heating production) they were included in the model.

An LCA on packaging may be performed with many other goals. For example, LCA may be used to explore the life cycle of a certain type of packaging and search for improvement possibilities. In such a case, it would *not* be a good choice to exclude certain parts of the life cycle.

Type of data

Related to the choice between partitioning and system expansion as a way of dealing with the allocation problem, is the choice between different types of data to represent the system. Let us use the packaging example again. If incineration is reduced due to increased recycling of packaging, heat will have to be delivered to the district heating system from some other source.

District heating systems are supplied with heat from a mixture of sources. Clearly, reduced heat deliveries from packaging waste would not affect all these in the same way, or to the same extent, but the marginal heat source would be affected first. Thus, data representing how the system reacts to changes are relevant for change-oriented studies, such as in our example. For other types of studies, data representing the average behaviour of the system are more relevant, which we will come back to in chapter 3. There, also other questions concerning choice of data, for example between site-specific data and data representing an average of a population of processes will be dealt with.

Impact assessment method

How results are presented is a matter to pay attention to when receiving LCA results. As we have seen so far, results may be presented as inventory results, characterisation results or weighted together as a one-dimensional index. Too much aggregation hides relevant information and introduces additional uncertainty, while too little aggregation drowns the interesting information in too much detail. The appropriate level of aggregation varies between applications and the time and competence available to those receiving the information, as discussed in the following examples:

The most aggregated type of product related environmental information is represented by the eco-label. In eco-labels the information is condensed into a *yes* or *no*, i.e. the label is granted or not. One of the reasons for this high degree of aggregation is that the information is used in a context (daily shopping) where there is very little time for each decision. In environmental product declarations, on the other hand, LCA data are presented as characterisation results (MSR 1999a). The intended audience is then not consumers, but usually professional purchasers with more time and specialised competence than the average consumers. More on this in chapter 10.

When the application consists of searching for improvement possibilities, it is our experience that the results need to be interpreted on several levels, both as inventory results and as impact assessment results.

For the development of complex products consisting of many different components made from many different materials (e.g. cars), environmental information on the components needs to be fairly highly aggregated. Thus many existing weighting methods were explicitly developed for product development purposes (i.a. Steen 1999; EDIP 1997; Goedkoop & Spriensma 1999). Product development has been identified as an important field of application for LCA and is reviewed in chapter 9.

An important part of impact assessment methods is the way environmental problems are modelled and measured. These models are called *characterisation methods* in LCA terminology. There are, however, important limitations of these models for the characterisation step that a reader of an LCA should be aware of when interpreting the results. The limitations are caused by simplified assumptions concerning the cause-effect chains of environmental problems as well as by lack of scientific knowledge. The most important ones are the following:

- Time and geography are usually disregarded in LCI. This means that there is no, or at least little and incomplete, information about where and when emissions take place. Since the actual impact of an emission depends among other things on when and where it takes place, LCIA only indicates potential impacts. However, research on more geographically differentiated impact assessment models is being conducted (e.g. Potting et al. 1998).

- When an emission is released a whole series of events is started such as dispersion, chemical degradation, exposure of organisms and effects on organisms. For most impact categories in LCIA the category indicators describe events early in the cause-effect chain. They may be difficult to understand and interpret. When presenting LCA results, one may very well have to answer questions such as "How many units of global warming potential is good for you?".

- Characterisation methods are much better developed and include less uncertain assumptions for some impact categories than for others. Global warming and depletion of stratospheric ozone occur on a global level. This means that the impact is the same irrespective of where the emission takes place. Impact assessment methods for these categories include less uncertain assumptions than for others. For some impact categories LCIA methods are still unsatisfactory. These are the impacts related to toxicity, use of resources and land use. For these impact categories there is a diversity of impacts included under each heading and thus a difficulty in finding a common framework to describe these impacts. There is also lack of scientific knowledge and data.

- Some environmental impacts are not easily captured in numbers. They are easily forgotten, for which reason *life cycle thinking* or qualitative LCA are important supplements.

The natural sciences cannot be a basis for prioritising between different kinds of environmental impacts, such as between effects on human health and extinction of a species. Weighting methods in LCA try to capture values held by humans concerning different environmental problems and from them create "yardsticks" to measure the relative severity of different environmental problems. Different ready-made weighting methods measure people's values in different ways. They also reflect different time horizons and geographical scales. Thus they convey different information. For example, the EPS method is based on willingness-to-pay to avoid environmental problems (Steen 1999), the EDIP method is based on political goals (EDIP 1997) and the ET-long indices are based on more ecologically defined targets (Eriksson et al. 1995).

Different applications – different methodology needs

From the overview of LCA methodology in this chapter it should be clear that there are many different applications of LCA and that different applications put different requirements on the methodology. That is why methodological choices in LCA are not arbitrary, but should be guided by the purpose of the study. Table 1.3 gives some

Table 1.3 Examples of how different applications have different needs for methodology.

Application	Requirement on methodology
Decision making, choice between alternative actions	Reflection of consequences of contemplated action
Market communication, e.g. environmental product declaration	"Fairness", possibility to compare
	Credibility and review processes require high transparency and thorough documentation in report to reviewer
Product development and purchasing (little time and competence of user of results)	Results presented with a high level of aggregation
Decisions on national level, e.g. on waste treatment strategies	Data representing national averages
Identification of improvement possibilities, own product	Site specific data

examples of requirements on methodology set by different applications. The list is neither complete nor categorised but given as an indication of the number and the types of methodological choices to be made when carrying out an LCA.

1.5 Summary and further reading

Several characteristics make LCA appealing to engineers and industry. It deals with environmental issues in a highly structured manner, it is quantitative, it is a tool focused on technical systems and it can handle several environmental issues at a time. Thus, trade-offs between different types of environmental impact and between different parts of the life cycle are made evident.

There are several different types of LCA applications, each with its particular methodological requirements. Our thesis is that methodological choices are governed by the application, although this is not always clearly acknowledged in many LCA manuals and guidelines. Moreover, it is also useful to distinguish between the LCA model and the LCA procedure. Four critical issues in LCA methodology determine the outcomes of an LCA study: definition of functional unit, system boundaries issues in general and allocation problems in particular, type of data used in the study, how the impact assessment is made. Any reader of an LCA report should be aware of the implications of these four issues.

LCA methodology has reached a certain maturity and an international standard, the ISO 14040 series, on LCA is now standard reference for anyone working with LCA. However, research is still going on concerning various parts of LCA methodology. The Society of Environmental Toxicology and Chemistry (www.setac.org) organises many of the scientific conferences in this field. It can therefore be expected that the LCA standard will be updated some time in the future.

A final word: the systematic way of working with LCA enables communication about large and complex environmental issues. Many find LCA studies somewhat complicated, but this is a case of LCA reflecting the complexities of our world. One must remember that LCA as such is not to blame.

2 Development of the LCA concept

One way of getting a grip on LCA is via study of the methodology. Another way of understanding LCA is through learning about its origin and the circumstances of the concept's development. Before LCA was known as LCA, it was known under many names: ecobalances, resource and environmental profile analysis (REPA), integral environmental analysis, environmental profiles, etc. Experience from application and methodological debates and over the years have shaped current LCA methodology. At a conference in 1991 a decision was actually made that the name of this concept should be Life Cycle Assessment. By 1997, the first standard for LCA methodology (ISO 14040) was issued by the International Organization for Standardization.

With time, when more and more environmental managers and policy-makers were getting acquainted with LCA, questions about when and how to use LCA were raised. Also there were other environmental methods and many found it difficult to make a choice. LCA came to be compared to other methods, such as Ecological Risk Assessment and Environmental Impact Assessment, in terms of scope, strengths and weaknesses. An overview of different types of LCA for different application as well as LCA's similarities and differences to other environmental methods is presented towards the end of this chapter (2.3. LCA in the environmental 'toolbox'). But before that, let us look at the development that made LCA what it is today.

2.1 Early LCA activities (1969–1989)

Of course there are some variations to the story of how it all started. It depends on who is telling it, but what is generally considered to be the first LCA study is a study for Coca-Cola conducted in 1969–1970 by the Midwest Research Institute in the US (Guinée 1995; Weidema 1997; Heiskanen 2000). Other independent initiatives from the same time can be identified. Some of the LCA pioneers have written their "LCA memoirs" on how their LCA work started (Boustead 1996; Hunt & Franklin 1996; Oberbacher et al. 1996). Other historical accounts describe the work of important groups or organisations (e.g. Gabathuler 1997) or the interactions between industry, policy-makers and academia in the LCA community (Heiskanen 2000).

Many remember the 1970s for the oil crisis and the energy debate and place the first LCAs in this context. In fact there was another, earlier and less remembered environmental debate about waste and packaging that was the driver behind the first LCAs. The book 'Limits to Growth' pointing out the problems associated with wasteful resource use (Meadows et al. 1972) is illustrative of the environmental debate before the oil crisis. Disposable packaging in the "throw-away" society was often a target in that debate. The first LCAs conducted between 1969 and 1972 were all studies on packaging and waste management. Thereby they predate the oil crisis, which emerged in 1973. Nevertheless, the oil crisis was important for LCA development in that it fuelled interest in further LCA studies. The combination of the debate on wasteful resource use and the oil crisis is probably why LCA came to be such a comprehensive methodology, including resources, energy, emissions and waste in the analysis.

Pioneers in USA

The story behind the first study in 1969 was that the Coca-Cola Company was considering whether they should manufacture beverage cans (Hunt & Franklin 1996). The company was looking at a number of issues related to packaging: environmental consequences of packaging manufacture, alternatives to beverage cans,

44

etc. Plastic bottles, refillable glass bottles and disposable containers were among the alternatives. The manager of the packaging function at Coca-Cola wanted an all-inclusive study that considered energy, material and environmental consequences of the entire packaging production, from raw material extraction to waste disposal. The reason for including both energy and material flows was that he saw that energy resources inter-related with materials use. For instance, the plastic bottles could be used as a source of energy when making glass bottles. The packaging manager went with his ideas to the Midwest Research Institute where Robert Hunt and William Franklin worked. They conducted what they called a Resource and Environmental Profile Analysis (REPA) for the Coca-Cola Company.

The Coca-Cola study was never published because of the confidential nature of the work – it was only used for internal business decisions. One of the outcomes was that the Coca-Cola Company gained comfort with the idea of switching from glass to plastic bottles (Hunt & Franklin 1996). This was a radical idea at the time because plastic had the reputation of an environmental villain.

About one year after the first study at MRI, Hunt & Franklin discovered projects with an approach similar to theirs at two universities in the US (Hunt & Franklin 1996). Both were studies on life cycle energy of beverage containers. One of them was conducted at Stanford University, the other at the University of Illinois. Energy studies had also been conducted at the US Department of Energy (Curran 1996). The work at MRI was different in that its scope went beyond energy issues and included resource use and environmental consequences as well.

Pioneers in the UK

The work at the University of Illinois, which was led by Professor Bruce Hannon, came to influence activities in the UK. In 1972, Dr Ian Boustead at the Materials Science Department at the Open University in the UK was writing a teaching text on silica glass production. Just before the text was to go to the printer, Boustead found a paper by Hannon (1972) reporting on the cumulative energy associated with the production of beverage containers. Boustead adapted Hannon's methodology and constructed a simple case study on milk bottles with some data from British glass manufacturers for the textbook (Boustead 1996).

At the time there was a fierce public debate about packaging and waste. An environmental organisation dumped empty non-returnable bottles on the doorstep of Schweppes' head office in London, and the Glass Manufacturers Federation decided to get some "definitive quantitative information" for their defence. The Glass Manufacturers Federation remembered Boustead, who had asked for data for the milk bottle example, and invited him to do an energy study on returnable and non-returnable beer bottles (Boustead 1996).

Pioneers in Germany

Packaging and waste issues were important drivers behind the first LCA work also in Germany. The packaging debate led the German Federal Ministry of Education and Science to ask for a study to elucidate the role of plastics in the growing problem of packaging waste. A group at the Batelle-Institut in Frankfurt-am-Main, an interdisciplinary think-tank, was contracted to do the work in 1972 (Oberbacher et al. 1996). The group had not originally envisioned the use of any LCA-type methodology, but this soon changed when a report by Franklin et al. (1972) came to their attention. After the Coca-Cola study, Franklin and colleagues had gone on to do a study on meat trays for the Mobil Chemical Company (Franklin et al. 1972). The report from this meat tray study got into the hands of the people at the Batelle-Institut. It inspired them to use the new methodology to find the packaging with the "smallest possible use of raw materials and energy and a minimum of environmental and economic consequences" (Oberbacher et al. 1996).

Pioneers in Sweden

Both the early British and German LCA work were inspired by projects in the US. In Sweden, inspiration was more local. The packaging company Tetra Pak wanted to introduce a PVC bottle (known as the Rigello bottle). The bottle had received a lot of criticism in the environmental debate. Not only was it disposable, it was also expected to become an important source of acidifying hydrogen chloride (HCl) emissions when burnt in waste incinerators. In the late 1960s the director of Tetra Pak contacted Gustav Sundström, an engineering consultant who planned and designed waste incinerators, to find out his opinion about the PVC bottle. Initially, Sundström was very negative towards it. According to his preliminary calculations, the amount of HCl would be very large and he expected it would cause high-temperature corrosion inside the waste incinerator. However, after a visit to Tetra Pak, Sundström realised he had made a mistake in his preliminary calculations; he had assumed that the plastic bottle had the same weight as a glass bottle. In fact, the plastic bottle was much lighter. He acknowledged his mistake to Tetra Pak, and went back to the office to recalculate. He also threw himself into the general public debate on the acidifying emissions of the bottles. He had noticed that the estimate put forward by the Swedish prime minister and the environmental secretary were around 1000 times too large and he contacted the largest daily newspaper in Sweden to point out their mistake. On behalf of Tetra Pak he conducted an emissions project to find out how the HCl emissions could be controlled. And as the packaging debate continued, Tetra Pak wanted another study in the beginning of the 1970s to find out how their packaging compared to other types of packaging. Sundström who by then was also planning and designing the waste incinerator for Malmö, in south Sweden, suggested that if they were to do such a comparison, it had to be a complete investigation from "cradle to grave" if it were to be a fair comparison. The central part of the study was an energy analysis with some information about resource use, waste and a few emissions. The study was finished and published in the spring of 1973, and the timing was such that the oil crisis was everywhere in the news. The immediate side effect of the study was that Malmö city decided that the waste incinerator also should be used to deliver the recovered energy to the city's district heating system (Sundström 2002).

Proliferation

The LCA concept (or rather REPAs or ecobalances) was not a widely known concept between 1970 and 1989, but because of the early packaging debate it came to be quite well known at least in the packaging industry and among policy-makers on waste management. The 1970s show examples of many packaging studies conducted for both private companies and public authorities.

Typically, one study led to another. In industry, new LCA studies often came about for reasons related to competition between industries. Boustead recalls, "When plastic bottles began to compete with glass bottles, we were invited to work with the plastics industry. Then when aluminium cans were introduced in competition with steel cans, we were asked into the steel and aluminium industries" (Boustead 1996). The other way the LCA concept spread was via a marketing mechanism. The packaging manufacturer Tetra Pak spread the idea of LCA to its customers, various breweries and dairies as a way of supporting them in the packaging debate. This led to Sundström carrying out studies for a Norwegian dairy (Oterholm et al. 1994) and for the Swedish brewery association (Sundström 1990), to name two.

Policy-makers in Germany, and also in the US, showed interest in LCA. At the US Environmental Protection Agency, a former employee of MRI commissioned a number of LCA studies from MRI between 1972 and 1974. (Many of these studies including the databases were reported publicly.) After three large studies on different types of beverage containers and disposable and reusable products, the US Environmental Protection Agency decided that using LCA as a regulatory tool was impractical. If reduction of solid waste and conservation of energy were important, then goals for waste reduction and energy conservation should be set rather than regulating thousands of specific products.

Because of the energy crisis there was intense interest in the energy part of the analysis. The US Federal Energy Agency published a study on solar energy in 1976. Boustead and Hancock published a Handbook of Industrial Energy Analysis (1979). Sundström conducted an energy analysis of milk packaging (1979).

Public interest in LCA waned when the energy crisis of the mid-1970s subsided. Although there was little public attention to LCA,

48

private businesses and industrial organisations were still interested. They used the LCA studies internally to give environmental perspective to their strategic planning and also to the design and planning of new products. There was never a time when the LCA consultants in the US, UK and Sweden were not working on LCA studies (Franklin & Hunt 1996; Boustead 1996; Sundström 2002). Between 1970 and 1989, Franklin and Hunt conducted more than 200 LCA studies (Franklin & Hunt 1996) and Sundström conducted around 100 LCA studies (Sundström 2002). An important circumstance that enabled the wider use of the LCA approach was that the public studies included all data on processes in the reports. These became important data sources for other LCA studies.

In the mid-1980s, environmental issues became more than ever a focus of public interest. The interest was spurred by environmental disasters such as the chemical accident in Bhopal in India (1984), the nuclear reactor explosion in Chernobyl (1986), the seal deaths in the North Sea (1988), the garbage barge in the US (1988) and the oil spill from the tanker Exxon Valdez (1989). "Green" parties were voted into parliaments in many European countries and environmental organisations like Greenpeace attracted many new members. Also, LCA resurfaced in the public debate, again in relation to packaging issues. Household waste consisted mostly of packaging waste and became an increasing problem since landfill space was becoming increasingly scarce. The Swiss conducted a large packaging study in 1984 (BUS 1984) in which the whole database was included in the report. The report was scrutinised by industry and other parties and drew a lot of criticism. This led to an update of the study being published in 1990 (BUWAL 1991). Nevertheless, soon after the Swiss published their first packaging study, many European countries followed, among others, Denmark in 1990 (Christiansen et al. 1990) and Sweden in 1991 (Tillman et al. 1991). When compared, the many packaging studies showed diverging results and somewhat different methodologies. This sparked a debate and started a new era of methodological discussion and development, which is the topic of section 2.2.

Early methodology

Most early studies were carried out by consultants for private companies and were not available to the public. Of course there were some exceptions: a couple of milk packaging studies (MRI 1977; Sundström 1979) and a comparison of plastic and paper carrier bags (Sundström 1989a,b,c) to name a few. Together with Hancock, Boustead compiled experiences from their many studies and published a Handbook of Industrial Energy Analysis in 1979 (Boustead & Hancock 1979). In addition there were the public studies conducted for authorities: the German study on packaging waste (Oberbacher et al. 1974) and a comparison of nine beverage containers for the US Environmental Protection Agency (Hunt & Franklin 1974). It is from these studies that we know what the early methodology was.

Early LCA calculations were time-consuming without modern computers. The typewritten reports consisted mostly of flowcharts, tables and data sheets. The methodology was in principle much the same as today even if terminology has developed. Terms such as inventory analysis and impact assessment were not used at the time. From the reports it is easy to identify what was used as the functional unit although the term as such did not exist at the time. Environmental impact was reported as the amount of energy and material resources used and the amount of waste produced. A limited number of emissions were reported, typically only SO_2, NO_x, CO_2 and particles. Emissions could even be reported as a "total amount of airborne or waterborne emissions" without listing the individual pollutants (see table 2.1). A simple form of impact assessment, the critical volume approach, was introduced (BUS 1984). Instead of reporting the amount of emissions, the volume of air or water needed to dilute emissions to harmless levels was reported.

Table 2.1 Extract from an early LCA report: "Resource and environmental profile analysis of Merlon polycarbonate refillable milk containers systems including specific comparisons with selected competitive container systems" (MRI 1977).

SUMMARY IMPACT DATA FOR 1,000 GALLONS OF MILK DELIVERED
(in one gallon containers by type of container system)

Impact category	Units	Milk container system								
		Refillable containers						Non-refillable containers		
		Glass bottle		HDPE bottle		Polycarbonate bottle		Plastic bottle	Paper-board carton	Plastic pouch
		5-trip	20-trip	5-trip	50-trip	5-trip	50-trip	1-trip	1-trip	1-trip
Raw materials	lb	954.15	242.97	21.88	9.20	72.68	14.28	17.70	238.88	2.34
Energy	106 BTU	7.42	2.90	4.98	1.56	8.86	1.95	8.78	6.20	3.59
Water	103 gal.	1.29	0.64	0.69	0.44	0.79	0.45	0.66	2.87	0.32
Industrial solid waste	cu ft	2.12	0.60	0.27	0.11	0.67	0.15	0.38	0.85	0.13
Atmospheric emissions	lb	32.67	15.07	19.80	8.81	31.5	9.97	30.86	26.08	14.02
Waterborne waste	lb	6.26	4.01	4.08	3.32	5.35	3.37	3.13	6.24	1.51
Post-consumer solid waste	cu ft	19.92	5.02	16.24	2.00	15.96	1.6	75.43	30.39	1.05

2.2 "… one of the most important tools for the 1990s …"

The 1990s can be characterised as a period of harmonisation of LCA methodology. After the first two decades, experience with LCA was mixed. Interest was strongly on the rise, but there was also criticism that LCA studies could be tailored to give the result you wanted. The quote below is typical of the time.

> "Life cycle analysis will emerge to be one of the most important tools for decision-making in the field of environmental management for the 1990s. However, present LCA techniques are fraught with some methodological problems and it is commonly felt that the scientific basis for assessing the environmental impact of products is still inadequate."
>
> *(IPRE – International Professional Association for Environmental Affairs, 1990)*

The 1990s also saw the first scientific conferences on LCA. The Society of Environmental Toxicology and Chemistry (SETAC), which is an academic society, started organising annual conferences on LCA where researchers and industry representatives could discuss and develop the methodology. SETAC also set up a number of workgroups to work on different parts of the LCA methodology between the conferences. This structured approach to discussing LCA helped to establish it as an academic field of study. In parallel, industry representatives organised their own workgroups on LCA. For example, the International Chamber of Commerce formed a workgroup in 1991 to develop recommendations for industry on how to work with LCA (WICE 1994). In Sweden, the Federation of Swedish Industries set up the Product Ecology Project in order to "develop simple and general LCA-based methods for industrial use" (PEP 1991; Ryding 1995).

LCA – a tool of great promise

The great interest in LCA can be explained by a shift in the focus of environmental work in industry. An idea that increasingly gained support in the beginning of the 1990s was that environmental pro-

Figure 2.1 A typical illustration used to promote a shift from the traditional focus on emissions from production sites to more product-oriented environmental strategies (SOU 1989).

tection should go beyond end-of-pipe strategies and emission control (see figure 2.1). Environmental optimisation of products was seen as a more effective path to environmental improvement than minimisation of emissions from industrial processes, especially for products that gave rise to pollution during use and as waste. In several countries, environmental authorities and policy-makers started calling for product-oriented environmental strategies in industry. In that context LCA was viewed as an appealing instrument. Not only was it product-oriented, it was also quantitative and thus seemingly objective. It was no longer necessary to rely on simple rules of thumb, such as "Re-use is better than recycling, which is better than single use". With LCA came the notion that it was possible to quantitatively compare alternatives in order to identify the environmentally preferred option. Moreover, it could deal with environmental issues in a structured way and it could handle several environmental issues at a time. At the same time, the amount of available data increased through the publication of case studies. The interest in LCA was thereby (relatively) easily converted into practice.

The need for LCA databases

There were great hopes that LCA could be used for product development (see also chapter 9). For example, within the Product Ecology Project there was a vision that design engineers should be able to make en environmental design decision in only five minutes using LCA software. This and other similar visions required easy access to data. Consequently projects with the aim of developing LCA databases were set up. Commercialisation of LCA software products was a related force in this development. Many LCA software products had emerged as by-products from some of the large European packaging studies and their successful commercialisation depended strongly on easy access to LCA data.

An international Society for the Promotion of Life Cycle Development (SPOLD) was formed in 1992 with the "public availability of life cycle inventory data" as its first priority (Hindle & de Oude 1996). The need for a publicly available LCI database was expressed not only within the Product Ecology Project and by SPOLD, but also by SETAC (1993) and the "Groupe de Sages" advising the European Commission on eco-labelling (Udo de Haes et al. 1994). People soon realised that before any databases were set up it was necessary to define formats and structures for their information content. The Scandinavians were first out with a database format for LCA called SPINE (Steen et al. 1995). It was implemented in the companies that were members of the Centre for Environmental Assessment of Products and Materials (CPM) in Sweden. A SPOLD format was also developed (Singhofen 1996; Singhofen et al. 1996). Since then, the SPINE and SPOLD formats have been transformed into an ISO standard for LCA data documentation format (ISO/TS14048 2002). The theme of LCA software products, data documentation and databases is further developed in chapter 8.

Criticism of LCA

There was also a great interest in using LCA for supporting environmental marketing claims (see also chapter 10). However, early cases of LCA in marketing led to serious concerns. Environmental organisations claimed that industry used LCA as smokescreens to attract the attention to the wrong environmental issues or to defend environmentally suspect products (Rosander 1992; SustainAbility 1993). The term *hired gun* was used for biased studies that favoured the product manufactured by those who had sponsored the LCA study. The suspicion that industry exploited the legitimacy of LCA in their marketing claims was based on cases of contradictory LCA studies. Typically, industry put forward similar LCA studies (on the same type of products) with divergent results. For example, a company in Denmark producing meat packaging trays made of foamed polystyrene had ordered an LCA study that showed that their plastic trays were environmentally superior to other types of meat packaging trays (ETI 1988). Soon afterward a German study describing cellulose pulp trays as environmentally superior (Fraunhofer 1989) was put forward.

Concerns about the inappropriate use of LCAs in marketing claims led a coalition of eleven state Attorney-Generals in the USA to issue a report in which they concluded that "the results of LCAs should not be used to advertise or promote specific products until *uniform* methods for conducting such assessments are developed and a consensus is reached among government, business, environmental and consumer groups on how this type of environmental comparison can be advertised non-deceptively" (ENDS 1991). Also environmental organisations expressed a need for greater standardisation of LCA methodologies (SustainAbility 1993). Such concerns were strong driving forces behind the efforts that led to the standardisation of LCA methodology.

Towards a uniform LCA methodology

With the increasing number of publicly reported LCA studies came the possibility to compare them. Similar studies with different results were examined and their methodologies were discussed. Not all discussions were solely critical. Some were more inquisitive in nature, aiming at understanding the roots of the differences. The Society for Environmental Toxicology and Chemistry (SETAC) provided a forum where researchers from universities and research institutes, environmental consultants and industry representatives met to share and discuss LCA experiences. Methodology discussions and development was intense and SETAC was instrumental in arranging a whole series of conferences, workshops and working groups during the 1990s. The goal of SETAC's LCA effort was to develop an international consensus on a "harmonised LCA methodology" (SETAC 1993). After seven international workshops and conferences between 1990 and 1993, the first guidelines for LCA were published in the *Code of Practice* (SETAC 1993). The tone in the Code of Practice is normative. It states that unless a study covers the entire life cycle and comprises goal and scope definition, inventory analysis, impact assessment and improvement assessment, by definition it cannot be called an LCA. Without an impact assessment, it is only an LCI, a life cycle inventory.

After publication of the Code of Practice, SETAC set up a number of working groups to speed up methodology development since the groups were active also between the conferences working on developing different parts of the LCA methodology. Work in such working groups within the context of SETAC is still going on, particularly within the field of impact assessment methodologies.

Also consensus-building continued after the publication of the Code of Practice. The next step was the standardisation of LCA methodology, which started in 1993 within the framework of the International Organization for Standardization. A whole series of LCA standards has been published since (see table 2.2).

Table 2.2 LCA documents published by the International Organization for Standardization (ISO 2003).

June 1997	ISO 14040 Life cycle assessment – principles and framework
October 1998	ISO 14041 Life cycle assessment – goal and scope definition and inventory analysis
March 2000	ISO 14042 Life cycle assessment – life cycle impact assessment
March 2000	ISO 14043 Life cycle assessment – life cycle interpretation
2002	ISO/TS14048 Life cycle assessment – data documentation format

Much of the work to develop the LCA methodology resulted in manuals, handbooks and guidelines, many of them quite inaccessible to the layman as they were written by researchers and experts for other researchers and experts. These publications are mostly normative in character, describing a rigid methodology applicable to a limited type of LCA study. With time, LCA has been shown to be applicable to a large range of products and it can used in many different contexts and for many different purposes. Increasing experience has led to a growing awareness that LCA methodology is quite flexible and that the LCA methodology needs to be adapted to the context and purpose of the specific study. This will probably lead to modifications in coming updates of the standard so that methodological recommendations better relate to the type of LCA application.

Methodological debates and development

The conferences started a process to define a methodological framework for LCA. However, in order to talk about LCA methodology it was also necessary to develop a terminology. Not even the term LCA was self-evident since the concept had had several names since the 1970s (e.g. ecobalances, REPAs). A debate at one of the first conferences (in Leiden, the Netherlands, 1991) (SETAC 1992) concerned whether the abbreviation LCA should stand for life cycle *analysis* or life cycle *assessment*. The latter term was chosen to underscore the fact that LCAs include subjective elements.

The majority of the discussions at conferences and workshops concerned the development of a description of LCA methodology. An overarching framework that named the different phases of an LCA study was soon produced and later developed. Figure 2.2 shows the development of the framework.

The concept of life cycle studies has developed over the years. In the 1970s and 1980s, life cycle studies had focused on the quantification of energy and materials used and wastes released into the environment throughout the life cycle, i.e. on what came to be called *inventory analysis*. Many of the LCA studies from the late 1980s and early 1990s had incorporated some kind of impact assessment. *Impact assessment* was brought into the framework in order to put the inventory into perspective, i.e. to understand the environmental relevance of the system's inputs and outputs. In turn, impact assessment consisted of three steps: classification, characterisation and valuation. Later, the description of the impact assessment phase became more detailed. It now consists of at least four steps: classification, characterisation, normalisation and weighting. The phases of goal definition and improvement assessment were included in the framework in the beginning. These two phases later developed into *goal and scope definition* and *interpretation*, respectively. Improvement assessment was originally included as a response to the criticism that many LCAs were "hired guns" and defensive in character. The inclusion of improvement assessment in the LCA framework was intended to emphasise that LCAs should be used for reducing environmental impacts and to ensure that LCAs were not used to justify a status quo. With time, improvement assessment came to be viewed as one of the many possible applications of LCA, not as an activity inherent in every LCA study.

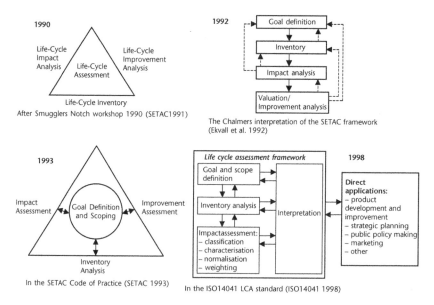

Figure 2.2 Development of the LCA framework. The early frameworks (1990 and 1993) are characterised by naming the steps in an LCA study. The later frameworks (1993 and 1998) also position the steps relative to each other.

58

Some of the methodological issues that have been the topic of both heated and lengthy debates concern the principles of allocation, impact assessment and the potential to simplify LCA work.

The allocation problem concerns how the environmental loads of a process are shared among the process' different products. Arguments for strict recommendations on how to partition the environmental loads as well as arguments for more open recommendations (that the methodological choice depends on the type of LCA study at hand) have been heard in the debate. The issue is not completely resolved. The ISO standard (ISO 14041 1998) is contradictory in that it both acknowledges the goal dependent element of methodological choices *and* prescribes an allocation procedure that ignores the goal dependent element. (The way to deal with the allocation problem is further described in chapter 4.)

A topic in the impact assessment debate is whether the methodology should describe potential impacts or real impacts. The difference between a potential and a real impact depends on the location of the impact. For example, acidifying emissions do not always lead to their maximum acidifying potential depending on the buffering capacity of lakes and soils. The advantage of describing environmental impacts on the level of potential impacts is that a general, natural science based methodology can be employed (e.g. acidifying potential of pollutants). A methodology that describes real impacts is of course more accurate. Its disadvantage is that more data (and work) are needed. In addition to data on emissions, also data on locations, receiving bodies and background concentrations of pollutants are needed for the environmental assessment. Nevertheless, attempts at developing site-dependent environmental impact assessment methods are being made, for example by Huijbregts (1999) and Potting et al. (1998) (see also chapter 5). Potential impact is a useful concept even if maximum impact is not always the result in practice. At least the description of the potential impact, which is synonymous with maximum possible impact, does not lead to underestimation of the environmental impact.

Another topic in the impact assessment debate concerns the extent to which natural science can be applied to impact assessment. At some point, subjective judgements have to be introduced to the interpretation of inventory results, for example, for setting priorities for environmental problems such as global warming and toxic impacts. The question is at what point and in what form subjective judgement is introduced. Disagreement on this matter has led to parallel development of several weighting methods.

A third issue in the impact assessment debate has been what counts as an environmental impact. According to the SETAC Code of Practice (1993) an LCA should assess the life cycle's impacts on *ecological health, human health* and *resource depletion.* In the handbook for the ISO standard (CML 2002), impact on *man-made environment* has been added to the list. An example of such an impact is the impact of acidification on buildings. The final word has probably not been said in this debate.

2.3 LCA in the environmental tool box

Towards the establishment of an LCA practice

The work to develop an LCA methodology has led to the establishment of LCA as an academic subject. Researchers using and developing LCA methodology or studying the use of LCA can be found at many universities. A sign of increasing research activity is the number of articles on LCA in academic journals (see figure 2.3). The field also developed its own journals, most notably the International Journal of Life Cycle Assessment. Moreover, LCA courses started being taught in the mid-1990s at some technical universities.

LCA application became more diverse in the 1990s, extending beyond packaging into food products, building materials and construction, chemicals, automobiles and their components and electronics, among other things. Moreover, the concept spread beyond Europe and North America. In 1991 an LCA Forum was established in Japan. It was later transformed into the LCA Society of Japan in 1997. LCA societies were also formed in India (in 1997), in Korea (in 1997) and in Australia (in 2001) (IntJLCA 2003).

Consequently, industry's adoption of LCA also became more widespread during the 1990s. Many companies started with LCA studies as an experimental activity in their environmental departments. So far LCA has mostly been used internally in the compa-

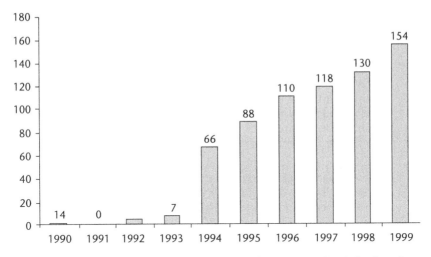

Figure 2.3 The number of LCA articles in academic press. (Statistics based on searches in the article databases of Science Citation Index, Compendex and ABI-Inform.)

nies, e.g. to develop an environmental overview of their production and supply-chain, in the product development process, for screening suppliers, etc. In the future, the use of LCA may further increase if LCA-based environmental product declaration systems gain popularity. Many larger industrial companies have their own LCA specialists and use LCA on a regular basis. The process of implementing LCA in industry is further described in chapter 13.

Different types of LCA for different applications

Recognition that there are different types of LCA has grown with increasing LCA experience. A diverse life cycle-based practice can be observed nowadays, ranging from large detailed LCA studies to simple LCA-based rules of thumb. In addition, *life cycle thinking* has come to be embraced more generally. It is a way of thinking that considers the cradle-to-grave implications of different activities without going into the details of an LCA study. The principle of life cycle thinking is often inscribed in the environmental policy of many companies. The following statements are found in the environmental policy of a pulp and paper company and a motor vehicle company, respectively:

> "The concept of product life cycles guides our environmental activities and provides the framework for our efforts. We expect the same commitment from our suppliers and partners so that at every stage, from raw material to the end product, the impact on the environment will be minimised."
>
> *(StoraEnso Environmental Report 2000)*

> "The company makes environmentally efficient and advanced technology available world-wide and brings this technology to bear over the full life cycle of its products."
>
> *(Volkswagen Environmental Report 2001/2002)*

Life cycle management is a concept closely related to life cycle thinking. Life cycle management is the managerial practices and organisational arrangements that apply life cycle thinking. This means that environmental concerns and work are co-ordinated in the whole life cycle instead of being independent concerns in each company. An organisation for the transfer of environmental information from suppliers to product developers and continuous environmental improvement in the whole life cycle are different examples of life cycle management. The company 3M has developed a life cycle management methodology, including the LCM screen in table 2.3, to help business units take a systematic approach to overall product responsibility (3M 1997).

Table 2.3 The LCM screen developed by 3M for the assessments of risks and opportunities throughout the various stages of a product's life cycle (3M 1997).

LCM stage Impact	Material acquisition	R&D operations	Manufacturing operations	Customer needs	
				Use	Disposal
Environment					
Energy/ resources					
Health					
Safety					

Life cycle thinking is also being applied in the realm of public policy making. An important example of this is the development of an Integrated Product Policy, IPP, in the EU (EC 2001). The IPP is an overarching policy programme that brings together and co-ordinates life-cycle-based policies in Europe such as producer take-back schemes and eco-labelling programmes.

Among the "ordinary" types of quantitative LCA studies, at least three types can be distinguished:

- LCA of the accounting type
- LCA of the change-oriented type
- stand-alone LCA

The first two on the list, LCA of the accounting type and the change-oriented type, are used for different types of comparison. Fairness in comparison puts requirements on methodology and chapter 3 describes these two types of LCA with regard to differences in methodology and types of application. In contrast, methodological requirements are less strict in the case of a stand-alone LCA and are therefore not described in chapter 3.

Stand-alone LCA is used to describe a single product, often in an exploratory way in order to get acquainted with some important environmental characteristics of that product. It is often used to identify the "hot spots" in the life cycle, i.e. which activities cause the greatest environmental impact. A survey of LCA practice in industry has shown that this type of LCA is probably the most common type of LCA (Frankl & Rubik 2000). A stand-alone LCA may also be the first, rough LCA, conducted before any more detailed studies are decided upon.

LCA studies of the accounting type are comparative and retrospective. This type of LCA is well suited for different types of eco-labelling and can be used in purchasing or procurement situations since these applications involve comparison of existing products. Environmental product declarations are a special type of environmental product information that builds on a highly specified LCA accounting methodology. Presently, eco-labelling schemes have been developed in many different contexts, by governmental bodies, environmental NGOs as well as by industry. Moreover, this is a type of application where the producers of LCA information are not identical to the users of the information. Eco-labelling and other types of LCA applications for market communication are further described in chapter 10.

LCA studies of the change-oriented type are comparative and pro-spective. This makes this type useful in product development, building design and process choices since decisions involves comparisons of options that may be implemented or produced in the future. This type of LCA can also be used for deciding on waste management options and recycling schemes. There are numerous environmental strategies for environmental improvement in all these fields, for example waste minimisation, material/chemical substitution, dematerialisation, pollution prevention, recycling/re-use and pollution control through end-of-pipe technology. Previous to LCA, hierarchies of environmental strategies (e.g. 're-use is always better than recycling, which is always better than pollution control ...') were means of guiding decision making. However, with the advent of LCA it became possible to compare and evaluate alternatives based in different environmental strategies. This represents an important use of LCA, which is dealt with in several chapters. Chapter 9 covers the use of LCA in relation to product design and development; chapter 11 the use of LCA in production, process design and other up-stream applications; chapter 12 the use of LCA in waste management and other down-stream applications.

To sum up, LCA comes in many shapes: life cycle thinking, as stand-alone descriptions, the accounting type and the change-oriented type. Examples of applications for different types of LCA methodology are presented in table 2.4. A closer look at the table reveals that the distinction between different fields of applications and types of LCA is not always strict. For example life cycle thinking as well as detailed LCAs may be used in product development depending on available resources and expectations on the results. In the case of general communication to customers and other stake-holders, both the accounting type and the change-oriented type of LCA can used depending on what is being communicated. The use-fulness of LCA in market communication is based on LCA providing an orderly structure for conveying complex environmental information about a complex product system if handled well. This is exemplified in the Akzo Nobel case in chapter 13. Further, the development of environmental product declarations require comparative, accounting-type LCA, whereas the actual environmental declaration of a particular product is based in a stand-alone LCA performed according to the specified criteria.

Table 2.4 Examples of life cycle approaches for different applications.

Type of LCA Producers/ users of LCA information	Life cycle thinking	Stand-alone (descriptive)	Accounting-type LCA (comparative and retrospective)	Change-oriented LCA (comparative and prospective)
Public policy makers / authorities:	– Development of environmental policies (e.g. IPP, producer take back schemes, recycling schemes and targets)	– Basis of development of producer take back schemes	– Governmental procurement – Development of eco-labelling criteria	– Basis for development of environmental policies (e.g. IPP, recycling schemes and targets)
Industry:	– Supply-chain management – Product development – Building design and construction	– Identification of "hot-spots" – Environmental product declaration (based on standardised methodology)	– Purchasing – Market communication – Development of methodological standard for environmental product declaration	– Product development – Building design and construction – Process choices & optimisation – Market communication
Environmental NGOs:	– Development of campaign ideas	– Critical evaluation of environmental strategies and measures	– Development of eco-labelling criteria	– Critical evaluation of environmental strategies and measures
Consumers:	– Life style choices		– Eco-labelling (as users)	

LCA relative to other environmental tools

Although many different types of issues and problems can be explored with LCA, it is not an all-purpose tool. Many other environmental tools exist. Environmental impact assessment and ecological risk assessment were mentioned in chapter 1. Table 2.5 also lists other tools used for environmental decision making. Not included in the list are tools with an economic focus, e.g. cost-benefit analysis and total cost accounting. From a user perspective, there may be many questions. How does LCA compare with the other environmental tools? What are the strengths and weaknesses of each tool? How can different tools be combined? In order to answer such questions it is necessary to examine the methodology of each tool. A methodological comparison of different tools looks into what the typical object of study is (product systems or something else), the level of detail in environmental assessment, type of data used (physical, monetary or qualitative information) and a number of other methodological dimensions (Baumann & Cowell 1999). This way of comparing environmental tools has also been used in compendiums of tools for environmental decision making (e.g. Moberg et al. 1999; Wrisberg et al. 2002).

Table 2.5 A selection of tools used for environmental decision making (based on Moberg et al. 1999 and Wrisberg et al. 2002). All tools have procedural elements, but the analytical tools are primarily defined by the principles of quantitative modelling while the procedural tools are defined by the structure of the work process.

Quantitative and analytical tools	Procedural tools
Life cycle assessment	Environmental management systems
MIPS	Environmental auditing
Material flow accounting	Concurrent ecodesign
Ecological footprint	Environmental impact assessment
Ecological risk assessment	

Many environmental tools are of the quantitative and analytical kind. LCA belongs to this category. The MIPS approach, material flow accounting and the ecological footprint are quite similar to LCA in the sense that they are used to describe systems of material flows. MIPS is used to study product systems, just like LCA. With MIPS, which stands for "material intensity per unit of service", it is sufficient to describe the material input to the system. It is thus a simpler tool than LCA in the sense that environmental impact has been approximated by material usage. Material flow accounting does not focus on product systems and differs from LCA in that it is used for describing the flows of a particular material within a region (e.g. a nation or a municipality) or an organisation (e.g. a corporation or a business sector). The ecological footprint is foremost a method for assessing and illustrating environmental impact. It can be used in combination with LCA to calculate the ecological footprint of a product but also together with material flow accounting to show the ecological footprint of a region. Ecological risk assessment is a more specialised environmental tool than LCA since it is mainly used for assessing the real and potential impacts of toxic substances.

Procedural tools are very different in character. They are used for organising integration of environmental concerns into various activities. Environmental management systems specify the way a company may organise its environmental efforts. A standardised environmental management system, such as ISO 14001, includes formulation of an environmental policy, development and implementation of an environmental plan, and eventually check-up of the environmental work and corrective actions. Environmental auditing is used in companies for evaluation of environmental efforts. Environmental auditing has become an integral part of environmental management systems, but can and has been conducted independently of these. In general environmental auditing is a series of activities, initiated by management to evaluate environmental performance, to check compliance with environmental legislation and to assess whether the management systems in place are effective. A method that can be used in product development is concurrent ecodesign. Put simply, the product developers bring together representatives of different parts of a product's life cycle so that they can give their respective environmental expertise. The representatives are usually found within the company and could be people in the purchasing, production, marketing and after-sales services units. Environmental impact assessment is different from the previously described procedural tools – it is the only one that is prescribed by law whenever an industrial plant, a road or another large development is planned. Of course legal requirements differ from country to country, but central to environmental impact assessment are detailed descriptions of local environmental impact caused by the development and the participatory process to bring out the opinions of the community.

Quantitative tools and procedural tools are often combined. Ecological risk assessment and LCA may be used within an environmental impact assessment; LCA and MIPS and ecological risk assessment in product development; material flow analysis and LCA in environmental auditing. The possible combinations are numerous. Which ones are relevant is derived from the context. Furthermore, trends affect environmental management and decision making – certain tools, often new ones, are more fashionable than others. Managers, decision makers and consultants thus have a special responsibility to assess the strengths and weaknesses of different tools and to decide on whether LCA is suitable or another tool is more appropriate for the occasion.

There are many more tools than those mentioned here. There are for example also economic tools, different forms of multi-criteria analysis, geographic information systems and scenario techniques. Generally, each tool has its own body of literature. This specialised literature is recommended for in-depth descriptions of the respective tools. For a survey of tools, the compilations "Analytical tools for environmental design and management in a systems perspective" (Wrisberg et al. 2002) and "Tools to aid environmental decision making" (Dale & English 1999) are suggested.

2.4 Summary and further reading

This chapter has presented the history of the LCA concept, with its roots in the waste debate and the energy crisis in the early 1970s. The accounts of some of the main characters in LCA history have been published in the International Journal of LCA. Hunt and Franklin (1996) wrote about the start in the US, Boustead (1996) about the start in the UK, Oberbacher et al. (1996) about the start in Germany and Gabathuler (1997) about how the Dutch scientists entered the LCA scene. The dissertation by Heiskanen (2000) provides an interesting overview of LCA activities and LCA politics in industry, academia and among public policy-makers. Examples of early LCA reports are not always easy to find since many were made for private companies. However, some of the public packaging studies (e.g. BUS 1984; BUWAL 1991; Christiansen et al. 1990; Tillman et al. 1991) and the handbook on industrial energy analysis by Boustead & Hancock (1979) may be found in libraries.

An important achievement during the 1990s is the publication of an LCA standard in the ISO 14040 series (ISO 14040 1997; ISO 14041 1998; ISO 14042 2000; ISO 14043 2000). The LCA standard has become a standard reference for anyone working with LCA. However, the first step towards the standard, the SETAC Code of Practice (SETAC 1993) is still interesting and valid reading.

The core of LCA, the flow modelling, has remained much the same since the beginning, while impact assessment methodology and informatics for LCA have seen most advances during the 1990s. Life cycle management is a more recent topic concerning application of LCA. The *International Journal of LCA* (www.scientificjournals.com) is an important source for those who want to follow the trends in LCA development. The journal has been publishing articles and commentaries on LCA methodology, reports of case studies and information about conferences since 1996. Those who want to take a more active part in LCA developments may turn to the *Society of Environmental Toxicology and Chemistry* (www.setac.org), which organises conferences on LCA methodology, working groups on unsolved methodological issues as well as case study seminars. Also the conference series on *Life Cycle Management* (Hunkeler et al. 2001) is interesting for those with an interest in matters concerning the usefulness of LCA in different types of application.

The usefulness of LCA is better understood if it is also seen in comparison with other environmental tools. For an exploration of the relationship between LCA and other environmental tools, the article by Baumann & Cowell (1998) represents a methodological starting point and the report compiled by Wrisberg et al. (2002) a more complete overview where different tools are applied in parallel and compared in case studies.

Part 2
LCA methodology

This part of the book enters more deeply into different parts of LCA methodology. The presentation covers general LCA methodology. Its application to different fields is presented in the next part of the book on LCA applications.

Chapter 3 deals with the act of setting up and designing an LCA study, i.e. the goal and scope definition phase in LCA methodology. Chapter 4 describes life cycle inventory analysis. In chapter 5 on life cycle impact assessment, methods and problems related to measuring environmental problems are described and discussed. Chapter 6 presents a number of examples of how to analyse and present LCA results. The art of reading an LCA report and scrutinising an LCA study is covered in chapter 7 on critical review. Finally, chapter 8 deals with data management issues, including LCA software packages, databases and formats for documentation of data.

There are also exercises that follow up on a number of chapters. The exercises are in the exercise part of the book.

3 Goal and scope definition

The goal of an LCA study is determined in the goal and scope definition phase of an LCA. Based on the goal, the scope and thus the requirements on the modelling to be done are specified. This is a crucial phase in LCA studies, since different purposes require different methodology, or vice versa, different methodology gives answers to different questions. However, this does not mean that the methodological choices of an LCA are arbitrary.

Ideally, if all choices and specifications are made in the goal and scope definition, and thus the requirements on the modelling are made clear enough, no or at least very few value choices should remain to be made during the subsequent LCA phases. In practice, LCA is an iterative process, and the need to make certain choices is often not evident from the beginning, but discovered during the course of the study. However, it is an advantage if as many of the choices as possible are foreseen and made at an early stage.

The goal and scope definition is a play between at least two actors, the commissioner and the practitioner. The commissioner initiates and pays for the study, whereas the practitioner (sometimes called the analyst) is the person or project group that actually carries out the study. The commissioner's role is to state the goal of the study and the practitioner's role is to know and to describe the implications of different methodological approaches. Between them, they should come up with a goal and scope definition resulting in a study that delivers answers to the "right" questions, i.e. the things the commissioner really wants to know more about.

This chapter describes how to define the *goal* of an LCA, which is closely related to the context in which it is done and then the *scope* which includes making choices concerning the methodology to use in the subsequent modelling. The chapter sorts out which methodological approaches provide answers to which types of question. In the last section it also gives some advice on *planning* an LCA project. Two exercises follow up on the content in this chapter. Exercise A focuses on a central part of the goal and scope definition, the definition of the *functional unit*, whereas exercise B covers the whole process of goal and scope definition.

3.1 Goal and context of the study

The ISO standard (ISO 14041 1998) states that the goal definition "shall unambiguously state the intended application, the reason for carrying out the study and the intended audience". All these things have to do with the context of the study, such as why it is done and how and by whom the results are going to be used.

Reasons for carrying out an LCA may for instance be to explore and learn about the life cycle. In other cases an LCA is intended to support product development or strategic planning. In yet other cases its intended use is marketing. The intended audience of course varies between applications and may consist of e.g. product developers, top management, authorities, customers or a combination of these categories.

Although it may not be so difficult to state the main application and the main audience of an LCA, it is not unusual that the initial goal is quite vague and formulated in general terms, such as "We want to do an LCA on our products/production" or "We want to know the environmental strengths and weaknesses of this product". It is necessary to transform such a general goal into a more specific purpose in order to be able to make relevant methodological choices in the subsequent modelling.

The purpose may be formulated as a question posed to the LCA study. Examples of such questions are the following:

- Where are the improvement possibilities in the life cycle of this product?
- Which are the activities in the life cycle that contribute the most to the environmental impact associated with this product?
- What would be the environmental consequences of changing certain processes in the life cycle in such and such a way?

- What would be the environmental consequences of using a secondary recycled raw material for this product, instead of the virgin material presently used?
- What is the environmentally preferable choice of products A, B and C used in application X?

3.2 Scope and modelling requirements

In this section we will go through all the choices that are necessary to make when deciding the scope of the study. These include the choice of which options to model, functional unit, choice of impact categories and method for impact assessment, system boundaries and principles for allocation and data quality requirements. They are all related to the modelling to be carried out.

Which options to model?

A choice that is closely related to stating the goal of the study is to define which specific products, product designs or process options are to be investigated. Think for instance about the difference between an LCA of the average laundry detergent used in Europe and an LCA of detergent X from supplier Y. The choice of which specific option to study is important in stand-alone LCAs of single products. It is even more so in comparative studies where it has to be ensured that compared alternatives really are technically comparative (see also the section on functional unit).

Initial flowchart

Already at a very early stage it is helpful to make a first general flowchart of the system to be studied. Such a first flowchart need not contain all the details of the life cycle. In fact, it may be an advantage if it is general enough to include all studied options or products in a comparative study. Figure 3.1 shows such an initial flowchart for the life cycle of detergents.

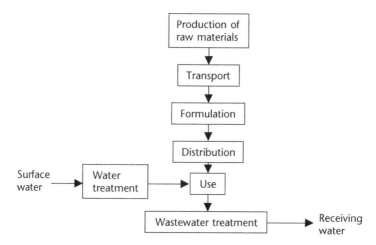

Figure 3.1   General and initial flowchart showing the life cycle of laundry detergents.

Functional unit

When the goal, the product(s) and the system have been decided on, it is time to start defining the functional unit. Do you remember the examples of functional units in chapter 1 (litres for beverage packaging, $m^2 \times$ year for flooring, person $\times$ km for passenger transportation and kg clean laundry for detergents)? The functional unit corresponds to a reference flow to which all other modelled flows of the system are related. This is why the functional unit needs to be quantitative. Which *specific* flow is the reference flow must also be pointed out in the flow chart.

However, there may be a lot of information that is not possible to include in crude quantitative metrics. Products or processes often fulfil more than just one function. For example, food provides nutritional value but it also gives pleasure and forestry produce timber but may also provide recreational areas. However, the LCA results may only be related to one reference flow. Therefore one of the functions must be chosen and represented by the functional unit.

For stand-alone studies (i.e. LCAs of single products), the definition of the functional unit is seldom critical. In comparative studies it may be a more difficult task since the functional unit is then used as the basis for comparison. The functional unit must represent the function of the compared options in a reasonably fair way. At the same time, the compared options may fulfil the function more or less well, or have functions or qualities in addition to the one described by the functional unit. For example, a parquet floor and a wall-to-wall carpet both serve as flooring, but the parquet floor may be considered more aesthetically pleasing and the carpet is better for noise reduction. One way of dealing with such differences in quality is to define a certain minimum level that all compared alternatives must fulfil. For example, for flooring a certain level of noise reduction may be required. Other examples are passenger transportation for which it may be required that all compared alternatives fulfil certain safety criteria and detergents for which what is meant by *clean* laundry may be stated. Another way, which must sometimes be reclined to, is to leave qualitative differences between compared alternatives out of the LCA calculations and simply describe them in words.

Choice of impact categories and method of impact assessment

The concepts *environment* and *environmental impact* imply a number of different things. In every LCA it is necessary to consider which environmental impacts to take into account. The ISO standard only gives headlines for impact categories: resource use, ecological consequences and human health (ISO 14040 1997). These must be interpreted in terms of more operational impact categories such as for example global warming, acidification and resource depletion. Impact category definition is one of the steps in impact assessment. We will discuss it further in chapter 5. There are a number of default lists of impact categories (described in chapter 5) that can be used. It is often recommended, for instance in the Dutch LCA handbook (CML 2002), that all relevant environmental impacts are considered.

Which inventory data to collect follows from the choice of impact categories as not all emissions contribute to all types of impacts.

How to interpret the results must also be decided. One may choose to stop after inventory and interpret inventory results directly. Such a study is called a life cycle inventory analysis instead of a life cycle assessment. Another option is to go through characterisation and interpret the results from that level. There are also the ready-made impact assessment methods going all the way to weighting. Impact assessment will be discussed in chapter 5 and different ways to interpret results in chapter 6.

Different types of LCA

It has been stressed that the methodological choices in LCA depend on the goal definition, the question being posed. Among LCA researchers there is a growing consensus that there are two main types of LCA (e.g. Frischknecht 1997; Baumann 1998; Weidema 1998; Tillman 2000; CML 2001). Terminology and the exact definition of concepts differ a bit between authors, but for our purposes we may call the two types of LCA *accounting* and *change-oriented*. (In chapter 2 we also introduced the stand-alone LCA. However, since methodological choices are usually less critical for stand-alone LCA, the methodological description in the following will focus on accounting and change-oriented LCAs.)

The accounting type of LCA answers questions of the type "What environmental impact can be associated with this product?" or even "What environmental impact can this product be held responsible for?" The change-oriented type of LCA compares the environmental consequences of alternative courses of action, through modelling effects of changes. It answers questions of the type "What would happen if ...?". Knowing what type of LCA is being done helps when setting system boundaries and choosing the type of data to represent the system. Which type of methodology goes with which type of LCA is summarised in table 3.1 (Tillman 2000). The subsequent sections will take us through the details in the table.

Table 3.1 Characteristics of accounting type and change-oriented LCI models (Tillman 2000).

Characteristic	Type of LCA	
	Accounting	Change-oriented
System boundaries	Additivity Completeness	Parts of system affected
Allocation procedure	Reflecting causes of system Partitioning	Reflecting effects of change System enlargement
Choice of data	Average	Marginal (at least in part)
System subdivision	–	Foreground & background

System boundaries

The principles of system boundary definition and allocation are decided during the goal and scope definition. However, one may have to wait to decide the exact details until enough information has been collected during inventory analysis.

System boundaries need to be specified in several dimensions (Tillman et al. 1994):

- Boundaries in relation to natural systems,
- Geographical boundaries,
- Time boundaries,
- Boundaries within the technical systems:
  - Boundaries related to production capital, personnel, etc. Cut-off criteria.
  - Boundaries in relation to other products' life cycles. Requires allocation procedures.

Boundaries in relation to natural systems

Where does the life cycle begin and end? Where is the product's "cradle" and where is its "grave"? On a general level, the activities included in the flow model of the technical system (the inventory model) are activities under human control. When a flow leaves (or enters) human control it also leaves (or enters) the technical sys-

79

tem. The boundary between the modelled technical system and the modelled surrounding natural system is also the boundary between the inventory analysis and impact assessment.

For non-renewable materials such as oil and minerals it is relatively easy to define the "cradle". The life cycle begins when the oil is pumped or the mineral extracted. For renewable resources, which may be divided into fund resources (e.g. forests and agricultural land) and flowing resources (e.g. solar radiation and freshwater streams), it is less easy to draw the boundaries between the technical system and the natural system. For example, is the soil part of nature or is it a technical production system, or perhaps both? This ambiguity is still not resolved in LCA methodology. That is part of the explanation why it is difficult to describe effects of land use in life cycle impact assessment (see chapter 5). However, some activities are definitely technical and thus should be included in the inventory model. Examples are operation of machinery for ploughing, sowing or planting, harvesting, addition of fertilisers and pesticides, as well as operation of solar cells and hydropower stations.

There are "graves" all along the life cycle, in the sense that waste in solid, liquid or gaseous form is released to the environment from all activities in the life cycle. Pollutant reducing devices such as flow gas cleaning and wastewater treatment are parts of the technical system, and thus included in the inventory model. So are waste treatment processes such as incineration plants.

Landfills, however, require extra methodological consideration. They are often controlled, e.g. the leachate collected and treated, but only for a certain time period and eventually they will be abandoned. In a sense, they have then moved from the technical system to the natural system without being moved geographically. One option, which is often recommended for describing landfills in LCA-terms, is to include emissions from landfills during a certain (surveyable) time period in the inventory result and account for the material remaining in the landfill after that time in a separate data category (Tillman et al. 1994; Nord 1995). The other option is to include the landfill in the technical system modelled during inventory until all material is degraded and dispersed, i.e. for infinite time (Finnveden et al. 1995).

Geographical boundaries

Geography matters in LCA for the following reasons:

- Different parts of a life cycle occur in different parts of the world.
- Infrastructure such as electricity production, waste management and transport systems vary from one region to another.
- The sensitivity of the environment to different pollutants varies in different geographical areas.

On the other hand, information about the location of processes is seldom handled in a detailed manner in LCA. This is due to the complexity of the systems studied where different parts of a life cycle may be located in many different places. In some cases, the origin of raw materials is simply unknown.

However, LCAs are usually geographically limited in one way or another. Let us look into a few examples: Consider a producer doing an LCA of a specific product. The product is produced at a specific location, but sold, used and treated as waste in the whole of the product's market area. In this case the production phase would be geographically delimited, but use and waste management less well defined geographically. Another example is when the consumption of a product in a certain area, e.g. a country, is used as a basis for delimitation. It allows for production outside the country, but use and waste management take place within the country. Such a study may be of interest for national authorities studying waste management options.

Time horizon

Change-oriented LCAs are prospective. They look forward in time since they are about alternative choices of action. The goal and scope definition must then consider with what time horizon the change is studied. Is it the consequences for the next two, five or twenty-five years that are at stake? It is also important to state the scale of change being considered.

Accounting LCAs ask what environmental impact a product may be made responsible for. Put simply, this means that they look backwards in time, that they are retrospective. This is perhaps to simplify things a bit too much, at least for long-lived products. For them it must be decided in what time perspective their production, use and waste treatment are to be studied and thus what type of data need be collected. If production data represent present time should then the data for the use phase and waste treatment also represent present time or should scenarios and assumptions about future use and waste treatment be made? Obviously, different questions are answered using these different approaches.

Cut-off criteria and boundaries relative to production capital, personnel, etc

Capital goods are buildings, machinery, vehicles etc used to produce the products studied. Whether environmental impact from production and maintenance of capital goods should be included in LCA has been debated. For accounting LCAs the guiding idea is often that the study should be as complete as possible and production and maintenance of capital goods thus be included. However, in practice it is rare that production of capital goods is included for reasons of feasibility (more data to collect). For certain applications conventions have been formulated, such as in the Swedish programme for environmental product declarations (MSR 1999a), in which production of capital goods is explicitly excluded.

For change-oriented LCAs, whether or not capital goods will be affected by the change has to be considered. Does the change imply investment in additional capital goods? If so, for which parts of the system? Capital goods not affected by the change being considered need not be modelled.

A topic that is similar to that of capital goods is that of personnel. Processes require personnel and personnel need food, transportation and so on. Personnel-related environmental impact is usually not included in LCA.

Over the years, there have been many debates in the LCA society on criteria for when a part of a life cycle may be cut off. As we will see, the term *cut-off* may be interpreted in several different ways. The first thing that comes to mind when cut-off is discussed is often whether the environmental impact of certain parts of the life cycle is *negligible* compared to the rest of the life cycle. Up-stream production of minor components may serve as an example. However, *relevance* may be as important a criterion for what to include, at least in change-oriented LCAs. Processes not affected by a change under consideration need not be included in such LCAs. A third type of system boundary that may be interpreted as cut-off is when it is simply decided not to model a system from *cradle-to-grave* but to use other types of system boundaries. An example of this is *cradle-to-gate* analysis, which includes only production, but not use and waste treatment. The last type of cut-off criterion is resource-related, i.e. parts of the life cycle are excluded for reasons of lack of time, data or financial resources. Such situations are often dealt with through reporting an inflow from another technical system as part of the inventory result. Reporting in this way signals that there are parts of the life cycle that have not been modelled and it allows for the addition of the missing parts at a later stage. Another option is to try to estimate the missing data.

The ISO standard (ISO 14041 1998) does not use the term cut-off. Instead it treats "Criteria for initial inclusion of inputs and outputs", stating that contribution to mass, energy use and environmental relevance (preferably all three) can be used as criteria for what to include and what to exclude.

Boundaries in relation to other products' life cycles and allocation

The life cycles of different products are linked in networks. Sometimes several products (or functions) share the same process(es). If the environmental load of those processes is to be expressed in relation to one function only then there is an *allocation problem*. This section gives the principles for allocation, since that is what can be decided on during the goal and scope definition. Specific operational allocation methods and examples are given in chapter 4 on inventory analysis.

There are three basic cases when allocation problems are encountered:

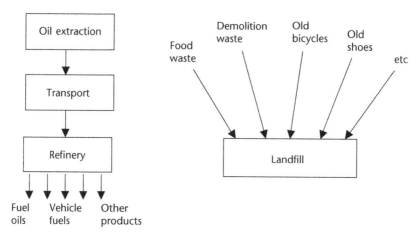

Figure 3.2 Examples of multi-output (refinery) and multi-input (landfill) processes.

1 Processes that result in several products (multi-output). As an example a refinery process is shown in figure 3.2. The allocation problem may be phrased as, "How much of the resource consumption and emissions of the process is associated with the different fuel oils, how much with the vehicle fuels, etc?"

2 Waste treatment processes that have input consisting of many different products (multi-input). A landfill is shown as an example in figure 3.2. A landfill has only one outflow of leachate. The allocation problem consists of how much of that leachate may be associated with the food waste, how much with the demolition waste, etc. The same type of problem is encountered for other waste treatment processes such as incineration of municipal waste and wastewater treatment.

3 Open loop recycling is when a product is recycled into a different product, as shown in figure 3.3. Open loop recycling usually involves quality losses. The following are examples of open loop recycling:

- Recycling of food packaging into other types of packaging materials.
- Recycling of energy from waste incineration.

84

- Recycling of steel scrap (from used cars for example) into rein-
forcement bars.

Only some of the activities in the open loop system are shared between the two products. These are those related to the production of the virgin material used in both products, the activities related to recycling such as the collection of the material to be recycled and the recycling process (e.g. cleaning, grinding, re-melting) and those related to the final waste treatment, in which material that has been used in both products is treated. The allocation problem in open loop recycling only involves these shared processes, which are shadowed in figure 3.3.

Allocation may sometimes be avoided through *increasing the level of detail* of the modelling. (This is true for multi-output and multi-input processes, but not for open loop recycling.) For example, not all the products of a refinery go through all distillery towers and other processes. This may be accounted for through modelling the refinery in greater detail. However, increasing the level of detail is

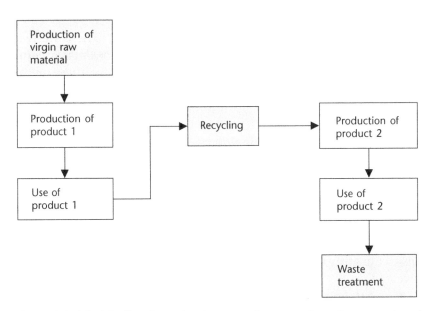

Figure 3.3 Principle flowchart showing open loop recycling. Processes shared between the two products are shadowed.

85

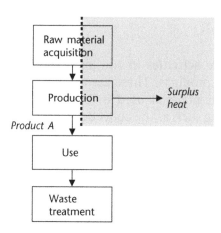

Figure 3.4 Allocation through partitioning. The resource consumption and emissions associated with the multiple process and the processes up-stream (partly shadowed) are divided between the two products.

not always applicable and even if it is, extra work and data are required.

Thus, more approaches to allocation are needed. There are two additional, principally different methods: *allocation through partitioning* and *system expansion*. In figure 3.4 and figure 3.5 these methods are exemplified for a system including an industrial process delivering industrial surplus heat to a district heating system.

Partitioning means that the resource consumption and emissions associated with the multiple process and the processes up-stream (partly shadowed in figure 3.4) are divided between the two products (product A and surplus heat). System expansion means that the industrial system is credited with the environmental load from the heat production that is avoided in the district heating system when it receives the surplus heat (figure 3.5). The reasoning behind it goes like this: "If the industrial system delivers more surplus heat to the district heating system, less heat need be produced from an alternative fuel".

It is our opinion that partitioning is applicable to accounting LCAs and system expansion is more relevant for LCAs modelling effects of changes (Baumann 1998; Tillman 2000). Partitioning is

86

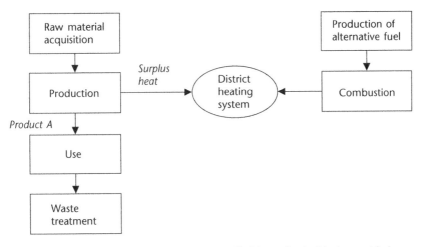

Figure 3.5 System expansion. The system studied is credited with the avoided production of heat from another source. The district heating system is not part of the modelled system, but the heat flows are followed up to a point where equal functions are delivered to the district heating system.

always feasible and it makes results from different LCA studies additive to one another. But uncertainty and sometimes even a degree of arbitrariness is often involved when deciding on the allocation partitioning factor.

If the question to the LCA is "What would be the environmental *consequences* of building a more efficient production process that also delivers surplus heat to the municipal district heating system?" then system expansion as illustrated in figure 3.5 is more appropriate than partitioning. A prerequisite for system expansion is that there exists an alternative way of producing the "extra" function(s). If the by-product is heat, as in our example, there are many alternative ways of producing heat. For other by-product this is not always the case. When applying system expansion an uncertainty is introduced concerning exactly how to model the additional processes. In our example (figure 3.5) we may ask what alternative fuel would be replaced if the industrial process delivered more heat. Would it be biomass, coal or oil? It has been shown that choices such as this may have a profound impact on the results of LCAs (Finnveden & Ekvall 1998).

In this chapter it has been argued that choice of allocation method should be based on what type of LCA is being done, accounting or change-oriented, which in turn is related to the purpose of the study. The ISO standard does not recognise such dependence between purpose of study and choice of allocation method, but recommends an order of preference between allocation methods. A short version of the ISO allocation procedure is as follows (ISO 14041 1998):

1 Whenever possible allocation should be avoided by:
   a) Increased level of detail of the model.
   b) System expansion.

2 Where allocation cannot be avoided the environmental loads should be partitioned between the system's different functions. Partitioning should reflect underlying physical relationships. The resulting allocation will not necessarily be in proportion to any simple measurement such as the mass or molar flow of co-products.

3 Where physical relationships alone cannot be established or used, allocation may be based on the other relationships between products, such as economic value of products.

System subdivision

For change-oriented LCAs, subdivision of the system into a foreground and a background system may be useful. (For accounting LCAs the concepts have less relevance since in this type of LCA all parts of the system are focused on equally.)

The *foreground system* consist of those processes on which measures may be taken concerning their selection or mode of operation as a result of decisions based on the study. The *background system* consists of all other modelled processes. These are influenced by measures taken in the foreground system (Clift et al. 1998).

The distinction between foreground and background system thus has to do with what part of the system is under the direct influence of the decision maker. Both the foreground and the background systems are affected by measures taken – the foreground directly,

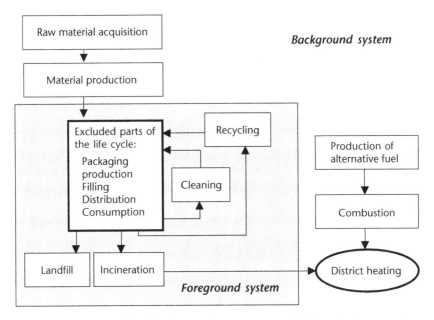

Figure 3.6 Foreground and background systems as applied to a study concerning waste treatment options for packaging waste.

the background indirectly. The effects on environmental impacts may be largest in the foreground or the background.

Applied to one of our examples from chapter 1, the packaging study, the boundary between foreground and background would be drawn as in figure 3.6. The foreground processes are those that the commissioners of the study, the national authorities, wanted to influence using the LCA study as support. These are the recycling and waste management processes. All other affected processes are in the background.

Subdivision of the system into foreground and background is helpful for choosing data with which to represent the system, especially concerning the choice between data representing average behaviour of a process (or mix of processes) and data representing response to incremental changes in production volume (marginal data). Different types of data may be used to model the foreground and background. This discussion takes us into the next section on data quality.

Data quality requirements

Depending on which data is used, the model to be built will give different views of reality. Different ambitions concerning data quality will also lead to different workloads when carrying out the study but of course also to different reliability in the results. Deciding on data quality requirements is thus an important activity during the goal and scope definition.

But what is data quality? The ISO standard (ISO 14041 1998) lists different aspects of data quality, which have been sorted under the headings *relevance, reliability* and *accessibility* in table 3.2 (Pålsson 1999).

Table 3.2 Different aspects of data quality (Pålsson 1999).

Relevance	Reliability	Accessibility
Time-related coverage	Precision	Reproducibility
Geographical coverage	Consistency	Consistency
Technology coverage		
Completeness		
Representativeness		

Relevance is the extent to which the data used represent what it is supposed to represent. The relevance of data may become a problem when availability of suitable data is limited and approximate data is "borrowed" from other LCA studies. There are different aspects to relevance, for example *time-related coverage* and *geographical coverage*, which are relatively easily grasped relevance concepts. If an LCA is being done in which current French consumer habits and waste management are of interest, then of course recent French data on consumer behaviour and waste management are more relevant than old British data.

Technology coverage includes the following aspects:

90

- Type of technology.
- Site-specific data versus average data.
- Marginal data versus average data.

The same product may be produced in many different ways using different technologies. A data set is of course more relevant if it represents the same type of technology as the one being modelled. It is more difficult to judge which is the more relevant type of data, an average over a number of similar processes or data from a specific plant. This depends on the goal and scope definition as demonstrated in the following example. Consider an LCA done by a producer of milk packaging wanting to study his own product. Assume that the product is produced in one plant only. Of course site-specific data are the most relevant to use to represent this plant. But which type of data is most relevant for production of the raw materials? If they are bought from specific suppliers that stay the same over time, then site-specific data for raw material production is also more relevant. On the other hand, if the raw materials come from varying sources, or if they are bought from a grid or on a spot-market, then an average over several suppliers will be more relevant. Also for use and waste treatment of the product, average data will be more relevant. Other goal definitions will lead to different answers concerning which is the most relevant, site-specific or average data. Try to think through for yourself what type of data would be most relevant for a) a municipality investigating how to best deal with milk packaging waste, and b) national authorities considering regulation of the waste treatment of milk packaging.

The choice between data describing how a process (or a production mix) behaves on the average and data that describes how the process (or production mix) reacts to small changes in production volume is usually referred to as the choice between average and marginal data. The debate on the average-marginal issue has been almost as intense as that on allocation. There is indeed a relationship. Modelling with marginal data answers question like "What would happen if more or less of the product was produced" (change-oriented) whereas LCAs using average data are more of the accounting type.

Depending on which choice is made the results of a study may vary extremely. For example, the average Swedish electricity production mix consists of about 50 % nuclear electricity and 50 % hydroelectricity with a minor proportion based on fossil fuel. The marginal production, on the other hand, is almost exclusively fossil fuel based. With such a large difference between the average and marginal production, the results of an LCA of an electricity intense product will vary considerably depending on if marginal or average electricity data are used.

Precision is perhaps the aspect that first comes to mind when *reliability* of data is mentioned. It concerns the numerical accuracy and uncertainty of data. But the reliability of data also depends on the *consistency* with which it has been collected and documented and on the competence of the person or organisation that collected the data. Data are more credible if they can be reviewed and that is only possible if they are documented transparently. Transparent documentation also supports the *reproducibility* of the results. We will come back to data documentation in chapter 8.

Assumptions and limitations

The ISO standard (ISO 14040 1997) states that assumptions should be considered and described in the goal and scope definition. Presumably, this goes for major assumptions and not for assumptions on individual data sets or the like. An example of an assumption to make in the goal and scope definition is an assumption about which the competing technology is when a system expansion is made.

The limitations of the study should also be stated. They may be the result of choices made in the scope definition, for example that the study is valid only for a certain geographical area or a certain time period. On the other hand, limitations may also be results of problems encountered later in the study such as failure to collect certain data.

3.3 Procedural aspects and planning of an LCA study

There are many different ways to go about conducting an LCA project. In this section we will go through some of the things to think about when setting up an LCA project. Most of the content in this section is based on case studies of how LCA projects were carried out in industry (Baumann 1998, see also chapter 13) and on our own experience from numerous LCA studies.

Reporting and critical review

The LCA standard (ISO 14040 1997) requires that in the goal and scope definition the required type and format of the report of the study should be decided on. Whether and what type of critical review will be performed is another choice. The standard states that if the intended use of the study is to support a comparative assertion to be disclosed to the public, a critical review *shall* be conducted.

There are different types of critical review processes such as review by internal experts, by external experts or by interested parties. It may be good advice to start contacting intended reviewers already during goal and scope definition, especially if a review by interested parties is intended. Chapter 7 will give further details on reviewing.

Actors in an LCA project

There is always a practitioner or an analyst performing an LCA study. The practitioner may be a single individual, but may also be a group of people. Of course if a project group is used, its work needs to be co-ordinated and procedures for communication within the group established.

Usually there is also a commissioner of an LCA, although there are examples of LCA studies carried out for research purposes without a clear commissioner. The goal and scope definition is a play between commissioner and practitioner. The commissioner states the goal of the LCA, why is it being done, what type of information is wanted, etc. However, the goal of a study as stated originally by a commissioner is often too vague to use as a basis for modelling requirements. The goal needs to be interpreted in terms of a more specific purpose before setting up modelling requirements. Usually it is the practitioner who has enough knowledge about LCA to rephrase the general goal as a specific purpose and based on that come up with the modelling requirements. Naturally, this needs to be done in a dialogue with the commissioner. Generally, the need for dialogue between commissioner and practitioner during goal and scope definition is underestimated.

Another aspect of the play between commissioner and practitioner concerns the planning of the project so that it will stay within budget constraints. The amount of time and effort it will take to perform an LCA depends to a large extent on data accessibility. If most of the data have already been collected in earlier studies and documented in a transparent way, less effort will be needed to model the system. When starting from scratch, data collection will be time consuming. The commissioner and practitioner must try to judge what is possible to achieve within the budget.

There may be multiple commissioners of a study. Compromises may then have to be made between what the different commissioners want as a result. For example, if the group of commissioners represent different parts of a life cycle such as raw material producers, assembly industry, etc they probably want different focuses of the study.

Since the largest amount of work spent on an LCA is usually on data collection, it is useful to plan the data collection in some detail. It is helpful to plan which data sources to use for which parts of the life cycle. For which processes should published data sources be used and for which processes should data be collected from production sites?

Data suppliers represent another type of actor in LCA projects. It is helpful to have a strategy for how they should be approached. Should they be offered any revenues in return for supplying data, such as access to the results? Should data suppliers be given the possibility to review how their data have been interpreted? How will confidentiality be dealt with? It is good advice to have answers to these questions before approaching data suppliers.

94

3.4 Summary and further reading

Having read this chapter you should be able to carry out exercises A and B. Exercise A is on the definition of the functional unit and exercise B takes you through a goal and scope definition, structured exactly as in this chapter.

The first step is to define the goal of the study, the "who-wants-to-know-what-about-what-and-for-what-reason", as clearly and precisely as possible. Based on that, the scope of the study is decided on and all the methodological choices made. They may be summarised in the following checklist:

- choice of which options to model,
- functional unit,
- choice of impact categories and method of impact assessment,
- accounting or change-oriented LCA?,
- system boundaries, in relation to
  - natural systems,
  - geographical boundaries,
  - time horizon,
  - production capital, personnel, etc,
  - other products' life cycles and allocation,
  - division into foreground and background system (when applicable).

Finally, there are procedural aspects to think about, such as how to report the study and the interplay between the different actors in an LCA project.

If you want to read more about goal and scope definition, the ISO 14041 standard (1998) is an important document. All the LCA guidelines also contain sections on goal and scope definition. Of these, the CML guide to the ISO standard on LCA (CML 2002) is the most recent. As for the more specific methodological choices, there is a huge literature on some of them, particularly on allocation. An entry here is the report from a SETAC conference on allocation (Huppes & Schneider 1994). There are of course ways other than the accounting/change-oriented distinction made in this chapter to classify LCAs in different types. A review of typologies has been given by Weidema (1998).

4 Inventory analysis

To make an inventory analysis means to construct a flow model of a technical system. The model is an incomplete mass and energy balance over the system, where only the environmentally relevant flows are considered. Environmentally indifferent flows such as diffuse heat and emissions of water vapour as a combustion product are not modelled. LCI models are usually static and linear, which means that time is not used as a variable and that all relationships are simplified to linear ones. Usually, the model is represented as a flow chart.

Activities of the life cycle inventory analysis (LCI) include:

1 Construction of the flowchart according to the system boundaries decided on in the goal and scope definition.
2 Data collection for all the activities in the product system followed by documentation of collected data.
3 Calculation of the environmental loads (resource use and pollutant emissions) of the system in relation to the functional unit.

This chapter describes how to construct an LCI model and carry out the calculations. It is a cumulative, sometimes even an iterative effort. As data get collected and more is learned about the studied system, it is sometimes necessary to revise decisions taken during the goal and scope definition. In practice then, the line between the goal and scope definition and the inventory analysis is not always as clear-cut as in the descriptions of the LCA procedure.

The first sections of the chapter present how to draw a flowchart, collect data and perform the calculations. The following sections discuss on a more detailed but practical level, some of the modelling aspects of inventory analysis. These are allocation, different ways to account for recycling rates, and how to account for energy in LCA.

There are also three exercises related to this chapter, covering the three main activities listed above. Exercise C is a simple exercise into flowchart construction and calculation of environmental loads. Exercise D concerns data collection and documentation and exercise E deals with the allocation problem. Exercises C, D and E, together with exercises A and B, train different parts of LCA methodology and provide a basis before undertaking any of the LCA projects in exercise H.

4.1 Construction of a flowchart

In the goal and scope definition, principles for system boundaries and other modelling requirements are decided on and usually also a first, general flowchart is developed. In the inventory analysis, this flowchart is elaborated on and given much more detail, showing all modelled activities and the flows between them. An example of a general flowchart, constructed during the goal and scope definition, was shown in figure 1.6, which relates to a study on waste management options for packaging waste for a number of packaging materials. In the inventory phase detailed flow charts were elaborated on for all the different packaging materials. The detailed flowchart for aluminium that was developed is shown in figure 4.1.

Flowcharts can sometimes be as simple as that in figure 4.2 (flowchart of wood flooring) although they usually are more complex. The complexity may arise from multiple recycling loops (as in figure 4.1) or from an industry structure, such as the petro-chemical industry, which is highly networked (see figure 4.3). A complex product consisting of many different components gives rise to a tree-like flowchart with a large number of branches. A simple example of such a flowchart is the detergent study discussed in chapter 1 (figure 1.2).

The inventory analysis, as most activities in LCA, is a cumulative and iterative process. This means that as more and more is learned about the system during data collection, the flowchart is revised and further elaborated. The process of making a flowchart is described in the following excerpt from a study on LCA practice (Baumann 1998a). In the studied LCA project two types of textile fibre were compared.

98

"The two LCA analysts knew who was the supplier to the viscose fibre producer, so they set out to draw a first flowchart of the viscose life cycle. TO, one of the LCA analysts, always consulted handbooks on chemical industry in the company library when drawing the flowcharts. It was no more than a day's work. He constructed the flowchart by looking for the raw materials; that is, he would start with the functional unit and trace the flow backwards. He said, 'I see to that the tree is more or less complete before I start "hunting" the suppliers.' ... Their first flowchart consisted of 18 industrial activities, of which 13 were in the main chain describing the life cycle of viscose from the forest to the waste treatment. The 5 side activities were activities such as 'production of process chemicals' and 'production of forestry fertilisers'. ... Some time later (after a visit to one of the data suppliers), a second flowchart was made. Their second flowchart concentrated on the viscose production; waste treatment activities were left out, and all process chemicals had been left out. Now, 35 industrial activities were included in the flowchart. ... TO commented on the difficulties of drawing flowcharts and collecting data. 'What you find out is that the world does not look as simple as in the flowcharts. What it boils down to with the suppliers is that they sometimes buy from their competitors when they don't have the capacity (to produce) themselves, and then they deliver to us. It doesn't matter how detailed you are, you still make generalisations.' ... In all, four flowcharts were made for the viscose fibre in the course of the study. The first one was a general one covering all main activities from cradle to grave. The waste treatment part was copied from another study on Swedish waste management. The two subsequent flowcharts were 'enlargements' with more detail and focus on the production and process chemicals. The fourth and last flowchart (consisting of 74 activities) was a compilation of the previous flowcharts and included all activities in the life cycle, even those for which no data had been obtained."

(from Baumann 1998a)

4.2 Data collection

Data collection is one of the most time consuming activities in LCA. Yet, very little has been written about how to carry out the data collection. LCA guidelines are typically concerned with what type of data to collect, thereby accidentally portraying the collection in itself as a rather unproblematic activity. In practice, data col-

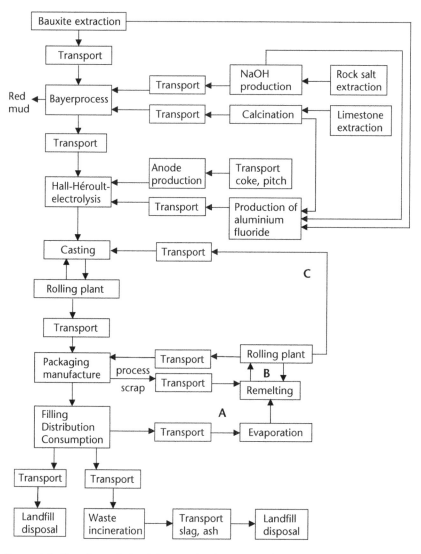

Figure 4.1 Flowchart of aluminium packaging material (from Tillman et al. 1991). This flowchart is complicated by the multiple recycling loops, recycling of packaging process scrap and packaging (A), recycling of rolling plant scrap (B) and recycling of excess remelted aluminium (C).

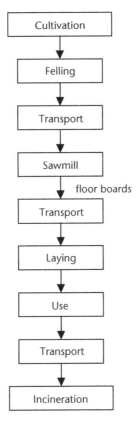

Figure 4.2 Flowchart for solid wood flooring (from Jönsson et al. 1995).

lection can be more of a matter of searching for data than merely collecting them. In the following, we will discuss how to go about finding LCA data. But first we give a short description of what data is to be collected.

Which data

Numerical data as well as descriptive, qualitative data need to be collected. The numerical data consist of data on the inputs to all modelled activities, and the outputs, i.e. amounts and types of (see figure 4.4):

101

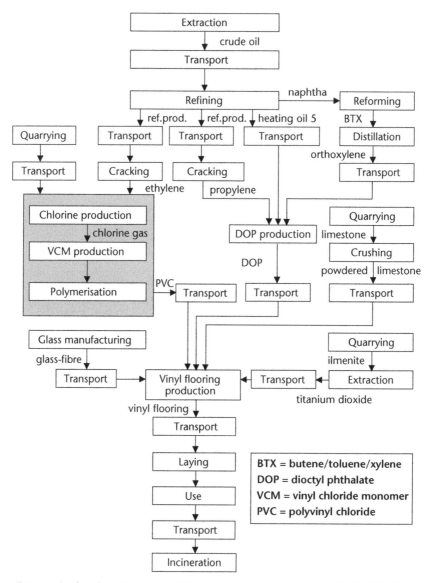

Figure 4.3 Flowchart for polyvinyl flooring (from Jönsson et al. 1995). This flow-chart is complicated by the network character of the petro-chemical industry.

- inputs of raw materials and energy, ancillary inputs and other physical inputs (for example 'land use'),
- products and
- emissions to air, water and land and other environmental aspects (for example noise).

In addition, data used to support allocation need to be collected. Such data may consist of relative prices of products. It may also consist of information on physical relationships between flows.

When collecting data concerning transports, distances and routing data are typically needed. They are then used together with generic data on energy use and emissions from different modes of transport.

Examples of qualitative information that needs to be collected are descriptions of the technology of the process, how and when emissions were measured, the geographical location of the process and where inflows come from and outflows go. It is especially important to know what system boundaries relate to a data set. Such qualitative information is needed when interpreting the collected data and judging its validity (for more information about data handling, see chapter 8).

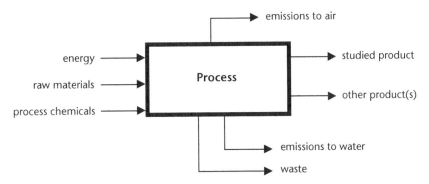

Figure 4.4 Typical categories of numerical data collected to describe processes. Examples of additional qualitative information are age of data, technology of the process, origin of raw materials, locality of process and impacted environment.

Data sources

One problem almost inherent to LCA is that no practitioner can be a technical expert on all the different technologies represented in a life cycle. As a consequence, practitioners may not always have direct access to relevant data sources. Instead, other people need to be asked. Table 4.1 illustrates the range of data collection procedures used in an LCA study on documentation systems (paper-based documentation compared with CD-ROM-based documentation) (Baumann 1998b). An explanation of the range of search strategies is that the studied product was not a core product of the company conducting the LCA. Thus no established channels to data suppliers were at hand. Instead, the LCA analyst turned to search for telephone numbers to "customer inquiries" on packaging labels ('browsing' in table 4.1) and to disassemble the product in order to weigh the constituent materials and components. Evidently, in this particular case the most successful way through which data was accessed was through personal tips, either from other data suppliers or from colleagues or acquaintances.

Table 4.1 Data search strategies and their success rates (from Baumann 1998b).

	Successful	Dead ends	Total
Browsing (e.g., in shops)	1	1	2
Phone directory	2	1	3
Experimental (e.g., weighing)	3	1	4
Tip from data supplier	7	1	8
Search library or www	2	no information	(2)
Tip from colleague or acquaintance	6	5	11
Unknown	1	1	2

In the following, some guidance on a more general level is given on where to search for LCI data. As illustrated by the example above, the presentation of possible data sources is in no way exhaustive.

When an LCA is performed on a company basis the first step in data collection (apart from collecting data on the company's own processes) is often to turn to the suppliers and ask for environmental data on the raw materials purchased. The outcome of such a request may vary greatly. Sometimes ready-made cradle-to-gate inventories are the result. More common, perhaps, is that data can be provided only for the processes operated by the supplier. Then data for processes further upstream have to be collected in some other way, either directly from producers of the raw materials or from other sources.

When the whole life cycle is modelled, (as opposed to cradle-to-gate studies) it is as important to collect data for downstream processes (customers, use phase and waste management) as the upstream processes. Data may be collected directly from customers and waste management companies (or waste water treatment facilities). However, often data representing averages are preferred for these stages in the life cycle.

Data is sometimes hard to come by for the use phase of a product. Consumer behaviour varies greatly and is not always known. For some products the same is true for product performance, for example the lifetime of products. Statistical studies of consumer behaviour and product performance are available for some products, but not all. As a proxy, results from tests of product performance are often used to represent the use phase.

There are also published LCI data. Several industrial branches have published LCI data through their branch organisations, usually cradle-to-gate average data. Databases are issued also by other organisations, and as parts of LCA software packages.

Reports from LCAs and similar projects is another type of data source. Some of these are publicly available, but many LCAs are conducted as internal company projects or by consultants, which is why reports of LCA may be difficult to find in libraries.

Openness regarding information on environmental performance of industrial processes varies between companies, between industrial branches and between countries. Openness also depends on how the data will be used (whether made public or not, for instance) and presumably also on who asks for the data. Already existing business relationships may facilitate data collection from suppliers.

No matter how thorough the LCA practitioner, there will always be data gaps in LCIs. Some of these may be filled with estimates and assumptions. Support for such estimates may be sought from e.g. technical experts or model calculations.

Planning for data collection

There are a number of things to think about before approaching data suppliers. These are given here as a checklist, which again does not claim to be exhaustive, but is intended for guidance.

• Think through for which activities in the life cycle site-specific data are necessary, and for which activities average data are preferred. Average data are preferably collected from sector organisations or from literature, whereas site-specific data usually must be collected directly from producers.
• Before approaching data suppliers, do your homework, i.e. inform yourself on a general level about the technology in question. In other words, be prepared for a dialogue with an expert.
• If doing an LCA on a company basis, think through how data suppliers who are also raw material suppliers are going to be approached. Should the first contact be taken directly by the LCA practitioner or should it go through the purchasing department that already has regular contacts with the suppliers?
• Have a strategy for handling confidentiality issues and proprietary information.
• Decide whether data suppliers will be given the opportunity to review how their data are interpreted.
• Decide whether a data collection sheet should be used, either as a questionnaire to the data supplier or as a checklist for the LCA analyst. Examples of data collection sheets are given in ISO 14041 (1998) and Carlson & Pålsson (1998).

Validation of data

ISO 14041 (1998) requires that a check of the validity of collected data is performed. Examples of such checks are comparison with other data sources and mass and energy balances. To check against the data quality requirements formulated in the goal and scope definition is also important, especially whether the data is relevant for the intended use. Does data represent the "right" (i.e. the required) type of technology? Does data represent a specific site when site specific data was required, and if it does, does it represent the site which was intended to be modelled? Are the system boundaries of the data set collected in line with what was required? Are the data too old to be considered still valid? Etcetera. However, validity checks are only possible if data is documented thoroughly enough (see chapter 8).

4.3 Calculation procedure

When the flowchart is drawn and the data collected, the calculations can finally be done! An LCI is calculated in the following steps:

1 *Normalise* data for all the activities for which data have been collected, i.e. relate the other inputs and outputs of that activity to one of the products (or input for waste treatment processes). In this first step, do not try to relate the flows to the functional unit, but treat every activity individually. The step is needed since LCI data very seldom comes in a format that directly "fits" into the calculations. Data is very often received as valid for a total, yearly, production. They need to be recalculated to be valid for, for example, 1 kg or 1 tonne of product. In practice, the step usually also involves conversion of units. In theory, the normalisation of data for single activities is a very simple operation, but in practice mistakes are often made and errors introduced in this step, e.g. when converting units.

2 Calculate the flows *linking* the activities in the flowchart, using the flow representing the functional unit as a reference. This is done by setting up relationships between inflows and outflows ("mass balances") for the individual activities in the flow chart and solving the resulting equation system. One of the equations is the one defining the reference flow.

3 Calculate the flows *passing the system boundary,* again as related to the flow representing the functional unit. This is a simple operation, since step 2 has given the size of the linking flows and step 1 the relation between different flows for each activity.

4 *Sum up* the resource use and emissions to the environment for the whole system.

5 *Document* the calculations.

The procedure is illustrated in the example in box 4.1.

107

Box 4.1. Inventory calculations

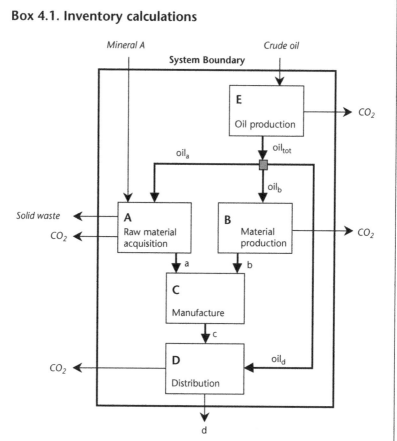

Figure 4.5 Flowchart. Bold arrows represent the flows linking the different activities in the life cycle. Thin arrows represent the flows passing the system boundaries, which summed up give the inventory result.

Consider the system represented by the flow chart in figure 4.5. The product c consists of a mineral raw material, a, and a plastic raw material, b. These two materials are assembled in process C, which uses no energy and has no emissions. The distribution of product c (activity D) requires energy in the form of *oil*, the combustion of which gives rise to emissions of carbon dioxide (CO_2). Use and waste treatment of the product is not modelled – the model is thus a cradle-to-gate inventory. The mineral raw material a, produced in process A, uses *mineral A* as a resource. The process requires *oil* and CO_2 is released. The plastic raw material *b* is produced from *oil* in process B. Part of the oil is combusted in the process, giving rise to CO_2 emissions. The *oil* used in activities A, B and D is produced in process E, which uses *crude oil* as a resource and also emits some CO_2.

The raw data, as collected, are shown in the first column in table 4.2. Process A uses 1000 tonnes of mineral A and 50 tonnes of oil per year and produces 800 tonnes *a*/year while emitting 150 tonnes of carbon dioxide and producing 200 tonnes of solid waste. Data for the processes B (material production), C (manufacture) and E (oil production) have similar formats. In contrast, the data for activity D, distribution, were not collected per annum, but the data found were given *per kg c*.

The first step of the calculations, normalisation, is shown in the second column. Normalisation simply means to relate the data to one tonne, or one kg (or other, optional, unit) of each activity's production (or input for waste treatment processes). For activity D, distribution, this was already how the data was given. For the remainder, the unit chosen for the normalised data was kg/kg product.

Next the flows linking the activities of the modelled system are calculated. The input data is used to formulate a system of equations describing the relationships between the flows, for example as follows:

$$oil_a = a \times 0.0625$$
$$oil_b = b \times 2.4$$
$$a + b = c$$
$$a / b = 0.25 / 0.75$$
$$c = 1$$
$$oil_d = d \times 7$$
$$oil_{tot} = oil_a + oil_b + oil_d$$

The *functional unit* is represented by the *reference flow 1 kg of c*. The definition of the reference flow is always one of the equations. Solving the set of equations results in the third column in table 4.2.

By now we know the flows out from each process per functional unit. We also know how the remaining flows relate to the output from each activity (i.e. the normalised data sets). The remaining flows are then easily calculated (column 4, table 4.2).

The inventory results for the whole system are then calculated as the sum of the flows passing the system boundary, as shown in the last section of table 4.2. Only the flows passing the system boundaries are part of this result. Not all of these are elementary, i.e. passing a system boundary between the technical system and the natural system. The product, flow *d*, goes to some other part of the technical system.

> The resulting data set may be seen as LCI data for a new, aggregated activity, which may be used in a subsequent LCI through linking one of its flows to models of other technical systems. However, the data for the new, aggregated activity is useful only if properly documented, i.e. only if system boundaries, allocation, computational procedures, etc, are documented. Documentation of calculations may be seen as the last step in the calculation procedure.

In practice, LCIs includes large amounts of data, for which reason dedicated LCA software tools are used for the calculations (for more information about these, see chapter 8). The tools use matrix inversion methods similar to what has been described above, or in some cases a sequential calculation of the inputs and outputs, with or without a number of iterations (CML 2002). Also linear programming has been used.

For small LCAs it may be as easy to solve the system of equations by hand (as recommended in exercise C) and then use an ordinary spreadsheet programme for the rest of the calculations, as out-lined in example 4.1. The advantage is that the practitioner then stays in full control of the calculations, whereas LCA software tools may contain hidden assumptions and the computational procedures are not always documented. The small LCA projects in exercises H1 to H10 are intended to be solved without the use of LCA software.

4.4 More about allocation

Allocation principles were discussed in chapter 3 on goal and scope definition, particularly the difference between partitioning and system enlargement. In the following we will discuss in more detail some of the allocation methods. But first let us repeat what the ISO 14041 standard (1998) says about allocation.

The standard puts down three principles concerning allocation, i.e. that activities shared between product systems must be identified before allocation, that the sum of allocated environmental loads shall equal the unallocated loads (the 100 % rule) and that

110

Table 4.2 Collected data for the system in figure 4.5 and stepwise calculations.

Activity A Raw material acquisition

	Data as collected	Normalised per activity	Linked flows, normalised to f.u.	Flows passing system boundary, normalised to f.u.
	tonne/year	kg/kg a	kg/kg c	kg/kg c
inflows				
mineral A	1 000	1.25		0.31
oil a	50	0.0625		
outflows				
a	800	1	0.016	
CO_2	150	0.1875		0.047
solid waste	200	0.25	0.25	0.0625

Activity B material aquisition

	Data as collected	Normalised per activity	Linked flows, normalised to f.u.	Flows passing system boundary, normalised to f.u.
	tonne/year	kg/kg b	kg/kg c	kg/kg c
inflows				
oil b	120 000	2.4	1.8	
outflows				
b	50 000	1	0.75	
CO_2	210 000	4.2		3.15

Activity C Manufacture

	Data as collected	Normalised per activity	Linked flows, normalised to f.u.	Flows passing system boundary, normalised to f.u.
	tonne/year	kg/kg c	kg/kg c	kg/kg c
inflows				
a	5 000	0.25	0.25	
b	15 000	0.75	0.75	
outflows				
c	20 000	1	1	

Activity D Distribution

	Data as collected	Normalised per activity	Linked flows, normalised to f.u.	Flows passing system boundary, normalised to f.u.
	tonne/year	kg/kg c	kg/kg c	kg/kg c
inflows				
c	1	1	1	
oil d	7	7	7	
outflows				
d	1	1		1
CO_2	21	21		21

Activity E Oil production

	Data as collected	Normalised per activity	Linked flows, normalised to f.u.	Flows passing system boundary, normalised to f.u.
	tonne/year	kg/kg oil	kg/kg c	kg/kg c
inflows				
crude oil	100 000	1.05		
outflows				
oil_{tot}	95 000	1	8.82	9.28
CO_2	15 000	0.16		1.39

Aggregated over system

	Flows passing system boundary, normalised to f.u.
	kg/kg c
inflows	
mineral A	0.31
crude oil	9.28
outflows	
CO_2	25.59
solid waste	0.0625
d	1

sensitivity analysis shall be carried out when several alternative allocation procedures seem possible. Then it sets out a procedure for dealing with allocation, as follows:

1 Whenever possible, allocation should be avoided by:
   a) increasing the level of detail of the model,
   b) expanding the system.

2 Where allocation cannot be avoided, the environmental loads should be partitioned between the system's "different products or functions in a way which reflects the underlying physical relationships between them; i.e. they shall reflect the way in which the inputs and outputs are changed by quantitative changes in the products or functions delivered by the system. The resulting allocation will not necessarily be in proportion to any simple measurement such as the mass or molar flow of co-products."

3 "Where physical relationship alone cannot be established or used as the basis for allocation, the inputs should be allocated between the products and functions in a way which reflects other relationships between them. For example, input and output data might be allocated between co-products in proportion to the economic value of the products."

Increased level of detail and system expansion have been discussed in chapter 3 and allocation in relation to economic value is not so difficult to understand. But what does it mean that allocation should reflect an underlying physical relationship? We will discuss some examples of allocation based on physical relationships in the following section, and then we will look into a selection of all the methods for allocation in open loop recycling that have been suggested.

Allocation based on physical relationship – examples

Allocation based on underlying physical relationships is often misunderstood as using the mass or molar ratio between outflows as a basis for allocation. However, the standard explicitly points out that this is not how the clause should be interpreted. Should allocation factors coincide with for instance the relative mass flows of co-products, this must be motivated by some technical-causal relationship. An example given in the ISO standard is cadmium emissions

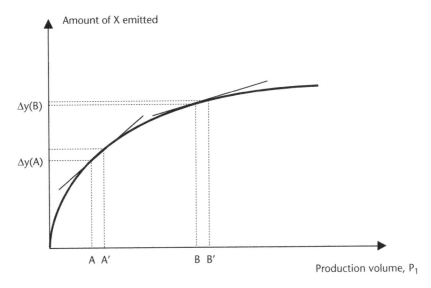

Figure 4.6 Example of a non-linear relationship between emission and production volume.

from waste incineration, which should only be allocated to cadmium containing products in the inflow to the incineration process. Another example is joint transportation of different products. Environmental load should be allocated between transported products on a mass basis if the loading of the vehicle is limited by weight and by volume if vehicle loading is limited by volume (ISO 14041 1998).

These examples are quite straightforward. However, the environmental load does not always depend linearly on the amount of product delivered by a process. Consider a process where the emission of pollutant X depends non-linearly on the production volume of product P_1, as in figure 4.6. Consider further that an LCA is conducted to support a decision on increasing production volume. If the process runs at point A, then an increase in production volume from A to A' will result in a much larger increase in emission of X than if production volume is increased from B to B'.

It has been suggested that allocation should be based on such non-linear behaviour of systems (Clift et al. 1999). However, it should be observed that allocation based on marginal response of a process violates the 100 % rule prescribed by the standard. It should further be noticed that the analysis underlying such an allocation is only valid for operation within the existing production capacity and can thus only accommodate certain scales of change.

Allocation in open loop recycling

Allocation in open loop recycling (OLR) has been one of the most debated issues in LCA methodology. A large number of methods have been suggested and doctoral dissertations have been written on the subject. We will give a brief overview of the flora of methods through applying a selection of methods to the example in box 4.2. The outcome is shown in figure 4.8. For a more complete picture and full references to the presented methods, see Ekvall & Tillman (1997).

A number of the allocation methods for open loop recycling (OLR) have been based on arguments about *fairness*, or expressed differently, on arguments about which product may be seen to be responsible, or *accountable*, for which activities in an OLR system. The cut-off method and methods that account for quality losses in the system may be put to this category. However, the two methods that most clearly belong to the fairness category are the ones based on arguments about whether "the problem" is that raw materials are extracted in the first place, and waste is thus inevitably produced or whether "the problem" rather is that when materials are not recycled, new, virgin materials must inevitably be extracted.

There are also more change-oriented methods based on arguments about what would happen if the recycling system is changed. These may be regarded as approximations of system enlargements. We will in the following first discuss the four fairness methods and then the two more change-oriented methods (i.e. the 50/50 method and the closed loop approximation). The results of all six methods when applied to the example in box 4.2 are shown in figure 4.8.

1 In the *cut-off method* only loads directly caused by a product are assigned to that product, i.e. virgin production is allocated to the first product, the first recycling process to the second product

114

Box 4.2 Open loop recycling

The example refers to an idealised open loop recycling system (figure 4.7). All material in product 1 is recycled into product 2. All material in product 2 is recycled into product 3. Product 2 and product 3 are produced from this recycled material only. The material in product 3 is not recycled after use. Only production of virgin material, recycling processes and final waste treatment are associated with more than one product and thus only the environmental loads of those processes need to be allocated between products. For simplification, only environmental loads of shared processes are considered in this example. These activities have the following environmental loads (only energy is considered):

$V1 = 5$ MJ/kg
$R1 = R2 = 3$ MJ/kg
$W3 = 1$ MJ/kg

The relative quality of the products are

$Q1 = 1$
$Q2 = 0.75$
$Q3 = 0.5$

The environmental load assigned to product 1 is denoted L1, the load assigned to product 2 L2 and the load assigned to product 3 L3.

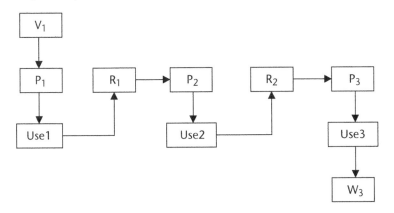

Figure 4.7 Simplified illustration of the processes and material flows in an idealised open loop recycling system. All material in product 1 is recycled into product 2. All material in product 2 is recycled into product 3. Product 2 and product 3 are produced from this recycled material only. The material in product 3 is not recycled after use (from Ekvall & Tillman 1997).

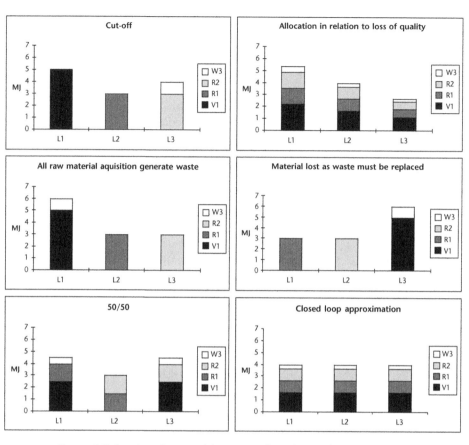

Figure 4.8 Results when applying a number of open loop recycling methods to example 4.2.

and the second recycling process and the waste treatment process are allocated to the last product (as also expressed by equations 1–3). The cut-off method is the easiest one to apply. No data from outside the life cycle of the investigated product are needed. As a refinement of the method, part of the recycling activities may be allocated down-stream in the recycling system.

$$L1 = V1 \qquad (1)$$
$$L2 = R1 \qquad (2)$$
$$L3 = R2 + W3 \qquad (3)$$

116

2 The environmental load may be assigned to the different products in relation to the *relative loss of quality* in each step. Various proposals have been made concerning exactly which processes should be allocated in this way. In the method presented in equations 4–6 and figure 4.8 loads from both production of virgin material, recycling processes and waste treatment are partitioned between all three products.

$$L1 = (Q1/(Q1+Q2+Q3)) \times (V1+R1+R2+W3) \qquad (4)$$
$$L2 = (Q2/(Q1+Q2+Q3)) \times (V1+R1+R2+W3) \qquad (5)$$
$$L3 = (Q3/(Q1+Q2+Q3)) \times (V1+R1+R2+W3) \qquad (6)$$

It is difficult to measure the quality of a material used in different products in an open loop recycling system. For example, if the first product is a PET bottle, the barrier properties are important. If the material is used as a textile material in a second life cycle, other material properties will be important for the quality of that product. If it is then finally used as a fuel, heat content will be decisive for quality in that application. Thus, it is probable that the only practical measure of quality in an open loop recycling system is economic value. The method, as presented in equations 4–6, requires knowledge and data about the whole recycling system.

3 Waste treatment may be seen an inevitable consequence of raw material extraction, in which case allocation according to equations 7–9 may seem fair.

$$L1 = V1 + W3 \qquad (7)$$
$$L2 = R1 \qquad (8)$$
$$L3 = R2 \qquad (9)$$

4 On the other hand, man-made materials may be seen as valuable resources that must be replaced by material from virgin resources if lost as waste. From this perspective the following allocation method may be formulated:

$$L1 = R1 \qquad (10)$$
$$L2 = R2 \qquad (11)$$
$$L3 = V1 + W3 \qquad (12)$$

Methods 3 and 4 both require data and knowledge about activities outside the life cycle of the product studied. Different incentives are built into these methods. Method 3, which regards waste treatment as the inevitable consequence of raw material extraction, promotes the use of recycled material (as long as the environmental impact from recycling is less than that from raw material production and waste treatment combined). Method 4, on the other hand, gives incentives for the development and production of recyclable products, whereas it gives no incentive for use of recycled material.

Instead of basing OLR allocation methods on arguments about which product in the system is responsible for what environmental impact, methods can be based on more change-oriented arguments. These are about what effects would be caused by changes in the recycling system. System expansion may be the answer to such arguments. However, due to uncertainties and data requirements system expansion may be difficult to apply to an OLR system. As a consequence, allocation methods have been developed that are approximations of system expansion.

5 The first of these is *approximation with closed loop recycling.* The approximation is valid for materials that do not loose too much quality when being recycled. Another underlying assumption is that the recycled material replaces virgin material without affecting recycling of other used material.

  When applied to the example in box 4.2 the *closed loop recycling approximation* may be expressed as

$$L1 = L2 = L3 = 1/3 \; V1 + 1/3 \; W3 + 1/3 \; (R1 + R2) \qquad (13)$$

The approximation may be applicable to materials such as metals, for which quality losses may be controlled in a recycling system through careful sorting and through keeping different fractions separated.

6 For degradable materials such as paper and plastics, which lose quality during recycling and thus cannot be recycled into the same product as easily, the closed loop approximation is less suitable. Under certain assumptions system expansion can be approximated by an allocation method called the 50/50-method. The 50/50-method is presented in more detail in Ekvall (1994) and in the Nordic Guidelines on LCA (Nord 1995). The main

118

assumption behind the method concerns the effects of increased recycling. It is assumed that recycled material replaces virgin material to 50 % and replaces other recycled material to 50 %.

Virgin material production and waste treatment are allocated to the first and the last product in equal proportions. Recycling processes are allocated to 50 % to the product upstream of the recycling process and to 50 % to the product downstream of the recycling process. Applied to the example in box 4.2 the method may be written as

$L1 = (V1 + W3)/2 + R1/2$ (14)
$L2 = (R1 + R2)/2$ (15)
$L3 = (V1 + W3)/2 + R2/2$ (16)

4.5 Accounting for recycling rate

There are a number of ways to express recycling rate, which may cause some confusion when conducting an LCA. In this section we will try to sort them out. The terminology is, however, not specific to LCA, but refer to any kind of description that involves recycling. The definitions in the following refer to figure 4.9 and are equally valid for material *recycling* (for example crushed glass re-melted to make new glass) and for *reuse* (for example glass bottles cleaned and used again).

Recycling rate (alternatively *reuse rate*) may refer to at least three different ratios; collection rate, recycling rate after losses during recycling and return rate. When discussing recycling rate it is important to know which one is referred to, so let us define them using figure 4.9:

Collection rate $= C = d/(c + d) \times 100$ %   (17)
Recycling rate after losses $= R = f/(c + d) \times 100$ %   (18)
Return rate $= RT = g/(g + a) \times 100$ %   (19)

There are examples of true closed loop recycling systems where material or products are returned to the same system after use and used for the same purpose again. Returnable bottle systems are an example, or systems with reuse of toner cartridges. Also the recycling of aluminium beverage packaging is quite a closed system, due to the specific quality requirements for aluminium for different applications. In such cases, $f = g$ and thus $R = RT$.

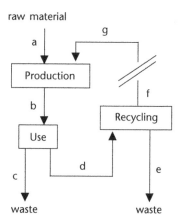

Figure 4.9 System with recycling. Flows are denoted a–g. Collection is included in recycling activities. Production of virgin raw material and treatment of waste are outside the system boundaries.

However, many material recycling systems are not truly closed, even if they are modelled as such in LCAs. This means that the rate at which recycled material is used in a production unit may differ from the recycling rate after losses of the same material. In such cases, $f \neq g$ and thus $R \neq RT$. This problem is encountered in exercise C, Beginner's LCA.

All the alternative ways to express recycling rate so far describe the degree to which a material is recycled. To complicate matters, recycling rate is sometimes expressed in an alternative manner, as the number of times a product or material is used before being disposed of, sometimes referred to as the *trip number*.

Trip number = N   (20)

Let us go on and see how trip number is related to recycling rate. The same system may be described with two alternative models, as in figure 4.10. In model A the recycling is described as a loop and in model B it is described as consecutive uses. If the two models in figure 4.10 are equivalent, then they must deliver the same function and must have the same inflows and outflows.

For simplicity, a closed loop recycling or reuse system is considered and losses during recycling are assumed to be negligible, implying that $C = R = RT$.

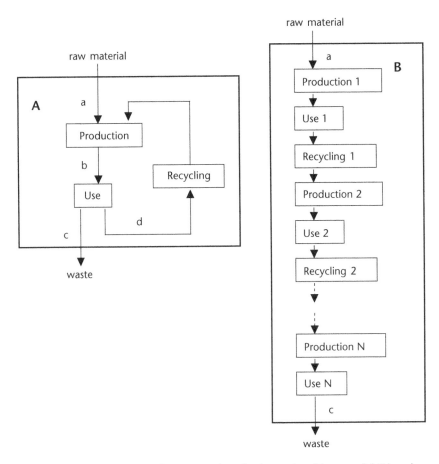

Figure 4.10 The same recycling system described as a closed loop model (A) and as a model with consecutive uses (B). Losses during recycling are assumed to be negligible. Collection is included in recycling activities. Production of virgin raw material and treatment of waste are outside the system boundaries.

Assume that the function delivered in model A equals 1. Then the function delivered on each trip in model B is $1/N$, which in turn implies that the inflow to each use-activity in model B is b/N.

Mass balance over 'use' in model A gives: $b = c + d$ (21)

Mass balance over 'use N' in model B gives: $b/N = c$ (22)

Combining these equations gives: $d = c(N-1)$ (23)

121

Box 4.3 Conversion between trip number and recycling rate

Of 100 items of a product, 60 % are reused once, and the remaining part goes to waste. Calculate the over-all recycling rate.

The question, as given, implicitly refers to a model as in figure 4.11 A. The assignment is to reformulate the example to a model as in figure 4.11 B, and calculate the recycling rate C in such a model.

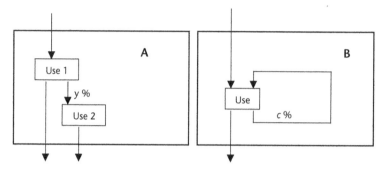

Figure 4.11 Recycling system described as a model with some of the products being used twice (A) and as a closed loop model (B).

In model A, a fraction denominated y delivers two functions (has trip number 2) whereas the remaining fraction only has a trip number of 1. The 100 items thus deliver $100(1+y)$ functions. The outflow from model A, which consists of both fractions, must equal the inflow and is thus 100 items.

If the models are equivalent, model B delivers the same number of functions as model A, i.e. $100(1+y)$ functions, implying that the total outflow from the use activity in B must be $100(1+y)$. We can set up the following equation for model B:

$C = (1-c) \times$ *total outflow from use* $= (1-c) \times 100(1 + y)$
$C = y/(1 + y) = 0.6/(1 + 0.6) = 37.5$ %

If we insert this last expression into expression (17), $C = d/(c + d)$ we get

$$C = 1-1/N \qquad (24)$$

or vice versa

$$N = 1/(1-C) \qquad (25)$$

Sometimes assumptions on how many times a product may be used are questioned. Since LCI results depend linearly on recycling rate, equation 25 shows that they are less sensitive to trip number the higher the trip number.

4.6 Accounting for energy use in LCI

In this section we will discuss some details of how to account for energy in LCI. Reasons for accounting for energy will be given and the risk of accounting for the same energy twice will be discussed. Finally, we will discuss how to account for feed-stock energy, i.e. the energy content of raw materials.

Energy use is always accounted for in LCI, but one could well ask why? Energy use as such does not cause environmental impact. Would it not be enough to account for mass flows (kg oil, coal, biomass, uranium etc) or the land used for hydropower? In principle, the answer is "yes", and this was actually what was done in example 4.1. However, there are a number of good reasons to account for energy use as such. One is that energy use is a type of parameter that is easy to communicate and, for better or for worse, it is often understood as a proxy for energy related environmental impact. A second, more practical reason is that energy data is relatively easy to collect. Emissions are not always measured, but some of them may be estimated from the energy use.

It may be argued that accounting for the same flows both in mass units and in energy units implies a double-counting. As far as the inventory analysis is concerned, this argument is invalid. To give the results of both mass and energy calculations simply means that two different properties of the same flows are reported. Double-counting does, however, occur if both properties are given weight in a consecutive interpretation, should for example weighting factors be applied to both mass and energy content of the same flow.

Energy flows in life cycles

Let us look into how energy generally flows in life cycles, using the schematic flowchart in figure 4.12. Raw materials that are extracted may either go into the product or they may be used for energy purposes. Some raw materials (e.g. fossil fuels, wood and crops) that go into products carry a heat content with them, which is then called feed-stock energy. Examples of raw materials without heat content are bauxite, iron ore and gravel.

Usually, the first process that meets a raw material is a separation, where different fractions of the raw material are separated from one another. By-products are generated and sometimes also waste. If the raw material has a heat content, so will the by-products and waste. Examples of products from such initial separation processes are the different refinery products from oil, the seed and the straw from crops, and the bark and the wood from round wood. Sometimes the heat content of the by-products is used in the further processing of the main product. This is the case for pulp production, for instance.

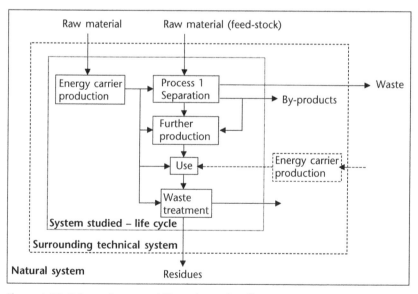

Figure 4.12 Schematic, general life cycle used to illustrate the energy flows in a life cycle. Transports are omitted for simplicity.

Additional energy is almost always required and consequently life cycles always include production of energy carriers, both fuels and electricity.

The last phase of a life cycle is waste treatment or waste water treatment. Such processes may deliver energy, for example through incineration or anaerobic digestion. Such recovered energy flows are not used within the life cycle studied, but pass the system boundary to surrounding technical systems. (They thereby cause an open loop recycling allocation problem.) The energy recovered in waste treatment processes usually has its origin in the raw material of the product studied. This is true for paper products originating from wood and food products originating from crops. It also holds for plastics, where energy released during incineration comes from the oil. However, a material such as aluminium, which is combustible if thin enough, has received its heat content not from bauxite, but as process energy during electrolysis.

What is reported as inventory results are the useful energy flows passing the system boundaries. Diffuse heat is disregarded. However, sometimes energy flows internal to the system are also reported. This is most common for electricity, which is sometimes reported as such, in parallel with the primary energy used to produce the electricity. (Primary energy means the energy extracted from the natural system for producing the electricity.) There is a risk of double-counting when such reporting is used, should internal flows (kWh electricity) by mistake be added to flows passing the system boundaries (MJ primary energy).

Feed-stock energy

The heat content of raw materials not used as an energy source is referred to as feed-stock energy (ISO 14041 1998). Referring to figure 4.12, feed-stock energy only refers to the raw material flow entering the material production chain. The energy content of raw materials for energy carrier production is not included in the concept. Accounting for feed-stock energy in LCA may cause double-counting if not done carefully. There are at least two possible ways to do so, as we will discuss in the following.

One method is to account for the heat content of the raw material when it passes the system boundary. If this method is used, care must be taken so that parts of that energy used in later stages of the life cycle as process energy are not accounted for twice. In addition, it may be necessary to allocate the energy content of the feed-stock between the main product and the by-products. A drawback of the method is that it does not distinguish between energy actually used during the life cycle and energy that is still available as a heat content in the product, possible to recover.

Alternatively, the heat content of the product or the material produced may be used to account for feed-stock energy. Then process energy that originates from the raw material must be accounted for separately. Depending on which data are available for the inventory analysis, this method often gives easier calculations. The method distinguishes between energy actually used during the life cycle and energy that is possible to recover from used products. Allocation procedures may be simplified if this method is used since by-products carry their energy content with them out of the system studied.

The main difference between the two methods is that the heat content of the raw material is accounted for in different categories. The overall result should be the same, provided allocation procedures do not cause differences.

Several waste treatment processes generate useful energy, which originates from the feed-stock of the materials going into the waste treatment process. Such energy is usually credited to the life cycle, through allocation or system enlargement. It should be noted that no such crediting may be done unless the feed-stock energy is accounted for.

4.7 Summary and further reading

This chapter has covered the practical detail of carrying out an LCI according to its procedure:

1 Construction of a flow chart according to the system boundaries decided on in the goal and scope definition.

2 Data collection for all the activities in the product system followed by documentation of collected data.
3 Calculation of the environmental loads (resource use and pollutant emissions) of the system in relation to the functional unit.

Having read the chapter, it is time to do exercise C, Beginner's LCA,
which will take you through all the computational steps of an LCA,
exercise D on data collection and exercise E, which is a computing
exercise on allocation.

The chapter has also given some more detail about different allocation methods. There exists a large number of possible ways to
allocate, especially in the case of open loop recycling. In the overview of open loop allocation methods, methods based on arguments about fairness are distinguished from more change-oriented
approaches. A more complete review of different allocation methods for open loop recycling may be found in Ekvall and Tillman
(1997). Discussion about allocation has been intense in the LCA
community. A good glimpse of the debate may be found in the proceedings from a SETAC workshop devoted to the subject (Huppes &
Schneider 1994).

In the last sections of the chapter, different ways to account for
recycling rate were discussed, along with methods to account for
energy use in LCI.

The chapter has described state-of-the art LCI methodology with
all its limitations and pitfalls. The normative reference to the LCI
methodology is of course the ISO standard (ISO 14041 1998).
Researchers are never content though, for which reason there are
on-going efforts to improve inventory methodology. One trend in
this line of research is towards more sophisticated modelling and
computational procedures. State-of-the art LCI models are steady
state models based on linear relationships only. This is of course a
simplification: reality is neither static nor linear. Consequently,
efforts have been made to include non-linearities in the models as
well as to build dynamic LCI-models. Also more sophisticated computational procedures have been deployed, particularly multi-
objective optimisation, as will be further described in chapter 11.

Another trend is to include relationships other than physical
ones in the models. Models of market behaviour have been used to
underpin allocation methods and economic input/output models

are being combined with LCI. The European network on environmental input-output analysis held its first meeting in 2001 (Suh
2001). LCI is also being developed towards including more types of
result parameters. Most attention has been paid to economic
parameters, typically cost parameters, but also parameters describing product performance have been included. Examples of such
models will be given in chapter 11.

5 Life cycle impact assessment

The phase of an LCA called life cycle impact assessment (LCIA) aims at describing the *environmental consequences* of the environmental loads quantified in the inventory analysis. The impact assessment is achieved by "translating" the environmental loads from the inventory results into environmental impacts, such as acidification, ozone depletion, effect on biodiversity, etc.

There are several reasons for this translation. For many, it is easier to relate to for example acidification consequences than to SO_2. The purpose is thus to make the results more environmentally relevant, comprehensible and easier to communicate. Another purpose is to improve the readability of the results. The number of inventory result parameters can range from 50 to 200 or more. This can make the inventory results difficult to grasp. Through the LCIA, the number of parameters can be reduced to approximately 15 by grouping the environmental loads of the inventory results into environmental impact categories, or even down to one by weighting across the impact categories. LCIA is also useful for making results more comparable. Comparability is a problem when alternatives have very different environmental profiles, as illustrated in figure 5.1. One of the products gives rise to more emissions of "ordinary" pollutants, and the other gives rise to more toxic ones. Which of the two has the least impact on the environment? Translating the inventory result parameters into more general impact categories is a way to transcend this incomparability.

In this chapter the problem of translating resource use and emissions into environmental impacts is described and discussed. The general categories of environmental impacts needing consideration in an LCA include *resource use, human health* and *ecological consequences*. There is widespread consensus on these overarching three categories, as evidenced by several documents (SETAC 1993;

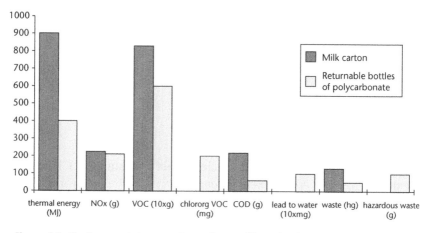

Figure 5.1 Environmental comparison of two milk packaging systems, milk cartons and returnable bottles made of polycarbonate plastic (only selected LCI parameters are shown). The basis of comparison is per 1000 l of milk (based on Tillman et al. 1991).

LCANET 1997; ISO 14040 1997), even if terminology varies. They may be called *safeguard subjects* or *areas of protection*. For practical reasons, the three categories are usually subdivided into more specific impact categories (global warming, acidification, ozone depletion, human toxicity, etc). This chapter also includes a description of the general structure of LCIA. The ISO has issued a standard also on LCIA (ISO 14042 2000), which is described in greater detail in section 5.2. In addition a number of "ready-made" LCIA methods are presented.

After reading this chapter, you should be able to carry out exercise F on impact assessment. It is an exercise in grouping resource use and emissions into impact categories. You should also be able to distinguish between the LCIA methods in appendices 2 and 3, i.e. to account for their difference in principle and underlying values.

130

5.1 What is an environmental impact?

What may at first seem to be a simple question with a self-evident answer can easily become more complicated the more you think about it.

To describe the environmental impacts of emissions and resource use quantitatively using the three categories resource use, human health and ecological consequences is not an uncomplicated affair. Environmental problems are complex and still not fully understood. As a consequence, different attempts at developing models to describe environmental impacts have led to different results. The complexity of the environmental problems is illustrated in figure 5.2 by the web-like cause-effect chains linking emission of pollutants to their consequences. One primary effect of a pollutant can be the cause of several secondary effects, or vice versa. Also illustrated in figure 5.2 is the possibility of feed-back effects.

As an example, consider the greenhouse effect. This effect is caused by several gases (CO_2, CH_4, N_2O, CFCs, etc). They all absorb thermal (infrared) radiation, which leads to a disturbed balance between the energy absorbed by the earth and the energy emitted by it. This change of the radiative forcing can be called a primary effect. It is a function of a substance's properties, its ability to absorb radiation, as well as its fate in the atmosphere. The change in radiative forcing is expected to change global temperature, which could be called a secondary effect. At this level enters an area-dependency since the temperature change will not be uniformly distributed over the earth. The temperature change is expected to lead to tertiary effects such as ice-melting, raised sea levels and changed weather patterns. These changes will in turn cause higher-order effects such as biodiversity changes in different ecosystems as well as various impacts on society (e.g. changed agricultural practices, flood refugees). So when the term "greenhouse effect" is used, what is actually being referred to, increased temperature, higher sea levels, or ...?

Given these cause-effect chains, it is possible to describe environmental impacts at different levels. Especially when describing environmental impacts as low-order effects, the fates of the pollutants are not considered. This means that the *potential* rather than the actual effects of the pollutants are described. However, this is a prac-

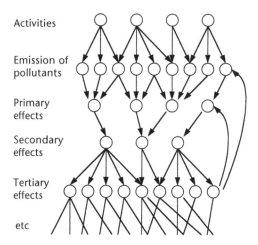

Activities

Emission of
pollutants

Primary
effects

Secondary
effects

Tertiary
effects

etc

Figure 5.2 Cause-effect chain of environmental impacts (after Finnveden et al. 1992).

tical way of avoiding the problem of having to add up environmental problems of the different geographical locations in a life cycle. As a result, global impacts are better dealt with than local impacts in LCAs.

Although there is widespread consensus that the impact on resource use, human health and ecology should be assessed, there are problems with this categorisation. One concerns the end-points of the cause-effect chains. A discussion on end-points relates to that pollution impacts not only nature, but also society, for example in the form of acid-rain induced corrosion on steel constructions and damages on cultural heritage. Therefore, it has been suggested that man-made environment should be the fourth safeguard subject. Another problem concerning the categorisation is to what extent the end-points of the cause-effect chains correspond to the three (or four) general categories and their sub-categories. Examples of tricky sub-categories are *work environment* and *aesthetics* (e.g. landscape scenery).

The trickiness is due to the lack of easily defined boundaries between the categories, which the following philosophical questions illustrate. Does assigning special weight to environmental impacts on humans lead to too much attention being paid to humans instead of to nature? And does it mean that humans are not part of nature? Is it sufficient to assess human toxicity in the category work environment or should stress, child labour and gender issues at the workplace also be included? Would an assessment of the landscape scenery lead to double-counting if also impacts on biodiversity were to be assessed? There is ambivalence concerning resource use. Some have argued that resource depletion is an economic and societal problem rather than an environmental one. If so, in the case of fossil fuels, an assessment of the size of the oil reserves leads to double-counting if also the emissions from oil combustion (i.a. CO_2) are assessed. One must therefore consider whether or not the definition of impact categories leads to double-counting or over-emphasis of certain environmental problems.

Given the numerous alternative ways of describing environmental impacts, different strategies can be chosen. One possibility is to trace pollutants through cause-effect chains and decide on what level to describe their environmental impact. This process is described in the ISO standard on impact assessment (ISO 14042 2000). However, this is generally too time-consuming, not to say too difficult for most people. An alternative that bypasses this problem is to use one or a few of the many "ready-to-use" LCIA methods that exist. In the context of an LCA study, this is what the LCA practitioner typically does. A way to view the ISO standard on LCIA is to see it as a standard for making "ready-to-use" LCIA methods. Some of these LCIA methods are presented and their respective underlying principles discussed in sections 5.3 and 5.4.

5.2 The different phases of life cycle impact assessment

The ISO standard for LCIA (ISO 14042) is detailed with regard to the number of sub-phases, as figure 5.3 shows. It contains the following:

- Impact category definition. Identification and selection of impact categories, models of cause-effect chains and their endpoints.

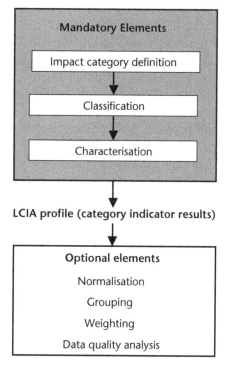

Figure 5.3 Life cycle impact assessment (LCIA) according to ISO 14042 (2000).

- Classification. Assignment of LCI result parameters to their respective impact category(ies).
- Characterisation. Calculation of the extent of the environmental impact per category.
- Normalisation. Relating the characterisation results to a reference value, for example relating the impacts of the studied product to the impacts of the total amount of pollutants emitted in a region.
- Grouping. Sorting and possibly ranking of the indicators.
- Weighting. Aggregation of characterisation results across impact categories.
- Data quality analysis. Includes sensitivity analysis among other things in order to obtain a better understanding of the reliability of the LCIA results.

134

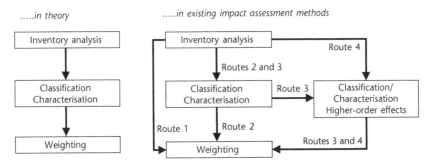

Figure 5.4 Impact assessment in theory and in practice. The different LCIA methods are represented by four different procedural routes.

Not all the sub-phases in the LCIA have the same level of importance. Some are mandatory while others are optional for an LCA. The subdivision between mandatory and optional elements reflects a desire to separate objective and subjective elements in the procedure, i.e. those based on natural science and those that are contextually defined.

The core LCIA sub-phases are classification, characterisation and weighting since these are the ones an LCA practitioner typically will have to deal with when performing an LCA study. When using ready-made LCIA methods many of the LCIA sub-phases are not executed by the LCIA practitioner since they are "inside" the LCIA method. As illustrated in figure 5.4, this leads to a perceived difference between the procedure as prescribed in the standard and how it appears to the LCA practitioner in practice.

Impact category definition

The set of impact categories is defined in the definition sub-phase. In practice this can be a specification of environmental impacts considered relevant in the goal and scope definition. Such a specification is sometimes based on what information was collected during the inventory analysis. Several things should be considered when deciding on which impact categories to include (Nord 1995; SETAC-Europe 1996; ISO 14042 2000):

- Completeness. The list of impact categories should cover all environmental problems of relevance, i.e. problems that are generally regarded as major environmental problems and also problems that may be of specific interest for the particular LCA study.
- Practicality. The list should not contain too many categories.
- Independence. The categories should be mutually independent in order to avoid double-counting.
- Possibility to integrate in the LCA calculations. This implies that it should be possible to link the LCI result parameters to chosen impact categories and characterisation methods.
- Environmental relevance. Indicators derived from characterisation methods should be environmentally relevant to the impact category and safeguard subjects.
- Scientific method. Characterisation methods should have scientific validity.

Some of these considerations may conflict with each other. For example, completeness and practicality may work in different directions.

Several suggestions on complete sets of impact categories can be found in the LCA literature. Tables 5.1, 5.2, 5.3 and 5.4 show four examples. They reflect differences in describing environmental impacts at different effect levels (primary, secondary, tertiary, etc). Tables 5.1 and 5.2 are similar in that their impact categories represent low-order effects, while those in table 5.3 represent higher-order effects. Both tables 5.1 and 5.2 point to the importance of including inventory results representing flows to and/or from other technical systems as these cannot be assigned to any of the impact categories. Table 5.4 shows a practical way of prioritising among impact categories. Despite the aspiration for objectivity, the set of impact categories in table 5.2 was decided on by the SETAC working group on LCIA by voting (LCANET 1997).

Table 5.1 List of impact categories according to Nordic Guidelines on Life-Cycle Assessment (Nord 1995). The categories can be further divided into sub-categories as noted in the footnotes.

Impact categories

1[a].	Resources – Energy and material
2.	Resources – Water
3.	Resources – Land (including wetlands)
4[b].	Human health – Toxicological impacts (excluding work environment)
5[b].	Human health – Non-toxicological impacts (excluding work environment)
6[b].	Human health impacts in work environment
7.	Ecological consequences – Global warming
8.	Ecological consequences – Depletion of stratospheric ozone
9.	Ecological consequences – Acidification
10.	Ecological consequences – Eutrophication
11.	Ecological consequences – Photo-oxidant formation
12.	Ecological consequences – Ecotoxicological impacts
13[c].	Ecological consequences – Habitat alterations and impacts on biodiversity
14[d].	Inflows which are not traced back
15[d].	Outflows which are not followed back

a This impact category can be divided into several sub-categories. For examples, a division can be made between energy and materials. Another division can be made between renewable and non-renewable resources. These choices can be made in relation to the choice of characterisation methods.

b Work environment is one among other exposure situations for humans. Here, it is suggested to treat this situation separately, partly because available characterisation methods often make this distinction.

c Several of the impact categories can cause "Habitat alterations and impacts on the biological diversity" as a second order effect. This impact category, however, is related to activities and emissions that have a direct impact on habitats and biodiversity.

d Not impact categories, but should be included.

Table 5.2 List of impact categories according to SETAC-Europe working group on life cycle impact assessment (SETAC-Europe 1996).

Impact categories

Input-related categories
1. Abiotic resources (deposits, funds, flows)
2. Biotic resources (funds)
3. Land

Pro memoria (flows to/from other technical systems)

Input-related (energy, materials, plantation wood, etc.)

Output-related (solid waste, etc.)

Output-related categories
4. Global warming
5. Depletion of stratospheric ozone
6. Human toxicological impacts
7. Ecotoxicological impacts
8. Photo-oxidant formation
9. Acidification
10. Eutrophication (incl. BOD and heat)
11. Odour
12. Noise
13. Radiation
14. Casualties

Table 5.3 The impact categories of the EPS system are called safeguard subjects (Ryding & Steen 1991; Steen & Ryding 1992; Steen 1999a).

Safeguard subjects

1. Human health
2. Biological diversity
3. Ecosystem production capacity (e.g. crops, wood, fish, meat)
4. Abiotic resources (e.g. fossil fuels, metals)
5. Cultural and recreational values (e.g. aesthetics, landscape scenery)

Table 5.4 Grouping of impact categories with regard to environmental relevance and availability of characterisation methods suggested in CML's guide to the ISO standards. Group A consists of those categories for which characterisation methods exist and which are included in most LCA studies. Group B categories may merit inclusion depending on the type of LCA study and availability of data. Group C categories need more research before they can be used in LCA studies (CML 2002).

A (baseline categories)	B (study-specific categories)	C (other categories)
Depletion of abiotic resources		Depletion of biotic resources
Impact of land use: – Land competition	Impact of land use: – Loss of life-support function – Loss of biodiversity	
Ecotoxicity: – Freshwater aquatic toxicity – Marine aquatic toxicity – Terrestrial toxicity	Ecotoxicity: – Freshwater sediment toxicity – Marine sediment toxicity	
Human toxicity	Odour: – Malodorous air	Odour: – Malodorous water
Climate change Stratospheric ozone depletion Photo-oxidant formation Acidification Eutrophication	Impact of ionising radiation Noise Waste heat Casualties	Desiccation Etc.

Classification

Classification simply means that the LCI result parameters are sorted and assigned to the various impact categories. This requires some knowledge of what kind of impacts pollutants and resource use lead to. Fortunately, published lists where various substances are listed per impact category are helpful (see e.g. appendix 2).

Certain environmental loads need to be assigned to more than one category. In the case of NO_x this parameter is assigned to the acidification category as well as to the eutrophication category. NO_x can even be assigned to three categories since a single NO_x molecule can first take part in chemical reactions leading to photo-oxidant formation. It can then cause the release of an acidifying hydrogen ion (H^+), and later contribute to eutrophication via the nitrogen atom. Such a multiple assignment is only made for effects that are independent of each other. If the effects are dependent on each other, for example global warming and global warming induced impacts on biodiversity, double assignment leads to double-counting. A warning to such double-counting is found in footnote c) to table 5.1: "Several of the impact categories can cause 'Habitat alterations and impacts on the biological diversity' as a second order effect. This impact category, however, is related to activities and emissions having a direct impact on habitats and biodiversity."

Characterisation

Characterisation is a quantitative step. The sizes of environmental impacts are calculated per category using *equivalency factors* defined while modelling the cause-effect chains. For example, all acidifying emissions (SO_2, NO_x, HCl, etc) in the LCI results are added up based on their equivalency factors, resulting in a sum indicating the extent of the acidification impact. The equivalency factors of the acidifying pollutants are defined by their common denominator: they all release H^+ (which causes the acidification). Each SO_2 molecule causes the release of two H^+ while each HCl molecule releases one H^+. Their molar equivalency factors are thus 2 and 1, respectively. Counting the number of hydrogen ions (H^+) released by acidifying pollutants says something about the *potential* impact of these pollutants, but nothing about their actual impact since information about where the acidifying pollutants are deposited is not taken into consideration here. If for example these pollutants are deposited in an area where the soil is rich in limestone the hydrogen ions are buffered and the acidifying impact is reduced.

The terminology concerning *equivalency factors* is quite varied in the LCA literature. They are sometimes called simply *equivalents* or *potentials*. In the ISO standard, the term *category indicators* is used. In other texts it is possible to read about *characterisation factors*.

The definition of characterisation methods with suitable equivalency factors is in principle based on the physico-chemical mechanisms of how different substances contribute to the different impact categories, i.e. based on the natural sciences. With equivalency factors based on physico-chemical mechanisms, the effects of deposition in geographical areas with different sensitivities to pollutants is disregarded, as exemplified in the case of acidifying pollutants. In other words, the potential impact represents the maximum impact. In practice, good characterisation methods exist for some of the impact categories (e.g. acidification) where the mechanisms are relatively simple and well known, and are less well developed for others (e.g. eco-toxicity) where the mechanisms are more complicated. An overview of various characterisation methods for the different impact categories is presented in section 5.3.

Normalisation

In the normalisation step, the characterisation results are related to (i.e. divided by) the actual (or predicted) magnitude for each impact category. The aim of this is to gain a better understanding of the magnitude of the environmental impacts caused by the system under study. With normalisation, it becomes possible to see when for example acidification impacts caused by the studied product are large in relation to total acidification impacts in the country where the product is produced and used. This relation is perhaps not so meaningful when the comparison is made between the impact per functional unit and the total impact in the region. It is more meaningful when the comparison is made between the total impact of the total use of the product and the total impact in the region.

Grouping

Grouping involves sorting the characterisation results into one or more sets. This can be useful for the analysis and the presentation of results. Examples of suitable group headings are *global / regional / local impacts*, and *impacts with high / medium / low priority*.

It is worth noting that although grouping is described in the context of LCIA in the ISO standard, grouping is also applicable when presenting LCI results. Grouping in the context of an LCI could for example mean that LCI result parameters are presented in the groups *emissions to air, emissions to water*, etc.

Weighting

Weighting can be defined as the qualitative or quantitative procedure where the relative importance of an environmental impact is weighted against all the other. The relative weights of the different impact categories are expressed by their *weighting factors*.

The methods for generating the weighting factors are predominantly based in the social sciences and on several kinds of principles (LCANET 1997; EEA 1997):

- Monetarisation. In this approach our values concerning the environment are described as the costs of various kinds of environmental damage or as the prices of various environmental goods. Economic valuation methodologies are concerned with how values are described for goods for which there is no market (and therefore no price). A "price" can be derived from individuals' willingness-to-pay (i.e. they are asked how much they are willing to pay to avoid extinction of a species, for example) or revealed by their behaviour (e.g. the difference in price of similar houses close to and far away from an airport reveals the cost of noise). This economic approach is based on the premises that social values are measured by the aggregation of individuals' preferences and that values of environmental qualities can be substituted by other commodities.
- Authorised targets. The difference between current levels of pollution and targeted levels can be used to derive weighting factors. Target levels can be formulated by national authorities as well as by companies. This approach could be said to be based on a distance-to-target thinking.
- Authoritative panels. Panels can be made up of scientific experts, government representatives, decision makers in a company and residents in an area, to name a few examples. Panel methods typically let the panellists describe and rank various types of impacts so that weighting factors representative for the panellists can be derived. Several techniques for deriving their weighting factors exist. Examples of such techniques are the Delphi technique and those building on multi-attribute utility theory.
- Proxies. In a proxy approach one or a few parameters are stated to be indicative for the total environmental impact. Examples of proxy parameters are *energy consumption* and *weight*.

- Technology abatement. The possibility of reducing environmental loads by using different technological abatement methods (e.g. filters, etc) can be used to set weighting factors. This approach could be said to be based on a distance-to-technically-feasible-target thinking.

Since ethical and ideological values are involved in the weighting element in LCIA, there will never be a consensus on these values. Many engineers therefore have an awkward relationship to weighting, and the use of weighting factors often lead to discussion about whether they are "scientifically correct" or not, whether the values are representative or not, etc. This awkwardness also relates to discussions of what is objective and what is subjective. Although our values concerning the environment are subjective, the methods for describing them as weighting factors are objective in the sense that the resulting weighting factors should in principle be empirically verifiable. In order not to trample on anyone's feelings, the ISO 14042 standard (2000) recommends that it may be ...

> "... desirable to use several different weighting factors and weighting methods and to conduct sensitivity analysis to assess the consequences on the LCIA results of different value choices and weighting methods. All weighting methods and operations used shall be documented to provide transparency."

Data quality analysis

Additional techniques and information may be needed to better understand the significance, uncertainty and sensitivity of the LCIA results. These techniques can also be used to guide the iterative procedure in LCAs. These techniques are used in order to identify (ISO 14042 2000):

- the most polluting activities in the life cycle (dominance analysis[1]),
- the most crucial inventory data, i.e. the data describing the activities in the life cycle for which slight changes in value change the ranking between compared alternatives (sensitivity analysis),

1   Dominance analysis is called gravity analysis in the ISO standard on LCA.

- the most crucial impact assessment data, i.e. data describing impact categories for which slight changes in value change the ranking between compared alternatives (sensitivity analysis),
- the significance of alternative methodological choices, e.g. different types of allocation (sensitivity analysis), and
- the degree of uncertainty in the results (uncertainty analysis). Uncertainty is introduced to the calculations when input data are estimates, intervals or probabilities.

These and other types of analyses, which are part of the interpretation phase of an LCA, are further described in chapter 6.

5.3 Characterisation methods

In this section we look more closely at characterisation methods, central for LCIA, since they translate environmental load into impact.

Characterisation methods in LCA are based on scientific methods, drawn from environmental chemistry, toxicology, ecology, etc, for describing environmental impacts. Characterisation methods for pollutants are often a combination of description of physico-chemical properties of the pollutants and modelling of the fate of the pollutants in the environment. For resources, land use, noise, casualties, etc, other modelling principles, based on occurrence or frequencies, are used.

The complexity of environmental systems has led to certain impact categories having several alternative characterisation models. There are also categories for which characterisation methods are missing or which have incomplete sets of equivalency factors. Research is in progress internationally to fill the gaps. A comprehensive overview of the development of characterisation methods can be found in the reports from the SETAC working group on impact assessment (SETAC-WIA2 2001) and the guide to the ISO standards on LCA assembled by the Centre of Environmental Science at Leiden University in the Netherlands (CML 2002).

Generally, the characterisation methods for many of the emission-caused impacts (acidification, eutrophication, global warming, etc) are more developed than those concerning for example resource use, land use and toxic substances. In practice, when characterisation methods are missing, characterised results need to be complemented with some kind of assessment of not characterised inventory results. Otherwise the impact assessment leads to over-emphasis of certain environmental impacts and neglect of others. It is also possible for the ambitious LCA practitioner with a good knowledge of environmental science to develop additional equivalency factors and new characterisation methods. This section presents some of the thinking and modelling underlying the different characterisation methods and problems concerning the different impact categories in LCA. The impact categories are described following the order of the SETAC-WIA2 list in table 5.2.

Resources

Resource depletion is one of the most debated topics concerning how impact assessment should be done. Consequently a wide variety of impact assessment methods have been developed. As yet there is no consensus on any of the methods and research is continuing. Furthermore, existing methods are incomplete in the sense that a limited number of resources are covered. To a large extent, the different methodologies differ in the way they regard resource depletion as an environmental problem. Some view a diminishing pool of resources as an environmental problem in itself; others view it as a societal problem, thus something outside the scope of LCA, and focus instead on the environmental impacts associated with resource extraction (mining, drilling, etc); others again focus on sustainable alternatives (SETAC-WIA2 2001; CML 2002).

Characterisation modelling differs depending on the type of resource. Resources can be divided into renewable and non-renewable resources (Nord 1995) or into abiotic and biotic resources (SETAC-WIA2 2001; CML 2002). Abiotic resources are those considered as non-living resources such as iron ore, crude oil and wind energy; biotic resources are "living", i.e. those with a biological character. Examples of biotic resources are forests, animals and plants. Resources such as peat and topsoil are difficult to classify since they are partly biotic and partly abiotic. Often peat is classified as abiotic while topsoil is classified as both biotic (for the organic part) and abiotic (for the mineral part) (SETAC-WIA2 2001). Also, a distinction between whether resources are deposits, funds and flows is often made. Deposits are resources that are not regenerated within human lifetimes, e.g. fossil fuels, minerals and clays. These are sometimes called non-renewable resources. Funds are resources that can be regenerated within human lifetimes, e.g. groundwater and topsoil. Flows are resources that are constantly regenerated, e.g. rivers, wind and solar energy (Finnveden 1996). Another term for flows is renewable resources.

There are no useful methods for impact assessment of flow resources yet, whereas several methods for deposit-type abiotic resources exist. A few characterisation methods for biotic resources have been suggested, but there is a need for more research (CML 2002).

When the decrease of the resource (of the *abiotic deposit* type) itself is deemed the key problem, characterisation modelling considers the size of reserves and extraction rates. This type of modelling is the basis for the equivalency factors for resources in appendix 2. Another way to look upon deposits takes thermodynamics as a point of departure and focuses on the useful reserves of energy or exergy (Finnveden & Östlund 1997; Ayres 1998). The characterisation methods grounded in thermodynamics are perhaps not frequently used. However, energy numbers are often reported in the characterisation results as a simple indicator of the depletion of different kinds of energy resources (deposits, flows, biotic, abiotic). Inventory results on energy usage have then typically been categorised and added up as for example total energy from fossil fuels, renewable energy sources and nuclear sources. A third way of assessing deposits is based on the possibility of resource extraction in the future. This can be done via assessment of additional environmental impacts due to mining of lower-grade deposits in the future, as in the Ecoindicator'99 method (Goedkoop & Spriensma 1999) presented in section 5.4 and appendix 3. It can also be done via estimation of environmental costs associated with substitution of current extraction processes with sustainable ones, as in the EPS2000 method (Steen 1999), also in section 5.4 and appendix 3.

A simple way to characterise *biotic resources* is based on categorisation, e.g. wood with/without a Forest Stewardship Council certifi-

146

cate and fish with/without a certificate for marine stewardship (CML 2002), but there are more sophisticated methods as well, distinguishing between *depletion* of abiotic resources and *impacts* on biodiversity. Characterisation models for depletion of biotic reserves (e.g. for fishing) can be based on the size of abiotic reserves and extraction and regeneration rates. So far, data is limited and useful sets of equivalents are not available. Characterisation methods on impacts on biodiversity cover for example risks of extinction of species as in the EPS2000 method (Steen 1999) (see section 5.4 and appendix 3). The state of biotic resources is sometimes related to land use, for example impacts on biodiversity following change in land use. Such aspects of biotic resources are usually covered by characterisation methods in the land use category.

Land use

Land use is another much debated topic within life cycle impact assessment. The category covers the actual use of land (occupancy) as well as changes in land use (transformation). Also, the extent to which land use and land transformation leads to changes in biodiversity and to life support functions (e.g. biological production) is handled by this category. Related to this is also the extent to which emissions lead to changed life support functions, for example to what extent CO_2 leads to fertilisation and increased biological production. All these aspects of land use are quite different in character, and there is yet no coherent approach to dealing with the whole issue of land use. International work groups, e.g. SETAC-WIA2, pursue this problem.

Characterisation of land use is made difficult by limited knowledge and data on the influence of land use on the environment in different parts of the world. A conceptual problem adds to the difficulties. Arguments have been put forward that certain aspects of land use, particularly occupancy, should be treated as a resource problem and that other aspects, for example impacts on biodiversity, should be treated as environmental impacts. Also, the distinction between land use as an inventory parameter and as an endpoint for environmental impact is confused. Useful characterisation methods are therefore few and each of them covers land-use-related impacts partially. The methods most widely used are probably those that are built-in in ready-made LCIA methods.

In the inventory, land use is measured as the area (in m^2) used by the different activities in the life cycle. The assessment of land use from the *occupancy* perspective is based on the fact that area is a limited resource since the surface of our planet is finite. The simplest way to characterise land use is to calculate the total land use (m^2) or total area of different types of land (for example m^2 forest, m^2 farmland and m^2 built-up land). However, since there is often competition between different uses of land, it becomes necessary to account for the length of time for which the land is occupied. To reflect increasing competition, occupancy is characterised as the area of exclusive land use for a given period of time (m^2 year).

The assessment of land use in the *transformation* perspective is related to the fact that a change in land use leads to a shift in the competition between different uses of land and to a change in land quality, e.g. from farmland to built-up land. Characterisation of change in land quality is complicated by that fact that assessment of change is relative. Transformation leads to land having either a higher or lower quality than before but it is still probably worse than its natural state, which could be defined either as its original state or the state to which it would recover. The relativity complicates characterisation and there is yet no easily applicable characterisation method for this aspect of land transformation.

Land use also leads to changes in biodiversity. However, there is a great lack of knowledge and data on mechanisms (CML 2002). Existing characterisation methods concentrate on loss of biodiversity in terms of reduction of the number of species, leaving out other aspects such as the type of species and types of ecosystems that are disappearing. Ready-made LCIA methods use different characterisation methods. In Ecoindicator'99 the characterisation modelling builds on a ratio between the number of plant species in the occupied area and the average number of plant species in the region. Although EPS2000 considers biodiversity, it characterises the impact of emissions on biodiversity. The impact of for example a toxic pollutant is characterised by the extent to which it contributes or affects the "normal" extinction rate, i.e. the number of species that become extinct during one year on a global basis.

148

The cycling of nutrients in an ecosystem, the water household, the generation of soil fertility and the microclimate are important life-supporting processes. Characterisation of their degradation is complex and practical characterisation methods assess only the impact on biological production. The free net primary production (the difference between the total primary biomass production in an area and the amount of biomass extracted from it by agricultural harvesting) has been suggested as the basis for characterising land-use impacts on life-support functions (SETAC-WIA2 2001). Impacts on biological production are also included in EPS2000, but these are related to emissions of fertilising CO_2 and toxic substances rather than land use as such.

Global warming

Climate change may lead to a broad range of impacts on ecosystems and our societies, but greenhouse gases have one property in common, which is useful for characterisation modelling in LCA. Characterisation of greenhouse gases is based on the extent to which they enhance the radiative forcing in the atmosphere, i.e. their capacity to absorb infrared radiation and thereby heat the atmosphere.

Carbon dioxide is not the only gas that causes climate change. Methane, chlorofluorocarbons (CFCs), nitrous oxide and other trace gases also absorb infrared radiation. Compared to CO_2, they absorb much more effectively. The potential contribution of a substance to climate change is expressed as its global warming potential (GWP). The GWP of a substance is defined as the ratio between the increased infrared absorption it causes and the increased infrared absorption caused by 1 kg of CO_2:

$GWP_{T,\,i} = \int a_i\, c_i\,(t)\ \mathrm{d}t\ /\ \int a_{CO_2}\, c_{CO_2}\,(t)\ \mathrm{d}t$, where a_i is the radiative forcing per unit concentration increase of greenhouse gas i (W/m^2 kg), $c_i\,(t)$ is the concentration of greenhouse gas i at time T after release (kg/m^3) and t is the time over which the integration is performed (year).

Because greenhouse gases have different life spans in the atmosphere, GWPs have been calculated for different time horizons. The GWPs used in LCA have been developed by the UN Intergovernmental Panel on Climate Change (IPCC). Their list of "provisional best estimates" of GWPs is updated periodically (CML 2002).

Besides the greenhouse gases, a number of other substances can also affect the radiative forcing. For example, aerosols formed from SO_2 emissions have a cooling effect. Their contribution may be significant but as yet there is no GWP for these.

Global warming potentials (GWPs) are listed in appendix 2.

Ozone depletion

Ozone (O_3) is a harmful pollutant in the lower atmosphere, damaging plants, human health and the built environment, but it is an essential substance in the upper atmosphere, the stratosphere, where it screens out more than 99 % of the dangerous ultraviolet radiation from the sun. Ozone depletion refers to the thinning of the stratospheric ozone layer as a result of various chlorinated and bromated substances, such as CFCs and halons (Harrison 1990).

Ozone occurs in trace amounts throughout the atmosphere with a peak concentration between about 20 and 25 km altitude, i.e. the lower stratosphere. If the ozone in a column of the atmosphere were concentrated in a thin shell surrounding the earth it would be about 3 mm thick (at atmospheric pressure). The ozone layer is maintained through a complex series of chemical reactions. Ozone is produced by the absorption of UV radiation by oxygen molecules; it is destroyed by ultra violet (UV) radiation, visible light and certain substances acting as catalysts, e.g. H, OH, NO, Cl and Br. The increased concentration of these catalysts increases the rate of ozone destruction during the time they remain in the stratosphere. The opposite effect is obtained by increased CO_2 emissions, which leads to lower stratospheric temperatures and hence slows down the ozone-destroying reactions.

The ozone depletion potentials (ODPs) used in LCA were developed by the World Meteorological Organisation (WMO) which updates its list of ODPs periodically (CML 2002). Owing to its complexity and incomplete understanding of ozone chemistry, a theoretical steady-state model is used to calculate the ozone depletion potential (ODP) of a substance. The standard ODP reflects the change in the stratospheric ozone column *in the steady-state* due to

150

amount of emission of that substance relative to that of CFC-11: $ODP_i = \delta[O_3]_i / \delta[O_3]_{CFC-11}$, where $\delta[O_3]$ represents the change in the ozone column for substance i and for CFC-11. OPDs exist for the most important chlorinated and bromated substances, but are still missing for a number of other substances that can influence the stratospheric ozone depletion.

Since it may take hundreds of years before steady-state is reached, it can sometimes be appropriate to use ODPs calculated for shorter time horizons, especially since the ozone depletion rate can be higher for many of the ozone-depleting substances in the short term.

Steady-state ODPs and time-dependent ODPs are listed in appendix 2.

Toxicity

Toxicity is another complicated impact category with a variety of characterisation methods. As yet there is no coherent framework for characterising the toxicological impacts pollutants, but research and methodology development is in progress internationally.

A reason why the toxicity category is complicated is that it includes many types of impacts and perhaps above all many substances. For example, organic solvents, heavy metals and pesticides all cause different types of toxic impact. Some substances cause neurological damage, others are carcinogenic, mutagenic, etc. Toxic substances tend to spread; pesticides used for agriculture can end up in waterways causing harm to aquatic organisms as well as making our drinking water unhealthy. The toxicity category is therefore often divided into human toxicity and eco-toxicity (CML 2002). Eco-toxicity, in turn, can be divided into aquatic toxicity and terrestrial toxicity. Furthermore, aquatic toxicity can be divided into freshwater and marine toxicity, and then there is also freshwater and marine sediment toxicity. Another way of proceeding is to differentiate between acute and chronic toxicity (Wenzel et al. 1997).

Important concepts in the characterisation of toxic substances are fate, exposure or intake and effect. The main difference between the many characterisation approaches concerns the definition of the effect and the extent to which the fate of the substances has been included. The more sophisticated the fate analysis, the more data is needed for developing the toxicity equivalent of a substance. The development of accurate methods is limited by, among other things, by the availability of fate, dose-effect and background data. This leads to a trade-off between accuracy and data requirements in the development of toxicity equivalents. Given the large number of chemicals used in our societies, we consequently need a large number of toxicity equivalents. The advantage of the simpler methods is that relatively many equivalents can be readily produced, although at the expense of accuracy.

Among the simpler approaches, without fate analysis, is the *critical volume approach*. A more sophisticated method, which builds on a generic fate analysis, is the *USES-LCA method* (Guinée et al. 1996; Huijbregts 1999). Attempts to include empirical data have also been made, for example in the *critical surface-time method* by Jolliet & Crettaz (1997). Standard laboratory toxicological data and models are in greater supply than empirical data. The USES-LCA model has been used to produce toxicity indicators for some 200 substances whereas the critical surface-time method only has around 20 indicators (CML 2002). The many "ready-to-use" LCIA methods (presented in more detail in the next section) build their indices on different approaches. The indices in the EDIP method are based on a rudimentary fate model. The Ecoindicator'99 method uses a simpler version of the USES-LCA method.

The critical volume approach uses environmental quality standards, which regulate maximum acceptable levels of pollution in terms of concentration. Examples of such standards are directives for water quality, occupational exposure, etc. Since these standards are expressed in concentration (e.g. mg/m^3), it is possible to calculate the volume of air or water needed to dilute an emission in order to reach the acceptable level. Hence the name of the approach, critical volume. The critical volumes for different emissions can then be added together. It is important to note which type of quality standard is used – some are more environmentally oriented, others are more health-oriented.

The USES-LCA has a global fate model that combines the regional, continental and global scales with arctic, temperate and tropical zones. Together with physico-chemical property factors of substances, the model can theoretically describe how a substance is

152

dispersed between soils, air and waters. The model is used to calculate the predicted environmental concentration (PEC) of a substance in air, water and soil. The PEC is then related to the predicted no-effect level (PNEC) of that substance to form a measure of the degree of impact, which is related to that of a reference substance. The reference substance is 1,4-dichlorobenzene, a known pesticide. The general equation for toxicity potentials is:

Toxicity potential$_{substance}$ = (PEC/PNEC)$_{substance}$ / (PEC/PNEC)$_{ref. substance}$

The USES-LCA model has been used to produce indicators for both aquatic and terrestrial toxicity as well as human toxicity. In the case of human toxicity, the predicted daily intake (PDI) replaces the PEC and the acceptable daily intake (ADI) the PNEC. Despite its level of sophistication, there are major uncertainties in the USES-LCA model, especially in its assessment of metals. Toxicity potentials are listed in appendix 2.

Photo-oxidant formation

Photo-oxidants are secondary pollutants formed in the lower atmosphere from NO$_x$ and hydrocarbons in the presence of sunlight. These substances are characteristic of photochemical smog, also known as summer smog or Los Angeles smog, a known cause of health problems such as irritation to respiratory systems and damage to vegetation. For example, the costs of smog for agriculture are substantial. Ozone is one of the most important photo-oxidants; others are peroxyacetyl nitrate (PAN), hydrogen peroxide and various aldehydes. The smog phenomenon is crucially dependent on meteorological conditions and the background concentrations of pollutants. It can extend from being a local problem to one on a regional, or even continental, scale when emissions of NO$_x$ and hydrocarbons are widespread and ozone is transported with the winds (Harrison 1990).

The methods mostly employed in LCAs focus on regional impacts, but there are also those that describe short-term local impacts during peak episodes. All methods calculate the estimated quantity of ozone formed photochemically by a given substance, but do so in different ways. The photo-oxidant creation potential

(POCP) of a substance is based in a 5-day trajectory model of pollutant transportation over Europe; the incremental reactivity (IR) of a substance is based in short-term scenarios (one day at the most) for urban areas in North America (CML 2002).

Ozone is formed when NO_x and sunlight are present. Ozone production is increased when the air also contains organic substances. Different hydrocarbons react at different rates and efficiencies. In the POCPs, the ozone production of a substance is described relative to that of a standard substance. The POCPs are usually expressed as ethylene equivalents. On the other hand IRs express the amount of ozone formed by a particular substance since the IR of a substance describes the change in ozone formation when a small amount of that substance is added to a base case pollution scenario. There are several types of IRs. For example, the highest incremental reactivity of the hydrocarbons is given by the MIRs (maximum incremental reactivity) and the reactivities leading to the highest peak ozone concentrations are given by the MORs (maximum ozone reactivity).

Since differences in background NO_x concentrations lead to different rates of ozone formation, there are both high-NO_x POCPs and low-NO_x POCPs. High-NO_x POCPs are usually the most relevant ones, but low-NO_x POCPs can be used in Scandinavia and other regions where the background concentration of NO_x is low (Nord 1995; CML 2002).

POCPs and IRs are given for specific hydrocarbons. This often leads to a practical problem in LCAs where hydrocarbon emissions are often presented as group parameters, e.g. VOCs (volatile organic carbons) or HCs (hydrocarbons). One solution is to use the average POCP or IR for specific groups of substances (e.g. aromatics, non-methane hydrocarbons, etc). Another is to identify what specific substances make up the "VOC mixture" during the inventory phase.

POCPs and IRs for NO_x and several hydrocarbons are listed in appendix 2.

Acidification

The major acidifying pollutants are SO_2, NO_x, HCl and NH_3. Acid rain is only one form in which acid deposition occurs. Fog, snow and dew also trap and deposit atmospheric pollutants. Furthermore, fallout of dry acidic particles and aerosols is converted to acids when they dissolve in surface water or contact moist tissues (e.g. in the lungs). Example of impacts are fish mortality in lakes, leaching of toxic metals out of soil and rocks, damage to forests and damage to building and monuments (Harrison 1990).

What acidifying pollutants have in common is that they form acidifying H^+ ions. A pollutant's potential for acidification can thus be measured by its capacity to form H^+ ions. This fact has been used for the characterisation modelling in LCA. The acidification potential (AP) is defined as the number of H^+ ions produced per kg substance relative to SO_2 ($AP_{substance} = n_{H+\,substance} / n_{H+\,SO_2}$) (CML/NOH 1992). The acidification potential thus reflects the maximum acidification a substance can cause. However, actual acidification varies depending on where the acidifying pollutants are deposited. The actual impact is governed by for example the buffering capacity of soil and waters, climatic conditions (amount of light and temperature) and rate of harvesting. Various approaches to accounting for local differences have been suggested but to date there are few easily applicable methods. The simplest solution is to disregard the impact of acidifying emissions in non-sensitive areas. Some regionalised impact assessment can be obtained by using the average acidification equivalents developed for Europe for three of the acidifying substances (SO_2, NO_x and NH_3) (Huijbregts 1999).

Acidification potentials for several acidifying substances are listed in appendix 2.

Eutrophication

Eutrophication is generally associated with the environmental impacts of excessively high levels of nutrients that lead to shifts in species composition and increased biological productivity, for example as algal blooms. In LCA, the eutrophication category, sometimes also called nutrification, covers not only the impacts of nutrients, but also those of degradable organic pollution and some-times also waste heat since they all affect biological productivity in some way (SETAC-WIA2 2001; CML 2002). These different pollut-ants have one aspect in common which is useful for characterisa-tion modelling, i.e. they all lead to oxygen consumption. Dis-charges of degradable organic matter into water are broken down by micro-organisms which utilise oxygen, resulting in lower oxy-gen levels in the water and detrimental effects on aquatic ecosys-tems. Flows of nutrients as well as waste heat into water lead to increased biological productivity and biomass formation, which in turn also lead to increased oxygen consumption when the biomass is being decomposed.

Eutrophication is a phenomenon that can influence terrestrial as well as aquatic ecosystems. Nitrogen (N) and phosphorus (P) are the two nutrients most implicated in eutrophication. Other substances are rarely constraints. In most terrestrial ecosystems, the amount of nitrogen is the limiting nutrient and an increase of nitrogen will stimulate plant growth. In aquatic ecosystems, phosphorus is nor-mally the limiting factor for growth in fresh waters, while nitrogen is the limiting factor in marine ecosystems. Nitrogen ending up in aquatic ecosystems comes from a number of different sources. Agri-cultural fertilisers and effluents from sewage works are major sources of nitrogen, but also parts of the atmospheric emissions of NO_x eventually end up in the aquatic ecosystems. The phosphorus in fertilisers is largely insoluble and relatively little is eroded from land into water. Most of the phosphorus comes instead from sewage effluents (Harrison 1990).

Since different ecosystems are limited by different nutrients, actual eutrophication varies geographically. This complicates char-acterisation. The simplest solution is to disregard the geographical variation. Eutrophication potentials then reflect the maximum eutrophying effect of a substance. Maximum eutrophication assumes that all airborne nutrients eventually end up in aquatic systems and includes all emissions of N and P substances to both air and water in the category together with the emissions of organic matter. Characterisation methods that account for geographical variations exist but have limited applicability, including for exam-ple only eutrophication of terrestrial systems caused by air emis-sions in Europe (Huijbregts 1999).

156

Calculation of eutrophication potentials is based on the proportions of nitrogen, phosphorus, carbon and oxygen in the average chemical formulae for aquatic biomass formation and decomposition. It takes 1 mole of phosphorus to form 1 mole of average aquatic biomass, $C_{106}H_{263}O_{110}N_{16}P$ (Stumm & Morgan 1981). Correspondingly it takes 16 moles of nitrogen to form 1 mole of average biomass. The decomposition of the biomass then requires oxygen. According to the molar ratios of the decompostion formula, the consumption of oxygen is 8.6 moles for each mole of nitrogen or 138 moles for each mole of phosphorus.

Since pollution of organic matter is often expressed as the biological oxygen demand (BOD) or chemical oxygen demand (COD), the oxygen consumption implied by organic pollution is therefore already given by the measured parameter. This means that the oxygen demand of organic pollution can be added to the calculated oxygen consumption of the decomposition following the nutrient-based biomass formation.

As yet there is no method for adding the impacts of waste heat to those of N and P substances and organic pollution. A simple alternative is to add up the amount of waste heat (in MJ) discharged into aquatic ecosystems separately. Waste heat is often disregarded in many LCA studies but it might be wise to assess the impacts of waste heat when discharges are considerable, such as discharges of waste heat from nuclear plants into water.

Eutrophication potentials are often expressed as PO_4^{3-}-equivalents, but given the molar ratios of the chemical formulae, PO_4^{3-}-equivalents can easily be converted into NO_3^- or O_2-equivalents. Eutrophication potentials are listed in appendix 2.

When characterisation methods are lacking

The inventory results may include several parameters that are difficult to characterise for various reasons. One reason may be that characterisation indicators are missing for some particular substances although the characterisation method exists. For example, equivalents are missing for the characterisation of the impact of SO_2 on global warming and the toxic impact of particulate matter (dust) and many chemicals. Another reason may be that useful characterisation methods are missing. This is the case for noise and radioactive substances, for which more research and methodology development is needed. (Some of the attempts to characterise these impacts are described below.) A third reason may be that the quantitative inventory result is missing, i.e. the existence of a pollutant is known but not the amount. This is the case for many toxic chemicals in LCAs. A fourth reason may be that the result parameter represents a flow to another technical system, one not investigated in the particular LCA study. The amount of recyclable material (in kg) or the amounts of different types of waste (in kg or m^3) are examples of such result parameters.

The way to deal with inventory results for which characterisation is unfeasible differs. Sometimes simple *ad hoc* characterisation methods can be developed within the scope of an LCA study. Another possibility is to look up and use characterisation methods still under development. However, it is more common to list the inventory results that are not characterised separately, in addition to the characterised ones. These inventory results are often sorted into categories and presented under different headings, such as *Flows not traced back to nature* or *Flows to other technical systems* and *Environmental loads for which characterisation methods are lacking*. A *red-flag characterisation* is also possible, i.e. to list the most harmful pollutants found but not quantified in the inventory analysis. However, it must be said that it is important to include these problematic parameters in the results in one way or another as it allows a qualitative interpretation of their impact. (Ways to present and interpret LCA results are further presented in chapter 6.)

Impacts of noise, odour, ionising radiation and casualties are often not found in LCAs since both inventory data and useful characterisation methods are missing (CML 2002). Attempts to include noise into LCA exist. Some are limited to road traffic (e.g. Müller-Wenk 1999) and thereby exclude among other things aircraft noise and noise from construction sites and industries. A more general method building on the production of sound (measured in Pa^{2}s) exists (CML/NOH 1992). This method characterises all sounds equally, also those not experienced as nuisances, e.g. remote sounds.

Detection levels for odorous substances can be measured relatively objectively, but the level when odour becomes a nuisance or

158

a problem is more individually determined. A relatively simple characterisation method building on the critical volume approach exists. It uses the odour threshold values (OTV) of different substances (CML/NOH 1992). The OTV is defined as the concentration at which 50 % of the population can detect the odour of a substance. With the OTV, the volume of air needed to dilute an odorous substance can be calculated.

Nuclear waste and certain types of concrete are examples of radioactive materials that can be encountered in the course of performing an LCA. The impact of a radioactive material is not easily characterised as it depends on the type of radiation (alpha, beta, gamma or neutron) it emits and on the material being irradiated. Characterisation methods focus either on the level of radioactivity or on the absorbed dose of radiation. The LCIA method Ecoindicator'99 includes the characterisation of ionising radiation.

Casualties in the LCA context refers to workplace related accidents and injuries. A simple way to account for these is to report the number of casualties, without distinguishing between the slightly injured or the gravely injured cases. A method to characterise casualties is included in EDIP, a LCIA method that includes the working environment impacts in its scope.

5.4 Ready-made LCIA methods

As mentioned earlier, there are a number of ready-made LCIA methods. The practical advantage of them is that the LCA practitioner does not need to go in-depth into the procedure of the different impact assessment steps (classification, characterisation, etc) since the environmental information for various pollutants and resources is aggregated to a *characterisation indicator* or even a single number, an *index*. The impact assessment procedure is, so to say, packaged inside the ready-made LCIA methods.

In the ready-made LCIA methods, the environmental harm of a pollutant or a resource is indicated relative other pollutants and resources. In other words, different environmental loads are "measured" on a common scale (yardstick). Each LCIA method has its particular measurement principle. In characterisation methods, the scale is based on physico-chemical properties of the pollutants, whereas weighting methods also use scales based on different ways of representing social preferences. Since characterisation methods were extensively dealt with in section 5.3, the following overview of ready-made LCIA methods will focus on LCIA methods that go beyond characterisation, i.e. all the way to weighting.

Characteristic for the weighting methods is that *all* environmental problems are "measured" on single scale. Since a single measuring scale is used, it is possible to calculate the total environmental impact of a system. It is obtained by multiplying all environmental loads of the system by their corresponding indices and summing them up. In principle, the result could very well be *42*[2] by chance.

Total environmental impact = load × index$_i$

where

i = all pollutants and resources used

In the LCA literature many LCIA methods are described in principle, but lists with indices for various substances have been developed only for a smaller number of them (Bengtsson 1998). The four LCIA methods described in the following (the Ecoindicator'99 method, the EPS method, the environmental themes method and the EDIP method) have such index lists (see appendix 3). Each of the four methods uses different means, i.e. weighting principles, to obtain the one-dimensional indices. Since determining the relative harm of different environmental impacts is a value-laden procedure, each method reflects different social values and preferences.

Ecoindicator'99

The Ecoindicator'99 method was developed so that designers and design engineers could work with environmental information in a simple format, i.e. single scores indices. The method is intended for internal use in companies, especially for product development applications (NOH 1996; Goedkoop et al. 1998). A first version was

2   The answer "42" plays an important part in the Hitch Hiker's Guide to the Galaxy when the main characters learn the importance of how to pose a question. The excerpt describing the defining moment is found in the preface.

published in 1995 (Ecoindicator'95), and Ecoindicator'99 is the updated and more complete version intended for Europe. Since spatial and temporal information is often lacking in LCIs, the constructors of Ecoindicator'99 compensated this lack by developing a model for assessing the average damage in Europe. This means that instead of looking at specific conditions for each emission (e.g. the fate of toxic substances, background concentrations), average conditions for Europe are considered.

As shown in figure 5.5, the Ecoindicator'99 method includes several steps. The first steps use natural sciences to calculate the environmental impact caused by the environmental loads from a product life cycle. The impact categories are ecosystem health, human health and resource use. In the next two steps average European data on exposure and effects are used to calculate the extent to which human and ecosystem health are affected. Then a weighting procedure is used to establish the seriousness of the damages to the ecosystem, human health and to the resource base. Cultural values determine the weighting factors, which are based on the distance-to-target principle where the target represents a low damage level, e.g. a maximum of 5 % ecosystem impairment.

Particular to this method is the use of cultural values. Weighting according to different cultural values in society means that weighting is done according to different attitudes to what counts as an environmental problem (i.e. when do we have a 5 % ecosystem impairment?). Three cultural perspectives are represented in Ecoindicator'99: the individualist, the hierarchist and the egalitarian perspectives. This leads to three sets of indices. These, in turn, can be combined to an average index list. According to the individualist view, only proven cause-effect relations are counted as environmental impacts. Also, a short-term perspective is applied. At the other extreme is the egalitarian view, where the precautionary principle is used consistently. This means that "nothing" is left out. In addition, a long-term perspective is applied. In between is the hierarchical view, which builds on facts backed up by some scientific and political bodies. These bodies should have sufficient recognition in the environmental community. The egalitarian perspective leads to most complete but at the same time also the most uncertain set of indices. Individualist, hierarchist and egalitarian Ecoindicator'99 indices are listed in appendix 3.

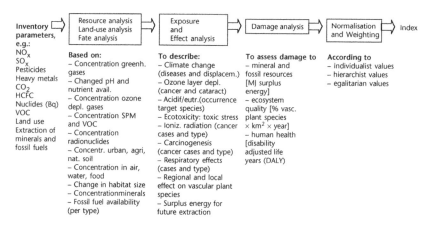

Figure 5.5 General representation of what is included in Ecoindicator'99 (based on Goedkoop & Spriensma 1999).

To record different cultural values, the constructors of Ecoindicator'99 used a panel (Goedkoop & Spriensma 1999). 365 members of a Swiss LCA interest group were questioned about their views and attitudes to environmental damages. The constructors recognise that the panel is not representative of the whole of Europe, but considered it useful for obtaining a first set of indices. Although the indices were developed for Europe, the methodology is generally applicable. Preliminary studies have been made to adapt the method in Japan and Colombia (Goedkoop & Spriensma 1999).

EPS

Like Ecoindicator'99, the EPS method was developed with the intention to supply designers and design engineers with single scores. However, EPS was developed earlier and in a more specific context. EPS, which stands for "environmental priority strategies in product design", was originally developed for the Volvo Car Corporation in Sweden by the Swedish Environmental Research Institute (Ryding & Steen 1991). The method was later revised and its weighting is now based on the definition of five safeguard subjects and the willingness-to-pay for protecting these safeguard subjects

162

(Steen & Ryding 1992; Steen 1999a). The five safeguard subjects, human health, biological diversity, ecosystem production capacity, abiotic resources, and cultural and recreational values listed in table 5.3 are based on the UN's Rio declaration. This reflects the intention to make EPS a generally applicable LCIA method. A list of EPS indices is found in appendix 3; a complete list is found in the EPS2000 report (Steen 1999b).

Each safeguard subject has several sub-categories, called unit effects. For example, the unit effects in the category of biological production are the pollution-caused *decreased production of 1 kg of crop seed or wood or fish*. Unit effects in the category of human health range from *excess death owing to pollution* and *severe nuisance owing to pollution*. Each unit effect has an economic value described by the willingness-to-pay to avoid the negative effects defined by the unit effect. The price of a unit effect is the equivalent of a weighting factor. The large uncertainties involved in determining environmental impacts has often led to the description of potential impacts in LCIA, often without indication of the size of the gap between the potential and the real environmental impacts. The approach used in the EPS method is an attempt to overcome this gap. Instead, EPS indices are supposed to reflect real environmental impacts, with each index accompanied by an uncertainty factor.

The calculation of an EPS index starts with a description of the extent of the impact of a pollutant on each unit effect; this is the equivalent of characterisation. The index is then obtained by multiplying the size of the impact per unit effect for each safeguard subject by the respective "price" of the unit effects and summing them. The calculation of an index for mercury (as air pollutant) in table 5.5 illustrates the method. For brevity, the calculation of the uncertainty factor has been excluded from the table.

Table 5.5 The matrix illustrates the calculation of an EPS index, using calculations for emission of mercury (Hg) to air as example (based on Steen 1999a, b).

	Characterisation		Weighting	
Safeguard subject	Global frequency × (or intensity)	Contribution of 1 × kg to global emissions	Value of unit effect =	SUM
HUMAN HEALTH	(affected persons/ year)	$(kg/year)^{-1}$	(euro/person × year)	
Reduced life expectancy	–		10 000 (per lost year)	
Severe morbidity	–		100 000	
Morbidity (as brain damage)	400 000 ×	1.2×10^{-8} ×	10 000 =	48.08
Severe nuisance	–		10 000	
Nuisance	–		100	
ECOSYSTEM PRODUCTION	(kg lost fish/year)	$(kg/year)^{-1}$	(euro/kg produce)	
Reduced fish or meat production (via fishing restrictions)	18 500 000 ×	1.2×10^{-8} ×	1 (/kg fish or meat) =	0.222
Reduced crop production	–		0.15 (/kg wheat, etc)	–
Reduced wood production	–		0.04 (/kg DS wood)	–
Reduced water production	–		0.03 (/kg drinking water)	–
BIODIVERSITY	(percent of 1 NEX*)	$(kg/year)^{-1}$	(euro/NEX)	
Extinction of species (via re-production)	0.01 ×	1.2×10^{-8} ×	110×10^{9} =	13.2
CULTURAL VALUES	(not yet defined)			–
ABIOTIC RESOURCES	(not applicable for emissions)			–
Sum	Environmental load unit (ELU)/kg Hg			61.5

* The safeguard subject *biodiversity* focuses of genetic resource value. The characterisation model is based on the extinction rate of "red-listed" species. The category indicator, normalised extinction of species (NEX), is dimensionless and is normalised with respect to the species extinct during 1990.

The EPS method counts both pollution and resource depletion as environmental impacts. In fact, resource depletion often weighs "heavier" in this method. The logic behind including resource depletion is that future generations should have the same possibilities with regard to availability of resources as present generations. Resource use is assessed by assessment of the pollution from resource acquisition that would be obtained if the resource were to be replaced by a sustainable resource. To illustrate the method, the calculation of an index for fossil oil is described. The sustainable alternative to fossil oil is assumed to be some kind of vegetable oil. It is thought that the potential production of vegetable oils may be enough to at least to substitute fossil oil as lubricant in machinery and raw material in chemical industry. Rape-seed oil being the most commonly discussed alternative to fossil oil is used as reference material to value fossil oil as resource. The calculation of an index for fossil oil is based on economic studies and LCA studies of rape-seed oil production; it is the sum of the environmental costs for emissions and resource use associated with rape-seed oil production and the direct cost of rape-seed oil production (Steen 1999b).

Environmental themes

The principles of the environmental themes method were developed in the Netherlands. In short, the method builds on a thematic classification and characterisation similar to those in tables 5.1 and 5.2, and add two more steps in which the environmental impacts are normalised and weighted. Themes usually are resource depletion and pollution, i.e. global warming, ozone depletion, photochemical oxidant formation, acidification, eutrophication, ecotoxicity and human toxicity.

The weights can be determined in different ways. In the original Dutch study, an expert panel defined the weighting factors (VCNI 1991). When the method was adapted to Swedish conditions the weights were derived from environmental targets in Swedish public environmental policy (Baumann & Rydberg 1994). These indices have a relatively short-term perspective since political environmental targets are set for 5–10 years ahead. Hence they are called ET-short. Another set of indices, ET-long, with a 20–100 year perspective has also been calculated for Swedish conditions (Eriksson et al. 1995). The environmental targets used for the long-term perspective are environmental critical loads, i.e. the maximum tolerable load in a geographical region.

In this method, the total environmental impact is calculated in three steps:

- the LCI results are sorted (classified) into selected environmental themes (impact assessment categories). By using a measure of the relative equivalency factor of the pollutants, the size of the impact, or rather the potential impact, is calculated per theme,
- the impact per theme is divided by the theme impact of the total pollution in a defined geographical area, usually a country. This normalisation results in an impact fraction, indicating how much the product contributes per theme to the environmental problems of the chosen geographical area,
- the impact fractions are summed to give a total impact after applying weighting factors that take into account the relative harm of the different environmental themes.

The steps can be formulated as an equation:

$$total\ impact = \Sigma\ weight_i \times \frac{\Sigma\ load_j \times eqv_{i,j}}{\Sigma\ load_{k,tot}}$$

where

i = environmental theme, e.g. acidification, ozone depletion etc;
$weight_i$ = weight factor of theme i;
$load_j$ = emission of substance j from the studied system;
$load_{k,tot}$ = total amount of pollutant k contributing to the theme;
$eqv_{i,j}$ = equivalence of product-related emission j within theme i;
$eqv_{i,k}$ = equivalence of substance k contributing to theme i.

This equation can be transformed into an equation to calculate the index of an environmental load:

$$index_j = \Sigma \left(\frac{weight_i \times eqv_{i,j}}{\Sigma\ load_{k,tot} \times eqv_{i,k}} \right)$$

EDIP

Similar to Ecoindicator'99 and EPS, EDIP was developed for use in product development processes. Methodologically, EDIP is similar to the environmental themes method since EDIP uses more or less the same impact categories: global warming, ozone depletion, acidification, eutrophication and waste. However, what distinguishes the EDIP method is the assessment of toxic substances and the attention to work environment (Wenzel et al. 1997).

There are many proposals for how toxicity can be dealt with in LCA. Generally, too much data is needed to produce toxicity equivalents in a scientifically comprehensive way. As a result there is a lack of toxicity equivalents. The EDIP constructors have attempted to produce a broad set of toxicity equivalents based on a relatively simple toxic impact model that does not need too much data. Their method was inspired by the EU technical guidelines for risk assessment of chemicals in the environment (Wenzel et al. 1997). The EDIP method distinguishes between ecotoxicity and human toxicity, and between acute and chronic toxicity. This results in three toxicity impact cateogories: persistent toxicity (for chronic toxicity), and ecotoxicity and human toxicity (for acute and local toxicity). The ecotoxicity equivalent of a substance is determined by its dispersion in the environment and its physico-chemical characteristics (e.g. its potential for bioconcentration, determined based on its octanol-water partitioning ratio). For human toxicity, our exposure to the toxic substances is also included (e.g. per cent of substance in air inhaled). The toxicity equivalents are expressed in m^3 of air, water or soil into which the emission should be diluted for its concentration to be so low that no toxicological effects could be expected.

In the EDIP method, weighting is done in three separate categories. For environmental impacts, the EDIP method uses Danish political targets. For resource use, the weighting is based on the relation between consumption and regeneration of reserves. For working environment, weighting is based on the probability of work injury and based on Danish statistics (Wenzel et al. 1997).

Other LCIA methods

In addition to the presented ready-made LCIA methods, there are a number of other methods for evaluating environmental impacts. Some of them were originally developed in order to simplify the LCA approach; others are simple methods for making an overall assessment of environmental impact. Many of them consequently use simple methodological approaches and describe overall environmental impact in terms of an easily understood physical or monetary parameter.

The environmental harm of emissions depends on the extent of their dilution in recipient bodies (air, water or ground). Accordingly, it is possible to calculate the *volume* of air or water or soil necessary to dilute emissions to harmless levels. The *critical volume approach* uses environmental and health quality standards to define "harmless" concentrations of pollutants for calculating the necessary volumes. As in the original Swiss study (BUS 1984), this approach can be used for the overall assessment of environmental loads, but it is nowadays mostly used for the assessment of toxic substances (see characterisation of toxic substances in section 5.3). The *molar method* (Schaltegger & Sturm 1991) is similar to the critical volume approach. The difference is that the necessary amount of air or water is given in numbers of moles and not as a volume.

Area-based approaches can also be found. These are similar to the volume-based approaches, but area has the advantage of being easier to relate to the finite space available on earth. The *critical surface-time approach* (Jolliet 1994; Jolliet & Crettaz 1997) uses environmental and health quality standards to determine the size of an area affected by pollution. The method also takes time into consideration by including the time for degradation of a pollutant. The impact is presented as *m^2year*. Area is also central to the *SPI method* (Narodoslawsky & Krotshek 1995) and the concept of the *ecological footprint* (Wackernagel & Rees 1996). These approaches present overall environmental impact as m^2, which includes the area needed for resource production, industrial plants and other facilities as well as that for the assimilation of pollutants and waste.

One-parameter methods, such as the SPI and the ecological footprint, are often called *proxy methods* for the reason that one parameter, for example area, is made to stand as an approximation of the overall environmental impact. *MIPS* (Schmidt-Bleek 1994) is another proxy method in which the amount of material is the proxy parameter as MIPS stands for "material intensity per service unit". (The term service unit is synonymous to functional unit.) All materials, irrespective of the type, are added up on a weight basis. Analysis is greatly simplified with this method since it is sufficient to concentrate on the mass flow in the life cycle without inventory-

168

© The authors and Studentlitteratur

ing all emissions. *Energy consumption reduction* is a proxy method introduced by Cramer et al. (1993). As the name implies, energy is at heart of this method. The energy parameter includes the energy consumption in the life cycle as well as the energy needed by for example end-of-pipe technology for reducing environmental impacts.

Money is a widely used parameter in public and private decision making and planning. The economic approach has also been transferred to LCA methodology and several methods that attach a monetary value to the environmental impacts of a life cycle can therefore be found. In addition to the EPS method presented in section 5.4, there is also the Tellus method (1992) and the DESC method (Krozer 1992). The weighting of environmental loads is based on the costs of controlling and reducing impacts down to target levels determined by environmental authorities.

Expert panels or *stakeholder panels* can also be used for making an overall assessment of the environmental impact. The Landbank panel method applies the Delphi method to LCA (Wilson & Jones 1994; Landbank 1996). The Delphi method is a stepwise method in which each member of the panel votes on the most serious environmental impacts and may then adjust their vote after having been presented the votes of the other panel members.

5.5 Comparison of LCIA methods

The comparison in table 5.5 shows that the environmental harm of a pollutant or resource is different in the different LCIA methods. The reason for this is that the different LCIA methods convey different types of information, be it society's priorities through political systems or captured through panels, through its individuals' economic priorities or be it the "priorities" of nature (expressed by critical loads). As these LCIA methods reflect different prioritisation principles, it is not possible to say generally that any of them is the most correct one.

Comparisons such as those in table 5.5 are useful to identify where different methods and values lead to large differences in LCA results. Although each LCIA method has its weighting principle,

Table 5.6 *Comparison of the relative harm of selected environmental loads (relative to CO_2) in three LCIA methods.*

	Ecoindicator'99	Environmental Themes – short	EPS
CO_2	0.00019 (/g)	0.0111 (/g)	0.0702 ELU/kg
CO_2	1	1	1
NO_x	416	356	2.32
SO_2	737	218	0.524
HC	63	293	–
PAH	4 842 195	177 477	6 952
Hg (air)	484 211	4 252 253	2 521
Hg (water)	4 842 105	2 837 378	–
N-tot	289	647	0.142
BOD	–	36	0.004

the method constructors' difficulties in finding enough and adequate data have sometimes led them to use default parameters in calculating their indices. The use of the ranking principle in product comparisons then becomes less consistent.

Why so many LCIA methods?

The complexity of environmental problems is one part of the answer to this question. Another part is that we as humans have widely diverging views on nature, the role of individuals and our possibilities to control society. Test yourself with the following questions (from Wandén 1993):

On your view of nature: Is nature robust or is it fragile? Is nature in constant flux, or is it evolving towards a climax?

On your view of humans: Are humans cultural beings or natural beings? Do humans have large freedom of action or do they have limited possibilities and freedom to act?

On your view of society: Does growth favour the environment, or does it harm the environment? Should society be organised in a market economy, in a decentralised small-scale economy or in planned economy?

The different LCIA methods represent, more or less clearly, different answers to these questions. Ecoindicator'99 gives probably the most explicit answers with the use of the three cultural perspectives.

In practice identification of values is further complicated by the fact that there is often a difference between expressed values and enacted values. There are multiple sayings that illustrate this kind of difference, for example "Do as I say and not as I do" and "Action speaks louder than words". The question is which are the most important ones, expressed values or enacted values? No matter how many LCIA methods are used, it is eventually the decision-maker, who will have to enact the decision. Together the different LCIA methods offer an overview of smaller, greater and more contentious environmental problems on which decision makers will have to take a stand and eventually make decisions.

Trends for the future …

Assessment of environmental impacts within the context of LCA is an area where there is still considerable research in progress. We will likely see new methods for complicated impact categories, such as toxicological impacts and land use in the future. There is for example large scale collaborative research programme, such as the European Omniitox project which is developing LCIA methods for toxic substances (Omniitox 2001). Moreover, the SETAC working group on impact assessment also points to new impact categories, such as the protection of the man-made environment, for which characterisation methods need developing (SETAC-WIA2 2001).

There is a general trend towards more sophisticated LCIA methods that allow more accurate assessment. The trend here is to develop LCIA methods that describe actual impacts rather than potential impacts. This means that a longer part of the cause-effect chain and higher-order effects has to be covered by the LCIA methods. Part of this trend is the development of methodology that takes better account of geographical differences in environmental background loads and sensitivity, for example the work of Potting and colleagues (1998) and Huijbregts (1999) who have developed geographically diversified characterisation indicators for acidifying and eutrophying substances. A similar trend is the adjustment of LCIA methods to different user contexts, for example, weighting methods that reflect the values in the company undertaking an LCA study rather than those of the general public (e.g. Miettinen & Hämäläinen 1997).

Hopefully, we will also see the development of a more coherent framework for impact assessment in the future. Within the Life Cycle Initiative, a collaboration between the United Nations Environmental Programme (UNEP) and SETAC, one of the aims is to develop and disseminate widely accepted LCIA methods for reliable and easy use of LCA (UNEP/SETAC 2000). A challenge for the future would be to combine different weighting approaches into a general framework where functional labels indicate the type of assessment principle that can be applied: potential/actual impacts, political/environmental/societal/corporate values, etc.

5.6 Summary and further reading

In this chapter we have seen that life cycle impact assessment (LCIA) consists of translating the life cycle inventory results (emissions and resource use) into environmental impacts. The procedure for doing this is described in detail in the standard ISO 14042 (2000) and includes the acts of classification, characterisation, normalisation and weighting, among others. In practice, the ordinary LCA analyst seldom overtly carries out all the acts of the procedure described in the standard since he or she is more likely to use some of the existing ready-made LCIA methods, either characterisation methods or weighting methods. These represent a more user-friendly format of the standard. However, knowledge of the LCIA procedure as described in the standard is useful for insightful application of the ready-made LCIA methods. For example, when using characterisation methods, the LCA analyst is required to first classify the life cycle inventory results. *Exercise F* on *classification* offers training on this particular aspect of life cycle impact assessment.

172

Knowledge of the standard is also useful when designing a new LCIA method.

To find out more about each LCIA method, it is best to turn to the original references. Concerning modelling deliberations in the construction of characterisation methods, the handbook on the ISO standard (CML 2002) presents detailed accounts for each impact category. The principles of Ecoindicator'99 are explained in an article by Goedkoop et al. (1998). The report by Goedkoop & Spriensma (1999) also presents all the underlying calculations on which the indices are based. Similarly, the reports by Steen (1999 a,b) provide exhaustive documentation on EPS2000. The latest version of the Environmental Theme method is presented in a report by Eriksson et al. (1995). A full description of the EDIP method can be found in the book by Wenzel & Hauschild (1998).

LCIA is one of the areas within LCA where a considerable amount of research is going on. Among the reasons for this are our incomplete understanding of environmental problems and the difficulties in prioritising among environmental problems. To follow on-going efforts concerning LCIA development and debate, it is worthwhile to study the outcomes of the SETAC working group on impact assessment (e.g. SETAC-WIA2 2001) and those of the LCInitiative co-organised by UNEP and SETAC (see www.uneptie.org/pc/sustain/lca/lcini.htm).

6 Interpretation and presentation of results

In a quantitative LCA, the number of result parameters after the inventory calculations may well be more than a hundred. It may not be easy to immediately make sense of all those numbers. It probably makes even less sense to present them in that way as results. In order to extract something meaningful out of the numbers it is necessary to "refine" the raw results in some way. One way of doing this is to present only a selection of the most important inventory result parameters in a bar diagram; another way is to present weighted impact assessment results. Alternative ways of analysing and presenting results is the topic of this chapter.

Refinement of raw results into useful, presentable and final results requires a process that may involve screening of the raw results, identification of critical data and assessments of the importance of missing data. The process of assessing results in order to draw conclusions is called *interpretation* in LCA terminology. The use of different types of diagrams is very helpful in this process. Evaluations of the robustness of conclusions drawn in an LCA study are also part of the interpretation phase. Such evaluations typically entail sensitivity analyses, uncertainty analyses and data quality assessments.

The term *life cycle interpretation* is defined in the ISO 14040 standard as the ...

> "... phase of life cycle assessment in which the findings of either the inventory analysis or the impact assessment, or both, are combined consistent with the defined goal and scope in order to reach conclusions and recommendations." (ISO 14040 1997)

The quoted ISO definition might unnecessarily narrow the field of possible conclusions in stating that conclusions should be consistent with the defined goal and scope. LCA studies often produce surprising, unexpected results, and therefore beyond the intended goal and scope. However, there is no reason why one should not give attention to unexpected results only because they are not in line with the defined goal of the study. Unexpected results usually offer great potential for learning, and the ability to make use of surprising results is an important element in LCA application, as will be seen in chapter 13. If the existence of unexpected results poses a problem according to a strict reading of the ISO standard, remember that it is always possible to reformulate the goal and scope since LCA is an iterative process.

The standard only describes the structure of the interpretation phase (as shown in figure 6.1) without prescribing any particular methods for analysing the results although some methods are suggested.

In this chapter, we have collected examples from many LCA studies to illustrate different ways to present results. This will hopefully give you ideas on how to analyse and present LCA results. The examples fall into two main categories (see table 6.1). In the first category, the format of the result presentation is decided by the character of the results. For example, sometimes an impact assessment is needed to draw conclusions; other times it is not and the inventory results are sufficient. Furthermore, the are different ways

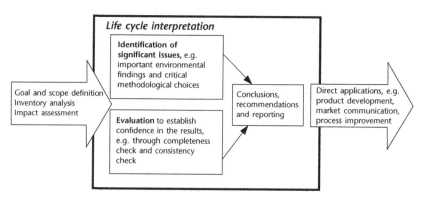

Figure 6.1 The structure of the interpretation phase in LCA (ISO 14043 2000).

176

to present qualitative results. In short, these examples present results with varying degree of detail. In the second category, the format of the results presentation is decided by a particular analytical purpose, e.g. the identification of the most polluting step in the life cycle, or the sensitivity of the overall results to changes in particular data. Although we have presented many examples in this chapter, you can probably come up with additional ways of how to analyse and present the results.

Table 6.1 Overview of result presentation formats.

Format decided by the character of results	
Section 6.1	Different level of detail: inventory results, impact assessment at the characterisation level, impact assessment results at the weighting level
Section 6.2	Qualitative data
	Qualitative data in otherwise quantitative studies

Format decided by analytical purposes	
Section 6.3	Identification of the most polluting step in the life cycle => dominance analysis
	Identification of the most problematic emission / environmental impact => contribution analysis
	Comparison of short-lived, single-use products with long-lived, multiple-use products => break-even analysis
	Identification of environmental impacts within sphere of responsibility / influence => decision maker analysis
Section 6.4	Testing the robustness of results:
	Check of effect of uncertain data => uncertainty analysis
	Check of effect of changes in most critical data => sensitivity analysis
	Check of effect of changes in scenarios => variation analysis

6.1 Quantitative results with varying level of detail

The results of an LCI are in the form of numerous parameters, many times more than a hundred. At the level of characterisation in impact assessment, the number of parameters has been reduced; the number of parameters equals the number of environmental categories (up to around 15). Further aggregation is possible (as seen in chapter 5) so that a single number, representing the total environmental impact, can be presented. Going all the way from inventory results to weighted results means that the number of result parameters is reduced and information has been aggregated, as illustrated in figure 6.2.

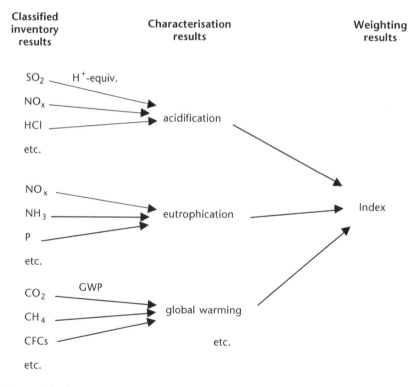

Figure 6.2 Illustration of the stepwise aggregation of information in LCA.

To illustrate the stepwise aggregation of information, results from the detergent study (Arvidsson 1995; used as example in chapter 1) are presented at the *inventory* level, the *characterisation* level and the *weighted* level. The detergent study consisted of a comparison of two detergents, and some examples are typical formats for result presentation in comparative studies.

Inventory results

All inventory result parameters in the study of the two detergent are presented in table 6.2. Since it was a relatively small study, there are only 63 result parameters and most parameters are common to both detergents. However, detergent 1 has three more result parameters than detergent 2. See if you can find them in the table.

Even if the inventory results are substantial, a table with all inventory parameters is often presented in the appendix of an LCA report. A selection of inventory result parameters is usually included in the main text part of the report. The selected results parameters are then often presented in a bar diagram, such as those in figures 6.3 and 6.4. Which inventory parameters to select is up to the analyst to decide. Typically the choice consists of a mix of the most common environmental loads, the most important (largest) environmental loads and particularly problematic environmental loads. It may be necessary to present the results in more than one diagram, each one conveying a different message. The diagram in figure 6.3 is a broad selection of inventory parameters. The diagram in figure 6.4 focuses on a particular group of parameters. Only the use of different types of energy is presented since energy is an important parameter for management of the industrial process.

Table 6.2 Full list of inventory cradle-to-gate results, quantitative comparison (in absolute numbers) of two detergents (Arvidsson 1995). The functional unit is 1 kg of detergent.

Compounds	Unit	Detergent 1	Detergent 2
Energy consumption			
1. Fossil fuel	MJ	11.60	9.70
2. Inherent energy	MJ	3.60	2.80
3. Electricity 50 %	MJ	4.40	3.30
4. Renewable fuel	MJ	1.00	0.60
5. Other energy type	MJ	0.04	0.02
Emissions into air			
6. CO_2	g	1500.00	1400.00
7. Particles	g	24.50	30.40
8. Fluorides	g	3.80	5.10
9. NO_x	g	5.30	4.40
10. Ashes	g	5.20	5.40
11. SO_2	g	3.80	2.90
12. HC	g	2.40	1.50
13. NH_3	g	0.90	1.00
14. CO	g	0.90	1.00
15. CH_4	g	0.40	0.60
16. Acetaldehyde	g	4.3×10^{-3}	4.3×10^{-3}
17. Ethylene Oxide	g	2.4×10^{-3}	3.1×10^{-3}
18. HAc	g	0.2	1.0×10^{-3}
19. HCl	g	9.8×10^{-4}	8.7×10^{-4}
20. N_2O	g	1.1×10^{-3}	6.6×10^{-4}
21. H_2S	g	5.6×10^{-4}	4.4×10^{-4}
22. Cl_2	g	6.5×10^{-4}	2.0×10^{-4}
23. Hg	g	1.9×10^{-6}	1.2×10^{-5}
24. HCFC 1301	g	3.1×10^{-7}	5.6×10^{-7}
Discharges into water			
25. Gypsum	g	370.00	500.00
26. Cl^-	g	38.00	44.00
27. Fluorides (aq)	g	5.70	7.60
28. TSS	g	6.30	5.00
29. COD	g	4.10	1.20
30. SO_4 (aq)	g	0.20	0.30
31. TDS	g	0.30	0.20
32. DSS	g	0.20	0.20
33. H_2SO_4	g	0.10	0.20
34. Tot-N	g	0.30	0.20
35. HCl (aq)	g	0.028	0.037
36. BOD	g	0.30	0.20
37. Oil (aq)	g	0.014	0.014
38. MCA (aq)	g	0.011	6.0×10^{-3}
39. Metals (aq)	g	0.042	0.047
40. HC (aq)	g	1.8×10^{-3}	2.0×10^{-3}
41. Tot-P	g	1.0×10^{-3}	1.0×10^{-3}

42.	Heavy metals	g	0.022	0.03
43.	DSO	g	3.0×10^{-4}	–
44.	Sulphur	g	7.5×10^{-5}	–
45.	Phenol	g	5.4×10^{-5}	5.6×10^{-5}
46.	TOC	g	6.3×10^{-6}	6.1×10^{-4}

Solid waste

47.	Solid, unspecified	g	530.00	520.00
48.	Waste, organic	g	8.90	1.70
49.	Waste, mineral	g	0.50	0.50
50.	Waste, radioactive	g	0.043	0.035
51.	Red sludge	g	0.089	0.083
52.	Covered mass	g	0.034	0.034
53.	Aluminium oxide	g	1.4×10^{-3}	0.10
54.	Salt	g	8.6×10^{-3}	8.0×10^{-3}

Resource use

55.	Cr	g	2.6×10^{-4}	8.7×10^{-4}
56.	B	g	2.2×10^{-3}	3.00
57.	Ni	g	0.017	–
58.	Al	g	0.048	0.04
59.	Fe ore	g	6.0×10^{-3}	6.1×10^{-3}
60.	S	g	0.60	0.30
61.	Oil	kg	0.36	0.29
62.	P	g	33	44.00
63.	Ag	g	1.2×10^{-5}	3.8×10^{-5}

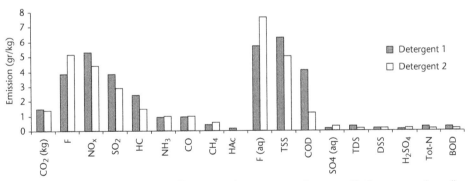

Figure 6.3 Selected cradle-to-gate inventory results, quantitative comparison (in absolute numbers) of two detergents (Arvidsson 1995).

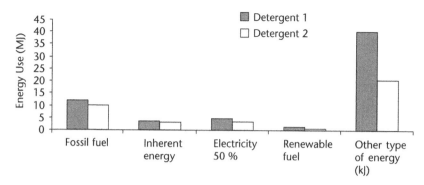

Figure 6.4 Selected cradle-to-gate inventory results focusing on energy parameters, quantitative comparison (in absolute numbers) of two detergents (Arvidsson 1995).

Results can be presented in a normalised form to facilitate comparison. This way results are presented relative to a norm rather than in absolute numbers, as in the previous examples. An example of normalised results for emissions to air and water for the two detergents is presented in figure 6.5. The results for detergent 1 have been set to 1 (one). The results for the detergent 2 are given relative to those of detergent 1. Now compare absolute and normalised results by comparing figures 6.3 and 6.5. It tends to be easier to

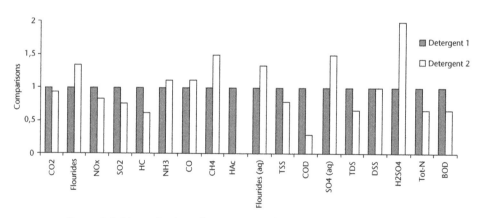

Figure 6.5 Normalised cradle-to-gate results show a relative comparison of two or more products. Here results for detergent 1 are set equal to 1, and all the results for detergent 2 are given relative to detergent 1 (Arvidsson 1995).

draw diagrams with normalised results because the magnitudes of bars are more even. However normalised results also hide the "real" (absolute) numbers, which is why normalised results are often found in reports in which results are partly confidential.

Table 6.2 and figures 6.3 and 6.5 all show that the results are inconclusive. None of the detergents consistently has the lowest environmental loads. It is therefore difficult to say which of the detergents causes the least environmental impact. An impact assessment is called for in such a situation.

Impact assessment – characterisation results

Presenting the results of the detergent study at the characterisation level allows for a more "total" result presentation. The step from the inventory to the characterisation level aggregates the information to the extent where all parameters can fit into one diagram. Figure 6.6 shows a comparison of normalised characterisation results for the two detergents. It shows clearly that detergent 2 is environmentally preferable to detergent 1. A few words of caution are needed here. Although aggregation condenses the information so that it more easily fits into one diagram, it also obscures the existence of

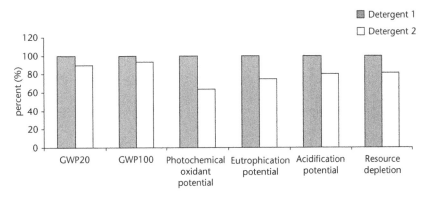

Figure 6.6 Normalised characterisation results of the detergent study (Arvidsson 1995). The diagram builds on "all" cradle-to-gate inventory result parameters although the existence of particularly problematic pollutants becomes obscured when aggregating. In this case, the results at the characterisation level allow a conclusion to be drawn.

183

particular pollutants, typically those that are considered problematic and in need of monitoring. Furthermore, the results at the characterisation level are total in the sense that only those inventory result whose parameters fit into the characterisation method are included. Among parameters that are left out one finds those that are considered relatively harmless (for example "salt", parameter 54 in table 6.2), relate to poorly developed impact assessment categories such as impacts of toxicity and land use (see further section 6.2) or represent material flows not traced back to nature.

Impact assessment – weighted results

The weighted results are not necessary to draw a conclusion in the case of the detergent study since the results were conclusive at the characterisation level. However, for the sake of exemplification, the results of the detergent study are also presented at the weighted level in figure 6.7.

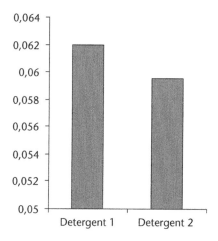

Figure 6.7 Simple bar diagram showing the total environmental impact according to the EPS weighting method for the cradle-to-gate results for the two detergents (based on Arvidsson 1995). The difference between the two detergents is clear but small.

Different audiences – different result presentation formats

The ability to support a conclusion is not the only determinant in the choice of a presentation format. The intended users or the intended audience of the results also plays a role.

Inventory results are typically more popular with people who understand chemical substance names and work in a process industry producing relatively simple products. The inventory result parameters resemble the process parameters used in the chemical, pulp and paper, and metallurgical industries. Detailed inventory result parameters can therefore be used for identifying the production processes that cause them.

In contrast, the manufacturing industry often uses highly aggregated results. One reason for wanting to condense the information is that the products are complex, consisting of an almost unsurveyable number of parts and materials. An additional reason is that designers and construction engineers have little time for and competence concerning complex environmental information. For example, Volvo works with environmental information about components in the format of LCA results weighted according to the EPS method. This way each material and component is environmentally described by a single number.

Characterisation results are often used in instances of communication to a more general audience. Results are then communicated in terms of environmental problems without going into the detail of chemical substance names. How many people would know that for example SO_2 should be understood as acidification and that CH_4 as greenhouse warming? In fact, characterisation results in a standardised format are used in environmental product declarations (see chapter 10).

6.2 Qualitative results

It is self-evident that a qualitative LCA study produces results of qualitative nature. However, most quantitative LCA studies also produce some results of qualitative nature. These two cases will be examined in this section.

Qualitative LCA studies

It is not always possible or even desirable to always conduct LCA studies of the quantitative kind. Qualitative studies may lose to quantitative studies with respect to detail and accuracy but they usually gain with respect to speed. At any rate, qualitative studies need not be less communicative or conclusive than quantitative studies. The results of a qualitative LCA study comparing three insulation materials is presented in figure 6.8. Technical and environmental information about each insulating material were given to a panel, in this case an environmental council group at the Swedish Building Research Agency. The three insulating materials were graded on a 7-step scale from little to large impact. The result of their evaluation is presented in figure 6.8.

In order to "evaluate" the evaluation, the same technical and environmental information given to the environmental council was also given to a group of students. Interestingly enough, the evaluation made by the students was identical to the one made by the environmental council. From this it can be inferred either that the qualitative technical and environmental information was conclusive enough for the two groups to make the same subjective evaluation, or that the technical and environmental information was biased.

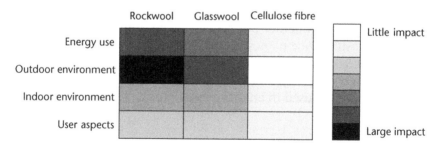

Figure 6.8 Qualitative comparison of three insulation materials. The evaluation was carried out by an environmental council of the Swedish Building Research Agency (Tillman & Svensson 1993).

Qualitative data in quantitative studies

The environmental impacts of many substances have not yet been characterised in LCA methodology. The consequence is that many inventory result parameters lack characterisation equivalents and/ or weighting indices. Since the result presentation cannot deal with these substances in a quantitative way, they have to be dealt with qualitatively. If not, they run the risk of being overlooked and forgotten about. A way to present a qualitative impact assessment for these substances is to present them in a *red flag* table. A red "flag" is raised for all those substance for which environmental impacts are not described. Table 6.3 shows a list of all inventory results in the detergent study (Arvidsson 1995) distinguishing between those without EPS index and those with an index.

It is possible to further analyse the red flag substances by categorising them, for example according to environmental regulation, which has put certain substances on phase-out lists. Counting the number of red flag substances listed in phase-out lists gives an indication of the seriousness of their environmental impact.

Table 6.3 Red flag table for the cradle-to-gate inventory result parameters of the detergent study (Arvidsson 1995). 35 parameters lack a weighting index (according to the EPS method) while 29 have an index (❣ indicates a red flag).

Compounds	Unit	Detergent 1	Detergent 2	Index (ELU/kg)
Energy consumption				
1. Fossil fuel	MJ	11.60	9.70	❣
2. Inherent energy	MJ	3.60	2.80	❣
3. Electricity 50 %	MJ	4.40	3.30	❣
4. Renewable fuel	MJ	1.00	0.60	❣
5. Other energy type	MJ	0.04	0.02	❣
Emissions into air				
6. CO_2	g	1500.00	1400.00	0.108
7. Particles	g	24.50	30.40	36.00
8. Fluorides	g	3.80	5.10	2.07
9. NO_x	g	5.30	4.40	2.13
10. Ashes	g	5.20	5.40	36.00
11. SO_2	g	3.80	2.90	3.27
12. HC	g	2.40	1.50	2.14
13. NH_3	g	0.90	1.00	2.90
14. CO	g	0.90	1.00	0.331
15. CH_4	g	0.40	0.60	2.72
16. Acetaldehyde	g	4.3×10^{-3}	4.3×10^{-3}	❣

187

17.	Ethylene Oxide	g	2.4×10^{-3}	3.1×10^{-3}	3.45
18.	HAc	g	0.20	1.0×10^{-3}	⁚
19.	HCl	g	9.8×10^{-4}	8.7×10^{-4}	2.13
20.	N_2O	g	1.1×10^{-3}	6.6×10^{-4}	38,3
21.	H_2S	g	5.6×10^{-4}	4.4×10^{-4}	6.89
22.	Cl_2	g	6.5×10^{-4}	2.0×10^{-4}	⁚
23.	Hg	g	1.9×10^{-6}	1.2×10^{-5}	61.4
24.	HCFC 1301	g	3.1×10^{-7}	5.6×10^{-7}	⁚

Discharges into water

25.	Gypsum	g	370.00	500.00	⁚
26.	Cl^-	g	38.00	44.00	⁚
27.	Fluorides (aq)	g	5.70	7.60	⁚
28.	TSS	g	6.30	5.00	⁚
29.	COD	g	4.10	1.20	1.01×10^{-3}
30.	SO_4 (aq)	g	0.20	0.30	⁚
31.	TDS	g	0.30	0.20	⁚
32.	DSS	g	0.20	0.20	⁚
33.	H_2SO_4	g	0.10	0.20	⁚
34.	Tot-N	g	0.30	0.20	-0.381
35.	HCl (aq)	g	0.028	0.037	⁚
36.	BOD	g	0.30	0.20	2.01×10^{-3}
37.	Oil (aq)	g	0.014	0.014	⁚
38.	MCA (aq)	g	0.011	6.0×10^{-3}	⁚
39.	Metals (aq)	g	0.042	0.047	⁚
40.	HC (aq)	g	1.8×10^{-3}	2.0×10^{-3}	⁚
41.	Tot-P	g	1.0×10^{-3}	1.0×10^{-3}	0.055
42.	Heavy metals	g	0.022	0.03	⁚
43.	DSO	g	3.0×10^{-4}	–	⁚
44.	Sulphur	g	7.5×10^{-5}	–	⁚
45.	Phenol	g	5.4×10^{-5}	5.6×10^{-5}	⁚
46.	TOC	g	6.3×10^{-6}	6.1×10^{-4}	⁚

Solid waste

47.	Solid, unspecified	g	530.00	520.00	⁚
48.	Waste, organic	g	8.90	1.70	⁚
49.	Waste, mineral	g	0.50	0.50	⁚
50.	Waste, radioactive	g	0.043	0.035	⁚
51.	Red sludge	g	0.089	0.083	⁚
52.	Covered mass	g	0.034	0.034	⁚
53.	Aluminium oxide	g	1.4×10^{-3}	0.10	⁚
54.	Salt	g	8.6×10^{-3}	8.0×10^{-3}	⁚

Resource use

55.	Cr	g	2.6×10^{-4}	8.7×10^{-4}	84.90
56.	B	g	2.2×10^{-3}	3.00	0.05
57.	Ni	g	0.017	–	160.00
58.	Al	g	0.048	0.04	0.439
59.	Fe ore	g	6.0×10^{-3}	6.1×10^{-3}	0.961
60.	S	g	0.60	0.30	0.1
61.	Oil	g	360	290	0.506
62.	P	g	33	44.00	4.47
63.	Ag	g	1.2×10^{-5}	3.8×10^{-5}	54000

6.3 Different purposes – different result presentations

Although the overall results are the main objective in comparisons, it is often interesting to analyse the results in a more detailed way. Instead of looking at the results at the level of the whole life cycle, it is possible to also look "inside" the life cycle, i.e. to look at the results for different parts of the life cycle. The analytical purpose of this can be either to identify for which activities in the life cycle improvements are most needed and/or which of them are controlled or at least under the influence of those conducting the LCA study.

In this section a few types of result analyses are presented. In the next section (6.4.) a different kind of result analysis, testing the robustness of results and conclusions, is presented.

Dominance analysis

A dominance analysis is used to investigate what parts of the life cycle give rise to the greatest (dominant) environmental impact. It is carried out by looking at the emissions (or the environmental impact) of each activity in the life cycle. This is done for one of the detergents in figure 6.9 where emissions to air are presented for each of the activities in its life cycle (processes from A to M and transports). The analysis allows for identifying where improvements are most wanted or needed. Figure 6.9 shows that processes D and I are the most dominant ones. Processes B, C, G and K are also important. Transports are important when targeting the NO_x emissions. A dominance analysis is equally useful for the identification of relatively unproblematic activities. This is important for example for a company wanting to know whether they are at risk of exposure in the environmental debate or if it is their own production processes or those of their suppliers that cause the greatest problems.

It is also possible to conduct a dominance analysis where activities in the lifecycle are grouped into more general categories, such as production, transports, use and waste management. This has

189

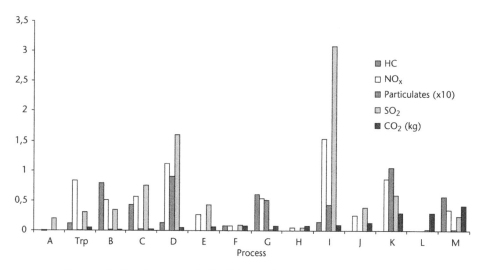

Figure 6.9 Dominance analysis of the cradle-to-gate results for a detergent (Arvidsson 1995).

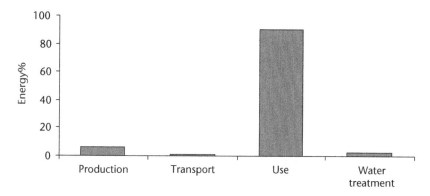

Figure 6.10 Dominance analysis concerning the use of energy in the different part of a detergent's life cycle (Arvidsson 1995). NB: Here, the analysis has been made on cradle-to-grave results.

been done for one of the detergents in our recurring example. From figure 6.10 it is clear that use of the detergent causes the greatest energy consumption. This means that the environmental impact of the detergent depends much on the consumer's behaviour with

190

regard to dosage, washing temperature and frequency of washing. The small difference between the two detergents (see figures 6.6 and 6.7) is of little importance in comparison to the importance of the consumer's behaviour.

Contribution analysis

A contribution analysis is very similar to a dominance analysis. The difference is to identify which environmental loads (instead of activities) contribute most to the total environmental impact. It is necessary to compare emissions and resource use on the characterisation level or the weighting level for this type of analysis. The results are quite often presented as percentages of the total, but other ways are also possible, for example as in figure 6.11. Figure 6.11 shows that CO_2 emissions and particles are the greatest contributors to the overall environmental impact according to EPS (note the scale factor of these two emissions). Problematic substances such as mercury have insignificant emissions. These conclu-

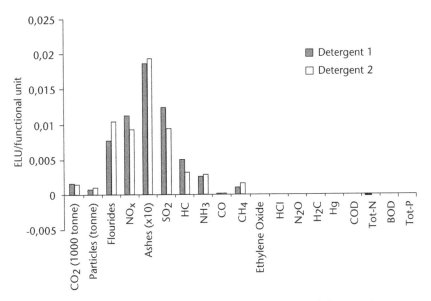

Figure 6.11 Contribution analysis of the cradle-to-gate result for two detergents (Arvidsson 1995).

sions are valid for both detergents. Figure 6.10 actually shows that the two detergents have quite similar environmental profiles.

Break-even analysis

A break-even analysis can be used to investigate trade-offs of environmental impacts that are related to the use of the studied products. Three examples illustrate this type of analysis. In the first and second examples, single-use products are compared with multiple-use products (paper/porcelain cups and non-refillable/refillable milk containers, respectively). The trade-off is between production with a relatively low environmental impact for the simpler, single-use products and the impact related to washing the multiple-use products. In the third example, car fenders made of different materials are compared. The trade-off is between the weight of the fender (the heavier the higher the impact from driving) and the recycling process, which can differ substantially for different materials.

To use porcelain cups only once, like paper cups, would be very wasteful. The question is how many times a porcelain cup must be

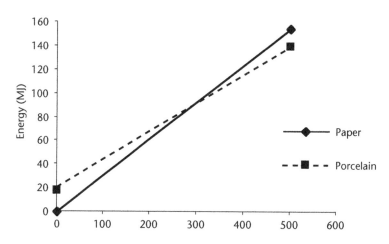

Figure 6.12 Break even analysis in a comparison of porcelain coffee mugs with single-use paper cups (van Eijk et al. 1991). The energy use is accumulated over the number of servings with paper cups/servings in porcelain cups.

used (inclusive of its washing up) before it becomes environmentally preferable to paper cups. This is perhaps not a meaningful question for a household, but it could be a meaningful question for a workplace or for an airline company. According to the results of a Dutch study presented in figure 6.12, a porcelain cup has to be used at least 300 times in order to be preferable to paper cups. Given the number of workdays in a year, it is not impossible for a porcelain cup in an office environment to be used more than 300 times in a year. Its environmental payback time would be a year in that case.

Our next example concerns a similar issue as in the paper cup/porcelain cup study. How many times should a refillable milk container be used for it to be environmentally preferred to non-refillable milk containers? According to an American study, a refillable milk container should be used at least 10 to 20 times for it to be environmentally preferred to single-use containers, see figure 6.13.

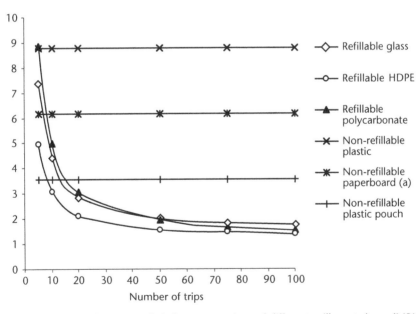

Figure 6.13 Break-even analysis in a comparison of different milk containers (MRI 1997). The energy use is presented per use of container. The energy use is the same each time a single-use milk container is used. For a refillable container, the energy use per use decreases with the number of times it is used. The refillable containers should be used at least 10 to 15 times to be environmentally preferred compared to the most preferred single-use milk container.

This figure illustrates an alternative way of presenting a break-even analysis. It shows the energy use per each use of a milk container assuming different numbers of trips for the refillable containers (instead of the energy use accumulated for each use, as in figure 6.12). In figure 6.13, the energy use is constant for the single-use milk container and it decreases per use for each extra time the refillable milk containers are used. So, if a refillable bottle is used twice, the energy per use (or trip) is about half compared to the energy use if it is used only once. Trip numbers between 10 and 20 correspond to recycling rates between 90 % and 95 %. (An explanation of recycling rates and trip numbers is found in chapter 4.)

The third example about car fenders (figure 6.14) resembles our first example in figure 6.12. in that the break-even is identified through the analysis of accumulated environmental impact associated with the use of the studied products. However, the trade-off situation is slightly different. After 15 000 km and the end of the car life, the fenders are recycled and the fender material can be used a second time (150 000–300 000 km). For the car fenders here, the trade-off is between the environmental impact from driving (the

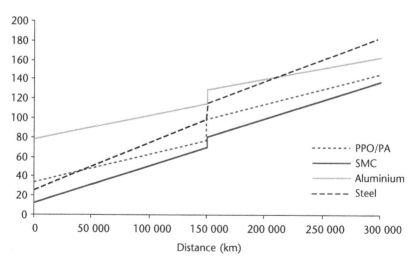

Figure 6.14 A break-even analysis for car fenders made of different materials evaluating the trade-off between their weight and recyclability (Saur et al. 1996).

heavier the fender, the greater its environmental impact) and the environmental impact from their recycling (recycling differs much for plastics and metals).

The heavier steel fender looses in the long run (top line at 300 000 km) in spite of its low environmental impact in production (at 0 km) and low-impact recycling. The aluminium fender is environmentally more "costly" to produce (top line at 0 km) but gains in the long run mostly thanks to being much lighter than the steel fender. The two fenders made of plastic composite materials (PPO/PA and SMC) have rather similar profiles. SMC fenders are slightly heavier than PPO/PA fenders (steeper slope of the line) but have better recycling characteristics (smaller step up at 150 000 km).

Decision maker analysis

The basis for this type of analysis is identification of the different companies and organisations that carry out the different activities in the technical system. This can be used by the commissioner of the study for identifying the extent to which environmental impact is under his/her control. In the example presented in figures 6.15 and 6.16, five levels of influence were identified, but the number of levels may of course vary from case to case.

The analysis in this particular example was made for SKF Sweden AB, a manufacturer of ball bearings. The SKF group is a large one. In addition to bearing manufacturers, producers of bearing components and producers of certain raw materials are also part of it. However, other raw material producers, transportation companies and packaging producers are not part of the SKF group. The degree of influence that SKF has over them varies and depends on how tightly they are bound to SKF through collaboration and/or supplier contracts. The environmental loads of the activities under the direct control of SKF, the commissioning company, represent the highest level of influence. The other levels of influence are determined by the degree of formalised collaboration with SKF, the lowest being little or no influence. Figure 6.14 shows the organisational owners of the activities in the flowchart, categorised according to different levels of influence. Figure 6.16 shows the distribution of environmental impacts over the five levels of influence.

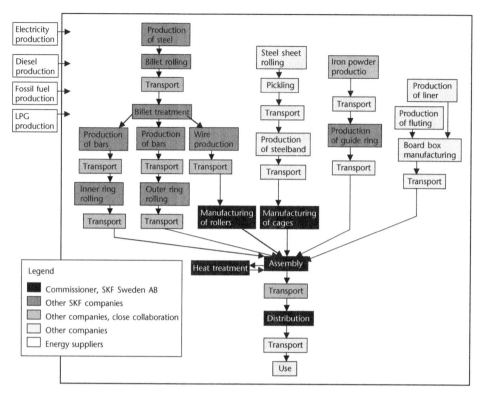

Figure 6.15 Decision maker analysis. Relationship between LCA commissioner and other companies involved in the production of spherical roller bearing.

6.4 Testing the robustness of the results

Any LCA study requires the collection of a large amount of information and data. Difficulties obtaining the most appropriate data are often encountered. Instead of site-specific data, one might have to resort to literature data or to estimated data. Instead of national averages, single-site data might have to suffice. The instances where approximate data are used can be many. This circumstance brings to the fore the need for testing the robustness of the results, i.e. to check whether conclusions hold even if critical and/or approximate data are changed. This type of analysis is called *evaluation* according to the ISO 14043 terminology (2000).

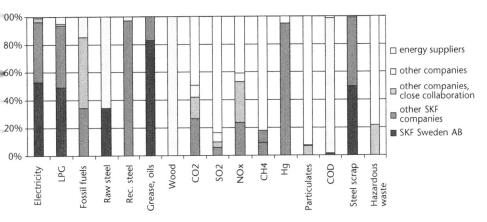

Figure 6.16 Decision maker analysis of selected inventory results for a spherical roller bearing (based on Ekdahl 2001). The diagram shows among other things that SKF Sweden AB stands for the majority of the electricity consumption, use of greases and oils and generation of steel scrap. To reduce emissions to air (CO_2, SO_2, NO_x and CH_4) the decision maker needs to influence the choice of energy suppliers. The commissioner at SKF Sweden AB must target other companies in the SKF group in order to reduce emissions of mercury (Hg).

Table 6.4 Overview of tests for checking the robustness of results and conclusions.

Type of test	Purpose of test
Completeness check	Check for data gaps in inventory, or completeness of impact assessment (to what extent does it cover all inventory result parameters).
Consistency check	Check appropriateness of life cycle modelling and methodological choices given the defined goal and scope (see further chapters 3–5)
Uncertainty analysis	Check of effect of uncertain data (ranges of data, estimates, approximations, etc)
Sensitivity analysis	Identification and check of effect of critical data
Variation analysis	Check of effect of alternative scenarios and life cycle models
Data quality assessment	Assessment of the degree of data gaps, approximate data and appropriate data

The robustness of the results and the conclusions is based not only on the data used in the calculations. It is also based on the range of alternative scenarios and/or products included in the comparison as well as choices made when methodological alternatives are possible as in the case of allocation.

Different robustness tests are listed in table 6.4 below. Some of the tests, such as completeness check, are rather self-explanatory, and will not be further described.

Uncertainty analysis

Uncertainty analysis deals with the effect of imprecise data on the results. The reason why data can be considered imprecise is that data for a particular material can range over an interval. The reasons for this are that the environmental performance of different suppliers varies or that production processes can operate under different conditions.

The interval in which the data can range can be an important piece of information for a comparison (see figure 6.17). A designer typically compares materials on a generic level. Even when the

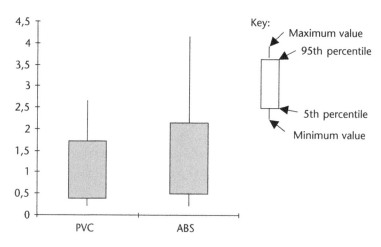

Figure 6.17 Uncertainty analysis presenting the range of environmental impact results for two plastic materials (Coulon et al. 1997).

average environmental impact is lower for one of the materials, the other might still be an environmentally good choice if it is possible to select one of the environmentally preferred suppliers.

In order to present an uncertainty analysis as in figure 6.17, it is necessary to collect all the varying data so that the interval and distribution can be established.

Sensitivity analysis

Uncertain data can be dealt with without additional, extensive data collection to establish the range of data. Sensitivity analysis can be done by systematically changing the input parameters. Those input parameters for which only a small change will lead to a reversal of the results (for example, the ranking of studied alternatives is changed) can be identified as the most critical ones. The need for accurate data for these parameters is therefore great. It is also possible to make this analysis on the level of process steps instead of at the level of individual parameters.

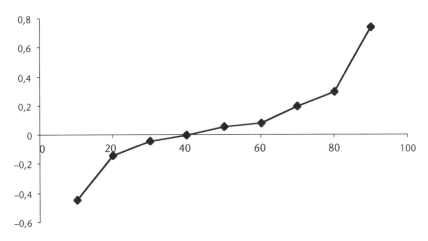

Figure 6.18 There is a 40 % probability that the cradle-to-gate results for detergent 2 will remain environmentally preferred those for detergent 1 (Arvidsson 1995). The Monte Carlo simulation systematically changed input variables in the impact assessment. The most critical parameters are those associated with global warming and the depletion of fossil and mineral resources.

A Monte Carlo simulation can be used for making a sensitivity analysis. Random numbers are multiplied by standard errors (geometric standard deviation) for each input data. A hundred simulations are then made to find out how the final result varies. The distribution of results is shown in diagrams such as that in figure 6.18. The diagram shows the probability of detergent 2 remaining environmentally preferred to detergent 1 when input data are changed. The Monte Carlo simulation also identifies those critical parameters for which small changes lead to reversed ranking of the compared alternatives. The critical parameters are identified by dividing their standard error by the factor that the respective input data has to be multiplied by in order to change the ranking. The most critical parameters are those with the highest ratios.

In this particular case (Arvidsson 1995), the sensitivity analysis was conducted on changes in the input data for environmental impact assessment in the EPS method, not on the inventory data. The most critical parameters (indices) in the EPS method are those on global warming and depletion of fossil and mineral resources.

Variation analysis

A variation analysis can be understood as an investigation of changing parts of the life cycle model, or changing "branches" on the "life cycle process tree". Two variation analyses are presented in the following.

Again using the detergent study (Arvidsson 1995) as an example, we will present a variation analysis that takes the large differences in energy generation in different countries (here, Sweden and Germany) as its starting point. The idea of conducting this particular variation analysis arose when it was seen that the use phase was dominant in the life cycle (see figure 6.10). In other words, this was unexpected and something not originally expressed in the goal and scope definition. Thus the further exploration of this issue can be expressed as: What difference does it make if the detergent is used in Germany or in Sweden? Implicit in this formulation is that the country of detergent production is unchanged and that certain transports change given the alternative countries of use. The impor-

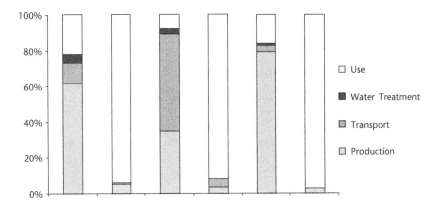

Figure 6.19 Proportion of energy-related emissions given the differences in the electricity generation in the countries where the detergent is used (Arvidsson 1995). Note the different proportions of the use phase in Sweden and Germany. Also note that the analysis is made on cradle-to-grave results.

tance of the country of use is illustrated in figure 6.19. The use of the detergent involves the use of washing machines. The electricity to run the washing machines can be generated in many different ways. Fossil fuels are important for German electricity generation in comparison to Sweden where hydroenergy and nuclear energy dominate.

Another possibility would have been to present variation analysis in absolute numbers instead of the relative numbers shown in figure 6.19. The effect of the different countries of use together with the country of production staying the same would perhaps have been accentuated.

Another interesting variation analysis, concerning newspaper production, is presented in figure 6.20. Starting from existing newspaper production, the authors (Rafenberg & Mayer 1998) explore the importance of various changes, for example changing to printing plates made of recycled aluminium or changing the type of paper or ink. This variation analysis made it possible to see which changes would lead to substantial reductions in environmental load and which would only lead to marginal changes.

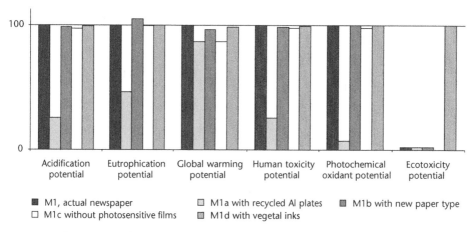

Figure 6.20 Changes (M1a-M1d) to the production of a newspaper (M1) were studied in a variation analysis (Rafenberg & Mayer 1998). The analysis shows that changing the printing plates leads to the greatest improvement.

6.5 Summary and further reading

This chapter has shown several examples of how to analyse and present LCA results. The act of analysing and presenting the results is called *interpretation* in the LCA framework. The ISO 14043 standard on interpretation describes the general structure of the interpretation phase but does not prescribe any methods for the analysis of results (ISO 14043 2000). In principle there are two types of analysis. The first concerns the results as such, i.e. the identification of significant issues. Several methods can be used to find the most polluting step in the life cycle, the most critical methodological choice, etc. The second type tests the robustness of the results – it is an evaluation of the results in order to establish confidence in the results. Here, tests of for example the consistency of methodological choices and completeness of data are made.

There is no specific literature about the interpretation of results, apart from the standard (ISO 14043 2000). To find more examples of how to analyse and present results, it is best to look in various LCA reports and be inspired by good and bad examples. Some examples are also found in the ISO 14043 standard (2000).

7 Critical review of LCA

At conferences in the early 1990s the suspicion was aired that LCA analysts were sometimes "hired guns", conducting LCAs that showed what the analyst had been paid to show. The remedies discerned were standardisation of the methodology and critical reviews of studies. Concern for *credibility* is thus one of the reasons for critical review of LCA studies.

There are additional reasons, however. For instance, critical review is a way to deal with *confidentiality*. If parts of the underlying data of an LCA study are confidential, but there is a need for credibility in line with what is rendered by a fully transparent report, a reviewer who has seen the full report, including the confidential data, may certify its validity.

Having read the preceding methodology chapters you will have realised that conducting an LCA is a more complex task than what one may think at first when meeting the conceptual idea of a cradle-to-grave analysis. It may involve many methodological choices. They must be made in a way that makes the study relevant with respect to its goal definition and allows it to fulfil its intended purpose. An LCA may also stretch over many different technology areas, some of which may be less familiar to the practitioner. LCA analysts may hence require *expert support* to assure the quality of their work. As a consequence, the role of a reviewer is sometimes more similar to that of a coach or sparring partner than that of an auditor.

Finally, LCAs may have implications for actors other than those directly involved in the study. For example, they may underpin decisions about policies or they may have commercial implications. In such cases, *involvement of the interested parties* in the review process is an option. If interested parties are involved in the framing of the study and have an influence on the choices made during its course, the chances increase that the results of the LCA will be taken into account in subsequent decision making processes.

For all these reasons critical review was a topic in several of the early LCA guidelines, notably the SETAC Code of Practice (SETAC 1993) and the Nordic Guidelines of LCA (Nord 1995). Later, it was regulated in the ISO 14040 standard (1997), where instructions are given concerning how to carry out a critical review and where critical review is mandatory for LCA studies intended to support "comparative assertions[1] disclosed to the public." Systematic documentation of review practice is limited, for which reason the preparation of this chapter has included interviews with experienced reviewers of LCA studies, complementing the documents referred to above.

The reasons *why* critical reviews of LCA studies are conducted have already been given. The remainder of the chapter will take us through *when* reviews are done, i.e. for what type of studies, with respect to *what* studies are evaluated and *how* reviews are done in terms of procedures. Finally, some experiences from reviewing practice will be given. Having read the chapter you should be well prepared to do exercise G on critical review.

7.1 *When* are LCAs reviewed critically?

What LCA studies are or should be subject to critical review? This is largely a decision for the commissioner of the study, with one important exception. As already mentioned, the ISO standard mandates that critical reviews be conducted for LCA studies used to support comparative assertions made public (ISO 14040 1997). We call this type of review as "full" ISO review. The standard also gives the form such a review should take. Otherwise, whether to have a critical review done or not, and in what form, is decided during the goal and scope definition (see chapter 3). In practice, the type of project that can bear the costs of a "full" ISO review is large projects in mul-

---

1   ISO 14040 (1997) defines comparative assertion as an "environmental claim regarding the superiority or equivalence of one product versus a competing product which performs the same function".

tinational companies or in international sector collaborations. However, the ISO mandate has not lead to keeping unreviewed LCA studies including comparisons from being published. There are many such studies and one may only speculate on the reasons. Perhaps it is sometimes not important to commissioners and practitioners to comply completely with the standard or perhaps the term "comparative assertion" is sometimes interpreted in a narrow sense.

When less formal reviews are made as part of a quality assurance procedure, internal or external experts may be used. For instance, some LCA consultancies practice internal review, i.e. a colleague that is not directly involved in the study at hand reviews the work. There are also examples where external LCA experts are used to review LCA studies that are conducted internally in companies. In such cases the role of the reviewer is more that of an adviser and less of an auditor.

LCAs underpinning environmental product declarations (EPDs) are always subject to external review. EPDs (which are further described in chapter 10) are LCA results intended to be communicated in market situations. They are published within the framework of an EPD programme. Within such programmes there are rules for what verification procedures are needed, although the rigidity of verification procedures differs between programmes. EPDs do not include comparisons in themselves as every EPD is a stand-alone LCA, but they are intended for comparison between similar products. To ensure such comparability, LCA methodology for EPD is much more strictly standardised than for other LCA applications. The review is intended to certify compliance with the methodology prescribed by the programme, among other things.

There is a link between the need for critical review and the transparency with which a study is reported, as pointed out in the Nordic guidelines on LCA (Nord 1995). A fully transparent report where all data, assumptions and methodological choices are openly reported may be read critically by anyone. Hence there is less need for a formal critical review of such studies. If, one the other hand, only aggregated results are reported, as in e.g. environmental product declarations, the need increases for independent verification that the prescribed methodology has been used, the data is appropriate and the calculations correct.

7.2 With respect to *what* are LCAs reviewed?

A critical review may be done with respect to a number of different criteria including the following evaluations:

- Are the methods used consistent with normative documents, i.e. in most cases the ISO standard?
- Are the methods used relevant with respect to the goal definition?
- Are the methods used scientifically and technically valid in more general terms?
- Are the data appropriate and reasonable?
- Are the calculations correct?
- Are the conclusions supported by the results of the study and do they not extend beyond identified limitations of the study?
- Is the report transparent?
- Does the report fulfil requirements made in normative documents, i.e. in most cases the ISO standards?

Not all types of reviews investigate all these issues. There are two types of quite comprehensive and formalised reviews (the "full" ISO review and the EPD review) that are quite different. We will start by looking into them and follow with a discussion of the content of other types of reviews.

Mandatory ISO review of public LCAs supporting comparative assertions

Critical reviews according to ISO, both compulsory and optional, are focused on the *methodology* and its consistency with the ISO standard and general scientific and technical validity, the *appropriateness of the data* used, that the *conclusions drawn* are really underpinned by the results and not beyond the limitations of the study and that the *report* is transparent and consistent. An ISO review is not primarily concerned with checking the calculations and numerical results, even though some reviewers evaluate those numerical relations that are easily checked.

For comparative public LCAs, i.e. the cases when review is mandatory (the "full" ISO review), the equivalence of the compared model systems is stressed when *methodology* is evaluated. The functional unit must be the same and methodological considerations equivalent, such as system boundaries, allocation procedures and data quality. Impact assessment must be conducted for a sufficiently comprehensive set of impact categories. Weighting, on the other hand, must not be used for this type of study, but comparisons made impact category per impact category (ISO 14040 1997; ISO 14041 1998; ISO 14042 2000).

The *requirements on reports* made available to parties other than the commissioner (third-party reports in ISO terminology) are extensive in the ISO standards. The overall requirement is that studies should be transparently reported, which means that results, methods, assumptions and limitations and data should be reported in a way that allows the reader to comprehend the complexities and trade-offs inherent in the LCA study and use the results in a manner consistent with the study goals. Put simply, all the information should be reported that would allow someone else to repeat the study. The standards include detailed lists of items to be reported in any third-party report, requirements that are made even more extensive for studies including comparative assertions. ISO 14040 (1997) gives the general requirements, ISO 14041 (1998) the requirements on what should be included when reporting goal definition and inventory analysis and ISO 14042 (2000) the requirements on reporting the impact assessment.

EPD review

Reviews of LCAs underpinning EPDs are quite different. The numerical results here come to the fore for at least two different reasons. Firstly, conclusions and comparisons are external to the EPD and are intended to be made by the customer. Correct numbers are thus a prerequisite for the customer to make valid comparisons. Secondly, EPDs are non-transparent aggregated LCA results. Thus the role of the reviewer becomes to certify that the reported numerical results are correct, based on the data and methods used. Thus, calculations are checked (on a sample test basis) and even the correspondence of the data used with the data in referenced sources is checked on a sample test basis (MSR 1999).

Review of LCAs for EPD purposes also differs from other types of reviews in that there are additional normative documents with respect to which the LCA is evaluated. These norms, which complement the ISO standards, are there to ensure comparability between EPDs of similar products. Relevance of methodological choices in relation to the goal definition is of no concern for the reviewer of an EPD-LCA. The purpose of the study is given and the methodology choices have already been made in the additional EPD norms. Compliance with them is what is evaluated by the reviewer.

Other types of reviews

Not all reviews include the same amount of the formalism as in the mandatory ISO reviews and the EPD reviews. ISO 14040 (1997) describes two other types of critical review, which are optional, *internal expert review* and *external expert review*. In them less attention may be given to formalities such as requirements on the report. Instead the review may focus on *methodology* issues, or *data issues*, or it may check *calculations* or concentrate on whether the *conclusions* are robust. The focus and the level of detail of the review may vary and is decided in the goal and scope definition.

Among *methodology* issues that may be brought to the fore are the following:

- Functional unit.
- Relevance of compared options, in cases of comparisons.
- Methods for impact assessment (e.g. what impact categories are used, whether weighting is applied or not, and if so using what weighting method is used).
- System boundaries and allocation procedures.
- Relevance of used data in relation to the study goal (average vs marginal, average vs site specific, age, geographic coverage ...).

When evaluating the methodology, relevance in relation to the purpose of the study is central. There are often assumptions underpinning many of the methodological choices, the relevance and validity of which may need to be checked. For example, assumptions about the equivalence in function between compared options or about the lifetime of products have implications for the choice of functional unit. When system enlargement is used there are always assumptions about what specific process is replaced, e.g. what fuel is replaced in the case of waste incineration and what material is replaced in the case of material recycling. Such assumptions have implications for the choice of data. In addition, in studies that include comparisons it is important to check that the methodological choices are equivalent between compared alternatives.

Data issues may include the relevance of the data used (which has already been listed above as a methodology issue), but may also concern the extent and consistency with which the data has been documented. Getting the data right is also a question of getting the models of the technical systems right, and a review of the data used may very well involve an expert on the technology modelled in the LCA.

To check all the *calculations* in an LCA essentially means to repeat the study, and is thus hardly possible within the framework of a critical review. What the reviewer may do is to check some impact categories or inventory parameters on a sample test basis. For instance, the environmental impact categories that are of major concern for the technology modelled in the LCA may be checked. It is also relatively easy to evaluate some key relationships such as fossil fuel use versus CO_2 emissions versus global warming potential. Finally, an experienced LCA reviewer has acquired a feeling for what orders of magnitude are reasonable.

The *conclusions*, finally, are important of course. Do the results really support the conclusions drawn? Does the study draw conclusions beyond the limits described in the scope of the study? Do uncertainty and sensitivity analyses underpin the conclusions?

7.3 *How* are critical reviews conducted?

As mentioned, the ISO standard distinguishes between three different types of critical reviews; internal expert review, external expert review and review by interested parties.

It is the latter type, review by interested parties, that is mandatory for public LCAs supporting comparative assertions. Such reviews are made by a panel of experts (comprising for example LCA expertise and expertise on the technology that is the subject of the study). According to the standard the panel may also include interested parties potentially affected by the conclusions of the study such as governmental agencies, environmental pressure groups (NGOs) and competitors (ISO 14040 1997). In practice, however, such stakeholder involvement is usually handled separately from the critical review, in a reference panel or steering group or similar arrangement.

Internal and external expert reviews are usually done by single individuals rather than expert panels.

A review may be conducted either as a more or less supporting activity that follows the whole LCA project or it may be done as an audit of a completed report. The ISO standard gives no advice on this matter. However, the SETAC Code of practice (1993) recommends that critical reviews of LCAs be conducted in parallel with the project. Reviewers should be engaged first during the goal and scope definition, then again at a stage where there are initial results and finally when the final report is being prepared. The influence of the SETAC Code of practice is shown by the fact that this is still how reviewers work in many cases.

Written review statements play an important role in the whole process. The more formal the review, the more weight is given to the statement. Review statements may be written in all three phases of a full-blown review process, i.e. goal and scope definition, preliminary results, final report. The ISO standard requires that review statements are included in the LCA report.

The considerations, the when, what and how, of critical review are summarised in table 7.1.

Table 7.1 Different kinds of critical reviews summarised.

		When	Mandatory ISO review	EPD review	Internal expert review	External expert review
What	Methods:					
	– in line with normative documents		X	X		
	– relevant with respect to goal definition		X	–		
	– scientifically and tech-nically valid		X	X		
	Data					
	– relevant		X	X		
	– valid		X	X		
	– document		X	X		
	Calculations correct		–	X		
	Conclusions					
	– supported by study results		X	–		
	– within study limitations		X	–		
	Report					
	– transparent		X	X[1]		
	– in line with detailed requirements in standards		X	–		
How	Interactive critical review process		Usually			
	Review of final report only		Usually not	X		

As decided in goal and scope definition (written diagonally across the Internal expert review and External expert review columns)

1) underlying LCA report required to be transparent, in contrast to published EPD.

7.4 Summary and further reading

In summary, critical reviews of LCA studies are intended to enhance their credibility and quality. Stakeholder involvement in the review process increases the chances that the results are taken into account in subsequent decision making.

Not all LCAs are subject to critical review, however. According to the ISO standard critical review is mandatory in cases of comparative assertions made public. LCAs underpinning environmental product declarations are also always reviewed. In other cases critical review is optional and may be conducted by internal or external experts.

LCA studies may be reviewed with respect to a number of different issues. These are summarised in table 7.1 and include methodology issues, data issues, calculations, validity of conclusions and transparency of the report. Not all aspects are evaluated in all types of studies, as also seen in table 7.1. As further described there are two main procedural types of reviews, interactive ones and those where only the final report is subject to review.

Having read this chapter you should be prepared to do exercise G, in which you will recognise table 7.1. The exercise consists of writing a review statement for an LCA. Review statements play an important role in the ISO standards.

Not much has been written about critical review, in spite of the importance placed on the topic. In cases where a full ISO review is conducted, the requirements and rules for reviews are scattered in the documents and all three of ISO 14040 (1997), ISO 14041 (1998) and ISO 14042 (2000) must be referred to. However, the standards give little support regarding the procedures of review processes. Instead the SETAC Code of Practice (1993) is still a valuable document in this respect.

8 LCA data management

Anyone about to conduct an LCA study might understand the importance of keeping good order in all the data. A lot of data is collected during the inventory phase from a number of sources, directly from suppliers as well as from the literature and various databases. Sometimes no data is available and one has even to come up with an estimate or make an approximation based on similar technology. Deciding on what data to use requires that it is possible to interpret exactly what the data stand for. Re-use of data from for example other LCA studies and LCA databases is greatly helped if data is well documented, e.g. the source, age and scope of data are known. To assist calculations, LCA software packages have been developed and several are available on the market. Many of them come with built-in databases. Eventually both collected data and results may have to be documented for future use and for the study to be transparent.

A schematic representation of the flow and handling of data in the course of an LCA study is presented in figure 8.1. The flow and handling of data starts with data collection, which was described in chapter 4. This chapter picks up the thread and continues with related data management issues, i.e. data documentation, LCA software packages and databases.

When learning to carry out LCA it is useful to carry out the modelling "by hand" and with simple spreadsheet software in order to have full control over the data, methodological choices and calculations. It may be difficult for the beginner to discern methodological choices (e.g. default allocation principle, default emission factors and default weighting method) that are built-in in an LCA software tool. Of course, when conducting LCAs professionally, it is not practical to carry out an LCA by hand. A software tool is then extremely helpful, even more so if it is in contact with inventory

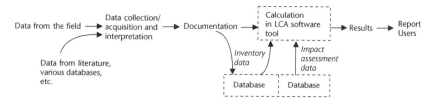

Figure 8.1 Flow and handling of data in the course of an LCA study.

and impact assessment databases. The overview of LCA software packages and databases presented in this chapter covers some of the most common packages and databases.

To support review, re-use and exchange of data, data must be documented in a consistent format or people will have difficulties in interpreting the meaning of data. An ISO specification for the life cycle data documentation format, ISO/TS 14048 (2002), has been developed for this purpose. It supports making transparent LCA studies and building up of databases that can communicate and transfer data from one database to another without any loss of information. Data documentation is dealt with in detail in the final section of this chapter and in exercise D.

8.1 LCA software packages

There are a number of LCA software packages available on the market. It would be difficult to come up with an accurate number, but an international survey identified at least 24 software packages (IRIS 2000). Some of them are designed to deal with any type of LCA but there are also software packages that have been designed for particular LCA applications or industrial sectors. In the survey, a distinction was made between software packages that support screening or qualitative LCA, LCA of the accounting type and "fullblown" LCA which may include networked flows and recycling loops (see figure 8.2). The classification is based on the *computational capacity* of the software tool and the extent to which the *quality of data* used in calculations can be reviewed (IRIS 2000). An LCA that include net-

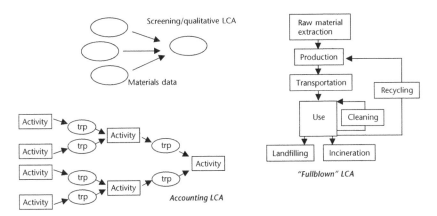

Figure 8.2 Screening LCA software packages use rough estimates for supplier and transport data. Accounting LCA software packages add up the parts of a product chain in tree-like structure. "Fullblown" LCA software packages allow networked and looped flows, such as recycling flows (based on IRIS 2000).

worked flows and loop flows requires a software tool with extensive mathematical capacity as it involves comprehensive system modelling compared to the other two types of LCA (see also section on calculation procedures in chapter 4). Accounting LCA, which is often used for eco-labelling and environmental product declarations, requires a software that allows transparent assessments so that the calculations and the quality of data can be undergo third party review. The remaining category, screening LCA software packages, can be used to make quick and rough LCAs, which is useful for example in product development. They allow an overview of the life cycle but do not produce assessments that are transparently documented.

Almost all of the software packages comply with the ISO14040 standards. Most of them include one or several weighting methods. The user may also define a weighting method and add it to the software package. However, this requires some amount of work. Most of the software packages communicate in English, but some of them communicate in another language as well, e.g. Danish, Dutch, French or German. There are also software packages that only communicate in Japanese.

215

There can be differences in the way the computational tool and the database are related to each other (see figure 8.3). Many software packages come with a database with inventory data and impact assessment data included. In some cases the software package comes with an integrated, yet empty database system and the data can then be bought separately. There are also LCA software packages that can rely on an external database that supports not only LCA but also other environmental applications. Such a database may be located centrally in a network. The advantage of having a system with an external database is that several LCA analysts and users can share a common pool of data. In the other case, each LCA analyst has his/her database stored in their own computer.

The price range for the software packages varies from free of charge up to 20 000 USD. The price is related to the size of the included database to some extent. The data included in such databases can be general or cover a particular industrial sector or geographical area.

The combination of different features and properties means that some of the software packages can be used quite generally while others have more specialised design, adapted for use in a particular industrial sector or type of application. An overview of some of the most common LCA software packages is presented in table 8.1. However, there are several more worth mentioning. Examples of software packages not included in the IRIS survey include ATHENA (Canada) and BEES (US). Both are made for the building industry.

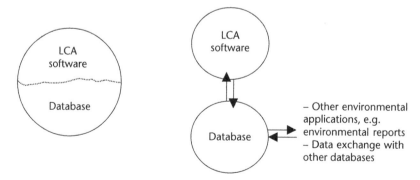

Figure 8.3 Two principally different ways the LCA software and database can be related.

Table 8.1 Examples of LCA software packages (based on IRIS 2000). (NB: Some of the software packages have been updated since the survey; the most recent version is given within brackets.)

Name of software	Country of origin	Type of LCA	Type of user	Result level	Demo available
The Boustead model 4.2 (4.4)	UK	Accounting & fullblown LCA	Design engineer Environmental engineer LCA expert	Inventory & characterisation	Yes
ECO-it 1.0	Netherlands	Screening LCA	Design engineer	Weighting	Yes
EDIP 2.11 beta (3.0 beta)	Denmark	Accounting & fullblown LCA	Design engineer LCA expert	Inventory, characterisation & weighting	No
EPS 4.0 Design System (EPS2000)	Sweden	Screening & accounting LCA	Design engineer Environmental engineer LCA expert	Inventory, characterisation & weighting	Yes
GaBi3 (4)	Germany	Fullblown LCA	LCA expert	Inventory, characterisation & weighting	Yes
GEMIS (4.13)	Germany	Screening & accounting LCA	Environmental engineer LCA expert	Characterisation	Yes
JEMAI-LCA	Japan	Fullblown LCA	Design engineer LCA expert	Inventory, characterisation & weighting	?
KCL Eco 3.0 (3.01)	Finland	Screening, accounting & fullblown LCA	Design engineer Environmental engineer LCA expert	Inventory, characterisation & weighting	Yes
LCA-iT4	Sweden	Screening, accounting & fullblown LCA	Design engineer Environmental engineer LCA expert	Inventory, characterisation & weighting	Yes
PEMS 4.6	UK	Screening, accounting & fullblown LCA	LCA expert	Inventory, characterisation & weighting	Yes
REGIS 2.1 (2.2)	Switzerland	Screening & accounting LCA	Environmental engineer LCA expert	Inventory, characterisation & weighting	Yes
Sima-Pro 4.0 (5.1)	Netherlands	Screening, accounting & fullblown LCA	Design engineer Environmental engineer LCA expert	Inventory, characterisation & weighting	Yes
TEAM™ (3.0)	France	Screening, accounting & fullblown LCA	Environmental engineer LCA expert	Inventory, characterisation & weighting	Yes
Umberto 3.5 (4.1)	Germany	Accounting & fullblown LCA	Design engineer Environmental engineer LCA expert	Inventory, characterisation & weighting	Yes

While ATHENA is intended for supporting construction design choices, BEES was developed mainly with the procurement process in mind. There are also software tools that combine LCA with economic input-output analysis, the EIO-LCA software by Espinosa et al. (1997), and with analytical hiearchy process as in the Pre-LCA tool by Ong et al. (2001). Tools particularly intended to be easy-to-use include e.g. the Easy-LCA tool (Suzuki 1998) and the EcoScan tool (TNO 2003). The scope of SPINE@CPM Data Tool does not include LCA calculations but it is worth mentioning nevertheless. It supports data acquisition and documentation in a standardised format and may be used by anyone for building up an LCI database, which in turn is compatible with those software tools that comply with the SPINE format (CPM 2003). A list of internet addresses to the home pages of many of the software packages mentioned in this chapter is found towards the end of this chapter.

8.2 LCA databases

Data collection is usually a time-consuming task, especially when one has to turn to many suppliers or locate data for "more remote" activities. In some applications, when a quick LCA screening is wanted, there is hardly any time for data collection. Of course, the individual LCA practitioner could, and often does, build up a sizeable database over time just through conducting LCAs. However, it is not efficient in the long run for each LCA practitioner collect and document data. The fear that data collection would hamper LCA implementation has led especially public authorities to call for public LCI databases since the beginning of the 1990s. Also industry have supported the setting-up of public LCI databases as they would make their own LCA work and data collection more efficient.

The challenge of building an LCI database is that it should be able to handle both individual industrial processes and aggregated cradle-to-gate systems in such a way that data can be re-used in many different ways (see figure 8.4). This requires that information on how processes are related must also be stored.

The earliest database initiatives stem from the many national packaging studies conducted in the early 1990s (see chapter 2). The

218

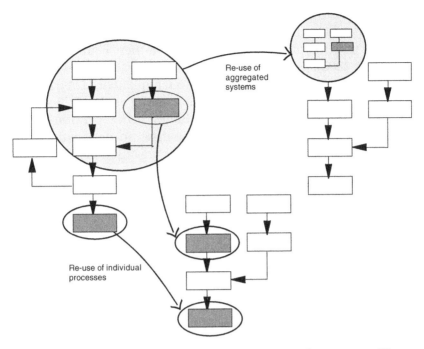

Figure 8.4 A good LCI database should have a structure that supports different ways of re-using data.

accomplishment of collecting large amounts of data for such studies fed the idea that public databases were possible. In several countries co-ordinated efforts are now being made to produce nationally representative and accessible databases. The intention is often to support LCA implementation, not only in large companies, but also in smaller and medium-sized companies as in the EU Cost Action 530 project (Norris & Notten 2002) and local government (e.g. Curran 2002). Such efforts typically involve collaborating organisations and some government funding. There are also international efforts for furthering LCA implementation, e.g. the *Life Cycle Initiative* co-ordinated by UNEP and SETAC. One of its aims is to support LCA implementation in developing countries (Udo de Haes et al. 2002). In the Asia Pacific region, steps are being taken towards achieving a public database applicable for the region, involving Japan, Korea, Chinese Taipei, Malaysia and Thailand (Norris & Notten 2002). One of the drivers for involving developing countries in the LCA community is an international demand for inventory data since much primary material production takes place in these countries (Norris & Notten 2002).

Also industry has taken initiatives to set up public LCA databases as a way of keeping control over the data being used in LCA studies. The increasing number of LCA studies being performed also increases the number of requests for data. To deal with this, a number of international industry sector organisations have sponsored the production of LCI databases with average data for their industry. Data from these databases is usually available for a fee.

Another type of data source is the data that comes with an LCA software package. In turn, this data often comes from studies conducted by the LCA practitioners linked to the software developers. Behind most LCA software developments one finds LCA researchers, industry practitioners and consultants who originally needed a tool to facilitate their LCA work. Handing over data became a way of "paying" for the development of software and database systems – a software package is more easily sold together with a database. Also for this type of data source there might be a fee involved to access data.

These various efforts have resulted in the existence of a number of LCI databases and to several more database projects being underway. An overview is presented in table 8.2. In addition, LCA reports in a way constitute databases. The US-EPA has supported the development of an LCA portal, LCAccess. Its *Global LCI Directory* provides numerous references to LCA studies as a way to support data collection. To what extent the different databases build on structures and formats that allow efficient re-use and exchange of data is presently not sufficiently known. It has therefore been suggested within the LCInitiative that a quality review of existing databases should be undertaken (LCInitiative 2002).

Table 8.2 Overview of existing databases and database projects underway (based on Norris & Notten 2002 and LCInitiative 2003).

	Existing	Underway
Public authorities, national and international level	Italy (the I-LCA db*), Switzerland (the BUWAL 250 db)	Australia, Canada (the Raw Materials db), Chinese Taipei, Europe (the Cost Action 530 collaboration), international (the CODATA collaboration), Japan (JEMAI), Korea, Sweden, Switzerland (the EcoInvent 2000 project), USA
Industrial sector organisations	Association of Plastics Manufacturers in Europe (APME), European Aluminium Association (EEA), European Federation of Corrugated Board Manufacturers (FEFCO), International Iron and Steel Institute (IISI) & Nickel Development Institute (NiD)	
Consultants and research institutes	Denmark (the EDIP db), Finland (the KCL-Eco db), France (the TEAM db), Germany (the GaBi db & the Umberto db), Sweden (the SPINE@CPM db & the LCAiT db), etc.	Austria, Denmark, France, Germany, Sweden, Switzerland, UK, USA

* db = database

Towards a common database format, ISO/TS 14048

In parallel with the early database projects grew the realisation that database development also required the development of *database format*. Two different, but similar database formats were developed, SPINE (Carlson et al. 1998) and SPOLD (Singhofen et al. 1996). Later, elements from both SPINE and SPOLD and experience from using them formed the base for ISO's technical specification for the LCA data documentation format, ISO/TS 14048 (2002). In short, ISO/TS 14048 is a standardised format for LCA data, be it on paper or in a database. It is based on a general model of a technical system and includes a whole vocabulary for describing data. It can therefore support the development of questionnaires used for data collection as well as design of LCA databases and electronic communication systems for LCA data. More on how the technical specification may influence data collection is presented in section 8.3.

In addition to the historical development leading to development of the SPINE and SPOLD formats and ISO/TS 14048 outlined in chapter 2 (section 2.2), a few words need to be said about the visions that are driving the efforts to standardise LCA data format.

For LCI databases to be used really efficiently, databases need to be able to communicate more "automatically" with each other and with LCA software. Data presented in one way in a particular database should not have to be interpreted and entered manually in another. However, in practice, an LCA practitioner acquiring data from a database has to check a number of things since terminology is not consistent across databases. For a data set named for example polyethylene production, the LCA practitioner needs to check whether the data set represents the cradle-to-gate system or just the unit process of polyethylene production. Also quantities and units have to be checked so that they are the same as those in the practitioners database and calculations. With a consistent data format across databases, data can be transferred without loss of information from one database to another and to LCA software. This would make data collection both quick and inexpensive. With a commonly accepted and widespread data format it would also be possible to build a network of databases instead of having a few centralised databases. The drawback of large centralised databases is that database managers have difficulties in knowing when there have been changes to production processes and thereby in keeping data up-to-date. Maintenance costs can be kept low by having databases close to where data is being "produced" and by documenting data according to the standard format from the beginning when it is collected.

Two examples of how people are trying to turn such visions into reality may be represented by the CPM data exchange project (Erixon 2000; Carlson et al. 2000) and the CODATA collaboration (in Norris & Notten 2002), both with the objective of facilitating the electronic exchange of data.

8.3 Documentation of LCA data according to ISO/TS 14048

Most often, the LCA practitioner cannot solely rely on obtaining data from LCI databases when conducting an LCA study and is thus forced to seek data from companies and in the literature. Sometimes data even has to be estimated. The collected data will most likely end up in the LCI database at the practitioner's workplace, for calculations and for archival reasons, but perhaps more importantly for future re-use of the data. Working efficiently with LCA data in the long run implies that extensive interpretation and re-interpretation of what collected data stands for ought to be kept to a minimum. It is therefore a good rule to document data correctly from the start. The standardised format for LCA data documentation defined in ISO/TS 14048 is useful for this purpose.

ISO/TS 14048 is an ISO technical specification, rather than a standard owing to the procedure of how it was developed. ISO/TS 14048 contains a list of requirements on documented data rather than a description of the procedure of documenting data. Furthermore, ISO/TS 14048 takes the inventory data specifications in ISO 14041 (see chapter 3) a couple of steps further by including requirements related to life cycle impact assessment and general environmental data management. The technical specification thus supports the building up of a more general environmental information system although it is primarily intended for LCI data documentation.

The documentation requirements are derived from general quality aspects of LCI results, i.e. the technical scope of the used data, its transparency and its applicability. The requirements are divided into several groups (see figure 8.5).

Each group is described through of a number of *data fields* into which information is entered (see table 8.3). The assignment of information to data fields is called *formatting*. It includes interpretation of the original information in terms of the data documentation format, structuring the original information into the data documentation format and entering structured information in the data fields (ISO/TS 14048 2002). To support the entering of structured information, the technical specification prescribes a *strict nomencla-*

223

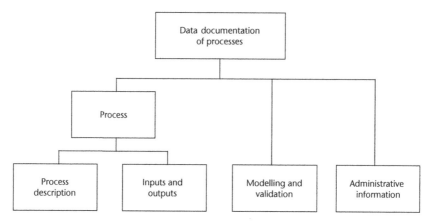

Figure 8.5 The structure of the data documentation format according to ISO/TS 14048 (2002).

ture, i.e. terminology, in certain data fields and a *user-defined nomenclature* in other data fields (see table 8.3). When working with the data documentation format, it is also important to make a clear distinction between a zero and an empty data field when entering information into a data field.

Working with data documentation during the inventory phase

What the documentation format shows is that the actual data, e.g. the emission data, need to be accompanied by a lot of information. Since it is during the inventory phase one has the greatest knowledge about different technical processes and subsystems included in the LCA it becomes an important reason for documenting data thoroughly right from the start. The documentation format may seem too detailed. However, the time spent on data documentation is repaid by the possibility of future shared use of data. Also for the individual LCA study, data documentation has its advantages: it is a preparation for reporting; it enables the simultaneous check of data quality and validity; it enables third party review of the LCA study. An additional advantage of having control over data is that it helps avoid double-counting since the technical scope of the data is

224

Table 8.3 A concentrated version of the data documentation format and requirements based on ISO/TS 14048 (2002) is presented on the next three pages.

Process description

Process	Name:	Descriptive name, e.g. "Combined heat and electricity plant with support system"
Class	Name:	Class to which the process belongs, e.g. electricity supply; enables data search. *User-defined nomenclature.*
	Reference:	Specification of the nomenclature from which the class name is chosen.
Quantitative reference	Type:	e.g. functional unit, reference flow, other flow. *The user may define additional terms.*
	Name:	The name of the quantitative reference, e.g. net production of electricity
	Unit:	The unit of the quantitative reference, e.g. kWh
	Amount:	The amount of the quantitative reference, e.g. 1
Technical scope:		e.g. cradle-to-gate, cradle-to-grave, gate-to-gate, gate-to-grave. *The user may define additional terms.*
Aggregation type:		i.e. non-aggregated, horizontally aggregated, vertically aggregated, both horizontally and vertically aggregated, or unknown. **Strict nomenclature.** (horizontal aggregation = average of several processes producing the same product; vertical aggregation = the sum of interconnected processes)
Technology	Short technology description:	Short description of the included technology.
	Technical content & functionality:	Detailed description of the individual operations and how they are technically and materially related so that data user can determine the technical relevance of the data.
	Technology picture:	e.g. a flowchart of the process.
	Process contents Included processes: Intermediate product flows – Source process: – Input & output source: – Input & output destination: – Destination process:	Relevant for processes that consist of a combination of unit processes and where documentation is provided for each process included in the aggregate. Includes references to the process identification numbers given in the section with 'Administrative information' and to input/output reference numbers given in the flow section.
	Operating conditions:	Explanation of the operating conditions of the process, i.e. actual (possibly non-linear) relations between inputs and outputs.
	Mathematical model Formulae: Name of variable: Value of variable:	The operating conditions may alternatively be documented as a model of the relations between inputs and outputs. One or several formulae may be given and the variables should be defined.
Valid time span	Start date:	The start of the valid time span in the format YYYY-MM-DD.
	End date:	The end of the valid time span in the format YYYY-MM-DD.
	Time-span description:	Description of the time the process is valid; is identical to the time of collection unless forecasts have been applied. Limitations can be set by changes in technology, improvements, etc.
Valid geography	Area name:	Name of the area according to two-letter code according to ISO 3166-1, e.g. Au for Australia. **Strict nomenclature.**
	Area description:	Description of the geographical area or location for which the process and data are valid; is identical to area of data collection unless extrapolation is made.
	Sites:	Address(es) to specified included site(s).
	GIS:	Geographical Information System (GIS) reference according to ISO 6709, e.g. Easting_301230 Northing_6263230. **Strict nomenclature.**
Data acquisition	Sampling procedure:	Description of the way the included processes have been selected from the population for which the data are valid.
	Sampling site:	The addresses of the sampled sites.
	No of sites:	The number of included sampled sites; relevant information for judging the uncertainty of data.
	Sample volume Absolute: Relative:	Total production volume of the sampled sites & the percentage (%) of the total volume of the population for which thte data is valid.)

Flows – inputs and outputs

Identification number:	A unique number to identify *each* specific input/output within the local data storage.
Direction (of flow):	i.e. input, output or non-flow-related aspect. ***Strict nomenclature.***
Group:	e.g. resource, raw material, energy, ancillary, emission, residues, co-product, product. *User may define additional terms.*
Receiving environment:	i.e. air, water, ground or technosphere. The technosphere is the receiving environment for non-elementary inputs/outputs. ***Strict nomenclature.***
Receiving environment specification:	e.g. agricultural air, forest air, high altitudes (>1000 m), indoor air, rural air, urban air, agricultural ground, forest ground, grassland ground, impediment ground, industrial ground, landfill ground, rural ground, urban ground, creek, fossil water, ground water, lake, marsh, ocean, pond, rapid, river, coastal waters, coastal ground, surface water, swamp, waterfall, technosphere. *User may define additional terms.*
Environment condition:	Free-text description of environmental conditions indicated above.
Geographical location:	Location where process(es), inputs and outputs occur; useful information for area-sensitive impact assessment.
Related external systems Origin of destination: Transport type: Information refer- ence:	Information on related, but not included processes, e.g. a raw material supplier and related transport. Includes identification of delivering/receiving process(es), name of transport supplier or transport type and references to contact persons or documents where this information is found.
Internal location	Information about the use of an input or output within a process system.
Name Substance name: Reference to nomen- clature: Name specification:	Name of the input/output flow according to a *defined nomenclature chosen by the user*, e.g. CAS numbers or SETAC nomenclature. Specification of the chosen nomenclature and additional name to simplify the understanding of the name may also be supplied.
Property Name of property: Unit of property Amount of property:	Relevant property(ies) of the input/output required for an LCA study, e.g. relative economic values of the different outputs for allowing allocation or temperature and pressure of a steam flow for calculating a steam flow's energy capacity. SI units have to used *(strict nomenclature).*
Amount Name: Unit – Symbol: – Explanation: Parameter – Name: – Value:	Indicate the distribution function used to describe an amount, e.g. range, mean, mode, range, single point. Each type of distribution function requires a specific set of parameters. Indicate the symbol representing the unit. If SI units are not, an explanation should be given. Indicate also what parameters are used to describe the specified distribution function, e.g, maximum and minimum value for a range, sample size, standard deviation, coefficient of variance. *User may define additional nomenclature.* This is where you eventually write the quantitative amount of the input or output flow in relation to the quantitative reference specified in the 'Process' section.
Mathematical relations Formulae: Name of variable: Value of variable:	The relations between input and output may be expressed by mathematical formulae. One or several formulae can be specified. Variables and values of variables should be defined.
Documentation Data collection (methods): Collection date: Data treatment: Reference to data source:	Short description of the data collection methods used, e.g. derived from continuous measurements, modelled from data describing a similar system, estimated. Date or period when the data was collected. Description of methods, sources and assumptions used to generate, recalculate or reformat the presented amounts. Specification of references used for data collection and treatment.

Modelling & validation

Intended application:	Indicate the application of the process data. This may indicate e.g. the level of quality ambition.
Information sources:	Describe the primary data sources, e.g. site measurements or secondary sources, e.g. reports.

Modelling principles
  Data selection principles:
  Adaptation principles:
  Modelling constants
  – Name:
  – Value:
	Indicate general principles used for the process modelling. Data selection principles include the basis of aggregated data. Adaptation principles refer to adjustments or extrapolations made to remodel the collected data to suit an LCI. Factors held constant in the process model, e.g. a constant recycling rate for paper regardless of the location. Modelling constants nomenclature: net calorific value, gross calorific value, recycling rate, process efficiency, yield rate, cut-off ratio, transportation distance. *User may add additional terms.*

Modelling choices
  Criteria for excluding
  elementary flows:
  Criteria for excluding inter-
  mediate product flows:
  Criteria for externalizing
  processes:
Allocations performed
  – Allocated co-products:
  – Allocation explanation:
Process expansion
  – Process included in
  expansion:
  – Process expansion
  explanation:
	Indicate modelling choices. Describe criteria for selecting, which elementary flows are included/excluded, which intermediate flows (i.e. non-elementary flows) are excluded or which technical subsystems are excluded. The information is useful for assessing the relevance of the data and the extent of data gaps.
	
	In the case of allocation, the type of allocation performed should be indicated and justified. The allocated co-products should be indicated. In the case of system expansion, here termed process expansion, an explanation and justification of the expansion should be given and the process(es) indicated.

Data quality statement:	Description of general and specific strengths and weaknesses of data quality. The data generator may be aware of e.g. data that were especially difficult to validate or interpret.

Validation
  Method:
  Procedure:
  Result:
  Validator:
	Indicate method used for validating data, e.g. on-site validation, recalculation, mass balance, cross-check with other source, proof-reading of data entries. *User may define additional terms.* A more detailed description of the validation procedure is given under 'procedure'. Indicate result of validation, e.g. an acceptable deviation of 3 % was found on raw material input versus product and waste. Indicate the name, the competence and address of the person performing the validation.

Other information:	e.g. advice on how to use the process or known limitations of the process.

Administrative information

Identification number:	A unique number used to identify the process, specified by the authority responsible for the identification number.
Registration authority:	Indicate the authority responsible for the identification number. The data supplier is responsible for the registration procedure to produce unique identification numbers.
Version number:	Can be used to identify updates of data for a specified process.
Data commissioner:	Indicate the person who commissioned the data collection/update.
Data generator:	Indicate the person/organisation responsible for modelling the process and compiling the data.
Data documentor:	Indicate the person responsible for entering the data into this documentation format.
Date completed:	The date when the data documentation was completed, edited or updated.
Publication:	Reference to a printed source where the original copy of this document may be found.
Copyright:	Indicate the person or organisation holding the copyright to the process documentation.
Access restrictions:	Indicate how the data may be spread, e.g. public or restricted access.

known and it thereby becomes clear whether data sets overlap or not. In the same way, it also helps having control over data gaps.

Data documentation is time-consuming. Experience from working with the SPINE format has been documented (Pålsson 1999). Her practical advice on avoiding unnecessary work when documenting LCI data is a good place to end this chapter:

- Secondary sources. When using secondary sources, such as different types of published reports, a lot of time goes into interpreting the material. Sometimes contacts are taken with the author of the report to clarify some issues. Inconsistencies in the original material may be corrected or additional information may be provided. In order to avoid duplication of effort it is important that any extra information arising from interpreting the material also is documented.

- Remodelling. It is not unusual that data describing a particular technical system is remodelled to better fit the format of an LCA. For example, data from environmental reports on an industrial plant may be remodelled into data describing a specific product produced in the plant. Assumptions and choices made in the remodelling need to be explained in the documentation to show that data has not been "tampered with" in an inappropriate way and to ensure trust in the original data supplier and in the intentions of the commissioner.

- Aggregated systems. Data on aggregated system are generally difficult to document without loss of vital information. Such systems are preferably divided into subsystems that are documented separately. If it is not possible to disaggregate the system, then the purpose of the study, system boundaries, use of allocation methods, etc, need to be carefully described so as to avoid future misinterpretation of data.

- Missing information. It may be difficult to obtain all the information required by the data documentation format. It is preferable to state that it has not been possible to acquire the information than to leave the data field empty. If possible, the reason why information is missing should also be documented as it helps a future data user to judge whether the data gap can be amended or not.

228

8.4 Summary and further reading

Carrying out an LCA study implies handling a lot of data. LCA software tools have been developed to facilitate LCA calculations. Several different types of LCA software tools can be found on the market (see table 8.1 and the list of internet addresses). Some of the tools are general LCA tools with great computing capacity; others are made for "quick and dirty" LCAs, useful for example for product development or procurement.

Data collection is a time-consuming activity. Data collection can be more time-efficient if data from one study can be re-used in another. This has been a driving force behind database development in the field of LCA. Developments concerning databases with the notion of national, central LCA databases in many countries. However, problems with maintenance and up-dating data have led to it being more reasonable to develop databases that are shared in smaller networks, e.g. a workplace, and that can communicate and exchange data on demand with other databases.

Database development has also led to the development of formats for storing and documenting LCA. This has implications for data collection in LCA during which collected data need to be well documented so that others can re-use the data. A technical specification on LCA data documentation has been developed through ISO (ISO/TS 14048 2002). Exercise D is an exercise on data documentation according to the ISO/TS 14048 format.

To find out more about data management issues, it is worthwhile to follow the activities of the LCInitiative (www.uneptie.org/pc/sustain/lcinitiative) and the Centre for Environmental Assessment of Product and Material Systems (www.cpm.chalmers.se and www.imi.chalmers.se).

Internet addresses to LCA resources and software suppliers

The ATHENA (Environmental Impact Estimator v.2.0, ATHENA™ Sustainable Materials Institute. http://www.athenasmi.ca, accessed April 2003.

BEES 3.0®. Building for Environmental and Economic Sustainability. http://www.bfrl.nist.gov/oae/software/bees.html, accessed April 2003.

CPM. Centre for Environmental Assessment of Product and Material Systems, http://www.cpm.chalmers.se/

The Boustead model v 4.4. Boustead Consulting Ltd, http://www.boustead-consulting.co.uk

ECO-it. Pré Consultants BV, http//www.pre.nl

EDIP PC tool v 3.0 beta. Danish Environmental Protection Agency & Institute for Product Development, Technical University of Denmark, http://www.mst.dk/activi/08030000.htm

EPS 2000 Design System. Assess Ecostrategy Scandinavia AB, http://www.assess.se

GaBi4. PE Product Engineering GmbH, http://www.gabi-software.com

GEMIS 4.13. Öko-Institut, http://www.oeko.de/service/gemis

IMI. Industrial Environmental Informatics, Chalmers University of Technology, http://www.imi.chalmers.se/

JEMAI-LCA. Japan Environmental Management Association for Industry, http://www.jemai.or.jp

KCL Eco 3.01. Finnish Pulp and Paper Research Institute, http://www.kcl.fi/eco

LCAiT 4. Chalmers Industriteknik, Ekologik, http://www.lcait.com

LCInititiative. UNEP/SETAC programme on life cycle inventory issues, www.uneptie.org/pc/sustain/lcinitiative

PEMS. Pira International, http://www.pira.co.uk/pack

REGIS 2.2. Sinum AG – Ecoperformance Systems, http://www.sinum.com

SimaPro 4.0. Pré Consultants BV, http//www.pre.nl

SPINE@CPM & SPINE@CPM Data Tool 3.0. CPM, Centre for environmental assessment of Product and Material systems, http://www.globalspine.com

SPOLD. Memorial site for the Society for Promotion of Life-cycle Assessment Development, http://www.spold.org/

TEAM™ 3.0. Ecobilan SA/PriceWaterhouseCoopers, http://www.ecobilan.com

Umberto 4.5. ifu, Institut für Umweltinformatik Hamburg GmbH & ifeu, Institut für Energie- und Umweltforschung Heidelberg GmbH, http://www.umberto.de

US-EPA. LCAccess, the LCA portal, http://www.epa.gov/ORD/NRMRL/lcaccess/

Part 3
LCA applications

LCA can be applied to many fields. This part of the book offers an overview of LCA applications. Product development is dealt with in chapter 9. Chapter 10 goes into the use of LCA in market communication, particularly the use of LCA for different types of eco-labelling. Chapters 11 and 12 cover applications upstream and downstream in the life cycle. More precisely, this means that chapter 11 presents an overview of LCA application related to industrial production, both in the process industry and in the manufacturing industry. LCA's relevance for procurement, supply chains and transportation is also brought up in chapter 11. Whereas chapter 11 deals with production, chapter 12 deals with the application of LCA to waste management issues such as choices between recycling, incineration and landfilling. The last chapter of the book presents accounts of how LCA projects are run in industry, covering both the organisation of an LCA project and the implementation of LCA activities in a company.

9 LCA and product development

Product design and development has been seen as the principal area of application of LCA since the early days of LCA. Of course other types of applications have been identified over the years, but the application of LCA to product development has received the most attention. An early vision of LCA application to product development described the 'five-minutes LCA' for any product developer to carry out using LCA software and databases (see also chapter 2). Since then, more diversified ways of using LCA to influence product design have evolved. There is now a great number of LCA based approaches to product design and several reports, books, handbooks and even doctoral dissertations have been published on this topic.

The focal point of LCA, the *product*, coincides with that of the product design and development process. This explains in part why the LCA community has brought LCA forward as a central tool for environmental adaption of product designs. The other part of the explanation is that product development is seen as a decisive activity for achieving sustainability in industrial society – most of the environmental attributes are determined and built into the product during the design stage when materials are selected and constructions designed. The advantage of life cycle based approaches in product development is that these can bring a holistic environmental perspective to the design deliberations.

This chapter aims at presenting an overview of different ways of using LCA and life cycle based approaches for the greening of product designs. Some consist of very simplified LCAs while others are more complex approaches depending on for what stage of the design process they are intended. To clarify the context an introductory description of the characteristics of ecodesign and product development is given. Suggestions about how to utilise LCA in product design are good in themselves but what counts is the extent to which they are put into practice. Therefore this chapter ends by examining some of the experiences of working with life cycle approaches in product development. This will hopefully be of help when implementing or evaluating application of life cycle approaches to product development.

9.1 Product development and environmental considerations

Product development is the process that precedes the production of a new product in a company or an organisation, e.g. a research institute, a consulting firm or a non-profit organisation. Each company has its own way of working with product development. Some companies have their own in-house designers while others may use external contracted designers or free-lancers, but the designers are not the only ones involved. Typically, product development is a multi-disciplinary activity involving people mainly from the marketing, design and manufacturing departments. So, depending on the discipline and the company, terminology and descriptions of product design and development processes vary. In any case, different phases can be discerned in this process, which involves defining needs, planning the structure, operation and appearance of a product and then planning these to fit efficient production, distribution and selling procedures (see figure 9.1). Far from all product development projects concern new product development. Many projects consist of updating existing product models and introducing product improvements. The early phases of product development are then less work intensive.

The introduction of ecodesign into this process is a challenge in practice. It consists of finding out in what form and at what points in the process environmental considerations should be made and by whom they are best carried out. One possibility is that ecodesign deliberations are mostly handled by the product developers them-

236

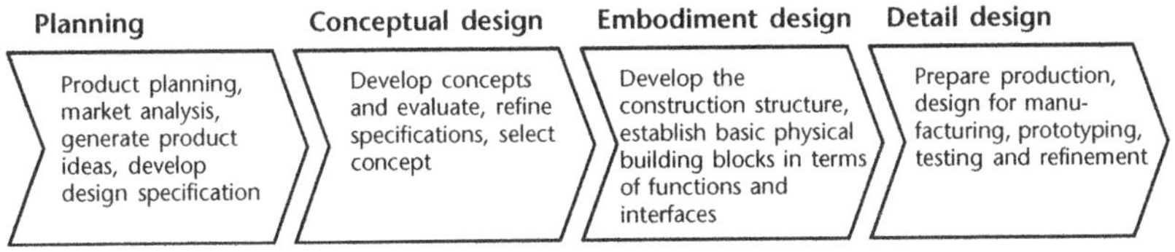

| Planning | Conceptual design | Embodiment design | Detail design |

Product planning, market analysis, generate product ideas, develop design specification

Develop concepts and evaluate, refine specifications, select concept

Develop the construction structure, establish basic physical building blocks in terms of functions and interfaces

Prepare production, design for manufacturing, prototyping, testing and refinement

Figure 9.1 General phases of the product development process, iterations omitted (based on Ulrich & Eppinger 1995, Brezet & van Hemel 1997 and Eder 2000).

selves while another is that environmental specialists are brought in to collaborate with the product developers. A consequence is that companies undergo a period of experimentation with the organisation of ecodesign and the use of tools such as LCA.

One of the important tasks during product development is the development of *design specifications* (see figure 9.1). Design specifications can be described as the customers' needs translated into precise, measurable detail about what the product has to do, without telling the product developers how to address it (Ulrich & Eppinger 1997). For example, a customer need identified in the market analysis can be "easy to install", which can be translated into "average installation time is 75 seconds" in the design specification. Study of *reference products* is also important. A benchmarking analysis of reference products provides additional input to the definition of design specifications. Each specification metric for the new design, e.g. 75 seconds, is typically defined in relation to how the competing products rate on the same issue. For complex products it may be difficult to meet all the initial design specifications, which means that the design specifications are often revised and refined after the concept selection (see figure 9.1).

When it comes to the design of products made by large-scale industry for mass production, product development is an extensive and complex process, both in terms of time and the number of people involved. Many products require three to five years and some take as long as ten years to be developed (Ulrich & Eppinger 1995). The collection of individuals developing a product form the *project team*, which in turn often consists of a *core team* and an *extended team*. The core team is usually small enough to meet in a conference room while the extended team may be quite sizeable, sometimes

237

including up to hundreds or thousands of members, some of them externally located in partner companies and suppliers. The costs are roughly proportional to the number or people involved and to the duration of the project. There are also costs for investing in new tooling and production equipment (Ulrich & Eppinger 1995).

Product development can also be described as a number of parallel processes and cross-functional collaborations that handle and co-ordinate a number of issues, environment being one of them (see figure 9.2). Two challenges characteristic of this process include *time pressure* and *trade-offs* between competing issues. Product development time has increasingly become a means of competition since firms not only compete on the basis of developing products that meet customers' needs well but also on getting the product faster and more efficiently to the market than others (Wheelwright & Clark 1992). Consequently, trade-off decisions must be made under time pressure and often without complete information (Ulrich & Eppinger 1995). Environmental requirements have to coexist with all the other requirements (Luttrop 1999).

Strategies and methods for adding an environmental dimension to product development are described in various handbooks on ecodesign, although the term for it varies. Examples of other names are Design for Environment (DfE), green product development and

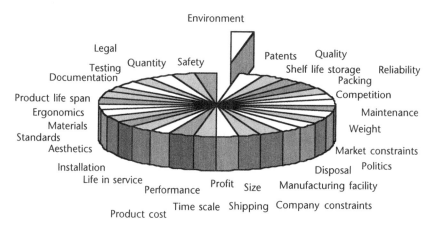

Figure 9.2 A multiplicity of issues must be handled in the product development process (Luttrop 1999).

238

ecological design. Ecodesign as a field has originally developed independently of LCA, but LCA has by now become a important element of ecodesign and some even speak of *life cycle design* (e.g. Keoleian & Menerey 1993). However, despite the varied terminology, the ultimate goal is much the same, i.e. to design products as though the environment matters and to minimise their direct and indirect environmental impact at every possible opportunity (Lewis & Gertsakis 2001).

A general opinion is that environmental considerations should start influencing the product development process as early as possible. Otherwise only small changes to the product design are possible for economic reasons (see figure 9.3). This leads to ecodesign being of different types depending on the level of innovation, ranging from incremental improvements to radical system innovations. At one end of the spectrum is *product improvement* that refers to environmental improvement without really changing the product technology. In *product redesign* the product concept generally stays the same, but parts of the product are developed further or replaced. This level of innovation includes for example design for

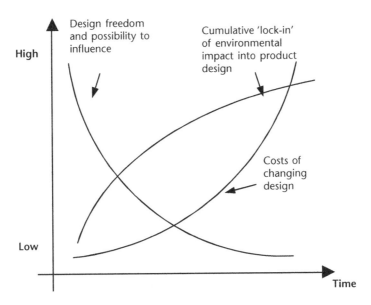

Figure 9.3 Conditions for ecodesign change during the product development process.

recycling. In *function innovation*, the product concept is changed, as in the example of paper-based correspondence changing to e-mail. At the other end of the spectrum one finds *system innovation* which implies changes in infrastructure and societal organisation required for new products and services, for example shifting from agriculture to industry based food production (Brezet 1997). Currently, however, most practical efforts consist of incremental improvements (Kärnä 1999). Interrelated with this, most ecodesign tools concentrate on environmental impact assessment while keeping the functionality of the product unchanged. Thereby they are especially well adapted to product improvement and redesign (Lagerstedt 2003).

Ecodesign tools

Ecodesign tools come in many sorts and kinds as complements to ordinary design tools. They fall into two broad categories: *creativity tools* and *analytic tools* (Lewis & Gertsakis 2001). Brainstorming is an example of a well-known creativity technique, but there are also tools that specifically support the generation of *environmentally-oriented* product ideas and concepts. For example the 10 Golden Ecodesign Rules and the ecostrategy wheel in figure 9.4 can be used to generate environmental options during brainstorming sessions. The many generated product ideas and concepts then need to be evaluated. This is where the analytical tools come in. There are many ecodesign tools of the analytical kind. Their purpose is to assist in identification and evaluation of environmental impacts of different design solutions. A simple analytical tool intended for assessment in the earlier stages of product development is the MET matrix, also in figure 9.4. LCA is typically used for analytical purposes although LCA based approaches can also support more creative processes, but more on this in the next section. Certain analytical tools may also support priority setting or the analysis of trade-offs. Experience has shown that management policies and procedures for integrating environmental considerations are crucial for ecodesign (Ehrenfeld & Lenox 1997; Kärnä 1999). Here a third type of tool is to be found, which consists of environmental management systems especially adapted to the product development proc-

240

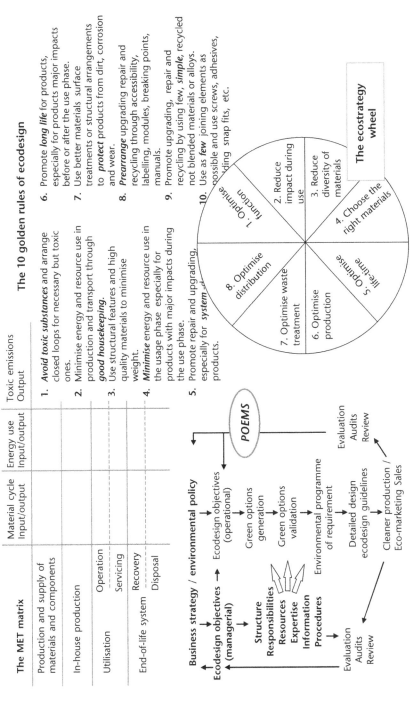

Figure 9.4 Four ecodesign tools. Creativity tools include the 10 Golden Rules of Ecodesign (Luttrop 1999) and the ecostrategy wheel (van Hemel 1995). A simple analytic tool is represented by the MET matrix (Brezet & van Hemel 1997) and an ecodesign management tool by P-OEMS (Brezet & Rocha 2001).

241

ess and embedded in the company's general environmental management system. An example of such a system is P-OEMS, the product-oriented environmental management system in figure 9.4.

9.2 LCA and life cycle based approaches for ecodesign

The dilemma of using "ordinary" quantitative LCA during product development is that there is a shortage of data and no concrete designs to study during the early design stages. Towards the later phases the problem is different: there is seldom enough time for conducting LCA studies. LCA is nevertheless a useful concept, foremost by bringing a holistic environmental perspective to ecodesign, thus enabling identification and analysis of environmental trade-offs such as material minimisation versus durability.

LCA is both time and data consuming and requires also some level of expertise. This means that it is difficult to integrate LCA in the product development process and some adaptation of the methodology is necessary. The road taken in most cases is simplification of the LCA methodology, at least the way it appears to the product developers. Life cycle influenced matrices, software tools and LCA-derived proxies and rules-of-thumb are different examples of simplified LCA. However, many forms of simplified LCA depend on a precursory full-scale LCA. Even if full-scale quantitative LCA is rarely applied directly in the product development process, it is often used as a basis for developing the more simplified LCA methods. Identification of major environmental product issues through a full-scale LCA provides direction as to what the simplified method should cover or concentrate on. The orientation that follows presents different types of life cycle tools for ecodesign and their application to different parts of the product development process.

Types of LCA-based ecodesign tools

Matrices. The MET matrix (Brezet & van Hemel 1997) is a good representative of matrices with a life cycle perspective. It was developed as a simple method for designers to systematically describe the environmental properties of a product. It covers the main life cycle stages and environmental impacts in a simplified way (see figure 9.4). Many companies and organisations, such as eco-labelling programmes, design their own matrices similar to the MET matrix but differing in degree of detail. There are two main approaches to filling such a matrix with information. One is to describe the environmental impact of a product in absolute terms, for example with short descriptive statements about materials used, recyclability, major environmental impacts, etc, complemented by some quantitative information on the amount of materials used, energy content of materials, etc. The quantitative information can be given in absolute numbers or on a scale, e.g. from 1 to 5 where 1 indicates a low amount or impact and 5 a large amount or impact. The descriptive matrices for each product then form the basis for an environmental ranking of the products. The other approach consists of making comparative assessments, in relative terms, between for example the new product and the existing product or between competing alternative designs directly in the matrix. In that case, the differences between the reference product and the alternatives can be expressed on a simple scale ranging from better to worse or with qualitative statements. A very different matrix approach is the Life Cycle Design Structure Matrix (LC-DSM) developed by Schlüter (2001). It builds on the design structure matrix (DSM) technique, in which all the relevant variables are noted on *both* the x-axis and the y-axis. In the LC-DSM it is the different stages in the product cycle that are listed on the two axes (Schlüter 2001). The relations between all variables, i.e. the life cycle stages, are then noted in the matrix. The strength of DSM technique is that it can be applied to large problems while maintaining a relatively good overview of the whole model. With the LC-DSM the design teams can create an environmental balance sheet for their products and components with changing level of detail during the product development process, supporting the identification of critical environmental issues.

A cross-section of LCA-based matrices from different sectors of industry has been collected by Graedel (1998). The main advantage of matrix LCA is that it is efficient, both in terms of time and resources (Greadel 1998; Lewis & Gertsakis 2001). It can be carried out by existing staff, but since the results are based on the knowledge of the designer, co-operation with the environmental staff is recommended, at least to begin with (IVF 2000). Depending on the type of matrix, matrix LCA can be used on different occasions during product development. Often these simplified assessment schemes are intended for the evaluation of product concepts and details, but there are matrices for earlier stages of product development as well. Poole and Simon have shown how a matrix LCA is applicable to product planning in the electronics industry (Poole & Simon 1997). Product planning is part of the early product development phase during which different design trends are analysed and evaluated. In analysis using their Abrigdged LCA matrix the trends towards for example increasing miniaturisation and more network solutions are assessed in a comparative way. The matrix is filled with statements about positive and negative effects of the different design trends and with cautionary notes, such as "miniaturisation of electronic product may complicate disassembly and recycling" (Poole & Simon 1997).

Dedicated software-based LCA. Time being a limiting factor in product development, special LCA software packages have been developed that allow "quick and dirty" LCAs. Examples of such dedicated software packages are Eco-IT, EcoScan, EPS and Idemat (internet addresses listed after this chapter). By providing data via built-in large material and process databases and by also having many methodological choices built in, these software packages allow a relatively quick execution of an LCA by the product developer himself. The database typically contains cradle-to-gate data. Allocation choices can thus be avoided since these are "built into" the data. Moreover, LCA results are given directly as weighted results according to a default life cycle impact assessment method. A quick LCA can thereby be carried out by drawing data from the existing database, cutting down on in-depth checks of its validity and where data is missing, replacing it with estimates and assumptions. These software tools belong to the class of analytical design tools. The main aim is to assist product developers in identifying environmental strengths and weaknesses of the designs and also issues that may need further investigation. Dedicated LCA software tools can be used during the conceptual design phase or later for the environmental analysis of product concepts and details, but it is also possible to carry out rough LCAs on reference products, thereby providing input to the generation of ideas in the earlier phases of product development.

Although not a dedicated software tool, artificial neural network-based LCA may be assigned to this category of computer-based models intended for the use of the designers themselves. The principle of artificial neural network (ANN) modelling is 'learning by example'. Applied to the context of LCA and product development, ANN-based LCA can be used to perform preliminary environmental assessments of concepts based on what is known of existing products. The ANN models are "trained" to obtain an approximate environmental performance for a new product concept. The design team queries the ANN model with attribute data for product concepts without having to define new LCA models. The Product Concept Descriptors developed by Sousa et al. (2000) represent a set of general attributes chosen so that they are usually known during the conceptual design, easily understood by product developers and logically linked to the environmental performance of products (Sousa et al. 2000). Some examples of such descriptors are mass [kg], material composition [%mass], life time [hours] and in use power consumption [watt]. In a way it can be said that ANN-based LCA modelling uses old LCAs of existing products as surrogate LCAs for the new product, but re-models them using the attributes of the new product.

"Ordinary" quantitative LCA. Although matrix LCA and LCA using dedicated software are quick, results may not be of sufficient quality or detail to support comprehensive and in-depth analysis of environmental trade-offs. In such cases it might be worthwhile to undertake "ordinary" quantitative LCA after all. However, the product developer will need the assistance of an environmental specialist for the execution of the LCA. The EDIP manual (Wenzel et al. 1997) provides a comprehensive methodology for environmental design for industrial products (hence, EDIP), which includes not only ordinary methodological instructions on LCA methodology but also guidance on how the environmental specialist and the designer may collaborate (see table 9.1). An LCA can inform product developers on three occasions. An LCA of reference product(s) can help define the environmental specification(s) for the product. LCAs can then evaluate product concepts and details and help in

selecting them. An LCA can be conducted if necessary to verify the design solution.

Another way of using "ordinary" quantitative LCA is more indirect. Instead of using it for product evaluations, it can be used to define rules-of-thumb and proxies.

Table 9.1 Distribution of tasks between the designer and the environmental specialist (adapted from Wenzel et al. 1997).

Tasks of the designer	Tasks of the environmental specialist
Environmental assessment of a reference product	
• Identify an existing or a theoretical product which can serve as a reference	• Identify the essential environmental impacts and their main causes
Environmental diagnosis of a reference product	
• Identify existing alternative design solutions in the reference product(s), including solutions found in competing products	• Simulate theoretical changes in the reference product or its product system and perform an LCA on them • Perform an LCA on specific alternatives, including competing products
• Together, identify environmental focus points in the reference product	
Specification of environmental goals	
• Analyse the consumers' environmental perceptions and priorities and make a projection of the analysis • Define the environmental specification(s) for the product	• (no task)
Design for Environment and LCA of new products	
• Create environmentally attractive product systems • Adapt the product environmentally to existing product systems • If feasible adapt the system environmentally to the product	• Perform environmental assessments of concepts • Perform environmental assessments of details, typically changes relative the reference product
Verification of design solutions	
• Verify that the environmental specification(s) and any other requirements are met	If necessary, perform an LCA on the designed product

LCA-derived rules-of-thumb and proxies. LCA-derived rules-of-thumb are simple design rules based on experience from "ordinary" quantitative LCA studies. Successive studies of a type of product may repeatedly reveal the same particular aspect as being the greatest source of environmental impact. Identification of this aspect forms the basis for defining a rule-of-thumb. For example, LCAs of cars tend to show that the greatest source of impact is the driving of the car. Unless there is an intention to change fuel and engine systems, an important lesson is that the environmental impact can be reduced through lowering the weight of the car since the weight affects fuel consumption. "Reduced environmental impact through lower weight" can thus be a guiding rule-of-thumb for the product developers. When designing buildings, a corresponding rule-of-thumb would be to see to it that energy consumption during the use phase of the building is as low as possible, which has implications for windows, insulation and ventilation among other things. The advantage of such simple design rules is that they are easily diffused in the design team and, in contrast to other life cycle approaches, do not require much education to apply.

Proxies, then, are simple metrics that measure and evaluate a product with respect to its critical environmental properties. Which metrics to use can be determined through "ordinary" quantitative LCA. For example, if weight has been identified as a critical factor, then an obvious metric could be kilograms. Proxies can thereby be used to follow up on the application of LCA-derived rules-of-thumb and other ecodesign guidelines. A well-known proxy is MIPS, which stands for material intensity per service unit (Schmidt-Bleek 1994). It measures the collective weight of different materials used throughout the life cycle. Another common proxy, often used in the building industry, is the cumulative energy use (often called either 'energy content' or 'embodied energy') since the production of many building materials is energy intensive (Lewis & Gertsakis 2001).

Combination tools. In addition to the plain life cycle approaches, there are also a number of methods that combine LCA with assessment of other aspects, such as technical performance or cost. The point of the combined tools is to help the design team with the trade-offs between environmental and other properties of the product. Without going into too much detail, these tools are both elaborate and simple at the same time – elaborate because the draw on several different methodologies and simple because they draw on methods and concepts already familiar to the designers. A tool that combines a functional characterisation of the product with environmental descriptors is the eco-functional matrix (Lagerstedt 2003). The functional characteristics represent different properties that are essential for product functionality and commercial viability, e.g. good ergonomics, aesthetics, reliability and price. Each functional category is evaluated on a scale from 0 to 10, indicating its importance. The environmental descriptors draw on those developed by Sousa et al. (2000) since they fit the design context by being logically linked to functional characteristics and expressed in terms easily understood by designers (Lagerstedt 2003). The environmental descriptors describe various environmental properties such as size [weight/volume], number of different materials, energy use and energy source on a scale from 0 to 10 indicating approximate environmental performance. The functional and environmental characteristics are then combined in a matrix through analysis of how functionality and environmental impact are interrelated, thereby addressing the dual aim of minimising environmental impact and maximising functionality.

The eco-functional matrix builds indirectly on LCA. However, there are combinations that involves a more direct application of LCA, e.g. the various approaches that combine Quality Function Deployment (QFD) and LCA (e.g. Olesen 1997, Masui et al. 2000). They represent attempts of taking customers' environmental demands into account when designing the product. This is done through observing and interviewing customers with regard to their reaction to environmental properties of a reference product and by performing an LCA of that product in parallel. However, product costs are also important and a combination that adds life cycle costing to QFD and LCA has also been put forward (Hanssen 1997).

LCA as a creativity tool. Most of the above mentioned LCA-based tools are of the analytical kind. For this reason it might be appropriate to highlight the use of LCA as a creativity tool to round off this overview of LCA-based ecodesign tools. Reverse LCA is an approach suggested by Graedel (1998). It develops the task of defining a functional unit into the more comprehensive analysis of the needs that the product is designed to fulfil. The term *reverse* refers to the fact that the need is examined in detail before any product design is characterised. In normal LCA the product is evaluated environmentally, but with RLCA one begins with the environmental characteristics of an ideal product and works backward to determine the

248

physical design that would best satisfy those characteristics. What makes RLCA a creativity tool is the focus on the needs rather than on the product, which encourages creative systems thinking and supports identification of opportunities for innovation.

Another creativity approach that has been alluded to in the preceding overview is the use of LCA studies of reference products as inputs to brainstorming sessions early on during product development. This can not only contribute to the generation of product ideas and concepts. Such inputs can also support more general environmental learning in the designers (Bakker 1995). Well presented LCAs of well chosen reference products and/or product systems provide the designers with comprehensive nuanced knowledge of the factors that determine the environmental properties of the products they work with. More importantly, such knowledge may influence and change the designers' mental frame of reference and add to the body of knowledge they apply "intuitively" in the design process. This type of learning may contribute more fundamentally to environmental product design than the rote application of evaluation tools.

There are thus a number of life cycle approaches, both analytical and creative and for the early, intermediate as well as the later stages of product development (see figure 9.5). However, it is not reasonable to use all approaches simultaneously. Designers tend to prefer qualitative tools that are quick and simple to use partly owing to the time pressure (McAloone 2000). Environmental life cycle considerations in product design are probably best supported by a well-balanced combination of a few of the approaches.

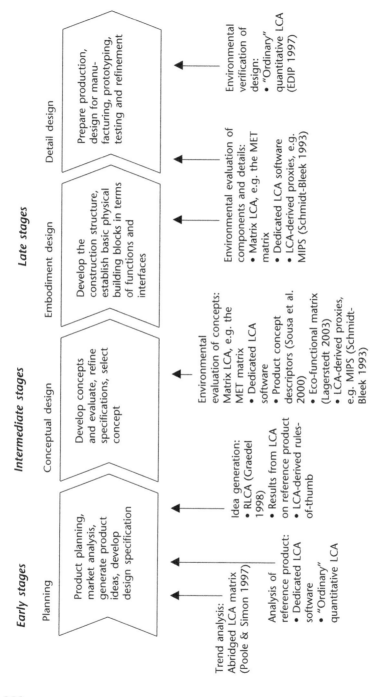

Figure 9.5 Timing of the use of different life cycle approaches in the product development process.

9.3 Ecodesign and LCA in product development in practice

Clearly, LCA can be used in many different ways in product development. The previous section has shown several examples of LCA based and LCA influenced methods. However, the mere existence of methods is not a guarantee of their integration into product development. Several studies show that LCA application in product development is far from being common practice in industry. A study of the state-of-the art of ecodesign in Europe (Tukker et al. 2000) showed that the most active parties developing and practising ecodesign were research institutes and universities. However, there are some large multinational companies that address the issue of ecodesign in a relatively comprehensive way, particularly in the fields of electrical and electronic goods, motor vehicles and packaging. In other companies, practical experiences have mainly consisted of experimental projects, without subsequent structured application (Kärnä 1999; Frankl & Rubik 2000) or are non-existent (Tukker et al. 2000). Particularly small and medium sized companies are lagging behind.

Another survey has studied the application of LCA to design and R&D[1] in a large multinational company that has worked with LCA since the beginning of the 1990s (Laestadius & Karlsson 2001). The company produces electrical equipment and machinery and can be considered to be at the forefront of LCA application. The survey produced some contradictory results. The technical, economic and environmental benefits of using LCA were modest and LCA activities seemed not to be integrated into normal operational activities, nor have they taken place with any frequency in product development projects. In spite of this, there was a very positive opinion about the future applicability and use of LCA. The majority of the respondents to the survey believed that LCA had come to stay and that it would become more useful in the future.

A third study (Frankl & Rubik 2000), this one on the use of LCA in industry in general showed that different tools are used for environmental improvement of products, e.g. LCA, checklists, etc. How-

---

1   Research and development

ever, the most frequently used method consisted of checking for compliance with legislation. Concerning LCA, several companies developed customised simplified assessment tools based on LCA after having conducted an LCA study or two. One such case is reported in chapter 13, the LGUT case.

Documentation of the practice of LCA in product development is thus limited since most efforts have gone into tool and methodology development and less on studying how they work in practice (Baumann et al. 2000). Drawing together some of what is known produces the following list of recommendations and critical issues.

LCA alone is not sufficient for ecodesign to take place. What is considered as a complete *toolbox* consists of (Tukker et al. 2000):

- up-to-date databases and easy-to-use and commonly accepted software tools,
- manuals with schemes and procedures assisting the implementation of ecodesign in companies, and
- simplified tools (checklists, design rules, etc) that are tailor-made with regard to the environmental properties of the product type and the industry.

Management and *motivation*, however, may be more important than sophisticated toolboxes (Ehrenfeld & Lenox 1997; Kärnä 1999; Johansson 2002). Characteristic of the frontrunner companies is their strategic commitment to environmental product development (Tukker et al. 2000). From this follows that environmental issues must be managed within the product development process. It is also important that management shows consistent behaviour (Ritzén 2000).

Even with a clear management commitment and an ecodesign toolbox, designers are still left with many uncertainties and trade-offs that they have to solve themselves. It is essential that environmental issues somehow capture the interest of product developers and their managers. *Support to designers* is therefore a critical issue. Important issues concern the organisation and division of ecodesign-related responsibilities and competence development (Ritzén 2000). The extent to which environmental specifications and deliberations are left to the designers to consider on their own or in cooperation with environmental specialists needs to be determined.

252

Concerning the development of competence, LCAs can be as a good a source for learning about what the main environmental issues relevant to product development. The holistic picture given by "ordinary" LCAs often leads to surprises and insights (Baumann 1998) and LCAs of well-chosen reference products and product systems are more conducive to lasting learning that LCAs that evaluate product concepts and detail (Bakker 1995).

9.4 Summary and further reading

Product development has been a central field of application for LCA for a long time. Numerous approaches based on LCA have been developed, ranging from detailed LCA to streamlined LCA. Figure 9.5 is a summary of LCA approaches for the product development process. Two books stand out in the LCA literature on ecodesign. The EDIP manual (Wenzel, Hauschild & Alting 1997) presents a way of working with detailed LCA in the product development process. The book by Graedel (1998) covers the topic of streamlined LCA.

Many of the LCA approaches have been developed independently of each other and it is not reasonable to use all of them. A well-balanced choice must be made. Unfortunately, less is known about how these different LCA approaches work in practice. There are studies that indicate that management and motivation may be more important than the actual tools. An accessible report on this has been written by Tukker et al. (2000).

To find out more about ecodesign tools and guidelines in general, the interested reader is recommended to turn to general handbooks on ecodesign, for example the guide to greener designs by Lewis and Gertsakis (2001), the seminal UNEP guideline on ecodesign by Brezet and van Hemel (1997) or the anthology on solutions for product and service development by Charter and Tischner (2001).

Internet sources

ECO-it. Pré Consultants BV, http//www.pre.nl

EcoScan 3.0. TNO Industrial Technology, Eindhoven, NL, http://www.ind.tno.nl/product_development/sustainable_concepts/ecoscan/index.html

EPS 2000 Design System. Assess Ecostrategy Scandinavia AB, http://www.assess.se

Idemat. Idemat Online, TU Delft,NL, http://www.io.tudelft.nl/research/dfs/idemat/

10 Green marketing and LCA

Figure 10.1 Collection of environmental communication instruments and symbols.

Do you recognise any of the symbols and logotypes above? They all have in common that they are used for environmental or sustainability communication when products are bought and sold. The flora of such symbols is extensive and sometimes confusing. Most of the symbols are voluntary and used for marketing purposes. These include the eco-labels (exemplified by the Canadian Environmental Choice, the German Blue Angel, the Indian Ecomark, the Japanese Eco Mark and the EU flower). There is a similar label that is not concerned with environmental issues but with global equity. Another voluntary environmental symbol that may be used on products is the EPD logo that tells us that the product has a certified environmental product declaration. Green product brands and the symbols used to promote them are a different type of voluntary information. As an example, the logo of Body Shop is shown in the figure. There are also compulsory labels. For example, the label for environmentally hazardous products, the dead fish and tree, is mandatory for some products. The German Grüne Punkt is sometimes mistaken for an eco-label, but all it tells us is that a fee for packaging take-back has been paid. Such compulsory, administrative or even negative labelling should not be confused with positive marketing instruments.

So what is marketing then? The Chartered Institute of Marketing defines marketing as "The management process responsible for identifying, anticipating and satisfying customer requirements profitably" (Peattie 1992). Marketing is thus oriented towards customers and the company's external environment. It includes the gathering and use of external information, particularly about customers and competitors. Product development, which in part is based on such information, is also part of marketing. For most products successful marketing requires that the product be differentiated from competing products. Finally, manipulation of the "marketing mix", i.e. the mix between the factors product, price, place and promotion, is an important element of marketing (Peattie 1992).

Product development was the subject of chapter 9 and will not be further discussed in this chapter. Instead, we will concentrate on environmental information flows between customers and suppliers and instruments to convey such information. We will also discuss in what way green marketing in general is related to LCA and in particular to what extent the standardised environmental marketing instruments (eco-labelling and environmental product declarations) are based on LCA.

10.1 What is green marketing?

Environmental communication on the market may be characterised as in figure 10.2, in which business-to-business communication and communication between business and consumers are differentiated. Business costumers often have a closer and more long-standing relationship with their suppliers as well as more time and competence available for purchasing decisions. Environmental product information to business customers may thus contain more

256

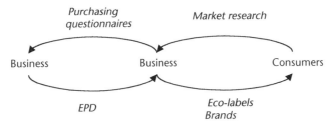

Figure 10.2 Environmental market communication and examples of the use of environmental market instruments.

detail and be more technical. For example, environmental product declarations (results from highly standardised LCAs) were developed mainly with business-to-business communication in mind. Their development was partly driven by suppliers receiving numerous questionnaires from their customers, requesting detailed environmental product information. In business-to-business market relations there is also room for more personal communication. Such an example is presented in chapter 13 (section 13.1, Akzo Nobel case) where an LCA analyst established personal contacts with his data suppliers in the supplying companies.

Consumers are usually addressed on a more collective basis than business costumers. They generally have less competence and time to judge the environmental performance of products, and are thus addressed with more simplified and aggregated information. Eco-labels are one example, but there is also a whole range of other means to convey an environmental image of a product. For instance, there are various "home-made" labels. Also the packaging or the design of the product as such may send a green message. Verbal claims may be used such as *compostable* or *recyclable* or *free from chemical X.*

Not all types of environmental market communication relate to products, however. Some activities are more related to companies, such as the implementation of environmental management systems and the reporting associated with such systems. Another example is the adoption of external codes of conduct, such as the Responsible Care programme of the chemical industry. Yet another example is when corporations form or join environmental associations such as the World Business Council for Sustainable Development.

Different types of information may be combined to build an image of a company and its products as environmentally sound. Such combinations are used for instance when environmental brands are created. Body Shop (the logo shown in figure 10.1) is often used as a textbook example of such environmental branding. In some cases the products sold under a green brand are eco-labelled, in other cases the company sets up its own criteria for what they consider to be an environmentally adapted product.

The green message may be communicated via a whole assortment of channels. Consumers meet logos and labels, graphical profiles, design of packaging and TV-commercials. Brochures and reports, exhibitions at fairs, speeches delivered at conferences along with information on company homepages target a more professional audience.

The double role of green marketing

Environmental marketing plays double roles (Schminke & Prösler 2001). From the perspective of the customer it may be seen as an environmental protection instrument, enabling environmentally aware purchasing choices thereby driving product development towards greener products. Such objectives are explicitly stated by the international standards on environmental labelling and declarations (ISO 14020 2000; see section 10.2 for a citation). It is also the underlying argument for e.g. environmental authorities in different countries and environmental NGOs to engage in eco-labelling programmes.

On the other hand, for producers sending environmental product information it is just yet another vehicle to promote the product, along with "normal" product information about function, cost and design. Due to the complexity of environmental issues and the relatively small experience with handling environmental information in marketing and purchasing situations there is a substantial risk that the information sent by the producer does not match the receiving customer's demand for information. Fore example, the information may be too condensed or too full of detail or it may

258

concern the "wrong" environmental issues. (For a further discussion about information mismatches between suppliers and customers see chapter 11).

There is also another way in which environmental market information may play double roles. On the one hand, it enables customers, whether consumers or professional purchases, to make environmentally aware choices and influence how products are produced. On the other hand, if the promotion of a product is "too" successful, environmental gains from improvements may be outweighed by an increase in total consumption volumes. Such effects are called rebound effects.

Marketing and LCA

It is probably fair to say that marketing has acted as a driver for the development of LCA methodology in general, and the standardisation of LCA in particular. In the early days of LCA, expectations were that LCA would make it possible to show that "my product is better than yours" in a quantitative, scientific and objective manner. However, such hopes were soon dashed, as environmental claims based on LCA were criticised on the grounds of ambiguities and gaps in methodology (e.g. system boundaries, choice of data, lack of impact assessment) (Sundbom Ridderstråle 1996). Further developed LCA methodology as well as standardised methodology was seen as the way forward.

LCA was standardised in the ISO 14040 series. However, the standard did not resolve all methodological obstacles to use of LCA for promotion of products. It contains restrictions and rules regarding LCAs used for *comparative assertions*. For example, such LCAs must be subject to critical review (ISO 14040 1997) and must not include weighting (ISO 14042 2000). Behind these restrictions lies the fact that market communication is but one of the many possible applications of LCA (see chapter 1) and that the general LCA standard must support LCAs also for other purposes and thus leave room for a variety of methodological choices.

In addition to the LCA standards, green marketing is addressed from another angle in the standard series on labelling and declarations (ISO 14020 1999), which we will come back to later in this chapter. These standards do not concern methodology as much as procedures related to "who may claim what on what grounds". LCA and life cycle considerations form an essential part of those grounds.

Without doubt, LCA and life cycle thinking has provided a systematic way to compile *product*-related environmental information. It is only natural that this has implications for marketing, as marketing is about products. For instance, it is evident that eco-labelling schemes (which are older than LCA) have gradually adopted the life cycle perspective. The ease with which the notion of a *life cycle* has been adopted may also be related to its similarities with the concept of *supply chains*. These are already channels for product related information (e.g. prices, technical quality) and it may not be so farfetched to add environmental information.

There are also ways, other than direct product information, to use LCA in marketing. Many examples may be found of companies communicating the fact that they work with LCA, as a way of showing that environmental issues are addressed in an ambitious manner.

10.2 Standardised environmental market communication

There are at least two prerequisites for environmental market information to fulfil its roles. One is that the information is acceptable and credible, and the other is that it is understandable and possible to grasp. In their communication activities, companies have to address these issues. One way is to use eco-labelling and environmental product declaration programmes.

Eco-labels identify the environmentally preferable products within a product category by means of a label. An eco-label may be granted when a product meets certain environmental criteria. Environmental product declarations are results from highly standardised LCAs intended to be communicated on the market.

Eco-labelling and environmental product declaration programmes offer standardised communication formats (a label or a

260

specific format for the LCA information) that are intended to make the information easier to grasp. The programmes include procedures to verify that the information is correct, which increase credibility. They also include procedures for involving stakeholders (producers, consumers, authorities, environmental NGOs, etc) when constructing the rules of the game, such as the criteria for which products may receive an eco-label. Such participatory processes are intended to increase acceptance. Among the drawbacks of eco-labelling and environmental product declarations are cost, time delays and the fact that standardised communication formats may miss their mark (e.g. require information on issues that are less relevant for a specific product or to a specific customer and leave other issues out).

Each eco-labelling programme or product declaration programme has its own specific norms and rules, but there are also ISO standards for environmental market instruments in the ISO 14020 series. In this chapter we will use ISO's classification for these instruments. The general principles are given in ISO 14020 (2000). What ISO calls *Type I environmental labelling* (ISO 14024 1999) is usually understood as eco-labelling. *Type II environmental labelling* (self-declared environmental claims) is covered by ISO 14021 (1999). *Type III environmental declarations*, finally, also called environmental product declarations, are covered by an ISO technical report, ISO/TR 14025 (2000). The type I and type III documents describe how to set up and operate a labelling or declaration *programme*, rather than setting up requirements on particular labels and declarations for specific product groups. The precise ISO definitions are given in box 10.1. All the ISO documents state that:

"the overall goal of environmental labels and declarations is, through communication of verifiable and accurate information, that is not misleading, on environmental aspects of products and services, to encourage the demand for and the supply of those products and services that cause less stress on the environment, thereby stimulating the potential for market-driven continuous environmental improvement".

Box 10.1 ISO definitions and terms

Type I environmental labelling – a voluntary, multiple-criteria-based third party programme that awards a license which authorizes the use of environmental labels on products indicating overall environmental preferability of a product within a particular product category based on life cycle considerations.

Type II environmental labelling (Self-declared environmental claims) – environmental claims that are made, without independent third-party certification, by manufacturers, importers, distributors, retailers or anyone likely to benefit from such a claim.

Type III environmental declaration – quantified environmental data for a product with pre-set categories of parameters based on the ISO 14040-series of standards, but not excluding additional environmental information within a type III environmental declaration programme.

Type III environmental declaration programme – voluntary process by which an industrial sector or independent body develops a type III environmental declaration, including setting minimum requirements, selecting categories of parameters, defining the involvement of third parties and the format for external communications.

Eco-labelling (type I)

Eco-labels identify the environmentally preferable products within a product category, i.e. they are positive statements. Authorisation to use an eco-label is granted by an independent (third-party) body, i.e. an eco-labelling programme. The information is conveyed by means of a symbol – a label. (Figure 10.1 shows the Canadian Environmental Choice label, the Indian Eco Mark, the EU flower, the German Blue Angel and the Japanese EcoMark.) Eco-labels thus represent the type of environmental product information that is the most condensed. If the product meets the requirements (which are multi-dimensional) a label may be granted and all that is communicated to the consumer is the label. This type of information is very fast and easy to grasp, which is important in many purchasing situations. Think for example about what amount of time and thought you yourself are spending on each product choice when doing your weekly shopping for food and consumer goods.

The roots of eco-labelling may be found in the growing global concern for the environment. As business realised that such concerns could be translated to market advantages a wide array of environmental claims emerged ("recyclable", "eco-friendly", "natural" etc). Concern for credibility and impartiality, along with the opportunity to use market forces to drive environmental improvement of products, led to the formation of third-party eco-labelling programmes. The first eco-labelling programme set up was the German Blue Angel, in 1977. In 2002, it had criteria for well over 100 product groups and some 3900 labelled products. The Nordic Swan was started in 1989 and the EU Flower in 1992. In North America, the Environmental Choice programme was started in 1988 in Canada and the US Green Seal in 1989. The Green Seal has over 300 labelled products and criteria for over forty product categories (2002). Also Japan was early setting up its eco-labelling programme, the EcoMark, in 1989. There are now eco-labelling programmes all over the world, although the industrialised part of the world dominates.[1]

There are labelling programmes that relate only to certain product groups, such as the labels for organically produced food and there are labelling programmes that cover only one or a few environmental aspects, such as energy labelling for white goods. However, in the following we will discuss "full-blown" eco-labelling programmes covering a wide range of different products and a wide range of environmental aspects. Most of these have some kind of publicly authorised status. They may either be operated by an authority or by an authorised private organisation. There are also eco-labelling programmes run by environmental NGOs (non-governmental organisations). Eco-labelling programmes may be operated on a national basis, such as the German Blue Angel and the Canadian Environmental Choice programme or on a regional basis

---

1 In 2002 the Global Eco-labelling Network had members from Brazil, Canada, Croatia, Czech Republic, Denmark, EU, Germany, Greece, Hong Kong, Hungary, India, Israel, Japan, Korea, Luxembourg, New Zealand, Norway, Taiwan, Spain, Sweden, Thailand, United Kingdom, and USA.

such as the Nordic Swan and the EU flower. Some programmes claim to comply with the ISO standard, but not all.

The procedures of an eco-labelling programme label are often strictly regulated. Of course they differ between programmes, but on a general level they include the same basic steps (GEN 1999):

1 Selection and definition of the group of products or services for which the label shall apply.
2 Development and adoption of environmental criteria for the product group. Criteria consist of the environmental requirements that products must fulfil in order to receive the label. An example of eco-labelling criteria for flooring will be given in the following section.
3 Application, certification and licensing. When the criteria have been decided upon, producers may apply for a license to use the label. They must then show that the product meets the criteria. A licence to use the label for a specified time period is issued by the eco-labelling programme for a fee.

Consultation with interested parties is a very important part of the first two steps, defining the product group and developing the criteria. The procedures differ between programmes, but may include publication of draft criteria, submissions from interested groups or individuals, public hearings, and review by stakeholder advisory committees. Among those consulted are environmental authorities, industry, environmental NGOs, consumer organisations and technical experts.

The relation between LCA and eco-labelling lies in the criteria setting. Most eco-labelling programmes refer to life cycle evaluations in their procedures for criteria setting, though not only formal, quantitative LCA is used.

The ISO 14024 standard (1999), which, as mentioned earlier, some but not all eco-labelling programmes comply with, requires that the criteria be based on *life cycle considerations* and gives the matrix in table 10.1 as an example to assist in the selection of criteria. Many eco-labelling programmes, as well as the ISO standard, also require that criteria be set up concerning the function of the product or service.

Table 10.1 Example of a product environmental criteria selection matrix (ISO 14024 1999).

Stages of the life cycle	Environmental input/output indicators					
	Energy	Resources	Emission to			Other
			Water	Air	Soil	
Resource extraction						
Production						
Distribution						
Use						
Disposal						

Example – eco-labelling criteria for flooring

In order to understand better how life cycle considerations may be used as a basis for eco-labelling, let us look into an example, the Nordic Swan eco-labelling criteria for flooring. For full details readers are referred to the criteria document (Nordic Ecolabelling 2002).

The definition of the product group to which the criteria apply is full of details. Only flooring for indoor use, laid on top of an underlying structural element may be labelled. The flooring must serve no structural purpose. It must contain at least 50 % renewable raw material. Only flooring made from solid materials is included in the product group, and flooring applied in liquid state and hardened afterwards is explicitly excluded.

The criteria are summarised in table 10.2. To make it easier to recognise the life cycle, the table has been compiled according to the main phases of the life cycle, although the criteria document is not strictly organised that way. As we can see, the criteria relate to raw material production, content of harmful substances, emissions of certain pollutants during production and/or use and energy use during production. The criteria for use and waste management are more indirect and concern general requirements on the flooring as such (wear resistance, possibility to recycle) and requirements on information to the customer. The argument for this is that use and discard lies outside the direct control of the producer.

Table 10.2 Summary of criteria for eco-labelling of flooring according to the Nordic Swan (based on Nordic Ecolabelling 2002). All percentages refer to percent by weight.

Life cycle phase	Scope of criteria	Criteria	Comments
Raw material production			
Wood production	Forestry	Minimum 30 % of the wood in the product must be third party certified in accordance with an applicable forestry standard. No raw materials may come from forests needing protection for biological and/or social reasons.	Applicable to flooring containing > 10 % wood. There are criteria for which forestry standards and certification systems are acceptable. Other means of proving sustainable forestry may be accepted.
Production of fibres			Applicable to flooring containing > 15 % spun fibres (normally carpets). At least 80 % of the fibres must comply.
– Production of fibres from bast plants (flax, hemp, jute, coconut and similar)	Cultivation (pesticides) Process emissions	The raw fibre must be cultivated without use of pesticides. When retting is applied, COD or TOC emissions must be reduced by at least 75 % (presumably the efficiency of emission control technology).	COD/TOC requirement not applicable to field retting or mechanical methods.
– Production of wool fibres	Pesticide content Process emissions Restrictions concerning washing agents	The content of certain pesticides must not exceed 50 µg/kg. The limit applies to each substance. Emissions of COD from washing the wool must not exceed 60 kg/tonne. APEO, LAS and EDTA must not be used for washing. Cleaning with organic solvents is not permitted.	The limited pesticides are specified in detail.
– Storage and transportation of fibres	Pesticide content	Chlorophenols and their salts and esters must not be used in the storage and transportation of flax or wool. Total content of these substances must not exceed 20 µg/kg.	Samples should be taken at least once per transport consignment.
Production of foam rubber	Process emissions Content of harmful substance	COD/TOC emissions must be reduced by 90 % (presumably the efficiency of emission control technology). Content of 1,3-butadiene must be less than 1 mg/kg latex.	
Flooring production	Content of substances harmful to health or environment	Substances classified as carcinogenic, harmful to reproduction, genetically harmful, or toxic, in any of the Nordic countries must not be present in the product. The content of such components must not exceed 0.1 % of the product. Raw materials classified as allergenic in any Nordic country must not exceed 0.1 % in the finished product. Total content of substances classified at environmentally harmful, in any of the Nordic countries or the EU: ≤ 2 % in total, ≤ 1 % for individual substances. In addition there is a list of substances that may not be actively added to the product.	

266

Life cycle phase	Scope of criteria	Criteria	Comments
	Formaldehyde emissions	Fulfilment of A or B: A. Formaldehyde emissions from finished product < 0.13 mg/m^3 air. C. Requirements on control of formaldehyde emissions during production of boards for the flooring.	Applies to floorings with a content of formaldehyde or formaldehyde emitting additives.
	VOC emissions	VOC (volatile organic compounds) emissions must not exceed 2 g/m^2 flooring.	Applies to emissions from production site. Does not apply to certain wooden floorings.
	Energy and resource consumption	Weighted sum of electricity and fuels must not exceed a certain number. Sulphur content in fossil fuels ≤ 0.1 %. CO_2 emissions ≤ 3.0 kg/m^2 flooring. Producer must work to increase the proportion of electricity from renewable sources.	There are detailed instructions concerning system boundaries, heat content of fuels, emissions factors etc for calculation of energy use and emissions.
Use phase			
	Product information	Recommendations concerning the following must follow the product (when applicable): Supporting constructive element, including moisture content Adhesive Welding method Cleaning agent/method Maintenance agent/method Area of application Possible means to prolong the duration of the flooring	
	Wear resistance	Classification of floorings and requirements on abrasion resistance in accordance with international standards	For details, see critera document (Nordic Ecolabelling 2002)
Waste management			
	Possibility to recycle	Recycling (e.g. incineration or reuse) must be possible by means of normal methods. Used flooring must not constitute "special waste" in any of the Nordic countries.	

As may be seen, the information required concerning harmful substances has a lot more detail than what is usually taken into account in an LCA. On the other hand, information on resource consumption is lacking, with the exception of some energy data.

Not shown in table 10.2 is that for every criterion there are detailed requirements on what documentation is required by the eco-labelling organisation in order for applicants to show that their product meets the criteria. In addition to the criteria summarised in the table, it is also required that holders of eco-labelling licences ensure that the product and its production comply with environmental regulations and that the eco-labelling criteria are met over time. They are also required to show that they have a plan for training marketing personnel.

Environmental product declarations (type III)

Environmental product declarations (EPD) are LCA results intended to be communicated in market situations. To ensure comparability between products the LCA methodology for EPD must be much more strictly standardised than for other LCA applications. In EPDs, the LCA results may be complemented by other types of environmental information.

EPD programmes are open to all products as long as the declaration meets criteria on used methodology, format for presentation, verification procedures, etc. Weighting of LCA results is not used and there are no predetermined performance levels (environmental criteria) as in type I eco-labelling. The idea is that judgements and comparisons between competing products should be made by the customer. The absence of predetermined performance levels is what makes EPD programmes open to all products, but at the same time it should be kept in mind that as an EPD is a *declaration* it says nothing about whether the product is environmentally preferable or not.

Credibility is an issue for any type of environmental information communicated in a market situation. In type III programmes this is dealt with through verification procedures (the rigidity of which may vary between programmes) and through consultation processes.

The concept of environmental product declarations is much more recent than that of eco-labelling. EPDs are still under development and harmonisation efforts are taking place. The first programme, the Swedish one, was launched in 1998. Consequently, the ISO text on Type III environmental declarations (ISO/TR 14025 2000) is not a normative document, but a technical report setting out and discussing various future possible developments. The global network for environmental product declarations[2] has fewer members than the eco-labelling network, and even fewer programmes are actually up and running[3]. In addition to the general EPD programmes there are programmes with similarities to EPD focused on certain sectors (the building sector and the pulp and paper sector).

Since EPD programmes are such a recent development they have used the internet from the beginning as their main information channel. Most of the general information on programmes is available via the Internet and the actual declarations are often published on the programme homepages. You will find a number of web-addresses at the end of this chapter.

The procedures to develop a type III declaration are described on a very general level in the ISO document (ISO/TR 14025 2000). In order to get a more concrete example we will look into the procedures of a specific type III programme, the Swedish one. As it was the first one launched it often serves as a point of reference when other programmes are set up. At the end of the section we will discuss how it relates to the general principles in ISO/TR 14025.

There are a number of documents governing what information an EPD according to the Swedish system should contain. First and foremost, the LCA behind it must comply with ISO 14040–43. More strict LCA methodology rules to which all EPDs according to the programme must adhere are laid down in the document regulating the programme (MSR 1999a). But products differ, for which reason variations and specifications of these rules applicable to product

2   Members of the Global type III environmental products declaration network (in 2002) come from Japan, Canada, Germany, Norway, Denmark, Republic of South Korea, Italy and Sweden.
3   Countries that had environmental product declaration programmes in operation in 2002: Canada, Japan, Norway, Sweden and South Korea.

groups are set down in a document called *product specific requirements* (PSR). For example, the functional unit for the product group is prescribed in the PSR. Also requirements on environmental information, other than what may be provided by the LCA, may be set out in the PSR. Such information may consist of a declaration of the content of the product, for example.

If you, as a producer, would like to publish an EPD according to the Swedish programme, this is what you would need to do:

1 Check if there are product specific requirements (PSR) for a product group into which your product would fit. If not, you will need to prepare a PSR document and get it accepted. PSRs are preferably developed by companies and organisations in co-operation with each other, but it is possible for a single company to prepare a PSR. Participatory procedures are recommended, and there are requirements for what consultation must take place as a minimum. The preparation of a PSR usually takes its point of departure in one or several LCAs already conducted for products in the product group. (Exercise H10 consists of doing an LCA for apples, upon which PSR may be based.)

2 Collect and calculate LCA-based and other types of environmental product information. The LCA must conform to the methodology in EPD requirements and the PSR, and even if there already is an LCA it may have to be modified. Possibly also other product related environmental information needs be compiled.

3 Compile the information for reporting as an EPD, consisting of the following:

   • Description of the company/organisation.
   • Description of the product or service (may include a declaration of content).
   • Environmental performance declaration, i.e. the LCA results. A particular EPD feature is that results are reported separately for the production phase (from raw material extraction to manufactured product at the factory gate, cradle-to-gate) and the use phase encompassing distribution to the market, use and waste management including recycling processes (gate-to-grave).
   • Other information from the producer, e.g. a recycling declaration, information on whether the product meets different

270

kinds of environmental, health and safety criteria and information about how the product should be handled during the
use phase.
- Information from the certification body, the period of validity
and the registration number.

4 Verify and register the EPD.
Verification is a very rigorous procedure in the Swedish programme. It must be conducted by an accredited certification
body[4], which is the same procedure as for certification of environmental management systems according to ISO or EMAS. The
certification body reviews and verifies both the full LCA report
and the information as reported in the EPD. Registration and
publication, finally, is conducted by the organisation operating
the programme. The EPDs are published on the internet.

What has been described above are the procedures of a specific EPD
programme, the Swedish one. Let us now look into how this programme relates to a more general picture, as described in ISO/TR
14025 (2000). As mentioned, ISO/TR 14025 does not have the status of a standard, but is a technical report to be applied provision-
ally so that information and experience from its practical use may
be collected. Regarding the roles of different actors (i.e. who does
what) ISO/TR 14025 is very open and presents perhaps more questions than answers. Particularly concerning the rigour in verification procedures there are many different options. The one adopted
by the Swedish EPD programme is the most rigorous one. However,
it comes out clear that type III environmental declarations require
some type of independent verification. The need for participatory
processes where interested parties are consulted is stressed in the
ISO report, although it is only suggested in which processes such
consultation may take place. Finally, the format for communication of LCA results is only discussed. In practice, formats differ
between programmes (Lee & Park 2001).

---

4   Accreditation means that an authority reviews and authorises a certification
    body to do certifications. The certification body then reviews the EPD and cer-
    tifies that the information is correct.

271

Example – PSR and EPD for flooring

Earlier we looked into eco-labelling criteria for flooring. In the same way let us look into an EPD for flooring and the PSR behind them.

The product group is defined in the PSR (MSR 1999b) as flooring, consisting of the sub-groups flooring material, screed and adhesives. Construction elements under the flooring are explicitly excluded.

The PSR prescribes LCA methodological choices of for example functional unit, system boundaries and allocation. For the use phase it is required that installation and maintenance be reported separately. Average data for the use phase are given (for example average energy consumption for vacuum cleaning) and it is required that they are used together with maintenance recommendations for the specific product. It is also required that the material content of the flooring is declared, for which there is a prescribed format. Finally, recommendations and information concerning recycling and waste management should be given. There are also requirements for information of more administrative character.

The example EPD is for a laminate floor called Pergo Golv, which comes in two versions, Family and Original. It is produced by Pergo AB (Pergo 2000). The environmental performance of the production phase (cradle-to-gate) is given as in table 10.

In addition to the cradle-to-gate data in the table, the EPD gives information about how the floor should be installed and maintained. The average energy use for distribution is given along with energy use for vacuum cleaning. Emissions of formaldehyde are presented (< 0.05 mg/m^2) and it is claimed that VOC emissions usually are under the detection limit (10 µg/m^2).

The content of the product is declared according to the format prescribed in the PSR. This includes the content of chemicals subject to regulation (formaldehyde in this case). Concerning waste management, it is recommended that the product be incinerated after use. The flooring is declared to be slowly biodegradable.

If we compare the PSR for flooring with the eco-labelling criteria in table 10.2, we can see that there are great similarities in information requirements. The main difference is of course that while the one presents absolute criteria the other only requires information on specific issues. Another important difference is that the PSR is

272

Table 10.3 Environmental performance declaration for the production phase as reported in the EPD for Pergo flooring (Pergo 2000).

	Pergo Family	Pergo Original	Unit
Resource use			
Non-renewable resources			
Material resources	0.840	0.988	kg/m^2
Energy resources	59	66	MJ/m^2
Renewable resources			
Material resources	1.019	1.090	kg/m^2
Energy resources	29	33	MJ/m^2
Recycled material			
Recycled material	–8.6	–7.5	MJ/m^2
Energy consumption			
Oil	10	12	MJ/m^2
Coal	3	3	MJ/m^2
Natural gas	22	25	MJ/m^2
Diesel	7	8	MJ/m^2
Electricity (Sweden)	15	16	MJ/m^2
Electricity (other)	2	2	MJ/m^2
Biofuel	29	33	MJ/m^2
Total energy consumption	88	99	MJ/m^2
Pollutant emissions			
Greenhouse gases	4 846	5 153	g/m^2 (CO_2-eqv)
Ozone depleting gases	0	0	g/m^2
Acidifying gases	29.1	30.5	g/m^2(SO_2- eqv)
Gases contributing to ground level ozone formation	2.39	2.39	g/m^2(ethene-eqv)
Emissions contributing to aquatic oxygen depletion	174	189	g/m^2(O_2-eqv)
Toxic susbstances	<0.1	<0.1	g/m^2
Other information			
Waste			
Hazardous waste	0.020	0.021	kg/m^2
Other waste	0.042	0.046	kg/m^2
Energy recovery			
Corresponding to energy content of the product	approx 100	approx 110	MJ/m^2

open to all types of flooring, while the eco-labelling is open only to floorings consisting of at least 50 % renewable material. In the eco-labelling criteria there are requirements on wood production taking place in a certain way, while there is no such information in the EPD. In the eco-labelling criteria there are detailed criteria limiting the use of certain well specified pesticides while toxic substances are only reported as total amount in the EPD.

The ISO standard on self-declared environmental claims (type II)

In addition to the standards for environmental product information verified by a third party (type I and type III), ISO has also developed a standard for self-declared environmental claims (type II) (ISO 14021 1999). Apart from increasing the potential for market-driven environmental improvement, it aims at correct and verifiable environmental claims, prevention of unwarranted claims and reduction of marketplace confusion. It covers self-declared claims for products, whether communicated as statements or symbols.

On a general level, the standard bars the use of vague claims such as *environmentally friendly*, *green* and *non-polluting*. Also the term *sustainability* is seen as being too undefined, and its use in product claims is excluded. The standard sets requirements on the use of other terms. For example, any claim must be accurate and not misleading, verified and specific regarding what environmental aspect is considered. Also the use of symbols is controlled.

The standard demands that any environmental claim made should be possible to verify and that an evaluation is conducted before the claim is made. The information needed to verify the claim must be documented and made available to anyone asking for it.

Finally, the standard regulates the use of 13 specific terms used in environmental product claims. Among the terms are *compostable*, *degradable*, *designed for disassembly*, *recyclable*, *recycled content*, *reduced resource consumption* and *waste reduction*.

10.3 Summary and further reading

In this chapter we have seen that LCA is related to marketing and market communication in various ways. The wish to use LCA to promote products has driven standardisation of LCA as such, but also of LCA-related market communication instruments such as eco-labelling and environmental product declarations. Companies also communicate the fact that they work with LCA as part of showing themselves to be environmentally responsible. However, market communication does not only include sending information. It also includes collection of information, e.g. about customers. So far, we have seen very little green market research, e.g. about consumer's environmental preferences. Readers wanting to further explore the topic of green marketing in general are referred to Peattie (1992).

In purchasing situations, environmental product information is used by customers, whether professional purchasers or private consumers. They are the intended recipients of the information compiled in for instance an eco-label or an EPD. As discussed briefly in this chapter, there is a potential risk of mismatches between customers' information needs and the information content in such standardised market communication instruments.

In this chapter we have also seen that there are two, partly intertwined, issues to think about when sending an environmental message to the market. One is the *complexity and multi-dimensionality of the concept "environment"*, which requires that competence is built into the communication process, either as knowledgeable people or as standards and procedures with high knowledge content. The complexity of environmental issues also makes any environmental message inherently value-laden. Choices have to be made regarding what environmental aspects to consider and how to weigh them against each other. The need for such choices and the issue of who has the legitimacy to make them is related to the other critical issue for environmental marketing, that of *credibility*. Not all senders of environmental information have the same credibility.

Nevertheless, there is a whole battery of communication means in which suppliers trust their own credibility. These range from "home-made" labels and environmental branding to personal contacts between suppliers and customers and ambitious environmental reports.

Eco-labelling and environmental product declaration programmes (third party programmes) offer credibility through independent verification procedures. They address the complexity of environmental issues through offering standardised communication formats. These are intended to make the information easier to grasp. Different types of programme differ in what role is taken by the third party. In eco-labelling, environmental evaluations are explicitly expressed in criteria documents issued by the labelling organisation. The criteria make it possible to condense the information to a very simple format, a label. In EPD programmes, on the other hand, an explicit aim is that the information be "objective". To as large an extent as possible weighting and other valuations are left to the customer. The role of the EPD programme is to verify that the information is correct. Among the drawbacks of eco-labelling and environmental product declaration schemes are cost, time delays and the risk of information mismatches.

Further readings on the different standardised environmental marketing instruments include the ISO 14020 series and the Ecolabelling guide issued by the Global ecolabelling network (GEN 1999). The homepages of the Global ecolabelling network and the Global type III environmental products declarations network are also informative. Adresses are given at the end of the chapter.

Inevitably the life cycle perspective has relevance for environmental product information. However, it may take on many different forms, from formal quantitative LCAs to more qualitative life cycle thinking. Let us end by concluding that in its many different forms environmental market information plays a key role in enabling market forces to drive environmentally adjusted product development and consumption. However, it is a double-edged sword that may increase total consumption volumes at the same time.

Internet sources

The Global Ecolabelling Network, www.gen.gr.jp.
Global Type III Environmental Products Declarations Network, GEDnet. http://www.environdec.com/gednet/
Canada – the EPDS programme. Terra Choice, www.terrachoice.ca
Japan – the JEMAI Type III programme. Japan Environmental Management Association for Industry. www.jemai.or.jp
Norway – the NHO Type III programme. Confederation of Norwegian Business and Industry, www.nho.no
South Korea – the KELA Type III programme. Korea Environmental Labelling Association, www.kela.or.kr
Sweden – the EPD system. Swedish Environmental Management Council. www.environdec.com.

276

11 LCA for production processes

Most LCA studies and areas of applications have traditionally centred on products as such. For example, product development has
been seen as a main application for LCA. Communication of environmental performance of products to customers has also been a
strong driver in the development and adoption of LCA. However,
products are not made without production processes. In this chapter we will look into the less mature area of how LCA may be used
to study processes, with the aim of improving their environmental
performance. We will concentrate on *production* processes, i.e. the
up-stream processes before the use phase, whereas LCA of waste
treatment processes (down-stream processes) is the subject of chapter 12.

Industrial production comprises both the process sector and the
manufacturing sector. Production characteristics are quite different
for the two sectors. LCA modelling and applications relevant for the
process sector and the manufacturing sector are therefore dealt with
separately in sections 11.1 and 11.2. Whereas the process sector
produces mainly substances, i.e. single components, mixtures,
blends and formulations, the manufacturing sector produces complex products assembled from large numbers of different materials
and components. The process sector includes the type of industry
that produces materials (e.g. steel and other metals, polymers, pulp
and paper, minerals), energy carriers like fuels and electricity and
chemicals, ranging from bulk production of staple chemicals to
production of specialised chemicals like pharmaceuticals. Also large
parts of the food industry are process based, for instance dairies and
breweries. The manufacturing industry includes among others
automotive industry, electronics and white goods. Owing to their

different character, LCA application differs for these two types of industrial production. An area for LCA in the process industry concerns process optimisation. The manufacturing industry, which has to manage flows of numerous components, shows much interest in the use of LCA for procurement and some interest in optimisation of the supply chain as a whole.

Experience from many LCA studies shows that the production of materials often causes a dominant proportion of the environmental impact of a product, whereas assembly often causes a very minor proportion. If a product requires energy during its use phase (e.g. cars, buildings or detergents) the use phase often dominates the environmental profile, whereas for a product used in a more "passive" manner (e.g. packaging or furniture) the production phase dominates, notably the production of materials. In spite of transportation being a major source of pollution in society, transportation and distribution often contribute less to the environmental impact than expected. This is discussed in section 11.3.

11.1 LCA for the process industry

LCA, being a type of modelling that connects processes with material and/or energy flows, has borrowed extensively from well-established chemical engineering practices. Terms such as *flowchart*, *unit process* and *reference flow* bear witness to the relationship. What is unique about LCA is its wide system boundaries (cradle-to-grave) and its focus on inflows and outflows from/to the environment. As a consequence, when LCA has been applied to process design or process analysis, the methodology has been even further inspired by, or merged with, more advanced approaches to process systems engineering, notably various optimisation approaches. We will start by looking into these methodologies in brief, without going into mathematical detail. Then we will concentrate on the applications for these methodologies, including cleaner production strategies such as search for improvement possibilities and optimisation of existing processes, regulatory applications and, finally, process design. The application of LCA to the analysis of processes is still quite immature and much research and development remains

278

before methods are readily available for any type of application. This means that the examples will be snap-shots of the areas that have been studied to date.

Methodologies

The simplest type of methodology is normal LCA, focusing on the production processes, or even only the production processes under direct control of the commissioner of the study. The concepts of foreground and background system (see chapter 3) are thus highly relevant for process LCAs. The foreground processes are those under the direct control of the commissioner and the background all other, indirectly influenced, processes. LCA studies that focus on production processes are often of the cradle-to-gate type. Sometimes they are even of the gate-to-gate type, i.e. *only* the foreground system is modelled, in which case it may be questioned whether they may still be called LCAs. They are then rather environmental flow models of industrial plants.

No decisions on processes, whether concerning design, investment or mode of operation, are made without considering economic performance and technical feasibility. Thus, traditional process systems engineering methods focus on cost and technology. Such methods have been complemented with environmental information. Originally, these took a site perspective in various waste minimisation techniques (Azapagic 1999) as well as in methods such as risk assessment and environmental impact assessment. However, in more recent developments the life cycle perspective has been adopted.

One example is a life cycle process model for cement production, in which environmental performance was simulated simultaneously with production cost and product quality (Gäbel et al. 2003). A life cycle perspective in the cradle-to-gate sense was used. The model of the foreground system, the cement manufacturing plant, was much more detailed and flexible than in normal LCA, whereas the background processes were modelled using standard LCA methodology. The model is illustrated in figure 11.1.

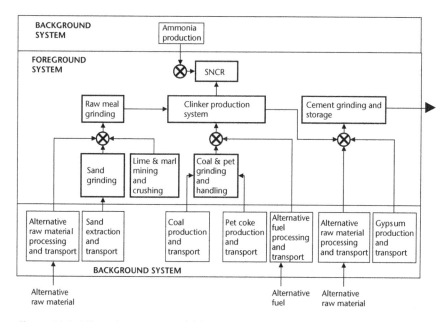

Figure 11.1 Life cycle process model for cement production (based on Gäbel et al. 2003).

Process engineering is often concerned with optimisation, normally with respect to economic objectives. There are several possibilities of applying optimisation also when environmental aspects are introduced. One possibility is to keep cost (or revenues) as the sole objective in the optimisation, and use environmental metrics as constraints or even just descriptively, as result parameters at the optimum solution. Conversely, environmental metrics may be used as objective functions and cost used as a constraint or a result parameter. Another, perhaps more balanced approach is multi-objective optimisation, in which several objective functions are used simultaneously (e.g. Azapagic & Clift 1999b; Alexander et al. 2000; Hoffman et al. 2001).

So, what is multi-objective optimisation? It means to optimise simultaneously with respect to a number of objectives (environmental and economic ones in this context). The result is not a single optimal point, but a multi-dimensional Pareto surface. On the Pareto surface no objective may be improved without worsening

280

the value of some other objective. Figure 11.2 shows an example of a Pareto "surface" where only two objective functions were used, in which case the surface is reduced to a curve. One is economic benefit, which it is an objective to maximize and the other is environmental impact, which conversely should be minimized. Anywhere along the curve, neither of the two objectives may be improved without worsening the other, e.g. by moving from point A to B. Point C, below the curve, is not Pareto optimal, since both environmental and economic performance may be improved by moving to point A. Pareto optimum does not necessarily mean that any of the objective functions is at the optimum obtained if the system is optimised with respect to the respective objectives individually. In multi-objective optimisation environmental metrics may be used on different levels: inventory parameters, impact assessment parameters or even further aggregated environmental information. Such aggregation may be achieved through applying LCA weighting methods, but there are also examples where other methods to aggregate environmental information have been used (e.g. Hoffman et al. 2001).

Trade-offs between different objectives are necessary. In cases where standard LCA methodology is used, information about eco-

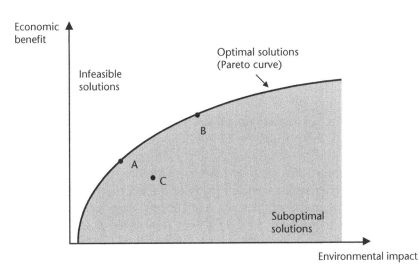

Figure 11.2 Schematic representation of a two-dimensional Pareto plot (adapted from Hoffman et al. 2001).

nomic performance and technical feasibility are external to the method. As always in LCA it is implicitly expected that environmental performance is traded off against economic and technical criteria in a decision making procedure external to the method. Also models like the cement production model described earlier leave the trade-off between different objectives to the decision makers. Multi-objective optimisation reduces the number of options, but still leaves a trade-off situation. There are procedures described in the literature where multi-objective optimisation is recommended to be followed by a more formalised decision procedure, a multi-criteria decision analysis (MCDA) step (e.g. Azapagic & Clift 1999a).

Multi-criteria decision analysis (MCDA) methods are formalised and structured ways to select between alternatives, basing the decision on a several criteria. They use matrices such as that in table 11.1, where the alternatives' performance is described according to a set of criteria/performance parameters.

Table 11.1 MCDA matrix.

Criteria / Alternatives	Criterion 1	Criterion 2	...	Criterion n
Alternative 1				
Alternative 2				
...				
Alternative n				

MCDA approaches aim at capturing the preferences of the decision maker and use them for the trade-off. Exactly how this is done differs between MCDA techniques, and the differences largely depend on what assumptions are made when modelling decision makers' preferences. There exist a wide variety of MCDA methods with varying degree of mathematical sophistication. They may largely be divided into those that weigh criteria (which is similar to how weighting is done in LCA) and those that use out-ranking approaches, for example by pair-wise comparison of alternatives (Guitouni & Martel 1998). There are also user-friendly software packages available for MCDA.

282

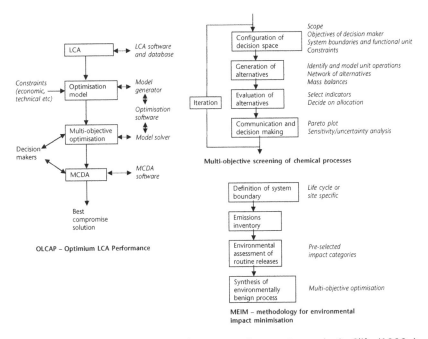

Figure 11.3 Process design procedures according to Azapagic & Clift (1999a) (OLCAP), Hoffman et al. (2001) (Multi-objective screening of chemical processes) and Pistikopoulus & Stefanis (1998) (MEIM).

Several researchers have embedded their modelling and optimisation schemes in formalised decision making procedures. Some of these are shown in figure 11.3. They all include LCA-type modelling, more or less sophisticated, and multi-objective optimisation, but vary in other respects. The procedure suggested by Hoffman et al. (2001) emphasises the problem definition phase with explicit expression of the decisions maker's objectives. The OLCAP method goes further than the others in the decision making phase, adding an MCDA step.

Applications

The chemical industry as well as other process industries have long been under pressure to reduce their environmental impact. This was first met by end-of-pipe solutions in the form of cleaning devices applied to outlet flows. Later, cleaner production strategies to reduce the production of waste and emissions were introduced. These include more integrated approaches such as modification of processes and internal recycling of waste streams. In the chemical industry such approaches are often called waste minimisation strategies. However, they take on a production site perspective and the risk that emissions are reduced at the site while being increased in other parts of the life cycle has motivated work on LCA and LCA-related process modelling. The life cycle approach in this work is usually limited to a cradle-to-gate perspective, which is motivated by the process industry being far up-stream in the production chain with their produce going into a wide variety of products.

Much of the work has been focused on methodology development and the number of applications is limited. These include search for improvement possibilities and optimisation of existing processes, applications related to regulation and the design and synthesis of new processes.

Search for improvement possibilities

One of the most common practical applications of LCA in general is the search for improvement possibilities. It is striking that when going through the literature on LCA of processes, the reported examples where LCA has been used to find improvement possibilities are almost all on work done internally in companies, or by researchers directly commissioned by an industry.

Ciba Specialty Chemicals have conducted LCAs on whole ranges of products (Bretz & Fankhauser 1997). The project as a whole was launched as a result of a new policy document striving for a new balance between economic, social and environmental responsibilities. The intended use of the LCAs is both internal (process improvement and optimisation) and external such as market communication and dialogue with authorities. The system is used both for calculating LCAs for existing products and for providing LCAs for processes under development in order to compare process alternatives.

The programme is impressive, covering over 1 700 products produced in approximately 1 600 processes from 4 700 raw materials/

284

intermediates. In order to be able to handle such massive amounts of information, a system was set up to extract data from existing information systems in the company, as well as from external data sources. In addition, methods to estimate data for intermediate raw materials were developed.

The life cycle process model for cement production (in figure 11.1) was developed by Cementa in collaboration with researchers. One of the explicit requirements on the model was to support company internal decisions in product and process development and strategic planning. For cement production, the main options to change the process lie in choice of raw materials (Gäbel et al. 2003). In contrast, in their case study of optimisation of the production of boron products, Azapagic and Clift (1999b) found the improvement possibilities in changing the mix in which the different boron products were produced. The boron study was also aimed at finding the environmental "hot spots" in the production chain. A similar study on vinyl chloride monomer (VCM) production was conducted by Stefanis et al. (1995). All these studies go beyond LCA in the sense that they include economic information (cost) in addition to the environmental information. The cement model also models product performance. Both the boron study and the VCM study included optimisation.

An application related to search for improvement possibilities is to use LCA to present already conducted improvements. Viotti et al. (1997) report on the environmental improvements over a ten-year period in the production of surfactant intermediates.

Regulatory applications

LCAs and similar models of processes may also be used in communication with authorities and in the formulation of governmental policies and regulations. For example, one of the requirements on the cement life cycle process model referred to above was that apart from internal uses it should be usable in dialogues with local authorities concerning operation permits.

Another regulatory application for process LCAs has been suggested in the context of IPPC, the EU directive on Integrated Pollution Prevention and Control (EC 1996). In the directive, the determination of Best Available Technology (BAT) is a critical issue. BATs are determined by expert groups on a European sector level and then serve as reference values for emission limits and operation permits (Gelderman et al. 1999). When BATs are chosen, the environment as a whole must be considered, and consequently LCA has been proposed as a method to determine BATs. Gelderman et al. (1999) propose that the impact assessment element of LCA is used to aggregate information on inflows to and outflows from the process being assessed. However, the life cycle system perspective (cradle-to-grave) is not necessarily used in their approach. Azapagic (1999), on the other hand, argues that wider system boundaries be used in the determination of BATs (or Best Practicable Environmental Option (BPEO), which is a similar concept in the British legislation). The argument put forward by Azapagic is that through considering only the emissions from the plant under study they may be reduced at the price of increased emissions in other parts of the life cycle.

Process design

Process design is similar to product design in the sense that in early development stages the number of options and the degrees of freedom are large and that they are gradually reduced as the design process moves forward (see figure 11.4). Hoffman et al. (2001) have suggested a methodology for multi-objective screening and evaluation of chemical processes in the early development phases. The methodology includes computer software where process alternatives are generated through the combination of unit operations such as reaction, absorption, distillation, cooling, combustion etc. These are combined to produce a large number of technically feasible production pathways, which are then screened according to environmental and economic criteria using Pareto plots. Hoffman et al. suggest an economic indicator based on net present value (which is the most common economic indicator for investment decisions) and a very broad environmental proxy parameter called MIPS (material input per unit of service). MIPS is the total material and energy use over the life cycle, similar to an LCA accounting only for resource use, which is aggregated into the broad classes abiotic resources, biotic resources, water, air, and soil. The argument for using MIPS is that knowledge about specific emissions and

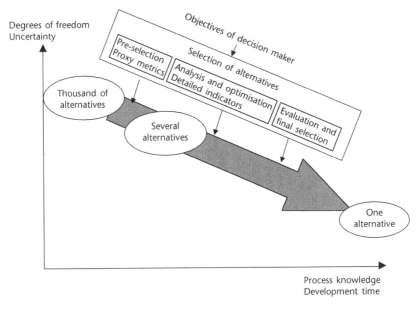

Figure 11.4 Three phases of process design and the selection of alternatives (adapted from Hoffman et al. 2001).

resource usages is very limited in the early development phases, and thus a proxy indicator is needed. Full LCA may be applied at a later stage, when the number of options has been reduced.

Chemicals may always be produced not only via different sets of unit operations but also via different reaction paths, i.e. via different intermediates. The more complex the chemical, the larger is the number of options. Environmental evaluation of reaction paths has been addressed using LCA or LCA-like approaches by for example Buxton et al. (1997) and Jödicke et al. (1999). Bretz and Fankhauser (1997) report on how Ciba Specialty Chemicals' used LCA to support the development of a new process route for production of DNS (4,4'-dinitro-2,2'-stilbenedisulphonic acid sodium salt). It is an intermediate for several of the company's products, mostly optical brighteners. A standard simulation tool for chemical processes (ASPEN) was used to estimate mass flows and energy requirements. These were then entered into the LCA system and an LCA was produced that showed that considerable environmental improvement could be achieved with the new synthesis route. The results were validated when the process came into operation in a new plant. Although the LCA tended to underestimate the environmental impact for both the new and the old process route, the relative improvement proved to be even higher in reality than in the LCA calculations.

The scheduling of the operation of processes operated in batches, as opposed to a continuous basis, present yet another decision space. LCA-models supporting environmentally conscious scheduling have been developed by Stefanis et al. (1997) and Berlin and Sonesson (2002). By coincidence, both studies concern dairy production.

11.2 LCA for manufacturing processes

In the previous section we have seen the application of LCA to optimisation decisions concerning production in the process industry. Although this type of application is less common, it is well in line with traditional environmental management in that its focus is on what can be done within the individual production facility. In practice when it comes to production in general, identification of "hot spots" is a more common use of LCA. The life cycle perspective, being well suited for looking at the whole product chain, is then used for identifying which production processes cause the greatest environmental impacts. This is exemplified by the detergent case study referred to in chapters 1 and 6. The identification of the "hot spots" is a first step towards improvement. However, to remedy them requires some form of interaction in the product chain, for example with suppliers, distributors or waste managers. Characteristic of the manufacturing industry is the huge supplier network, often called the supply chain. In the following we will explore the producer-supplier interaction in the procurement process, the interaction with suppliers, distributors, retailers etc in the management of the supply chain and the application of LCA in these contexts. Other types of interactions also take place in the supply chain, e.g. producers and suppliers collaborating for ecodesign and

288

producers communicating with the market, but these topics are dealt with in chapters 9 and 10.

Supply chains

Manufacturers of complex products such as cars and electronics have relatively little direct control of the emissions from production. An estimate for electronic products is that suppliers contribute 60–70 % of the total environmental load in the production. The assembly itself causes only limited environmental impact. With the current trend of increased outsourcing of production, the suppliers' part of the environmental impact is likely to increase in the future (Stevels 2002). This underscores the importance of looking at the whole supply chain when considering environmental efforts in the manufacturing industry.

Similarly to LCA, the supply chain concept grew out of the recognition that improvement of the individual supply chain stages did not lead to improvement of the chain as a whole. A difference between LCA and supply chain management is that performance measures for supply chains have traditionally been concerned with customer satisfaction or cost (Beamon 1999) whereas LCA focuses on environmental performance. However, decisions on who to partner with, what to outsource, number of suppliers, number of distribution centres, organisation of collection and recycling have both environmental and business implications.

The traditional definition of a supply chain describes it as an integrated manufacturing process wherein raw materials are converted into final products, then delivered to customers via distribution, retail, or both (Gattorna & Walters 1996; Beamon 1999). The traditional supply chain thus includes only those activities associated with manufacturing, from raw material acquisition to final product delivery. Lately, with increasing recycling in our society, the supply chain concept has come to also include recycling logistics and collection systems (see figure 11.5). Design and analysis of the supply chain has primarily focused on optimising the procurement process and the distribution of products (Beamon 1999). Common topics include for example determining which plants will produce which products, which distribution centres will serve which customers,

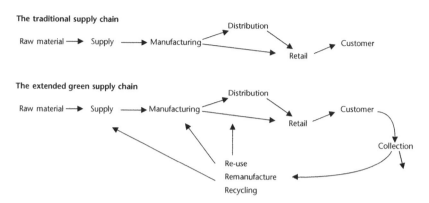

Figure 11.5 Environmental requirements have led to an extension of the traditional supply chain concept with the result that the scope of the extended supply chain overlaps with that of LCA – both have the whole product chain in focus.

critical aspects of the supplier-producer relationship, inventory levels and number of product types held in inventory.

A comprehensive research review revealed that there is very little experience of making environmental assessments of supply chains (Abukhader & Jönson 2003). Research has focused more on for example the introduction of environmental management systems and the impact of recycling on logistical costs. Life cycle thinking is nevertheless a suitable basis for the greening of the supply chain. Not only does it introduce an environmental dimension to the supply chain it also supports the extended supply chain concept which includes the logistics for recycling.

Several researchers even claim that it is necessary to consider the environmental life cycle perspective in order to achieve cost efficient changes to supply chains (Beamon 1999; Westkämper et al. 2001). In spite of this, life cycle thinking and LCA are rarely mentioned in discussions concerning the greening of supply chains. Moreover, the terminology in the literature for denoting the greening of supply chains is varied. It may be part of life cycle management (Pedersen 2001; Westkämper et al. 2001) or industrial ecology (Clift et al. 2001) or it may be called product stewardship (Lamming & Hampson 1996), sustainable supply network management (Young & Kielkiewicz-Young 2001), product chain responsibility

290

(Meinders & Meuffels 2001) or just simply green supply chains (Stevels 2002; Sarkis 2003) or environmental supply chain management (Nagel 2000). A term frequently used for the recovery part of the life cycle is reverse logistics (e.g. Sarkis 2003; Tsoulfas et al. 2002). In contrast to "ordinary" logistics, which deals with the distribution of products to multiple localities, reverse logistics is concerned with the organisation of the *collection* of products, often in the context of recycling or re-use.

The diverse terminology and the scarce documentation of experience of LCA in this field can be seen as signs that this is a relatively new topic and much remains to be done. Even so, it is clear that life cycle thinking and LCA can contribute to efforts on greening supply chains and that several uses of LCA are possible, for example:

- to measure the environmental performance of the supply chain,
- to identify where environmental efforts are most needed, i.e. identification of "hot spots",
- to shift focus in process and product engineering from process optimisation to supply chain optimisation (Meinders & Meuffels 2001; Pedersen 2001),
- to make environmental assessments of different logistical solutions, e.g. of reverse logistics (Tsoulfas et al. 2002) or the introduction of e-commerce (Abukhader 2003),
- to support life cycle design and planning, either through ecodesign partnerships with suppliers or through environmentally aware choices of construction materials and suppliers or both (Westkämper et al. 2001),
- to support life cycle design and product chain management decisions whether to recycle, remanufacture from re-useable parts, upgrade, etc.,
- to provide a framework for environmental communication from and to suppliers and customers, to decide on what environmental information to disseminate, collect and analyse (Meinders & Meuffels 2001), and
- to train suppliers on their contribution to the life cycle impacts of the product/service (Young & Kielkiewicz-Young 2001).

To achieve both cost-efficient and competitive environmental improvements in supply chains, LCA and life cycle management need to be complemented with other tools and strategies. The literature suggests for example environmental management systems, checklists, life cycle costing, shared environmental savings and open-book trading between supplier and client, cross-functional teams, etc. Several authors also point to the need for information about quantity and quality of virgin and recycled materials and components as well as their location among other things. They propose various information system tools (software tools and databases) for storing and sharing information among the many actors in the supply chain (e.g. Westkämper et al. 2001; Li et al. 2002). Such tools are now emerging both in the automotive and the electronics industries to support producer responsibility efforts and end-of-life management.

Procurement

Procurement has been given an important role in realisation of environmental efforts. Since it is the purchasing department that actually buys materials and products, it is in a strategic position to reduce environmental impact through incoming products and materials. Purchasers are in the position to effect environmental improvement through environmentally informed procurement choices. Moreover, through the volume of their purchases, they exert considerable influence on the market. In industry, green procurement depends on product design and can thus further enhance environmental design choices of materials and technologies by picking only those suppliers with the best environmental performance. However, attention to environmental qualities is a relatively new aspect in the procurement process and the ways to use LCA in this context are relatively experimental.

Figure 11.6 Typical parameters to assess the suitability of a product or service (based on EGPN 2003 and Nagel 2003).

The public sector is often expected to be in the forefront of green procurement. One reason is that, being environmental regulators, they should also set a good example to not lose credibility. Another reason is that governments and public administrations are the largest single buyers in a national market and their choices have considerable impact. This has led to the issue of public policies and regulations promoting green purchasing by the OECD, the EU and in the US (OECD 2002; EGPN 2003; US-EPA 1998). Green purchasing is rarely a policy area in its own right in companies unlike public authorities. The incentives for green procurement in private industry stem to a greater extent from market demands, cost saving potentials, commitment to an environmental policy or design strategy. In contrast to the public sector, industrial companies are intermediate consumers in that they convert raw materials into industrial products. Companies thus purchase "pre-consumer" goods, i.e. materials and components, whereas in the public sector up to 75 % of the expenses relate to consumable goods and the rest to infrastructure investments.

Professional purchasers differ from consumers in their capacity to procure goods in large quantities. Professional purchasers also represent corporate interests and their purchasing decisions reflect current product needs in their organisations. Purchasers have several tasks, which include:

- Managing the flow of incoming products.
- Managing existing stores and assessing their cost.
- Working with suppliers towards reliable business relationships.
- Performing actual purchasing.
- Selecting those suppliers that offer the most favourable conditions.
- Co-operating with various business departments in formulating their product needs.
- Co-ordinating action with financial controllers and obtaining authorisation for purchases.

In short, purchasing is about obtaining the right quantity, in the right quality, at the right time and from the right source. Some organisations distinguish between *product specifiers*, who assess and select goods, and *purchasers* who manage the actual purchase.

293

Guidelines for environmental purchasing could include for example a set of criteria for selecting the most appropriate product alternative. Such guidelines may also include specification of environmentally preferred products and services, methods of examining suppliers' environmental management, rating their environmental performance and building environmental clauses into contracts. LCA is one of several environmental tools that support green purchasing. Others are for example life cycle costing, lists of banned substances and questionnaires asking about various criteria such as recycled content, energy use, use of environmental management systems etc (Berg & Thompson 1997; EGPN 2003). The advantage of the life cycle perspective is that it provides a framework for gathering and analysing environmental information on products. LCA also highlights trade-offs that must be made among various criteria (Todd 1997; EGPN 2003). The challenge is to break down the overall LCA performance of a product to criteria relevant for the direct supplier. It may be so that the most environmental impact is caused by suppliers further upstream and not by the company's direct supplier (Nagel 2000).

There are two main applications of LCA to procurement. One is supplier selection and the other is product selection. A famous example of *supplier selection* is Scott Paper's environmental screening of its suppliers. Scott Paper compared their 40 pulp suppliers by means of LCA (see figure 11.7). The comparison showed among other things that the difference in CO_2 emission (per tonne pulp) varied greatly. Although all the suppliers delivered pulp for paper tissue, they did so with varying environmental performance. Scott Paper Ltd used the information to drop several of its suppliers from the list of approved suppliers and continued purchasing pulp from those remaining on the list (ENDS 1992).

BEES is a software tool for LCA-based *product selection*. It is aimed at the construction industry and was developed with support from the US EPA Environmentally Preferable Purchasing (EPP) programme. Its database contains both generic and brand-specific products. To date, nearly 200 building products and elements are included (BEES 2003). BEES measures the environmental performance of the products using LCA. Economic performance is also measured. Life cycle costing, which covers the costs of initial investment, operation, maintenance and disposal, is used for this

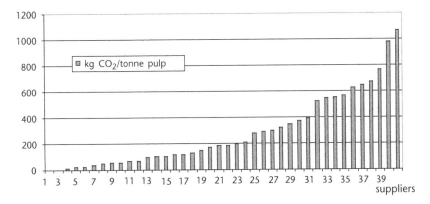

Figure 11.7 LCA-based screening of Scott Paper's pulp suppliers. The results were used to select suppliers for the list of approved suppliers (ENDS 1992).

purpose. This way, purchasers can determine if the cheapest product is also economical in the long run and if more environmental products are justified by being more durable even if they are more expensive. The software then uses multi-attribute decision analysis to combine environmental and economic performance into one overall performance measure (Lippiatt & Boyles 2001).

Some suppliers receive so many environmental inquiries from their different customers and potential customers that they feel compelled to do something to support the sales process (cf. Craig & Shiovitz 1997). Different customer may ask for more or less similar information, but use different questionnaires. Also, the time available for a supplier to prepare a procurement bid is often too short for the sales and marketing departments to investigate the environmental characteristics of their products. In response to this, some suppliers have started using environmental product declarations (EPDs) to accompany the products. The idea is that an EPD contains enough environmental information on the whole life cycle of the product to cover most customer inquiries. (For a description of EPD development, see chapter 10.)

So far, the use of LCA-based approaches in procurement is limited in practice. Purchasers are often unclear about what they should base their environmental purchasing decision on (Solér 1998; Verschor & Reijnders 1999; EGPN 2003). Several product assessment

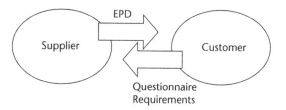

Figure 11.8 Some suppliers use environmental product declarations (EPDs) to deal with an increasing number of environmental inquiries from customers.

schemes exist in parallel, and standard procedures for LCA in procurement are missing. To overcome obstacles it is necessary for environmental purchasing to be in line with the company's or the public administration's overall policy and well integrated in the procurement routines. Purchasers face challenges in interpreting environmental product information that accompanies the product in terms of the needs of the purchasing company. Environmental education for those involved in sales and procurement together with adaptation of product-related environmental information to better fit the needs in procurement will be required for increased use of LCA-based approaches in this field.

11.3 Transportation and logistics

The contribution of transport to the overall environmental impact of a product is modest in many LCA studies. This is perhaps a reason why little attention has been paid to logistics in the field of LCA in spite of transportation being a major polluter in society. Most LCA studies related to transport concern the life cycles of different fuels. Many of them compare fossil fuels with alternative fuels such as ethanol or natural gas in the case of passenger cars (e.g. MacLean & Lave 2003; Röder 2001) but there are studies that focus on heavy goods fuels and transports (e.g. Sheehan et al. 1996; Fet et al. 2000; NTM 2002). Some studies, sometimes called "well-to-wheel" studies, look at engine and powertrain life cycles in addition to fuel life cycles in order to account for the technological differences that dif-

296

ferent fuels entail. For example, internal combustion engines differ greatly from fuel cells and it would be insufficient to just compare the life cycles of the fuels.

Many of the LCAs on fuels have been used to develop emission factors, i.e. average levels of emissions per tonne-kilometre for various modes of transportation. Such emission factors are used in most LCA studies for calculating the amount of transport emissions. Examples of emission factors are found in table 11.2 and in appendix 1. When developing emission factors for different modes of transport, assumptions on exploited capacity, type of engine and fuel quality and average age of fleet are made. Moreover, technological development and regulatory requirements have greatly influenced emission levels from transports. Examples of how much emission factors can vary are shown in table 11.2. The message here is that one must therefore be careful to pick emission factors appropriate for the study at hand.

Table 11.2 Examples of changes in emission factors for truck transports owing to technological development and stricter regulatory requirements.

		Energy requirements (MJ/tonne km)	CO_2 (g/tonne km)	CO (g/tonne km)	NO_x (g/tonne km)	SO_2 (g/tonne km)	Particulates (g/tonne km)
Truck, long distance transport	1991	1	78.6	0.30	1.30	0.154	0.10
	2002	0.72	52	0.046	0.33	0.013	0.0057
Truck, urban traffic	1991	2.7	212	0.81	3.52	0.42	0.27
	2002	2.41	176	0.15	1.1	0.043	0.019

Source: Tillman et al 1991. Source: NTM 2002. Vehicles manufactured later than 2000 (euro 3)

The transport sector is one of the most important sources of pollution. Transports (passenger and freight) accounted for 28 % of CO_2 and 63 % of NO_x emitted within the EU (EC 1999). While CO_2 emissions from industry in the EU decreased by 12 % between 1990 and 1999, CO_2 emissions from transport increased by 21 % during the same period. Development concerning engine technology and fuels have led to cleaner conbustion and reduced SO_2, NO_x, CO and particulate emissions but not CO_2 emissions as long as fossil fuels are used. Within the transport sector, efforts to reduce environmental impacts from transportation have mostly centred on reducing energy use in various transportation modes (truck, rail, airfreight and boat) (Vanek & Morlok 2000). In spite of substantial improvements in the technological efficiency of transportation modes, the freight transportation sector has been found to have the fastest growth in energy use compared to all other sectors from 1970 to 1995 in the US (Vanek & Morlok 2000). Growth in average length of haul for shipments, increasing complexity of supply chains and the increasing importance of imports and exports in the total mix of goods have all contributed to the increase.

Such numbers clearly indicate that environmental improvements in freight transportation are needed and that different supply chains and logistical solutions ought to be an issue worthy of analysis in LCA studies. Transport emissions may be small for many product groups, but they are considerable for certain types of products, for example food products, wood products and clothing (Vanek & Morlok 2000). For example, clothing had a large use of transportation energy, of the order of 70 % of the energy use for production. An LCA study focusing on transport systems for bananas showed a total of fossil CO_2 emissions of 135 g for one banana, which is almost equal to the weight of the banana itself (Bäckström 1999). What these product groups have in common is that during their use phase energy use is limited. Another product group with sizable transport emissions is building products owing to their weight.

Environmental improvements to supply chains and logistics are called for, especially for these product groups. However, for any product group, improving production and logistics are by no means mutually exclusive, and a combination of improvement efforts can lead to the most efficient outcome.

As mentioned earlier, little attention has been paid to logistics and supply chain issues in the field of LCA (Abukhader & Jönson 2003). Some methodological problems need to be resolved in order to facilitate analysis of these issues within the scope of an LCA study. To begin with, transportation and logistical systems need to be better mapped during the life cycle inventory analysis. In many cases transport is dealt with by measuring the distance on a map instead of describing more realistic transport, which includes among other things exploited capacities, distribution centres and

298

transshipments. Another problem concerns existing emission factors. The assumptions introduced in emission factors may have led to simplifications that render emission factors not sophisticated or flexible enough to accurately describe transport systems (Bäckström 1999; Fet et al. 2000). Also, different goods are often transported simultaneously but delivered to different locations. Sometimes goods are also transported together with passengers as in the case of ferries and aeroplanes. The choice of allocation method will therefore introduce considerable variation. Ordinary allocation methods used in LCAs, such as partitioning by weight or economic value, have been considered inadequate and more sophisticated allocation methods have been suggested, e.g. by Bäckström (1999).

11.4 Summary and further reading

In one sense the process industry was early in adopting LCA. Among the early LCAs were those on packaging, which included production processes. There have also been many sector initiatives to develop databases and average data for materials such as polymers and metals. Also for electricity production extensive LCAs were conducted in several countries. This early work on LCA of production processes was largely driven by information needs further down-stream in the life cycle. For example, many of the packaging studies concerned evaluations of recycling schemes, implying studies with a focus on waste management. Also product development, which has been seen as a major application of LCA, focuses on decisions further down-stream than material production processes. Thus the data derived for these purposes were often sector averages, useful for the down-stream applications but less useful for the process industry itself in its work to improve its environmental performance. Instead more site-specific approaches, such as waste minimisation and cleaner production strategies, were used.

However, the argument has been made many times that such site-specific approaches entail the risk that improvements in one part if the life cycle are outweighed by increased environmental impact in other parts. Thus the life cycle perspective has been introduced also for process design and improvement. For such applications, more detailed process models than those of standard LCA are needed. In addition, as LCA has at least one of its roots in chemical engineering practice, it was near at hand to merge LCA with more advanced modelling approaches, which among other things include economic and technical criteria and optimisation routines. However, a "full" life cycle perspective (cradle-to-grave) is very seldom (if ever) found in such studies. Instead they are of the cradle-to-gate type. This is hardly surprising, since cradle-to-gate are the parts of the life cycle that those responsible for e.g. material production are able to influence.

There may be other reasons for the process industry's readiness to adopt LCA (and similar approaches). This is a type of industry that has long been under pressure to improve its environmental performance and it thus has the competence to discuss environmental matters with external stakeholders. LCA offers a new perspective, not a new agenda. The process industry also has the competence to adopt LCA through its ability to handle flow models as well as chemistry.

The application of LCA to the analysis of processes is still quite immature. The literature is somewhat scattered and to a large extent consists of case study descriptions. However, a comprehensive review of the area has been presented by Azapagic (1999). Bretz and Fankhauser (1997) give a good example of industrial practice.

As already mentioned, the manufacturing industry has seen product development as the main application for LCA. Issues concerning procurement, production planning and supply chains have only recently been subject to environmental assessment, although in a limited manner. Moreover, there is a need for life cycle models that are better adapted to these applications and those related to transportation and logistics. Consequently, literature for further reading is also limited. However, the European Green Purchasing Network (www.epe.be) is a source of information on green procurement issues and the Network for Transport and the Environment (www.ntm.a.se) one on environmental performance and problems of transportation.

12 LCA and waste management

As described in chapter 2, issues about packaging and packaging waste were the main drivers behind the early development of LCA during the 1970s. Also the "second wave" of LCA from the mid-1980s to the early 1990s was largely driven by concern for waste in general, and packaging waste in particular. As we will see in this chapter, issues about waste management and recycling are a recurring theme of LCA. However, the scope has broadened and many more types of waste have been subject to LCA studies. For instance, sewage treatment and the handling of sewage sludge have been studied in a way that is very similar to the studies of solid waste. Also hazardous waste has been the subject of LCA studies. Recycling and reuse of a large variety of products and materials are central themes in many LCAs, but they may also come in as sub-issues of LCAs that are focused on more production-related issues.

In this chapter we use the term *waste management* in a very broad sense, implying any type of handling of a *used* product, ranging from reuse of the product, to material recycling, to energy recovery or to landfill depositing. Further on, we will not only refer to management of solid waste, but also to treatment of wastewater.

Most of this chapter will deal with LCA of post-consumer waste, i.e. the types of waste that consist of used products that have fulfilled their functions. Not all waste is of that type, however. There is also waste that emanates from industrial production processes.

A special feature of the area 'LCAs and waste management' is the existence of generic waste management models. These consist of a set of generic models of unit processes such as collection, landfilling, incineration and composting which may be combined to represent a specific waste management system. Some of these models are based purely on LCA, whereas others include cost and may be more advanced in their computational capacities. There are also cost optimisation models that have been complemented with environmental information drawing on LCA methodology.

LCA studies of various types of waste management essentially ask the same question: "Which waste treatment option is the better one, from an environmental point of view?" In the terms we used in chapter 3, they deal with waste management as the foreground system. However, there is another stream of research on LCA and waste treatment in which the goal is to model waste treatment processes to generate data for LCA studies in general, i.e. studies that include waste management as a background system. We will have a short look into this line of research in this chapter, but the main focus will be on LCA and LCA-related modelling that compare or even optimise different ways to manage waste.

12.1 LCA of waste management

A very common comparison in LCAs of waste treatment is between some kind of conventional process, such as landfilling or conventional sewage treatment, where a mixed waste stream is treated, and alternatives where the waste is separated into different fractions that are treated separately with the aim of reducing environmental impact through recycling of the fractions. Figure 12.1 depicts such options, on a very general level, equally valid for solid waste and wastewater. The separation may be done at source, in which case the different fractions must be collected separately, or it may be done centrally, in which case the collection is done before the separation. The term *collection* is here used in a very general sense and implies both collection by truck and conduction in sewers. The compared treatment options may range from cleaning (or similar) of a used product to make it fit for reuse, to recycling of materials (to be used in the same type of product as they originated from or to be used in some other application where a lower material quality is acceptable) or to energy recovery. In this type of studies the environmental benefits from recycling must often be traded off against the environmental impact from increased transportation.

302

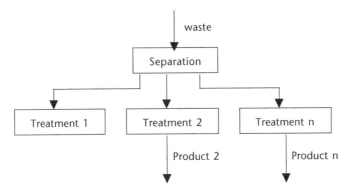

Figure 12.1 Options compared in LCAs of waste treatment, on a general level.

However, a flowchart such as the one in figure 12.1 is not enough to compare the different options. It does not allow fair comparison since some of the options produce useful products, which may be heat, electricity, different materials or in the case of wastewater treatment plant nutrients, thereby constituting an open loop recycling allocation problem. In "waste-LCAs" this is very often dealt with through system expansion, as shown in figure 12.2. As discussed in chapter 3, it may be difficult to know which would be the alternative production of the products, but the approach is still valid and valuable, since it takes the systems effects into account, i.e. the effects in a larger system.

Another common approach is to study not whole waste flows, but rather individual materials, exploring the potential environmental gains from keeping the material separate from other materials, thereby enabling recycling of the material to higher quality products than what would otherwise be possible. An example of a flowchart resulting from such an approach is shown in figure 12.3. It is valid for a polymer material for which many different recycling options exist, ranging from reuse of the products, to mechanical recycling of the material, to de-polymerisation (possible for some polymers), to pyrolysis, which recovers a mixture of lower molecular weight compounds for reprocessing or to recovery of fuels.

The approach is very similar to the one taken in the packaging study referred to in chapter 1 (figures 1.6 and 1.7, Tillman et al.

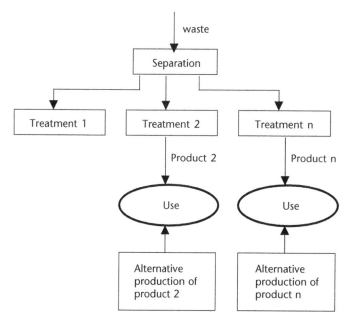

Figure 12.2 General LCA flowchart for comparison of waste treatment options. The use phase of the recycled products is not modelled.

1991) although only heat recovery, mechanical recycling and reuse were considered in that study. Several of the LCA projects in exercise H are of this type and some actually emanate from the packaging study.

Application of LCA to different types of waste

In the following we will briefly look into the different types of waste that have been studied with LCA. This overview is in no way complete, but rather intended to give examples of the very broad range of end-of-life systems that LCA may be applied to.

As mentioned, many of the early LCA efforts were on *packaging* and driven by concern for increasing amounts of waste and limited space to landfill it. Examples include two national Swiss studies (BUS 1984 and BUWAL 1991), a Danish one (Christianssen et al.

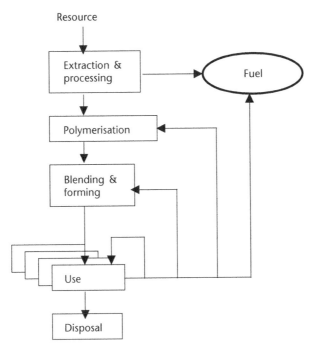

Figure 12.3 General LCA model of including many different recycling options for a polymer material kept separated from other waste flows (adapted from Mellor et al. 2002).

1990) and a Swedish one (Tillman et al. 1991). Also recycling versus incineration of paper has been an issue on which many LCAs were done (for an overview see Finnveden & Ekvall 1998). Studies of a similar kind have later been carried out in developing countries, for example South Korea (Song & Hyun 1999) and India (Sharma 2000).

New objects of study at a somewhat later stage were *wastewater systems* with their potential to recycle plant nutrients. The debated issue of disposal of sewage sludge came then to the fore. Many of the studies concern either sludge treatment and disposal or comparison between conventional sewage systems with systems that separate different fractions of the waste water, in particular urine separation (Lundin 2003). An example of a general flowchart for an LCA comparing separating options with conventional wastewater treatment is given in figure 12.4. See if you can find the similarities

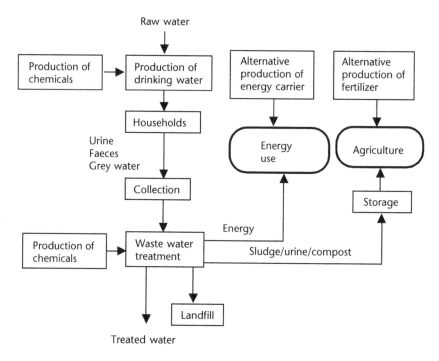

Figure 12.4 Flowchart from an LCA study comparing conventional wastewater treatment with options where wastewater fractions are separated at the source. Drinking water production was included in the systems since different options required different amounts of water for flushing toilets (Tillman et al. 1998).

between it and the even more general flowchart in figure 12.2. See also if you can decide on which parts of the system would be the foreground system and which would be the background system. (The concepts are defined in chapter 3).

Treatment of *hazardous waste* has been the subject of a Dutch project, where LCAs where conducted for seven different types of waste (Tukker 1999). The LCAs were carried in the context of a strategic environmental impact assessment of a national hazardous waste management plan. The goal of the LCAs was to identify treatment technologies that could be used as a reference or a "minimum standard". LCA was found to be a suitable tool for assessing the treatment of the types of hazardous waste that are incinerated in

306

one way or another, mainly solvents and oils of various kinds. Also in these studies system enlargement was used as a way to deal with the open loop recycling issue. For the types of waste that are disposed of in landfills LCA was deemed an unsuitable tool due to the great uncertainties concerning leaching in landfills and the uncertainties in the LCIA categories human toxicity and eco-toxicity.

Much hazardous waste (though not all) emanates from production processes rather than consists of used products. There are other examples where LCAs have been carried out on *industrial waste products*, e.g. used sulphuric acid (Brunn et al. 1996) and used catalysts (Baumann 1992). Though not from an industrial production system but from an agricultural one, manure is also a type of production waste. It has been studied with LCA by Sandars et al. (2003). All the studies mentioned have in common that they compare different options for recycling the waste products. From an LCA methodology point of view, recycling industrial waste is a bit different from recycling post-consumer waste. Recycling industrial waste creates a system with a by-product rather than an open loop recycling system since open loop recycling, as we have used the term in this book, implies several consecutive *uses* of a product or material.

Kerr and Ryan (2001) have studied "waste" of a completely different nature, *end-of-life* products that are *remanufactured* into new products. Their study concerned Xerox Corporation's famous remanufacturing system for used photocopiers. The results of the LCA showed savings in energy, materials and water use and amounts of waste and emissions of CO_2 in the range of 19–27 % for the types of photocopiers that were remanufactured as entire machines. However, that is not how it is done any longer. Instead, the photocopiers are built up from modules, and remanufacturing focuses on modules and parts. This new design strategy has been based on the earlier experience of disassembly and remanufacturing. For this type of system the savings in resource use and environmental impact over the life cycle amounted to 38–68 %, depending on the parameter regarded.

LCA modelling of recycling systems involving *metals*, finally, presents a challenge. The reason is that LCA models are usually static, i.e. they do not consider time as a variable. Metals, however, are often used in long-lived products and the stocks of many metals in society are constantly increasing. This is not taken into consideration in mainstream LCA. In order to overcome such limitations in the methodology, McLaren et al. (2000) have developed a framework for environmental assessment of recycling systems that include dynamic and non-linear characteristics of recycling systems.

LCA-based generic waste management models

A special feature of the field of LCA of waste is the occurrence of generic waste management models. Most of these include features beyond mainstream LCA, such as cost calculation, optimisation possibilities and aspects of substance flow analysis. In the following we will look into a selection of these models. More comprehensive reviews of models for integrated waste management may be found in e.g. Ljunggren Söderman (2000) and in Fiorucci et al. (2003).

The development of generic models for integrated waste management has been driven by pressure to reduce waste volumes and increase recycling, gradually implemented in regulatory systems. Examples include recycling targets, taxation on waste going to landfills, or even bans on landfill for certain types of waste. Municipal waste management plans have been made compulsory in several countries.

The models typically consist of a library of generic models of the unit processes used in waste management, such as collection, landfilling, incineration, composting, and anaerobic digestion. These may be combined by the user to represent a specific waste management system, whether an existing one or one that is a possible future option. It is also typical for this type of model that more data specifying the composition and quality of the different waste streams is included than in normal LCA. Sometimes this is done to an extent that the models are more substance flow analysis (SFA) models than LCA models. The reason for such detail in the description of waste flows is that it enables the models of unit processes to compute outflows as functions of the composition of the waste being treated. In one case the detailed information on flow properties is even used to let the model direct different waste fractions to different types of recycling, depending on material quality (Mellor et al. 2002). Some of the models are presented as being part of decision support systems, including multi-objective optimisation and multi-criteria decision analysis (MCDA), in a fashion similar to what has been discussed in chapter 11 (see figure 11.3).

Most of the models target municipalities and their need for waste management planning. For example, the US EPA has developed a tool intended to be used by those responsible for planning the management of municipal solid waste (Weitz et al. 1999). The tool is presented as a decision support tool featuring a database with LCI data and cost data for waste treatment processes, i.e. the foreground system processes, and data for background system processes such as production of energy carriers and materials. These may be combined by the user to produce a model of a waste management system. The tool includes an optimisation routine, optimising on both environmental and cost parameters. Other models that stem from LCA are the ISWM (integrated solid waste management) (White et al. 1995), and a Canadian model which has been based on it (Mirza 1995). MIMES-Waste is a Swedish waste management model. Originally it had a municipal scope (Sundberg & Wene 1988). It is based on cost optimisation but includes environmental aspects. Later developments of the model have been influenced by LCA in various respects and the model now covers also regional and national scopes (Ljunggren Söderman 2000). ORWARE is a model with a largely municipal scope. It may be described as a combination of LCA and substance flow analysis. In addition to municipal solid waste it also includes sewage (Eriksson et al. 2002).

CHAMP (Mellor et al. 2002) differs from the integrated waste management models in that it does not specifically target municipal waste management where a whole range of more or less well defined classes of waste comprising mixtures of many different materials is treated. Instead it takes the perspective of a specific material, and is intended to support decisions concerning the optimal management and recycling of that material under the condition that it is kept separate from other materials. It was developed for polymers and enables modelling the flow of a material through successive uses (see figure 12.3). It includes cost and environmental aspects on a life cycle basis. It is part of a decision support system including multi-objective optimisation and multi-criteria decision analysis (as described in chapter 11). Special features are that it includes modelling of logistics (including reversed logistics) and that it keeps track of material quality, thereby controlling the destiny of different material fractions. The potential user group of CHAMP is wider (and thus less well defined) than that of the integrated waste management models. The results can be relevant for material producers ("Is recycled material a suitable raw material?"), manufacturing industry ("Should our products be designed in a way that allows for disassembly of parts for remanufacture or separation of materials for recycling?") and policy makers introducing policies driving recycling and for waste managers ("What degree of separation of different materials results in useful fractions?").

12.2 Waste treatment in LCA

So far in this chapter we have discussed LCAs and LCA models intended to support decision making concerning waste management options, i.e. LCAs with waste management as the foreground system. However, waste treatment is of relevance to almost all LCAs, as waste treatment forms part of any full cradle-to-grave life cycle. Many early LCAs omitted the waste treatment stage, particularly landfills, because there were no data available, and simply reported the amount of solid waste produced. This was felt not to be satisfactory and it was argued that instead landfills should be regarded as technical processes to be modelled in the inventory analysis. Thus a number of projects set out to develop generic LCA data for waste treatment processes.

One such project is presented by Finnveden et al. (1995) and Sundqvist et al. (1997). It covered landfill disposal and incineration. A selection of the data it generated data may be found in appendix 1. A similar German project is reported by Kremer et al. (1998) and Bez et al. (1998). A model that generates LCA data for landfills has also been produced by Nielsen and Hauschild (1998), further presented in Nielsen et al. (1998).

From a methodological point of view, waste treatment has presented a challenge to LCA. One of the issues has been *open loop recycling*, which we have discussed in chapter 4 and will not discuss any further here. In addition to the open loop problem, waste treatment processes also present a *multi-input allocation* problem. The chal-

310

lenge has been to model waste processes in such a way that emissions, etc, may be related to the individual products and materials constituting the inflow. For landfills, finally, the *time horizon* is an issue.

Processes in landfills are much slower than industrial production processes. As waste is degraded, the chemical conditions inside the landfill change, which in turn influences degradation and leaching of the remaining material. Studies into LCA and waste treatment have concluded that there are two time frames that are relevant when describing landfills in LCA terms. The surveyable time period is approximately a century. During this period methane formation diminishes. After that the landfill goes into a pseudo steady state during which all changes occur much more slowly. The other time perspective of relevance is infinite, when all the material in the landfill is degraded and dispersed. Most of the data presented cover the surveyable time period.

The multi-input allocation problem of waste treatment processes occurs because many different waste products are mixed in the same process. There has been a general agreement in the LCA community that allocation in waste treatment process should be based on physical causalities to as great an extent as possible, for example through allocating releases of heavy metals only to those inflows that contain heavy metals. The approach taken to waste incineration by Sundqvist et al. (1997) was to divide the emissions into product-related and process-related ones. The product-related emissions come from a specific material or product and are emitted if they are not trapped in the bottom ash or in the flue gas cleaning system. Examples include carbon dioxide, sulphur oxides, hydrochloric acid and heavy metals. Process-related emissions are caused not so much by the components in the waste as by the conditions under which the process is run. Examples include carbon monoxide and polyaromatic hydrocarbons (PAHs). Some emissions are both product and process derived, notably nitrogen oxides. Product-related emissions are easier to allocate to specific products whereas process-related emissions require understanding of both process technology and operating conditions.

It should be noted that even if most LCA researchers seem to agree that waste treatment, including landfills, should be seen as part of the technical system and thus modelled in the inventory analysis, different methodologies are not totally coherent. Some weighting methods, such as the Weighted Environmental Themes (WET) method include different classes of waste as parameters to be weighted (see appendix 3). The implications are that the WET method regards waste management as taking place in the natural system, thus modelled in the impact assessment. This is inconsistent with what seems like a general consensus that waste treatment processes are part of the technical system. However, the approach is helpful when inventory data is missing.

12.3 Summary and further readings

As we have seen in this chapter there are two ways in which waste management may be studied in LCA. In one approach the waste management system is the foreground system. Studies of this type are used to support planning of waste management. Waste management may also be a background system in LCAs that are focused on some other issue. For those types of study, generic data are needed.

The type of study that is intended to support waste management planning is often concerned with the consequences of recycling options, in which case system expansion is the natural choice of method to deal with the open loop recycling problem. For this type of application there exist waste management models that include features beyond mainstream LCA, such as cost calculation and optimisation. An international workshop on such models was held in 1998 (Sundberg et al. 1998). A more recent overview may be found in Ljunggren Söderman (2000).

For LCAs where waste treatment is a background system efforts have been made to generate generic waste treatment data. However, for more uncommon types of waste (different classes of industrial waste, hazardous waste, ashes and slag, etc) generic data may still be difficult to find.

An important step in the development of LCA and waste treatment was the workshop held in 1995 (Finnveden & Huppes 1995). The area is being pursued in an international expert group on LCA for integrated waste management, as reported by Thomas and McDougall (2003).

312

13 Organising LCA activities in a company

Given that LCA is such an ambitious method, it is intriguing that companies work with it since it takes them outside their normal area of responsibility. The LCA methodology sends them looking for more than the environmental impacts of their own production processes. It sends them looking for the environmental impacts also at suppliers' facilities, the suppliers' suppliers and more remote industries. This chapter presents you with a glimpse at the practice of LCA in industry by presenting cases of LCA projects. An overview of the cases is listed in table 13.1.

The cases represent real LCA projects. They describe, among other things, the LCA analysts' troubles and surprises, the different phases of their projects and the usefulness of dominance analyses. The cases show that LCA studies can serve many different purposes, some of which are intended and others unexpected and made up as they go along. An LCA study can support decision making by providing the decision makers with a rational comparison, or serve a learning purpose when the LCA is exploratory, or be the basis for communication with customers and/or suppliers. It is even possible that a single LCA study has all these purposes at once. What purpose an LCA study actually will serve depends to some extent on whether the company is a beginner at LCA, has gained some experience or developed a routine.

The companies involved in the presented cases are more or less newcomers to the field of LCA. Consequently, the cases present not only the LCA projects as such but also the process of deciding whether to continue working with LCA or not, i.e. the implementation process. The cases represent a selection of different views on the usefulness of LCA and different strategies for implementation in different industries (Baumann 1998a & 1998b; Frankl & Rubik 2000). However, there are also commonalities, especially with regard to general patterns of implementation and perceptions on usefulness. The process of implementation, with its social and organisational "mechanisms" that move companies from being beginners to applying LCA routinely, is described in some detail towards the end of this chapter. The understanding of this process will help you judge the maturity of LCA activities in a company and perhaps also define your professional role if you come to work as an LCA analyst.

Table 13.1 Overview of cases of LCA projects.

Process industry (chemical): an LCA study of 2 types of fibres (section 13.1.)

Manufacturing industry (electronics): an LCA study of product documentation systems (13.2.)

Service/manufacturing industry (energy/electronics): an LCA study of an electricity meter (13.3)

Process industry (hygiene products): an LCA study of packaging systems (13.4.)

13.1 An LCA project in a process industry

This particular LCA project was conducted in a company that was a part of a large Swedish chemical corporation, which merged with a Dutch corporation during the course of the project (Baumann 1998a). The merger that took place in 1994 was relatively undramatic from the perspective of the LCA project. It did not affect the course of the project, nor did it result in any substantial changes in the company's environmental policy and its dedication to the Responsible Care programme of the chemical industry. The merger led to changes in company names, but for sake of simplicity, the company is called Akzo Nobel Surface Chemistry in the following.

The LCA project consisted of a study comparing viscose and polypropylene fibres in a non-woven application. In short, it was initiated by the "viscose niche" at Akzo Nobel Surface Chemistry, and conducted in collaboration with the "non-woven group" at the Swedish Institute for Fibres and Polymers (IFP).

314   © The authors and Studentlitteratur

Akzo Nobel Surface Chemistry, headquartered in Stenungsund on the Swedish West Coast, had at the time 20 plants/sites around the world. The viscose niche was their producer of process chemicals for viscose fibre production. Also tensides and flotation agents for the minerals mining industry were produced among other things. Akzo Nobel Surface Chemistry was a sub-business unit within the Chemicals business unit, which in turn was one of four business units within Akzo Nobel. The others were pharma, coatings and fibres. Akzo Nobel was in 1995 an international company with more than 70 000 employees in 50 countries, headquarters in Arnhem in the Netherlands and a turnover of 21.5 billion NLG.

Initiation of the LCA project

A clear start of the LCA project is difficult to identify. The members of the non-woven group at IFP had heard about an LCA study conducted at a European branch institute, but they were unable to get hold of it. LCA had therefore been a topic for general discussion for some time among them. One of the members of the group was the viscose niche manager at Akzo Nobel. He was an enterprising person and someone who was also very curious about LCA. In the spring of 1993, he met separately with the IFP director to discuss the possibility for IFP to conduct an LCA study for Akzo Nobel. Several suggestions were discussed, among others a comparison of different types of viscose production. It was thought that the programme leader of the non-woven group was going to do the study, and he started immediately to collect and study LCA literature.

During the summer, it was decided that the project was to be a non-woven group project (rather than one commissioned by Akzo Nobel). The ambition to define an LCA study of interest to all the group members decided the object of study: a comparison of viscose (a wood-based fibre) and a synthetic fibre. (The members of this group were producers of different types of fibres and process chemicals for these as well as manufacturers of non-woven applications.) The viscose niche manager, who also was the organiser of an international conference series for the viscose industry, suggested that the LCA project should be presented at the next conference in May 1994. To this they all agreed.

Figure 13.1 The viscose niche manager is stressed by the slow progress of the LCA study.

What the viscose niche manager at Akzo Nobel hoped for was that the LCA study would inject some optimism in the viscose industry. Not only did it have a poor environmental reputation because of its problems with carbondisulfide, CS_2 (a toxic and explosive chemical), it was also losing market shares to the synthetic fibres. Nevertheless, the viscose niche manager was hopeful. After all, the viscose fibre came from a renewable resource.

By November, the viscose niche manager was frustrated since the LCA study had made little progress at IFP. Fortunately he had found an "LCA specialist" within his company. It was a young man recently employed on a short-term contract after having finished his MSc Diploma project (an LCA study). The environmental manager, who had hired the young man to work on another LCA project, had plans and ideas for LCA activities within Akzo Nobel. For instance, he had already set up an informal LCA steering group. He agreed to let the viscose niche manager use the young LCA specialist as an advisor in the project at IFP. Although a beginner, he was deemed more experienced than the LCA analyst at IFP. The viscose niche manager then called IFP: "We've got someone who could assist you."

The environmental manager at Akzo Nobel Surface Chemistry is an important person although he mostly stayed in the background; he even called himself a "mole". He had often felt that traditional environmental work "got stuck" and when he had discovered LCA, he had felt that it offered something new: a systematic way to look at a product's whole environmental impact and a way to avoid suboptimisation. He let the viscose niche manager use the LCA analyst as much as necessary, even though the LCA analyst was already involved in another project, since he wanted the young LCA ana-

316

lyst to become established on his own merits. He also wanted LCA to be of relevance to more than him and the young LCA analyst. For this reason he had started an informal LCA committee. It gave a forum through which LCA results could be disseminated continuously and where they could discuss LCA activities outside the formal hierarchical organisation. The LCA committee consisted of various "key persons" (an R&D manager, a chemicals expert, a production manager and a marketing person). Before the merger, our "mole" is the environmental manager at Berol Nobel. After the merger, he is the environmental officer of the production plant. Despite this change, he remains in charge of the LCA committee. Thereby he stays in contact with the LCA analyst and the project the whole time.

Conducting the project

When the two LCA analysts first met, the one from Akzo Nobel soon realised that he had to be more active than an advisor if the study was to be finished in time. He began with explaining to IFP's LCA analyst that the fibres could not be analysed "just like that"; they had to be analysed in an application. They decided then to study viscose and polypropylene (PP) fibres in a diaper cover application (the surface that keeps baby's bottom dry). Polypropylene had 96 % of this market, viscose the rest. It was also decided that a detailed LCA study and proper LCA methodology ("all the way to weighting") were aims in themselves. A weighting method, familiar to them at the time, was chosen: EPS (Ryding & Steen 1991). After this, they decided on the functional unit, drew the flowcharts, identified data sources, etc. Although the Akzo Nobel LCA analyst was supposed to be an advisor, he had more time and experience than the IFP LCA analyst. In this he saw his chance: if he saw to make it a good study, it would help get both LCA and him established within Akzo Nobel. He summarised the situation: "They started, then I took over".

The two LCA analysts met approximately once a month. Their data collection turned out to become a trade: data from data suppliers were obtained in exchange for results when the study was finished. The Akzo Nobel LCA analyst also tried to obtain a more per-

Figure 13.2 When the two LCA analysts got together the study progressed rapidly.

sonal relationship with data suppliers or to use established channels, such as those of the purchasing department with many of Akzo Nobel's suppliers. The idea to use established channels had come from his manager. The thought was that established channels would provide a normal and undisturbing way of collecting data. The total time spent on the project by Akzo Nobel's LCA analyst was approximately 20 % of his working hours for half a year. Estimated on basis of data collection activities, the Akzo Nobel LCA analyst did most of the work.

By the time they were busy with the data collection, the informal LCA committee at Akzo Nobel had come to realise that their LCA analyst was more involved than an advisor, and reminded him of their priorities (the other ongoing LCA project at Akzo Nobel).

LCA results

The two LCA analysts computed preliminary results whenever new data arrived. In the beginning, the results were in favour of PP. Later, when more data had been collected, the results were in favour of viscose. The reason is that EPS puts much weight on the use of fossil resources. The IFP LCA analyst took the results quite literally, and told one of the non-woven group members that "viscose is better than PP". This was unexpected and sensitive information since PP dominated the market. The "PP members" of IFP's non-woven group reacted strongly and there was talk of stopping the presentation at the viscose conference. The non-woven group resolved the problem at an emergency telephone conference: results were not to be weighted with the EPS valuation method. Instead, results would be presented

318

in a less aggregated form, as inventory results and characterisation results. This would avoid discussions about weighting methods in place of a discussion about the results. A revised manuscript was faxed to each non-woven group member. The approval to the presentation was given the day before the conference.

Figure 13.3 Characterisation results were presented at the conference.

The conference presentation was a success. The study showed that CS_2 was a smaller environmental problem than expected in comparison to other environmental impacts in the viscose life cycle. Also, the overall difference between viscose and PP was much smaller than expected. This was good news for the viscose industry – it meant that it was worthwhile to develop the viscose process.

With the presentation, the LCA project was formally over. Nevertheless, the LCA analyst at Akzo Nobel took it further and he decided on his own to make a more detailed analysis of the results. Of the around 100 steps in the viscose life cycle, only a handful mattered (none of them were Akzo Nobel steps). He quickly put together a report and presented the results internally at Akzo Nobel Surface Chemistry (i.a. to the informal LCA committee). He also gave feedback to several data suppliers. In fact, the LCA analyst frequently used the viscose example in other presentations afterwards. Especially the dominance analysis was considered effective in communicating the usefulness of LCA.

When presenting the results, he always tried to show that the LCA results were surprising and interesting. To one of the data suppliers, he showed that NO_x emissions from their pulp mill were smaller than those from their forestry transportation. His impression was that "It was something they had never thought of before". Later, this data supplier started a logistics project to reduce emissions from transports. Another part of his disseminating strategy

319

Figure 13.4 The LCA analyst is busy making the most of the LCA study.

was to refer to the image of the chemical industry. Everybody within the industry knew that the chemical industry was an environmental villain in the eye of the general public, and he explained that with LCA came a possibility to identify new possibilities for improvement since LCA could show a company's part in the overall picture. In combination with Einstein's saying that 'today's problem are caused by old thinking, and that it takes new thinking to resolve them', he made himself a position when talking to older managers. The LCA analyst was eventually given 25 minutes to present his work for the members of the Chemicals' Board. Two weeks later he received full employment as LCA specialist and the existence of the LCA committee was formalised.

The project was generally considered successful. Akzo Nobel Surface Chemistry also started a transportation project. It led to a switch from trucks to railroad on certain distances. Several new LCA projects were started afterwards. For example, the satisfied viscose niche manager commissioned an update of the viscose results a couple of years later, but that's another story.

Comments

Much can be said about this "tortuous" project, but only a few points about its purposes will be made. Noticeable is that the project served many purposes. Looking only at Akzo Nobel Surface Chemistry, the project was driven partly by research-based curiosity, partly by experienced inadequacies with other environmental

320

tools. The environmental manager spoke about the greatness of the tool; the viscose niche manager was intrigued by it; an environmental officer at the pulp mill found it "fun" and wanted to learn more. A more formal reason was market communication ("inject some optimism in the viscose industry"). In addition, the LCA analyst saw the project as an opportunity to establish himself and LCA methodology within the company. To round off, the project led to expected as well as several unexpected, spin-off outcomes (new LCA projects, transportation projects, a formalised LCA organisation). This indicates that LCA was used for *organisational learning* rather than as support for a single decision.

Akzo Nobel's LCA analyst played an important role for the company's continued work with LCA. Although the project was formally ended after the conference, he kept communicating the usefulness of the LCA study. This shows that he had a conscious plan for introducing LCA, which he shared with his manager. It can be said that both worked in an *entrepreneurial* manner. Other examples of their entrepreneurial strategies are their data collection strategies, their dissemination strategies and the way they work to obtain a mandate from management. Their own explanation to why they could act so freely was the a "decentralisation culture" in the company.

Since the ending of this particular project, LCA activities have become further established and integrated in the activities of the company. Three years later (1997/1998), a second person was employed to work with LCA at Akzo Nobel Surface Chemistry and the LCA committee was reformed into the Environmental Strategy Group.

13.2 An LCA project in a manufacturing industry

In 1996, a product specialist with part-time environmental responsibilities at Ericsson Business Communication (a part of Business Networks), initiated an LCA project (Baumann 1998b). The project consisted of a comparison of alternative media for product documentation for one of their products, a business telephone switching exchange. The documentation describes how the switching exchange is set up, operated, constructed and integrated in the national telecommunications network.

Ericsson is a large international corporation in the telecommunications business. In 1996, at the time of the LCA project, it had 94 000 employees, of which 44 000 were in Sweden, and it was divided in 5 business areas: Radio, Public Telecom, Business Networks, Components and Microwave Systems. Privatisation of the telecommunications markets throughout the world had caused considerable changes to the market situation. From having had a market with only a few hundred customers on a national level, Ericsson struggled at the time of the project to adapt to a new situation with several millions of private customers. It also underwent a remarkable growth: the turnover had increased 5-fold over 10 years. In its environmental policy, a general commitment to life cycle thinking is made (Ericsson 1996).

Initiation of the LCA project

A chance meeting by the coffee machine in the communal coffee room with a documentation specialist triggered the project. A documentation specialist told enthusiastically the product specialist about a vivid environmental discussion at their latest meeting at the documentation department. The reason for the environmental discussion was that the documentation group were looking for new arguments. The project to modernise the product documentation system had gone on for a long time but with little success. Instead of the 60 000 pages in some 80 ring binders, the documentation specialist wanted the information about business telephone switching exchanges on some electronic medium (e.g. on disk, CD, or www). Unfortunately, neither technical nor economic arguments had convinced the product managers. However, the document specialist had started to think of using morally "unchallengeable" environmental arguments since he had realised that there was an environmental side to the modernisation (reduced use of paper).

At the time of this chance meeting by the coffee machine, the product specialist was on the lookout for ideas for LCA projects. He

322

had started to work with environmental matters on part-time after many years in the business and had attended some short courses and seminars to learn about environmental issues and management. At one of these, in 1994, he was introduced to LCA and had become enthusiastic; LCA was product-oriented which suited him as a product specialist, and it was quantitative which he thought appealed to the many engineers at Ericsson. He was convinced that LCA was the only technique to look at a product's environmental impact. After the coffee, the product specialist thought that he should make use of the situation; it was the first time that someone had approached him to talk about environmental matters spontaneously. He therefore started to plan for an LCA project to promote a modernisation of the documentation system.

The planned LCA study was not the first one within the corporation although it was the first within this particular business area. The product specialist thought that the company's earlier LCAs did not live up to proper LCA practice, and he wanted to use the project as an opportunity to introduce proper LCA methodology to the company. In his view, proper LCA methodology adhered to ISO 14040. To obtain this, he wanted to co-operate with CPM (Centre for Environmental Assessment of Product and Material Systems, an industry-university collaboration for the development of LCA methodology). He also wanted to use a particular LCA software. His plans for large-scale implementation of LCA were based on the use of this software since it could also be used for building up an internal corporate-wide LCA database. To sum up, the LCA study was conducted at the department of the product specialist, not at the documentation department.

Figure 13.5 The product specialist finds an opportunity to make an LCA study.

Figure 13.6 The LCA analyst has a hard time with the LCA software.

Conducting the study

An LCA analyst, i.e. a student who was looking for a MSc Diploma project, was recruited via CPM in September 1996. He spent approximately 2 weeks studying the LCA concept, which was new to him. The ISO standard was soon abandoned since the LCA analyst did not find it instructive. Instead, reports of other LCA studies were studied. In line with the ambition to conduct a proper LCA study, it was decided that it should go all the way to weighting. Three weighting methods (EPS, the ecoscarcity method and the environmental themes method) were used for sake of comparison. Then, around 2 months were spent on data collection. Since product documentation is not a core product, data suppliers were difficult to identify. Many, rather creative search strategies were used (see table 4.1). Finally, around 2 months were spent on making the calculations with the requested software. The calculations took so long because of the many bugs in the software and the LCA analyst was in contact with the software suppliers several times. This led to 3 new upgraded versions of the software during the time of the project.

LCA results

In March 1997, it was time to present the results. The tradition was to invite various people within the business unit, but the product specialist was eager to launch LCA on a larger scale and sent out a corporate-wide invitation to the seminar. However, he had a problem with conventional wisdom on environmental problems at Ericsson. The interest for environmental issues was low and the general

324

opinion was that the company did not really have any environmental problems thanks to the continuing miniaturisation of electronic products. In the corporate environmental report, it said *"Our technology is in itself adapted to the environment ..."* The product specialist chose to not challenge the notion of the environmental superiority of electronic products. Instead of setting out to prove that the company indeed had environmental problems he said that the study would provide proof of what people within Ericsson already knew (i.e. the environmental superiority of electronic products). He also referred to environmental questions coming from customers and claimed that these types of studies were necessary to provide the answers to those questions.

The LCA study showed that CDs caused much less environmental harm than ring binders (1:700). Such a large difference was unexpected, and so was the overview of the whole documentation system provided by the LCA. Each set of 80 ring binders could be replaced by a single CD. A change would therefore lead to a substantial weight reduction. Since the documentation was transported by air to the customers, weight was of great importance. Apart from that, the plastic cover of the ring binders and the paper production stood for a relatively large part of the overall emissions. Through the LCA, the documentation people acquired a technical overview of the documentation system, which thus far had been missing. In turn, this led to a discussion of choices of different types of CDs and transportation. The study also put the documentation system on the agenda of the product managers. The product specialist was eager to show the results and got the project presented in the annual corporate environmental report of 1996 although the project was not finished until 1997.

With the project, the product specialist had gone from part-time to fulltime on environmental matters. His corporate-wide promotion of LCA activities made his nearest manager react. The LCA seminar gave the manager the opportunity to call for a meeting with the corporate environmental manager and the business area's environmental manager to discuss the division of tasks, responsibilities and costs related to the LCA activities between business areas and central corporate units. This resulted in that an LCA group was formed at the business unit around the product specialist. The project also managed to put documentation systems on the agenda of the product managers – it had long been an overlooked area. The ring binders had started to be replaced by CDs before the project was ended. After the presentation of the project in the corporate environmental report, technical newspapers reported on similar modernisations of product documentation systems in other business units at Ericsson.

Comments

Two reasons lay behind the project. From the perspective of the documentation people, internal political reasons were at the fore: to find new arguments for modernising the product documentation system. From the perspective of the product specialist, the launching of LCA was at the fore. The outcomes of the project were manyfold: increased knowledge, discussion about areas of responsibility, networking, etc. The outcomes were to a large extent unexpected and came in addition to the original purposes of the LCA project. This indicates a process of organisational learning in which learning how to deal with environmental issues and with the product documentation as a system took place. In hindsight, the result that one CD is environmentally superior to 80 ring binders seems to be a predictable one. However, a lack of overview of the technical parts of the different documentation systems and the deliberations about what exactly was going to replace the ring binders led to that the LCA results never were expected.

Ericsson had made some kind of general commitment to LCA (e.g. in its environmental policy and through its membership in CPM). A couple of LCA studies had previously been conducted within various business areas. However, not until the activities of the product specialist and the presentation of the results did the LCA activities start to become co-ordinated. The ardent activities of the product specialist make him an LCA entrepreneur. Not only did he initiate LCA activities within his own business area, but also within the corporation as a whole. The initiative to set up a corporate-wide LCA database and the corporate-wide invitation to the seminar are also telling examples. Furthermore, the LCA study on documentation systems would never have taken place if it had not been for the product specialist. The documentation specialist actually never commissioned the LCA study. Moreover, the product specialist also thought he had to push the LCA activities forward much on his own, without much help from management.

The way the LCA study was motivated at the seminar, as a proof of the company's environmental virtue, is an example of how the LCA entrepreneur *situationally adapts* the rhetorics and the implementation strategy.

13.3 An LCA project in a service/ manufacturing industry

The LCA project in this case was conducted at Landis & Gyr Utilities (LGUT), a provider of systems and services for energy management of for example heating, ventilation and air conditioning. The company also produces energy-related equipment (meters, thermostats, valves, etc) and counters for payphones which employed a similar technology as some of the energy-related equipment. In 1996, at the time of the LCA project, the company had around 5 300 employees and its turnover was 625 million euro (Frankl & Rubik 2000). LGUT was in 1996 part of the Electrowatt group but has later been merged. (In 1998, it became Landis & Staefa and a part of Siemens).

Since the company's products and services help save energy, it was felt within the company that they had a certain obligation to reduce the environmental impact from their products and production processes. An important driver for the development of the corporate environmental policy was Stephan Schmidheiny, main shareholder at the time and also internationally known for his environmental initiatives. For instance, he was a major actor in setting up the World Business Council for Sustainable Development.

The LCA project

A few LCA studies had already been carried out within Landis & Gyr in Switzerland. The LCA project in this case was an exploratory study of an electricity meter. Electricity meters measure the use of electric energy of households and plants. They have to be very precise since energy billing is based on the measurements of the meters. The electricity meter was chosen for an LCA study for its relatively simple material content, so that the collection of inventory data would be manageable. It was foreseen that LCAs for more complicated products would be conducted in the future.

The motivation for the study was to find out which parts of the life cycle of the electricity meter caused the greatest environmental impact. There had been discussions between the environmental manager and the product designers about environmental priorities. The environmental manager assumed that the company's production, i.e. the actual assembly of electricity meters, caused a relatively low environmental impact. However, it was unclear to him whether it was the energy use during the use of the meter or the production of the materials and components of the meter that caused the greatest environmental impact. The product designers argued that the meter's use of energy during its lifetime was irrelevant since it was a thousand times lower than the electricity it measured. The environmental manager decided then to carry out the LCA study of the electricity meter himself. This was possible since he had a budget for identifying tools for more environmental product development. The LCA study was thus used for finding arguments to convince the product designers to consider environmental aspects during product design.

The results

The results of the LCA study showed that most of the environmental impacts were associated with the energy used during a meter's lifetime. This is due to its long lifetime (up to 30 years). The conclusion was that this should be addressed through the product design process. The results also initiated the development of an electricity meter with a 10–15 % lower energy use.

Afterwards, plans for further LCA studies were more or less abandoned. Among the reasons was that it seemed that LCA studies of their products led to similar results: so far they had all identified energy usage as the most important aspect. Another reason was that the LCA methodology was not well adapted to the work process of the product designers. It was too time-consuming and too rigid to fit into the creative phase of the design process. To replace standard LCA, the company developed their own environmental tool for the product development process. The new tool was named PEP (Product Eco-Performance), and it was based on the results of their previous LCA studies. The tool was a sort of checklist of environmental criteria important from a life cycle perspective. The environmental criteria were for example material efficiency, emission of hazardous substances, energy usage and recyclability. Each criterion was rated from 1 to 5 (1 for minimum requirement to 5 for high-performance environmental product) and then added together to form an overall environmental score for each product. In the design process, the product developer then compared the PEP score of the actual design with the target PEP score, i.e. the lowest acceptable PEP score for the design.

Comments

Although no further standard LCA studies were planned, basic life cycle thinking remained. The fact, that several criteria in the PEP tool were LCA-based, show the importance of LCA even if standard LCA studies are not conducted continuously. (For more on LCA and product development, see chapter 9.)

13.4 An LCA project in a consumer goods industry

Weleda AG produces pharmaceuticals and products for personal hygiene. The company uses only natural ingredients since it is rooted in the anthroposophical philosophy of Rudolf Steiner where humans and nature should co-exist in harmony. At Weleda, it is assumed that the products themselves are environmentally harmless thanks to the natural ingredients. Any environmental impact is therefore thought to come from either the production processes or the packaging. At the time of the LCA project, Weleda AG had almost 1 000 employees and was headquartered in Switzerland. The

LCA project was conducted at the company's biggest subsidiary located in Schwäbisch Gmünd in Germany. The German part of Weleda had around 500 employees and a turnover of 60 million euro (1996) (Frankl & Rubik 2000).

Initiation of the LCA project

In 1995, external environmental consultants conducted an LCA study for Weleda in Germany. The study concerned packaging systems and it was conducted in response to a public debate in Germany about the environmental problems of packaging. Packaging was considered problematic because of its large part of the household wastes and the perceived lack of space for more landfills. During the debate Weleda was confronted with many questions from customers. When trying to answer, it became clear that knowledge was incomplete within the company and the need for an LCA study emerged. The environmental manager knew of "small" LCA studies on packaging made by colleagues in Switzerland, but these were considered insufficient since packaging materials and the views on packaging were different in Germany and Switzerland. The company decided eventually to hire an external consultant since internal know-how of LCA was missing.

An LCA study was set up to compare Weleda's traditional packaging with synthetic alternatives, i.e. aluminium tubes with an alternative polyethylene (PE) tube, and glass bottles with alternative PET bottles. A change to synthetic packaging material was wanted above all for market reasons. Synthetic toothpaste tubes and bottles had become standard packaging material on the market and Weleda in Germany wanted to follow this trend, but not without checking the environmental consequences through a comprehensive LCA. And although Weleda in Switzerland and France had started to use PET bottles, Weleda in Germany was reluctant to follow their example given the on-going German packaging debate.

330

The LCA study and its results

The LCAs were modelled generally from cradle to grave following the ISO standard, which existed in a draft version at the time. The environmental officer at Weleda assisted in the data collection. He co-ordinated the internal data and channelled data from the suppliers. The impact assessment was conducted as far as the characterisation step. In addition to the ordinary quantitative impact categories, human toxicity and land use were evaluated qualitatively.

The results showed that the PE tube was better than the aluminium tube for most impact categories. All in all, the results were considered clearly in favour of the PE tube. However, it was thought that Weleda could not switch to PE tubes for product quality reasons. The advantage of the aluminium tube is that it deforms when squeezed, thereby preventing air from entering and microbes to grow inside the tube. Since preservatives are not used in Weleda's product, the company decided instead to try to modify the formula of toothpaste to suit PE tubes.

The results for the bottles were not as clear. The 200 ml PET bottle had generally the best results, but the brown glass bottle was not far behind. The consultants recommended the brown glass bottle since it was more recyclable than the PET bottle. Weleda chose then to keep the brown glass bottles until recycling of plastics had improved.

By the time of the completion of the LCA study, there was no clear commitment to continue working with LCA in the company. Several arguments were put forward. The LCA study was considered as "illuminating", but the LCA methodology dubious, mostly because of the perceived manipulability of LCA results. In addition, the data collection was considered too time-consuming. After the study, the company still lacked know-how to independently carry out LCAs. Weleda's environmental officer had assisted in the data collection, but the external consultant had carried out most of the work. Furthermore, Weleda seemed to view LCA as a competing rather than a complementing tool. For procurement, the company preferred to use its own ABC method. For product development, checklists and market surveys were mostly used. This together with the notion that their products were environmentally harmless led to the need for LCA was deemed small.

331

Comments

In short, Weleda's test of LCA was not wholly successful for LCA. The LCA study became a stand-alone project without continuation. The use of an external consultant certainly limited the company's possibility to learn about the potentials of LCA methodology. However, the intention to learn about LCA was not at the fore since the LCA study was commissioned in response to a public debate, not from a need to develop the environmental practices in the company.

13.5 Organising LCA projects

We now shift the focus from each individual LCA projects to looking at the four LCA projects collectively. Examination of the four described LCA projects show that there are some general traits concerning how one can organise work with LCA. There are at least two aspects to the organisation of LCA work. The first concerns what LCA methodology looks like in practice. The other aspect relate to that the projects can also be seen as telling examples of the general state of LCA activities in the companies. This latter aspect will be dealt with in the next section (13.6) on LCA implementation. Here, we will take a closer look at what characterises an LCA project in practice.

When comparing the LCA projects, it can be seen that their contexts differ greatly. For example, in the chemical industry, there is a general opinion that it is a "dirty" business whereas the electronic industry is seen as "clean". However, there are also similarities. Most LCA studies lead to more outcomes than expected.

When analysing each project, it becomes clear that the descriptions of LCA practice in the cases convey a slightly different picture of what is problematic than the more theoretical descriptions of LCA methodology found in for example the ISO standards. A striking difference between the descriptions of the LCA projects and written LCA methodologies is the lack of people in the latter. Each case describes different actors with different roles in the LCA projects, but descriptions of 'who is to do what?' are hard to find in the written methodologies. This is probably the explanation to why theoretical studies of LCA did not lead far in both the Akzo Nobel and the Ericsson cases (an "LCA advisor" was called in and the ISO standard was abandoned, respectively). Learning by doing has been a better way for these companies.

In the following, the most prominent activities in the LCA projects will be described according to the ordinary LCA framework.

Initiation of the LCA project

The initiation of an LCA project is not strictly a part of the LCA framework. The process of starting a project is seldom straightforward. It is nevertheless important for the design of the study. The Akzo Nobel case is a good example of this. The possibility of a project was loosely discussed. Several project ideas were discussed at different times and among different people. When did the project actually start? A single occasion when it is decided to conduct an LCA project is difficult to identify. Various circumstances led to that synthetic fibres and fibres from a renewable resource were to be compared. And, it took a long time until the goal and scope formalised the comparison of viscose and PP fibres in a diaper application.

Goal and scope definition

There is in practice often a clear role division between those who make the goal definition and those who make the scope definition. This is very clear in the Akzo Nobel and the Ericsson cases. The goal is typically defined by the commissioners of the LCA study. They are the ones with a general idea of what should be investigated, but they often lack LCA expertise. This means that it is difficult for them to scope the LCA study, i.e. to assess whether the idea is possible to model in LCA terms. Instead it is the LCA analyst that "translates" the general idea into LCA language, i.e. defines the functional unit, the requirements on the LCA model, decides on the type of data that will be needed, etc.

Strangely enough, the activity to decide on the object of study is not mentioned in LCA standards. Of course, it is up to the investigators to decide on what to study, but given that there are different types of LCA studies (comparative, explorative, etc), this lapse is worth mentioning. All cases presented earlier consisted of comparative studies, except in the LGUT case where an explorative study was conducted. The choice of object of study is to some extent governed by the complexity of a company's product. Akzo Nobel represents the process industry, which produces relatively simple, bulk-type products. Ericsson and LGUT are representatives of manufacturing industry, with complex products, consisting of numerous materials and components. The LCA study in the Akzo Nobel case concerned one of their important products, while the LCA study in the Ericsson case concerned something "unimportant", not even a regular product. Also in the LGUT case, the choice was governed by the criteria that the product should be as simple as possible rather than having an important position on the market. This is understandable since their core products are very complex. For the manufacturing industry, it is easier to start with studying something less complex, such as separate components, the simplest product or a even documentation system, as in the Ericsson case, before whole, core products are studied.

Inventory analysis

The cases show that the most prominent activities of the inventory analysis are the data collection and the running of the LCA software. A substantial amount of time is spent on calculating, updating the calculations and producing results diagrams. Unless the LCA software makes the wrong calculations, as in the Ericsson case, the LCA analysts seldom mention this part of the work. A greater problem is the acquisition of data.

Standardised questionnaires were not used in any of the cases. The LCA analyst's strategies for data search in the Ericsson case range from more or less random searching the telephone directory to dis-assemblying the product and weighing its components (see table 4.1). In the Akzo Nobel case, in which a core product was studied, data suppliers were more obvious and the ordinary channels between the company's purchasing department and the suppliers could be used. But even in this case, the co-operation of the data suppliers is not guaranteed, since there is no benefit related to the hand-ing out of data. Therefore a trade often takes place in these situations. For example the suppliers are suggested to give data in exchange for access to the LCA results later when the study is over. A personal, friendly relationship with the potential data supplier will at least facilitate the negotiation of access to data and also possibly speed up the data delivery. Again it is worth mentioning that activities for gathering data are little described in LCA standards and manuals.

Methodological problems pertaining to allocation and system boundaries did not cause much problem to the LCA analysts in the described cases. The reason behind this somewhat unexpected observation is unclear. Possibly the LCA studies were relatively sim-ple or the LCA analysts were confident in their command of LCA methodology.

Impact assessment and interpretation

In the beginning of an LCA project, the commissioner often defines the type of impact assessment in a general way. For example, it may be decided during the goal definition that the LCA methodology should be comprehensive, follow standards or go "all the way to weighting". The LCA analyst plays an important role in the process of drawing conclusions, working with the "raw" results from inven-tory analysis, refining them and deciding on whether the results are sufficient or not. In the Weleda case, the normal impact categories were judged insufficient and were therefore complemented with a qualitative assessment for certain impact categories. In the end, the various audiences governs the format of the results presentation more than decisions early on during the goal and scope definition. This is very clear in the Akzo Nobel case. Also here, the LCA analyst plays an important role, suggesting and sometimes also deciding on how the result presentation should be adapted to each audience.

Purposes and outcomes of LCA projects

The typical LCA project has multiple purposes. These can be general learning, obtaining material for market communication, supporting decision processes or even political processes. Some of the purposes will be stated in the beginning of the project, some will be added towards the end as spin-offs. There are often more informal reasons than formal reasons for an LCA project. It is often the case that the formal reason is stated in the goal and scope definition, but the many informal reasons are also important for the actual design of the LCA project. For example, in the Ericsson case, the product specialist commissioned the LCA study on product documentation since he was eager to test LCA – the documentation manager actually never asked for help.

An LCA study is often a "large" study, containing a lot of information and with enough material for many conclusions. This is a reason why an LCA study may lead to more outcomes than originally planned for. What the actual outcomes will be depends on how open the involved actors are to surprises. Openness to surprise will help them to act on unexpected results.

There can be two types of outcomes of an LCA: physical outcomes and intangible outcomes. Among the "physical" outcomes are for example changes to production process or logistics, change of product composition or packaging. Such physical changes do take place, although not necessarily where they were planned or expected from the beginning. The changed logistics in the Akzo Nobel case are good examples of this.

Among the intangible outcomes are all the new insights an LCA study can lead to. An important type of learning is illustrated in the Akzo Nobel case. The company found out its environmental position in the supply chain and that their own production processes contributed very little to the overall environmental impact. Certain learnings will affect the way things are done in the company. In the LGUT case, the LCA project led to that LCA-based rules of thumb were developed for the product designers. Other intangible outcomes are organisational changes (for example the formation of an LCA group as in the Akzo Nobel and Ericsson cases) and messages to external stakeholders (for example market communication to the viscose industry in the Akzo Nobel case and the presentation in the environmental report in the Ericsson case).

The companies seem to find LCA useful in spite of the ambitious and demanding methodology. LCA has after all a unique advantage of providing a systematic overview of complex systems. This, in turn, enables a company to position itself in the product system. LCA also gives the company a framework for communicating complex environmental information. The bird's-eye view given by LCA studies give companies both important opportunities for learning and a preparedness for discussion of environmental matters with external stakeholders, be it customers, suppliers or authorities.

13.6 Implementing LCA

Just because LCA has been invented does not mean that companies will start working with it. Similarly, just because a company has tested LCA does not automatically mean that it will continue with it. The companies described in this chapter are all relative beginners at LCA. In most cases, the LCA project represents an attempt to introduce LCA into the normal activities of the companies. Success in not given beforehand, as is seen in the Weleda case. Some of the factors important for LCA implementation are examined in the following.

Studies on how organisations "behave" have shown that there are general patterns to implementation processes. For example, implementation is a process that can be divided into several phases. Each phase has its typical traits. This is useful since it also means that the process for implementing LCA is similar to other implementation processes. The general knowledge about these processes will help us characterise the different phases of LCA implementation. This can be useful for assessing the state or "maturity" of LCA activities in a company, be it if you start working there as an LCA analyst, become involved as an environmental consultant or as a data supplier. Moreover, a general understanding of implementation processes is always useful as it provides guidance for the implementation of any new routine or idea.

The theoretical term for an implementation process is *institutionalisation* within organisation theory. To institutionalise means to make something institutional. Organisations, rules and processes that are social givens to which we have to adapt to can be called institutions. Examples of institutions are the church, schools, money for payments, routines and traditions. Using the terminology of institutionalisation theory (Tolbert & Zucker 1996) the implementation process can be divided in the following way:

Stages of the institutionalisation process:
Innovation —> Habitualisation —> Objectification —> Sedimentation

The habitualisation stage includes the initial adoption of an innovation or a novel idea (here, LCA) within an organisation (here, a company or even the whole of industry). Often only a small part of the company is involved (in the case of LCA, typically the environmental department). To habituate means to accustom, to become a habit. In the next phase, the objectification, the new idea (i.e. LCA) begins to spread within the company. To objectify means to present something as an "real" object, which cannot be ignored in the same way as a vague, new idea. This is a crucial phase since it is usually during this phase that the future of the novelty is determined, whether it will stay or be abandoned. The implementation is over when the novelty (i.e. LCA) has become routine and taken for granted – the innovation is then said to be sedimented.

Habitualisation – initial adoption of LCA

During the first phase, the habitualisation, it is necessary that certain people in a company feel a real need for LCA in order for the company to take on LCA. At this early stage, technical and economic factors together with internal political arrangements largely predict adoption. Examples of such factors are the presence of an environmental debate as in the chemical industry, the presence of a specific environmental problem (e.g. carbondisulfide in the viscose industry), dissatisfaction with existing environmental tools and a pressure from the market (e.g. questions from customers). Concerning internal political arrangements, the picture is mixed. LCA can be introduced in a top-down manner but also in a bottom-up approach. The way LCA is introduced internally depends to some extent on the culture in the company, the sector and the country. In some Scandinavian cases, a bottom-up introduction of LCA has been observed. This is the case in Akzo Nobel Surface Chemistry when environmental officers and engineers start working with LCA without seeking support and a mandate for the LCA activities until later. In many cases, LCA is introduced by corporate management. Such a top-down approach can for example be observed in the LGUT case.

Early on, the LCA adopters are few. Knowledge among non-adopters of what constitutes an LCA study is typically very small at this early stage. In other words, those not directly involved in LCA activities have probably never heard about LCA. Since people in the same profession or people in the same industry often share a common core of knowledge and ideas, the adoption of a given innovation may, and often does, occur in close co-operation with other organisations. Here, example of such co-operation was seen between Ericsson and CPM in the case of the LCA study on documentation systems, and between the companies in the non-woven group at IFP in the viscose/PP LCA project. Imitation may follow from such association, but this is not necessarily so since there is yet no consensus on the general utility of LCA at this stage. This means that early adopters of LCA are/were companies in somewhat similar circumstances but without similar ways of working with LCA.

Apart from the decision to take up LCA, also some kind of organised ways of working with LCA start to develop. However, the structures are typically short-lived in the beginning. An example of how short-lived these early "LCA organisations" are comes from the Akzo Nobel case: an informal reference group without name was set up to support a specific LCA project. This informal group lasted only approximately six months and reformed itself at the time of the viscose/PP LCA project. The group then named itself "LCA committee", but it was still informal. It became formally recognised some time well after the viscose/PP LCA project was finished.

Objectification – developing a consensus around the use of LCA

For the LCA implementation process to move on after the initial adoption of LCA, a consensus regarding the use of LCA has to develop. The development of such a consensus is most crucial for the routine use of LCA. The development of consensus has to address the development of *general and shared* understanding of what LCA is and what it should be used for. This is necessary. Otherwise the use of LCA will not expand beyond the small circle of LCA enthusiasts. Consensus can emerge through two different mechanisms.

One mechanism works through *monitoring*, i.e. gathering of information about LCA activities in a company's business surroundings. Monitoring is a way for a company to confirm its adoption of LCA or to assess the risk of adoption. If a company sees that for example its competitors are working with LCA, then it must also be right for them to work with LCA. The Ericsson case study provides an example of how the monitoring mechanism works. At the presentation of the results of the LCA study, the project leader thought it was important to also present CPM to the invited colleagues. CPM had many other industrial companies engaged in LCA activities as members. Presenting CPM showed that even if the LCA activities were new and unknown to most people at Ericsson, such activities were not unusual in Swedish industry. The implicit logic was that if "all other" companies are working with LCA, why should not Ericsson do it as well?

Monitoring activities can be more or less direct. In the Akzo Nobel case, monitoring is more indirect. All the non-woven group members at IFP knew about an LCA study conducted at European level. The problem was that they could not get hold of it, and their only possibility to obtain similar information as their European competitors was to conduct a similar study.

The second mechanism works through a *champion* who can promote LCA, i.e. the person called LCA entrepreneur in the cases. They are most easily recognised by the self-imposed responsibility to promote LCA activities (report writing and dissemination of results in the Akzo Nobel case, and corporate-wide initiatives in the Ericsson case). The LCA entrepreneur might be someone with a material stake in the LCA implementation, be it a permanent job as in the case of Akzo Nobel, or someone with a strong environmental interest. To be successful, the LCA entrepreneur has to show that the use of LCA will help solving a generally acknowledged problem within the organisation. The way this is done depends on the situation. There has to be a *situational adaptation* to the context. At Akzo Nobel, LCA is justified as a means to improve the poor envi-

340

ronmental reputation of the chemical industry. At Ericsson, LCA is justified as a means to prove the environmental advantages of the electronics industry.

The LCA entrepreneur also needs to develop strategies to make LCA a part of the normal activities in the company. For example the entrepreneur may conduct LCA studies wherever possible, rather than defining LCA studies for the environmentally or strategically most important product areas. The entrepreneur can also attempt to stimulate an LCA interest (the element of surprise in presentations of LCA results at Akzo Nobel), which is thought to create a demand for LCA in the organisation. The entrepreneur is also busy accumulating evidence on the usefulness of LCA and disseminating successful examples (dissemination of LCA results to various data suppliers in the Akzo Nobel case and to the environmental report in the Ericsson case).

LCA companies in the objectification phase often promote LCA and at the same time monitor the accumulation of evidence of its utility. The use of LCA during this phase has a somewhat fashion-like quality. Technical, economic or political factors are no longer as important. Whether other companies work with LCA or not is more important. With more and more becoming engaged in LCA activities, LCA users become with time a more heterogeneous group. Organisational structures built up for working with LCA are still relatively short-lived. They may last perhaps a couple of years as in the case of the LCA committee at Akzo Nobel before it was transformed into a Strategic Environmental committee.

Sedimentation – LCA activities have become taken for granted

Sedimentation is characterised by that the promotion of LCA and the accumulation of evidence have stopped. By now, there is a formal structure for working with LCA and there is no longer any need for an LCA entrepreneur to push the development. This means that the use of LCA has become taken for granted and there are routines for when to conduct LCA studies. The form of LCA may vary, be it standard LCA studies, as LCA-based rules of thumb or as simple

LCA-based green design tools as in the LGUT case. What is essential is that the LCA work has become taken for granted, or even expected, and that the LCA activities will survive even if the LCA people in the company change.

From learning to doing – how far have we come?

There is still some way to go from learning to doing since there is still much experimenting with LCA in different forms and applications in industry. Surveys show that the number of companies that work with LCA vary between 5 % and 40 % of industry depending on the country and the type of companies covered by the survey (Baumann 1995; Frankl & Rubik 2000). LCA as a standard operating procedure can be found in a few cases, but it is still not spread widely in industry. No observations of quantitative LCA studies conducted on a routine basis were made in any of the 20 cases studies documented in a European project, although it had a strong foothold in some of the studied companies (Frankl & Rubik 2000). Whether a company would continue, alter or abandon LCA usage seems to be related to:

- how well surprises are acted upon and the situational adaptation is made;
- if results in subsequent LCA studies are too similar, there is a probability that LCA use will be much simplified (e.g. will appear as LCA-based guidelines as in the LGUT case). To some extent, this is related to the size of the company, or rather the diversity of its products and operations. LCA application can continue to offer new insights in larger companies with broad product ranges;
- if the study is triggered by external debate and external consultants were used (as in the Weleda case), there is a probability that LCA will be abandoned since in-house knowledge about the tool remains limited.

It is not sufficient to justify LCA in its own right. LCA also needs to be justified in its organisational context. This means that identical implementation recipes will not work everywhere, since there are

342

parts of the implementation process that calls for a situational adaptation. How well the situational adaptation is made is crucial for the continuation of the LCA activities. Here, the LCA entrepreneurs have an important role to play.

13.7 Summary and further reading

This chapter has presented some examples of how real LCA projects happen in industry. Although the LCA concept is spreading, LCA work has not yet become routine procedure in industry. Companies tend to experiment, testing LCA on new products and new fields of application. This means that LCA projects often lead to learning and even surprising insights, perhaps also disappointment. In many companies, one may find an LCA entrepreneur, i.e. someone who actively and enthusiastically promotes LCA, and who is important for the process of implementing LCA. To read more about LCA implementation, the book reporting from the EU project on the use of LCA in industry (Frankl & Rubik 2000) is suggested. LCA in practice raises many issues in relation to organisation and business ('who is to do what?', 'for whom?', 'what is the business relevance?', etc.), issues that are typically not dealt with in methodological handbooks and standards. Those who want to enter more deeply into these issues pertaining to LCA in practice can find many leads through the LCM conference series on life cycle management. The LCA conference series does not yet have its own website, but a report from the first one (Hunkeler et al. 2001) is available in the International Journal of LCA.

14 Bibliography

3M (1997). *3M Environmental Management System. Life Cycle Management*. 3M, St Paul, MN, USA.

Abukhader, Sajed M (2003). *The environmental implications of electronic commerce. The assessment approach problem*. Licentiate thesis, Division of Packaging Logistics, Lund University, Lund, Sweden.

Abukhader, Sajed M & Gunilla Jönson (2003). "Logistics and the environment: Is it an established subject?" Submitted to *International Journal of Logistics and Research and Applications*.

Alexander, Brett, Geoff Barton, Jim Petrie & Jose Romagnoli (2000). "Process synthesis and optimisation tools for environmental design: methodology and structure". *Computers and Chemical Engineering, vol 24*, pp 1195–1200.

Arvidsson, Peter (1995). *LCA-rapport Tvättmedel (LCA report on detergents)*. Akzo Nobel Surface Chemistry, Stenungsund, Sweden.

Ayres, Robert (1998). "Eco-thermodynamics: economics and the second law". *Ecological Economics*, vol 26, no 2, pp 189–209.

Azapagic, Adisa (1999). "Life cycle assessment and its application to process selection, design and optimisation". *Chemical Engineering Journal*, vol 73, pp 1–21.

Azapagic, Adisa & Roland Clift (1999a). "The application of life cycle assessment to process optimisation". *Computers and Chemical Engineering*, vol 23, pp 1509–1526.

Azapagic, Adisa & Roland Clift (1999b). "Life cycle assessment and multiobjective optimisation". *Journal of Cleaner Production*, vol 7, pp 135–143.

Bakker, Conny (1995). *Environmental information for industrial designers*. PhD thesis. Technical University Delft, NL. Bakker, Fransen van de Puttestraat 77, Rotterdam, NL.

Baumann, Henrikke (1992). *LCA: Jämförelse och värdering av miljöpåverkan för behandling av förbrukad katalysatormassa från kataly-*

tisk kracker (RCCU). (LCA: Comparison and assessment of environmental impact for treatment of used catalyst from catalytic cracker (RCCU)). Rapport 1992:1, CIT Ekologik, Göteborg, Sweden.

Baumann, Henrikke. (1995). *Decision Making and Life Cycle Assessment*. Licentiate thesis, Chalmers University of Technology, Göteborg, Sweden.

Baumann, Henrikke. (1998). *Life cycle assessment and decision making. Theories and practices*. PhD thesis, Chalmers University of Technology, Göteborg, Sweden. Also as AFR report 183, Swedish Waste Research Council, Stockholm.

Baumann, Henrikke (1998a). "LCA at Akzo Nobel: A Phoenix." In H Baumann, *Life Cycle Assessment and Decision Making. Theories and Practices*. PhD thesis, Chalmers University of Technology, Göteborg.

Baumann, Henrikke (1998b). "LCA at Ericsson: A Beginning." In H Baumann, *Life Cycle Assessment and Decision Making. Theories and Practices*. PhD thesis, Chalmers University of Technology, Göteborg.

Baumann, Henrikke, Frank Boons & Annica Bragd (2002). "Mapping the green product development field: engineering, policy and business perspectives". *Journal of Cleaner Production*, vol 10, no 5, pp 409–425.

Baumann, Henrikke & Sarah J Cowell (1998). "An Evaluative Framework for Conceptual and Analytical Approaches Used in Environmental Management". *Greener Management International*, vol 26, pp 109–122.

Baumann, Henrikke & Tomas Rydberg (1994). "Life Cycle Assessment: Comparison of Three Methods for Impact Analysis and Valuation". *Journal of Cleaner Production*, vol 2, no 1, pp 13–20.

Beamon, Benita M (1999). "Designing the green supply chain." *Logistics Information Management*, vol 12, no 4, pp 332–342.

BEES (2003). *BEES 3.0®. Building for Environmental and Economic Sustainability*. http://www.bfrl.nist.gov/oae/software/bees.html, accessed April 2003.

Bengtsson, Magnus (1998). *Värderingsmetoder i LCA. Metoder för viktning av olika slags miljöpåverkan – en översikt*. CPM report 1998:1. Centre for Environmental Assessment of Product and Material Systems, Chalmers University of Technology, Göteborg, Sweden.

Berg, J Karla & Dixon Thompson (1997). "Environmental purchasing guidelines for organizations." *Proceedings of the Air & Waste Management Association's 90th Annual Meeting*, June 8–13, 1997, Toronto, Ontario, Canada.

Berlin, Johanna & Ulf Sonesson (2002). "Design and construction of an environmental process management model for the dairy industry". In Berlin, J (2002), *Environmental systems analysis of dairy production*. Licentiate thesis, Environmental Systems Analysis, Chalmers University of Technology, Göteborg, Sweden.

Bez, Jürgen, Michael Heyde & Gertaud Goldhan (1998). "Waste treatment in product specific life cycle inventories. An approach to material-related modelling. Part II: Sanitary landfill." *International Journal of LCA*, vol 3, no 2, pp 100–105.

Boustead, I & GF Hancock (1979). *Handbook of industrial energy analysis*. Ellis Horwood, Chichester, UK.

Boustead, Ian (1996). "LCA—How it Came About: The Beginning in the UK". *International Journal of LCA*, vol 1, no 1, pp 4–7.

Bretz, Rolf & Peter Fankhauser (1997). "Life cycle assessment of chemical production processes: A tool for ecological optimization". *Chimia*, vol 51, no 5, pp 213–217.

Brezet, Han (1997). "Dynamics in ecodesign practice". *Industry and environment*, vol 20, no 1–2, pp 21–24.

Brezet, Han & Carolien van Hemel (1997). *Ecodesign—a promising approach to sustainable production and consumption*. United Nations Environment Programme, Industry and Environment, Paris, France.

Brezet, Han & Cristina Rocha (2001). "Towards a model for product-oriented environmental management systems". In Chartner, M & U Tischner (eds) (2001), *Sustainable solutions. Developing products and services for the future*, pp 243–262. Greenleaf Publishing, Sheffield, UK.

Brunn, Hilmar, Rolf Bretz, Peter Fankhauser, Thomas Spengler & Otto Rentz (1996). "LCA in decision making processes. What should be done with used sulfuric acid?" *Internation Journal of LCA*, vol 1, no 3, pp 221–225.

BUS (1984). *Oekobilanz von Packstoffen*. Schriftenreihe Umwelt 24, Bundesamt für Umweltschutz, Bern, Switzerland.

BUWAL (1991). *Oekobilanz von Packstoffen. Stand 1990.* Shriftenreihe Umwelt nr 132, Bundesamt für Umwelt, Wald und Landschaft, Bern, Switzerland.

Buxton, A, AG Livingston & EN Pistikopoulus (1997). "Reaction path synthesis for environmental impact minimization". *Computers and Chemical Engineering*, vol 21 (suppl), pp S959–S964.

Bäckström, Sebastian (1999). *Environmental performance calculation in transport LCI. Allocation method design issues.* Licentiate thesis. Report 45, Department of Transportation and Logistics, Chalmers University of Technology, Göteborg, Sweden.

Carlson, Raul (1994). *Design and implementation of a database for use in the life cycle inventory stage of environmental life cycle assessments.* Master's thesis, Department of Computing Science & Department of Technical Environmental Planning, Chalmers University of Technology, Göteborg, Sweden.

Carlson, Raul, Maria Erixon & Ann-Christin Pålsson (2000). *Establishment of trade structures for LCI data.* CPM report 2000:3, Centre for environmental assessment of product and material systems, Chalmers University of Technology, Göteborg, Sweden.

Carlson, Raul, Göran Löfgren & Bengt Steen (1995). *SPINE: A relational database structure for life cycle assessment.* IVL report B1227, the Swedish Environmental Research Institute, Göteborg, Sweden.

Carlson, Raul & Ann-Christin Pålsson (1998). *Establishment of CPM's LCA database.* CPM report 1998:3, Centre for Environmental Assessment of Product and Material systems, Chalmers University of Technology, Göteborg, Sweden.

Carlson, Raul, Anne-Marie Tillman, Bengt Steen & Göran Löfgren (1998). "LCI data modelling and a database design". *International Journal of LCA*, vol 3, no 2, pp 106–113.

Chartner, Martin & Ursula Tischner (eds) (2001). *Sustainable solutions. Developing products and services for the future.* Greenleaf Publishing, Sheffield, UK.

Christiansen, K, A Grove, LE Hansen, L Hoffman, AA Jensen, K Pommer & A Schmidt (1990). *Miljøvurdering av PVC og udvalgte alternative materialer.* (Environmental evaluation of PVC and selected alternative materials.) Miljøprojekt 54, Miljøstyrelsen, Copenhagen, Denmark.

Clift, Roland, Rolf Frischknecht, Gjalt Huppes, Anne-Marie Tillman & Bo Weidema (1999). Report from the SETAC Working Group on the Inventory Enhancement. *SETAC-Europe News*, vol 10, no 3, pp 14–20.

Clift, Roland, Warren Mellor, Elizabeth Mellor, Adisa Azapagic & Gary Stevens (2001). "Chain management of polymers: a new approach to decision-support modelling." *1st International Conference on Life Cycle Management*, August 27–29, 2001, Copenhagen, Denmark, pp 183–186.

CML (2002). *Life cycle assessment. An operational guide to the ISO standards.* Editor: Jeroen Guinée, Centrum Milieukunde Leiden (CML), Leiden University, NL. Kluwer, Dordrecht, NL.

CML/NOH (1992). *Environmental life cycle assessments of products. Guide and Backgrounds.* Contributing authors: R Heijungs, J Guinée, G Huppes, RM Lankreijer, HA Udo de Haes, A Wegener Sleeswijk, AMM Ansems, PG Eggels, R van Duin & HP de Goede. NOH reports 9266 and 9267. The National Reuse of Waste Programme (NOH), the Netherlands.

Coulon, Remi, Vincent Camobreco, Helene Teulon & Jacques Besnainou (1997). "Data Quality and Uncertainty in LCI." *International Journal of LCA*, vol 2, no 3, pp 178–182.

Craig, Erin & Aime Shiovitz (1997). "Not another questionnaire! How Sun Microsystems tackled its customer environmental inquiry response problem using quality processes." *Proceedings of the 1997 IEEE International Symposium on Electronics and the Environment*, pp 267–271.

Cramer, J, J Quakernaat & T Dokter (1993). *Theory and practice of integrated chain management.* TNO, Apeldoorn, NL.

Curran, Mary Ann (1996). *Environmental Life Cycle Assessment.* McGraw-Hill, New York, NY, USA.

Curran, Mary Ann (2002). "The emerging focus on life-cycle assessment in the US Environmental Protection Agency." *Journal of the Franklin Institute*, vol 8, no 4–6, pp 287–290.

Dale, Virginia H & Mary R English (eds) (1999). *Tools to aid environmental decision making.* Springer, New York, NY, USA.

EC (1996). Council directive 91/61/EC. "Concerning integrated pollution prevention and control". *Official Journal of the European Commission*, no L257.

EC (1999). Commission of the European Communities, Transport statistics, at http://europa.eu.int/comm/energy_transport/etif/ list_of_tables.html#TRANSPORT.

EC (2001). *Green paper on Integrated Product Policy.* Com(2001) 68 final, Commission of the European Communities, Brussels, Belgium.

EDIP (1997). Wenzel, Henrik, Michael Hauschild & Leo Alting. *Environmental Assessment of Products, volume 1.* Chapman & Hall, London, UK.

Eder, WE (2000). "Designing and life cycle engineering—a systematic approach to designing". *Proceedings of the Institute of Mechanical Engineers part B Journal of Engineering Manufacture,* vol 215, pp 657–672.

EEA (1997). *Life cycle assessment. A guide to approaches, experiences and information sources.* Contributing authors: AA Jensen, J Elkington, K Christiansen, L Hoffmann, BT Møller, A Schmidt & F van Dijk. The European Environment Agency, Copenhagen, Denmark.

EGPN (2003). *Green purchasing in Europe.* The EPE workbook series, the European Green Purchasing Network. European Partners for the Environment, http://www.epe.be, accessed April 2003.

Ehrenfeld, John & Michael Lenox (1997). "The development and implementation of DfE programmes". *Journal of Sustainable Product Design,* issue 1, pp 17–27.

Ekdahl, Åsa (2001). *Life cycle assessment on SKF's spherical roller bearing.* ESA report 2001:1, Environmental Systems Analysis, Chalmers University of Technology, Göteborg, Sweden.

Ekvall, Tomas (1994). "Principles for allocation at multi-output processes and cascade recycling". In G Huppes & F Schneider (eds), *Proceedings of the European Workshop on Allocation in LCA.* Leiden, February 1994, pp 91–101. SETAC-Europe, Brussels, Belgium.

Ekvall, Tomas & Anne-Marie Tillman. "Open-loop recycling: criteria for allocation procedures". *International Journal of LCA,* vol 2, no 3, pp 155–162.

Ekvall, Tomas, Henrikke Baumann, Göran Svensson, Thomas Rydberg & Anne-Marie Tillman (1992). "Life-cycle assessment: Pilot study on inventory methodology and data bases". In *Product Life Cycle Assessment—Principles and methodology,* Nord 1992:9, pp

350

132–171. The Nordic Council of Ministers, Copenhagen, Denmark.

ENDS (1991). "Curbs urged on use of life cycle analysis in marketing". *ENDS report*, no 198, Environmental Data Services (ENDS), London, UK.

ENDS (1992). "Scott Ltd Cleans up Paper Chain". *ENDS report*, no 214, p 17, Environmental Data Services (ENDS), London, UK.

Ericsson (1996). *Ericsson Corporate Environmental Report*. Stockholm, Sweden.

Eriksson, Elin, Viveca Johannisson & Tomas Rydberg (1995). *Comparison of four valuation methods*. Chalmers Industriteknik, Göteborg, Sweden.

Eriksson, O, B Frostell, A Björklund, G Assefa, J-O Sundqvist, J Granath, M Carlsson, A Baky & L Tyselius (2002). "ORWARE—a simulation tool for waste management." *Resources, Conservation and Recycling*, vol 26, pp 287–307.

Erixon, Maria (ed) (2000). *Facilitating data exchange between LCA software involving the data documenation system SPINE*. CPM report 2000:2, Centre for environmental assessment of product and material systems, Chalmers University of Technology, Göteborg, Sweden.

ETI (1988). *Simplificert sammandrag av ETI-undersøgelsen af 22.11.1988. Miljøvurdering af emballager*. (Short version of the ETI environmental study of meat packaging.) For Myging AS. Emballage og Transportinstituttet, Denmark.

Espinosa, Octavio Juarez, James Garrett & Chris Hendrickson (1997). "Software tool for economic input-output life cycle assessment". *American Society of Mechanical Engineers, Design Engineering Division (publication)*, vol 94, pp 215–222.

Fet, Annik Magerholm, Ottar Michelsen & Tommy Johnsen (2000). *Environmental performance of transportation. A comparative study*. IØT report nr 3/2000, Department of industrial economics and technology management, Norwegian University of Science and Technology, Trondheim, Norway.

Finnveden, Göran, Ann-Christine Albertsson, Jaak Berenson, Erik Eriksson, Lars Olof Höglund & Jan-Olov Sundqvist (1995). "Solid waste treatment within the framework of life-cycle assessment." *Journal of Cleaner Production*, vol 3, no 4, pp 189–199.

Finnveden, Göran, Yvonne Andersson-Sköld, Mats-Ola Samuelsson, Lars Zetterberg & Lars-Gunnar Lindfors (1992). "Classification (Impact Analysis) in Connection with Life Cycle Assessment—A Preliminary Study". In *Product Life Cycle Assessment—Principles and Methodology*, Nord 1992:2. Nordic Council of Ministers, Copenhagen, Denmark.

Finnveden, Göran & Tomas Ekvall (1998). "Life-cycle assessment as a decision-support tool—The case of recycling versus incineration of paper". *Resources, Conservation and Recycling*, vol 24, no 3–4, pp 235–256.

Finnveden, Göran & Per Östlund (1997). "Exergies of natural resources in life cycle assessment and other applications". *Energy*, vol 22, no 9, pp 923–931.

Fiorucci, Paolo, Riccardo Minnciardi, Michela Robba & Roberto Sacile (2003). "Solid waste management and application of a decision support system". *Resources, Conservation and Recycling*, vol 37, pp 301–328.

Frankl, Paolo & Frieder Rubik (eds) (2000). *Life Cycle Assessment in Industry and Business. Adoption Patterns, Applications and Implications.* Contributing authors: M Bartolomeo, H Baumann, T Beckman, A von Dänicken, P Frankl, F Leone, U Meier, R Mirulla, F Rubik & R Wolff. Springer Verlag, Berlin, Germany.

Franklin, WE et al. (1972). *Project No. 35540.* Midwest Research Institute, Kansas City, Kansas, USA. (In Oberbacher et al. 1996.) Also as Franklin W & R Hunt (1972). *Environmental impacts of polystyrene and molded pulp meat trays. A summary.* Mobil Chemical Company, Macedon, NY, USA. (In Franklin & Hunt 1996)

Fraunhofer (1989). *Økosammenligning. Træslibbakke; bakke af skummet polystyren.* (Environmental comparison. Cellulose trays and trays of foamed polystyrene.) For Omni-Pac Ekco GmbH. Fraunhofer Institut, München, Germany.

Frischknecht, Rolf (1997). "Goal and scope definition and inventory analysis". In HA Udo de Haes & N Wrisberg (eds), *LCANET—European Network for Strategic Life Cycle Assessment Research and Development.* LCA Documents vol 1. Eco-Informa Press, Bayreuth, Germany.

Gabathuler, Heinz (1997). "The CML Story. How Environmental Sciences Entered the LCA Debate". *International Journal of LCA*, vol 2, no 4, pp 187–194.

Gäbel, Karin, Peter Forsberg & Anne-Marie Tillman (2003). "Life-cycle based process model for simulating environmental performance, product performance and cost in cement production." *Journal of Cleaner Production*, vol 12, no 1, pp 77.

Gattorna, JL & DW Walters (1996). *Managing the supply chain.* Macmillan Press, Basingstoke, UK.

Gelderman, Jutta, Christina Jahn, Thomas Spengler & Otto Rentz (1999). "Proposal for an integrated approach for the assessment of cross-media aspects relevant for the determination of 'best available technologies' (BAT) in the European Union." *International Journal of LCA*, vol 4, no 2, pp 94–106.

GEN (1999). *The ecolabelling guide.* Global Ecolabelling Network.

Goedkoop, Mark & Renilde Spriensma (1999). *The Eco-indicator'99. A damage oriented method for Life Cycle Impact Assessment. Methodology Report (Oct 1999).* PRé Consultants, Amersfoort, NL.

Goedkoop, Mark, Patrick Hofstetter, Ruedi Müller-Wenk & Renilde Spriemsma (1998). "The Ecoindicator'98 explained". *International Journal of LCA*, vol 3, no 6, pp 352–360.

Graedel, Thomas E (1998). *Streamlined life cycle assessment.* Prentice-Hall, Upper Saddle River, NJ, USA.

Guinée, Jeroen B (1995). *Development of a methodology for the environmental life-cycle assessment of products. With a case study on margarines.* PhD thesis, Leiden University, the Netherlands.

Guitouni, Adel & Jean-Marc Martel (1998). "Tentative guidelines to help choosing an appropriate MCDA method". *European Journal of Operational Research*, vol 109, pp 501–521.

Hannon, Bruce M (1972). *System Energy and Recycling: A Study of the Beverage Container Industry.* ASME paper no 72-WA/Ener3. The American Society of Mechanical Engineers, New York, NY, USA.

Hanssen, Ole-Jørgen (1997). *Sustainable industrial product systems.* PhD thesis, Norwegian University of Science and Technology, Trondheim. AR 20.97 Østfold Research Foundation, Fredrikstad, Norway.

Harrison, Roy M (1990). *Pollution: Causes, effects & control.* 2nd edition. The Royal Society of Chemistry, Cambridge, UK.

Heiskanen, Eva (2000). *Translations of an Environmental Technique: Institutionalization of the Life Cycle Approach in Business, Policy and Research Networks.* A-178, Acta Universitatis Oeconomicae Helsingiensis, Helsinki School of Economics and Business Administration.

Hindle, Peter & Nick Tieme de Oude (1996). "SPOLD: Society for the Promotion of Life Cycle Development". *International Journal of LCA*, vol 1, no 1, pp 55–56.

Hoffman, Volker H, Konrad Hungerbühler & Gregory J McRae (2001). "Multi-objective screening and evaluation of chemical process technologies". *Industrial Chemical Engineering Research*, vol 40, pp 4513–4524.

Huijbregts, Mark (1999). *Life cycle impact assessment of acidifying and eutrophying air pollutants. Calculation of characterisation factors with RAINS-LCA.* Interfaculty Department of Environmental Science, University of Amsterdam, Amsterdam, NL.

Hunkeler, David, Gerald Rebitzer, Allan Astrup Jensen & Manuele Margni (2001). "Life Cycle Management: Bridging the gap between science and application. Report from LCM2001—first international conference on life cycle management." *International Journal of LCA*, vol 6, no, 6, pp 384–390.

Hunt RG & WE Franklin (1974). *Resource and environmental profile analysis of nine beverage container alternatives.* EPA report 530/SW-91c, US Environmental Protection Agency. (In Franklin & Hunt 1996)

Hunt, Robert G & Willam E Franklin (1996). "LCA—How it came about: Personal reflections on the origin and the development of LCA in the USA". *International Journal of LCA*, vol 1, no 3, pp 147–150.

Huppes, Gjalt & François Schneider (eds) (1994). Proceedings of the European Workshop on allocation in LCA. 24–25 February 1994, Leiden, the Netherlands. SETAC-Europe, Brussels, Belgium.

IntJLCA (2003). Links to LCA societies on the website of the International Journal of LCA. (http://www.scientificjournals.com, accessed February 2003.)

IPRE (1990). Brochure material. International Professional Association for Environmental Affairs.

IRIS (2000). *LCA software survey.* Industrial Research Institutes in Sweden (IRIS), participating institutes: IVF (IVF report 00824) Mölndal, IVL (report B1390) Stockholm, CPM & SIK (report SR 672) Göteborg, Sweden.

354

ISO (2003). International Organization for Standardization, Geneva, Switzerland. (http://www.iso.org, accessed February 2003)

ISO 14020 (2000). *Environmental labels and declarations—General principles.* International Organization for Standardization, Geneva, Switzerland.

ISO 14021 (1999). *Environmental labels and declarations—Self-declared environmental claims (Type II environmental labelling).* International Organization for Standardization, Geneva, Switzerland.

ISO 14024 (1999). *Environmental labels and declarations—Type I environmental labelling—Principles and procedures.* International Organization for Standardization, Geneva, Switzerland.

ISO/TR 14025 (2000). *Environmental labels and declarations—Type III environmental declarations.* International Organization for Standardization, Geneva, Switzerland.

ISO 14040 (1997). *Environmental Management—Life Cycle Assessment—Principles and framework.* International Organization for Standardization, Geneva, Switzerland.

ISO 14041 (1998). *Environmental Management—Life Cycle Assessment—Goal and Scope Definition and Inventory Analysis.* International Organization for Standardization, Geneva, Switzerland.

ISO 14042 (2000). *Environmental Management—Life Cycle Assessment—Life Cycle Impact Assessment.* International Organization for Standardization, Geneva, Switzerland.

ISO 14043 (2000). *Environmental Management—Life Cycle Assessment—Life Cycle Interpretation.* International Organization for Standardization, Geneva, Switzerland.

ISO/TS 14048 (2002). *Environmental management—Life cycle assessment—Data documentation format.* International Organization for Standardization, Geneva, Switzerland.

IVF (2000). *Miljöverktyg – en sammanställning av 17 metoder.* (Environmental tools. A compilation of 17 methods.) IVF report 00825, IVF Industrial Research and Development Corporation, Mölndal, Sweden.

Jödicke, Gerald, Oliver Zenklausen, André Weidenhaupt & Konrad Hungerbühler (1999). "Developing environmentally-sound processes in the chemical industry: a case study on pharmaceutical intermediates". *Journal of Cleaner Production*, vol 7, pp 159–166.

Jolliet, Olivier (1994). "Critical surface-time: an evaluation method for LCA". In *Proceedings of the 4ᵗʰ SETAC-Europe Congress*, 11–14 April 1994, Free University, Brussels, Belgium.

Jolliet, O & P Crettaz (1997). *Critical Surface-Time 95*. Swiss Federal Institute of Technology, Lausanne, Switzerland.

Jönsson, Åsa (1995). *Life cycle assessment of flooring materials. A case study and methodolocial considerations*. Licentiate thesis. TMP report 1995:3, Technical Environmental Planning, Chalmers University of Technology, Göteborg, Sweden.

Jönsson, Åsa, Anne-Marie Tillman & Torbjörn Svensson (1995). *Life-cycle assessment of flooring materials. A comparison of linoleum, vinyl flooring and solid-pine flooring*. Report A5:1995, Swedish Council for Building Research, Stockholm, Sweden.

Keoleian, Gregory A & Dan Menerey (1993). *Life cycle design guidance manual*. National Pollution Prevention Center, University of Michigan, Ann Arbor, MI, US.

Kerr, Wendy & Chris Ryan (2001). "Eco-efficiency gains from remanufacturing. A case study of photocopier remanufacturing at Fuji Xerox Australia." *Journal of Cleaner Production*, vol 9, pp 75–91.

Kremer, Markus, Gertraud Goldhan & Michael Heyde (1998). "Waste treatment in product specific life cycle inventories. An approach to material-related modelling. Part I: Incineration." *International Journal of LCA*, vol 3, no 1, pp 47–55.

Krozer, Joram (1992). *Decision model for Environmental Strategies of Corporations (DESC)*. TME, Haag, NL.

Kärnä, Anna (1999). *Managing environmental issues from design to disposal—a chain reaction? Experiences of product chain actors in the Finnish electrical and electronics industry*. Licentiate thesis, Department of Management, Helsinki School of Economics and Business Administration. SET, Federation of Finnish Electrical and Electronics Industry, Helsinki, Finland.

Lagerstedt, Jessica (2003). *Functional and environmental factors in early phases of product development—Eco-Functional Matrix*. PhD thesis. TRITA-MMK 2003:1, Department of Machine Design, Royal Institute of Technology, Stockholm, Sweden.

Lamming, R & J Hampson (1996). "The environment as a supply chain issue." *British Journal of Management*, vol 7 (special issue), pp S45–S62.

Landbank (1996). *Evaluating environmental interventions in Finland, Sweden and Norway.* Landbank Environmental Research & Consulting, London, UK.

LCANET (1997). *A strategic research programme for life cycle assessment. Final document for the concerted action LCANET (European Network for Strategic LCA Research and Development).* Authors/editors: N Wrisberg, HA Udo de Haes, R Clift, R Frischknecht, L Grisel, P Hofstetter, AA Jensen, L-G Lindfors, F Schmidt-Bleek & H Stiller. LCA documents vol 1. Eco-Informa Press, Bayreuth, Germany.

Lee, K M & Park (2001). "Application of life-cycle assessment to type III environmental declarations". *Environmental Management,* vol 28, no 4, pp 533–546.

Lewis, Helen & John Gertsakis (2001). *Design + environment. A global guide to designing greener goods.* Contributing authors: Tim Grant, Nicola Morelli & Andrew Sweatman. Greenleaf Publishing, Sheffield, UK.

Li, Jianzhi, Zong Gao & Hong J Zhang (2002). "Plug and play information sharing architecture and its application in green supply chain management." *Proceedings of the 2002 IEEE International Symposium on Electronics and the Environment,* pp 157–162.

LCInititiative (2003). *Draft final report of the LCI definition study (version 7a, March 2003).* The LCI program of the Life Cycle Initiative, UN Environmental Program & Society for Environmental Toxicology and Chemistry. Contributing authors: G Norris, P Notten, M-A Wolf, T Ramjeawan, T Grant, R Frischknecht, G Huppes, R Carlson, P Arena & H von Blotnitz. http://www.uneptie.org/pc/sustain/lcinitiative/, accessed April 2003.

Lippiatt, Barbara C & Amy S Boyles (2001). "Using BEES to select cost-effective green products." *International Journal of LCA,* vol 6, no 2, pp 76–80.

Ljunggren Söderman, Maria (2000). *A systems engineering approach to national waste management.* PhD thesis, Chalmers University of Technology, Göteborg, Sweden.

Lundin, Margareta (2003). *Indicators for measuring the sustainability of urban water systems—a life cycle apporach.* PhD thesis, Chalmers University of Technology, Göteborg, Sweden.

Luttrop, Conrad (1999). "Eco-design in early product development". *Proceedings of R'99, Recovery, Recycling, Reintegration,* Geneva, Switzerland.

MacLean, Heather L & Lester B Lave (2003). "Evaluating automobile fuel/propulsion system technologies." *Progress in Energy and Combustion Science*, vol 29, no 1, pp 1–69.

McAloone, Tim C (2000). *Industrial application of environmentally conscious design.* Professional Engineering Publishing, London, UK.

McLaren, Jake, Stuart Parkinsson & Tim Jackson (2000). "Modelling material cascades—frameworks for the environmental assessment of recycling systems." *Resources, Conservation and Recycling*, vol 31,pp 83–104.

Mazui, K, S Aizawa, T Sakao & A Inaba (2000). "Design for environment in early stage of product development using Quality Function Deployment." *Proceedings of Joint International Congress and Exhibition Electronic Goes Green 2000+, vol 1.* Technical Lectures, Berlin, Germany.

Meadows, DL & DH Meadows, J Randers & WW Behrens III (1972). *The Limits to Growth.* Universe Books, New York, NY, USA.

Meinders, Herman & Mariëlle Meuffels (2001). "Product chain responsibility. An industry perspective." *Corporate Environmental Strategy*, vol 8, no 4, pp 348–354.

Mellor, Warren, Elisabeth Wright, Roland Clift, Adisa Azapagic & Gary Stevens (2002). "A mathematical model and decision-support framework for material recovery, recycling and cascaded use." *Chemical Engineering Science*, vol 57, pp 4697–4713.

Miettinen, Pauli & Raimo P Hämäläinen (1997). "How to benefit from decision analysis in environmental life cycle assessment (LCA)." *European Journal of Operational Research*, vol 102, no 2, pp 279–294.

Mirza, R (1998). "A life cycle inventory tool for integrated waste management: A municipal focus". In J Sundberg, T Nybrant & Å Silvertun (eds), *Proceedings from the International Workshop Systems Engineering Models for Waste Management, Gothenburg, Sweden, February 1998.* AFR report 229, Swedish Environmental Protection Agency, Stockholm, Sweden.

Moberg, Åsa, Göran Finnveden, Jessica Johansson & Peter Steen (1999). *Miljösystemanalytiska verktyg. En introduktion med koppling till beslutssituationer.* (Environmental systems analysis tools. An introduction and in relation to decision making). AFR report 251,

Swedish Waste ResearchCouncil, Swedish Environmental Protection Agency, Stockholm, Sweden.

MRI (1977). *Resource and environmental profile analysis of Merlon polycarbonate refillable milk container systems including specific comparisons with selected competitive container systems.* MRI project 4382-D, final report December 9, 1977. Midwest Research Institute, Kansas City, Missouri, USA.

MSR (1999a*). Requirements for environmental product declarations (EPD). An application of ISO/TR 14025 Type III environmental declarations.* MSR 1999:2, AB Svenska Miljöstyrningsrådet (Swedish Environmental Management Council), Stockholm, Sweden.

MSR (1999b). *Produktspecifika utgångspunkter för certifierade miljövarudeklarationer för golvytmaterial, golvavjämning och golvlim.* PSR 1999:5, AB Svenska Miljöstyrningsrådet (Swedish Environmental Management Council), Stockholm, Sweden.

Müller-Wenk, Ruedi (1999). *Life cycle impact assessment of road transport noise.* IWÖ-diskussionsbeitrag nr 77, IWÖ-HSG, St Gallen, Switzerland.

Nagel, MH (2000). "Environmental supply-chain management versus life cycle analysis (LCA) method Ecoindicator'95: a relative business perspective versus an absolute environmental perspective." *Proceedings of the 2000 IEEE International Symposium on Electronics and the Environment,* pp 118–123.

Nagel, MH (2003). "Managing the environmental performance of production facilities in the electronics industry: much more than the application of the concept of cleaner production". *Journal of Cleaner Production,* vol 11, pp 11–26.

Narodoslawsky, Michael & Christian Krotshek (1995). "The Sustainable Process Index (SPI): Evaluating processes according to environmental comparability". *Journal of Hazardous Materials,* vol 41, pp 383–397.

Nielsen, Per, Stephan Exner, Anne-Mette Jørgennsen & Michael Hauschild (1998). "Product specific emissions for municipal solid waste landfills. Part II: Presentation and verification of the computer tool LCA-LAND." *International Journal of LCA,* vol 3, no 4, pp 225–236.

Nielsen, Per & Michael Hauschild (1998). "Product specific emissions for municipal solid waste landfills. Part I: Landfill model." *International Journal of LCA,* vol 3, no 3, pp 158–168.

NOH (1996). *The Ecoindicator'95 final report.* NOH report 9523, National Reuse of Waste Research Programme (NOH), the Netherlands.

Nord (1995). *Nordic guidelines on life-cycle assessment.* Contributing authors: Lars-Gunnar Lindfors, Kim Christiansen, Leif Hoffman, Yrjö Virtanen, Vesa Juntilla, Ole-Jørgen Hanssen, Anne Rønning, Tomas Ekvall & Göran Finnveden. Nord 1995:20, The Nordic Council of Ministers, Copenhagen, Denmark.

Nordic Ecolabelling (2002). *Ecolabelling of floorings. Criteria document.* Version 3.0, 14 March 2002-14 December 2002.

NTM (2002). *NTM – Nätverket för transporter och miljö* (The Network for Transport and the Environment), http://www.ntm.a.se, accessed March 2002.

Oberbacher, Bonifaz, Hansjörg Nikodem & Walter Klöppfer (1996). "LCA—How it came about: An early systems analysis of packaging for liquids". *International Journal of LCA*, vol 1, no 2, pp 62–65.

OECD (2002). *OECD governments agree to take the lead on buying "green".* News release 23 January 2002, Organisation for Economic Cooperation and Development, http://www.oecd.org.

Olesen, J (1997). "Environmental QFD—the creation of project focus". *Proceedings of the International Conferences on Engineering Design*, Tampere, Finland.

Ong, SK, TH Koh & AYC Nee (2001). "Assessing the environmental impact of materials processing techniques using an analytical hierarchy process method." *Journal of Material Processing Technology*, vol 113, no 1–3, pp 424–431.

Oterholm, B, Ø Løkkeberg & G Sundström (1994). *Livsløpsanalyse av ulike emballasjesystemer for konsummelkprodukter.* (LCA of different milk packaging options.) TINE Norwegian Dairies BA, Oslo, Norway.

Peattie, K (1992). *Green marketing.* Pitman Publishing, London, UK.

Pedersen, Claus Stig (2001). "What is new in LCM?" *1st International Conference on Life Cycle Management*, August 27–29, 2001, Copenhagen, Denmark, pp 3–6.

PEP (1991). *Produkters ekologi – från vaggan till graven.* (Product ecology—from cradle to grave.) Project application for the Product Ecology Project from Federation of Swedish Industries, Swedish Environmental Research Institute and Chalmers Industriteknik to the Swedish Waste Research Council, 14 October 1991.

Pergo (2000). *Certifierad miljövarudeklaration for Pergo Golv (Certified environmental product declaration for Pergo Golv)*. Registered by AB Svenska Miljöstyrningsrådet, registration number S-P-00007.

Pistikopoulos, EN & SK Stefanis (1998). "Optimal solvent design for environmental impact minimisation". *Computers and Chemical Engineering*, vol 22, no 7, pp 717–733.

Poole, Stephen & Matthew Simon (1997). "Technological trends, product design and the environment". *Design Studies*, vol 18, no 3, pp 237–248.

Potting, J, W Schöpp, K Blok & M Hauschild (1998). "Site-dependent life-cycle impact assessment of acidification." *Journal of Industrial Ecology*, vol 2, no 2, pp 63–87.

Powell, Jane C, David W Pearce & Amelia L Craighill (1997). "Approaches to Valuation in LCA Impact Assessment". *International Journal of LCA*, vol 2, no 1, pp 11–15.

Pålsson, Ann-Christin. (1999). *Introduction and guide to LCA data documentation using the CPM documentation criteria and the SPINE format*. CPM report 1999:1, Centre for Environmental Assessment of Products and Material Systems (CPM), Chalmers University of Technology, Göteborg, Sweden.

Rafenberg, Christophe & Eric Mayer (1998). "Life cycle of the newspaper 'Le Monde'." *International Journal of LCA*, vol 3, no 3, pp 131–144.

Ritzén, Sofia (2000). *Integrating environmental aspects into product development—proactive measures*. PhD thesis. TRITA-MMK 2000:6, Department of Machine Design, Design, Royal Institute of Technology, Stockholm, Sweden.

Rosander, Per (1992). "Tänk nytt och bli en vinnare!" (Think new and become a winner!) *Kemisk tidskrift*, no 10, p 42.

Ryding, Sven-Olof & Bengt Steen (1991). *EPS-systemet. Ett PC-baserat system för utveckling och tillämpning av miljöstrategiska prioriteringar i produktutvecklingen*. (The EPS system. A PC-based system for development and application of environmental priority strategies in product development.) IVL report B1022. The Swedish Environmental Research Institute (IVL), Göteborg.

Ryding, Sven-Olof (ed) (1995). *Miljöanpassad produktutveckling*. (Environmental product development.) Federation of Swedish Industries, Stockholm, Sweden.

Röder, Alexander (2001). *Integration of life cycle assessment and energy planning models for the evaluation of car powertrains and fuels.* PhD thesis, Diss ETH no 14291. Swiss Federal Institute of Technology, Zürich, Switzerland.

Sandars, DL, E Audsley, C Canate, TR Cumby, IM Scotford & AG Williams (2003). "Environmental benefits of livestock manure management practices and technology by life cycle assessment." *Biosystems engineering,* vol 84, no 3, pp 267–2281.

Sarkis, Joseph (2003). "A strategic decision framework for green supply chain management." *Journal of Cleaner Production,* vol 11, pp 397–409.

Saur, Konrad, Johannes Gediga, Jens Hesselbach, Manfred Schuckert & Peter Eyerer (1996). "Life cycle assessment as an engineering tool in the automotive industry." *International Journal of LCA,* vol 1, no 1, pp 15–21.

Schaltegger, S & A Sturm (1991). *Methodik der ökologischen Rechnungslegung in Unternehmen.* WWZ-studien nr 33, Wirtschaftswissenschaftliches Zentrum der Universität Basel, Basel, Switzerland.

Schlüter, Frank (2001). *On the integration of environmental aspects into early product development—life cycle design structure matrix.* Licentiate thesis. TRITA-MML 2001:02, Department of Machine Design, Royal Institute of Technology, Stockholm, Sweden.

Schmidt-Bleek, Friedrich (1994). *Wieviel Umwelt braucht der Mensch?: MIPS – das Mass für ökologisches Wirtschaften.* Birkhäuser Verlag, Berlin, Germany.

Schminke, E & M Prösler (2001). "Using LCA results in green marketing—a case study." *LCM 2001, 1st international conference on life cycle management,* Aug 27–29, 2001, Copenhagen, Denmark.

SETAC (1991). *A technical framework for LCA.* Report of the workshop in Smuggler's Notch, Vermont, 18–23 August 1990. Society of Environmental Toxicology and Chemistry & SETAC Foundation for Environmental Education, Washington, DC, USA.

SETAC (1992). *Life-cycle assessment.* Report from the SETAC workshop on LCA inventory, classification, valuation and databases, 2–3 December 1991, Leiden, the Netherlands. Society of Environmental Toxicology and Chemistry, Brussels, Belgium.

SETAC (1993). *Guidelines for life-cycle assessment: A 'Code of Practice'.* Editors: F Consoli, D Allen, I Boustead, J Fava, W Franklin, AA Jensen, N de Oude, R Parrish, R Perriman, D Postlethwaite, B

Quay, J Séguin, B Vigon. Society of Environmental Toxicology and Chemistry, Brussels, Belgium & Pensacola, FL, USA.

SETAC-Europe (1996). *Towards a methodology for life cycle impact assessment. Report from the SETAC-Europe working group on impact assessment.* Editor: HA Udo de Haes. Society of Environmental Toxicology and Chemistry, Brussels, Belgium.

SETAC-WIA2 (2001). *Impact assessment of resources and land use.* Editors: E Lindeijer, R Müller-Wenk & B Steen; Contributors: M Baitz, J Broers, C Cederberg, G Finnveden, M van Houten, T Köllner, B Mattson, J May, L Mila i Canals, I Renner & B Weidema.

Sharma, Vinod K (2000). "Wastepaper in Mumbai (India). An approach for abridged life cycle assessment." *International Journal of LCA*, vol 5, no 1, pp 12–18.

Singhofen, Axel (1996). *Introduction into a common format for life-cycle inventory data.* Status report, SPOLD, Brussels, Belgium.

Singhofen, Axel, Christine R Hemming, Bo P Weidema, Laurent Grisel, Rolf Bretz, Bea de Smet & David Russell (1996). "Development of a common format for life-cycle inventory data". *International Journal of LCA*, vol 1, no 3, pp 171–178.

Solér, Cecilia (1998). *Rekommendationer for kommunikation av miljömärkning typ III inom ramen för ISO14000. Rapport av steg 2.* (Recommendations for communication of ecolabelling type III in the ISO14000 framework. Report from step 2.) Göteborg Research Institute, School of Economics and Commercial Law, Göteborg University, Göteborg, Sweden.

Song, Hyun-Seob & Jae Chun Hyun (1999). "A study on the comparison of the various waste management scenarios for PET bottles using the life-cycle assessment (LCA) methodology." *Resources, Conservation and Recycling*, vol 27, pp 267–284.

SOU (1989). *Miljöprojekt Göteborg: för ett renare Hisingen.* (Environmental reform project Göteborg: for a cleaner Hisingen.) Statens offentliga utredningar, Allmänna förlaget, Stockholm, Sweden.

Sousa, Inês, Julie L Eisenhard & David Wallace (2000). "Approximate life cycle assessment of product concepts using learning systems". *Journal of Industrial Ecology*, vol 4, no 4, pp 61–81.

Steen, Bengt (1999a). *A systematic approach to environmental priority strategies in product development (EPS). Version 2000—General system characteristics.* CPM report 1999:4, Centre for Environmental

Assessment of Products and Material Systems, Chalmers University of Technology, Göteborg, Sweden.

Steen, Bengt (1999b). *A systematic approach to environmental priority strategies in product development (EPS). Version 2000—Model and data of the default method.* CPM report 1999:5, Centre for Environmental Assessment of Products and Material Systems, Chalmers University of Technology, Göteborg, Sweden.

Steen, Bengt, Raul Carlson & Göran Löfgren (1995). *SPINE, a relation database structure for life cycle assessment.* IVL report B 1227, Swedish Environmental Research Institute (IVL), Göteborg, Sweden.

Steen, Bengt & Sven-Olof Ryding (1992). *The EPS Enviro-Accounting Method. An application of environmental accounting principles for evaluation and valuation in product design.* IVL report B1080, The Swedish Environmental Research Institute (IVL), Göteborg. Also as AFR report 11, Swedish Waste Research Council (AFR), Stockholm, Sweden.

Stefanis, SK, AG Livingston & EN Pistikopoulos (1995). "Minimizing the environmental impact of process plants: A process systems methodology". *Computers and Chemical Engineering,* vol 19 (suppl), pp S39–S44.

Stefanis, SK, AG Livingston & EN Pistikopoulos (1997). "Environmental impact considerations in the optimal design and scheduling of batch processes". *Computers and Chemical Engineering,* vol 21, no 10, pp 1073–1094.

Stevels, Ab (2002). "Green supply chain management: much more than questionnaires and ISO 14001." *Proceedings of the 2002 IEEE International Symposium on Electronics and the Environment,* pp 96–100.

StoraEnso (2000). *Responsibility. Environmental report 2000.* StoraEnso Oyj, Helsinki, Finland.

Stumm, W & JJ Morgan (1981). Aquatic chemistry. Introduction emphasizing chemical equilibria in natural water (2nd ed). Wiley, New York, NY, US.

Suh, Sangwon (ed) 2001. *Proceedings of the European network on environmental input-output analysis. 1st meeting.* 8 May 2001, Madrid, Spain. CML, Leiden University, Leiden, The Netherlands. Downloadable from www.leidenuniv.nl/interfac/cml.

Sundberg, Johan & Claes-Otto Wene (1988). "Mimes—a model for integrating the material flow with the energy system." In M Korhonen (ed), *Proceeding from VTT symposium on non-waste technology, Espoo, Finland 20–23 1988.* Technical Research Centre of Finland, Espoo, Finland.

Sundbom Ridderstråle, Ulrika (1996). *Life cycle assessment in marketing—a survey of the present situation.* TEP report 1996:12, Technical environmental planning, Chalmers University of Technology, Göteborg, Sweden.

Sundqvist, Jan-Olof, Göran Finnveden, Håkan Stripple, Ann-Christine Albertsson, Sigbritt Karlsson, Jaak Berendson & Lars-Olof Höglund (1997). *Life Cycle Assessment and Solid Waste—Stage 2.* AFR report 173, Swedish Environmental Protection Agency, Stockholm, Sweden.

Sundström, Gustav (1979). *Mjölkförpackningarna och energin.* (Milk-packaging and energy.) G Sundström AB, Malmö, Sweden.

Sundström, Gustav (1989). *Energiförbrukningen för bärkassar av polyeten och papper.* (Energy consumption of carrier bags of polyethylene and paper.) G Sundström AB, Malmö, Sweden.

Sundström, Gustav (1989). *Luftföroreningar vid tillverkning och distribution av bärkassar av polyeten och papper.* (Emissions to air from the production and distribution of carrier bags of polyethylene and paper.) G Sundström AB, Malmö, Sweden.

Sundström, Gustav (1989). *Vatten föroreningar vid tillverkning och distribution av bärkassar av polyeten och papper.* (Water emissions from the production and distribution of carrier bags of polyethylene and paper.) G Sundström AB, Malmö, Sweden.

Sundström, Gustav (1990). *Energiförbrukning och miljöbelastning för distributionssystem för öl och läsk i Sverige.* (Energy consumption and environmental loads of distribution of beer and soft drinks in Sweden.) Swedish Brewery Association, Stockholm, Sweden.

Sundström, Gustav (2002). Personal communication, 13 February 2002. Bjärred, Sweden.

SustainAbility (1993). *The LCA sourcebook. A European guide to life-cycle assessment.* Published in collaboration with the Society for the promotion of LCA development (SPOLD) and Business in the Environment. SustainAbility Ltd, London, UK.

Suzuki, Haruo (1998). "Development of life cycle assessment software 'Easy-LCA'." *Nihon Enerugi Gakkaishi/Journal of the Japan Institute of Energy,* vol 77, no 10, pp 974–980.

Tellus (1992). *The Tellus packaging study.* Tellus Institute, Boston, MA, US.

Tillman, Anne-Marie (2000). "Significance of decision making for LCA methodology". *Environmental Impact Assessment Review,* vol 20, no 1, pp 113–123.

Tillman, Anne-Marie, Henrikke Baumann, Elin Eriksson & Tomas Rydberg (1991). *Miljön och förpackningarna. Livscykelanalyser av förpackningsmaterial.* SOU 1991:77, Statens offentliga utredningar, Allmänna Förlaget, Stockholm, Sweden. Also as *Life cycle analysis of selected packaging materials. Quantification of environmental loadings.* Translation of SOU 1991:77. Chalmers Industriteknik, Göteborg, Sweden 1992.

Tillman, Anne-Marie, Tomas Ekvall, Henrikke Bauman & Thomas Rydberg (1994*).* "Choice of system boundaries in life cycle assessment." *Journal of Cleaner Production,* vol 2, no 1, pp 21–29.

Tillman, Anne-Marie & Torbjörn Svensson (1993). *Miljökonsekvenser av ny energiteknik. Solceller, absorptionsvärmepumpar, energihushållning.* (Environmental consequences of new energy technology. Photovoltaics, heat pumps, energy saving methods.) BFR T4:1993, Byggforskningsrådet, Stockholm, Sweden.

Tillman, Anne-Marie, Mikael Svingby & Henrik Lundström (1998). "Life cycle assessment of municipal waste water systems." *International Journal of LCA,* vol 3, no 3, pp 145–157.

Todd, Joel Ann (1997). "The application of the LCA concept to environmental procurement/environmental shopping." *Proceedings of the Air & Waste Management Association's 90th Annual Meeting,* June 8–13, 1997, Toronto, Ontario, Canada.

Tolbert, Pamela S & Lynne G Zucker (1996). "The institutionalisation of institutional theory". In Stewart R Clegg, Cynthia Hardy & Walter R Nord (eds), *Handbook of Organization Studies,* chapter 1.6, pp 175–190. Sage, London, UK.

Tsoulfas, Giannis T, Costas P Pappis & Stefan Minner (2002). "An environmental analysis of the reverse supply chain of SLI batteries." *Resources, Conservation and Recycling,* vol 36, no 2, pp 135–154.

Tukker, Arnold (1999). "Life cycle assessments for waste, part I: Overview, methodology and scooping process. Strategic EIA for the Dutch national hazardous waste management plan 1997–2007". *International Journal of LCA,* vol 4, no 5, pp 275–281.

366

Tukker, Arnold, Erik Haag & Peter Eder (2000). *Eco-design: European state of the art. Part I: Comparative analysis and conclusions.* EUR19583EN, European Commission Joint Research Centre, Institute for Prospective Technological Studies, Sevilla, Spain.

Udo de Haes, Helias A, et al. (1994). *Guidelines for the application of life-cycle assessment in the European Union ecolabelling programme.* SPOLD, Brussels, Belgium.

Udo de Haes, Helias A, Olivier Joilliet, Gregory A Norris & Konrad Saur (2002). "Backgrounds, aims and scope." *International Journal of LCA*, vol 7, no 4, pp 192–195.

Ulrich, Karl T & Steven D Eppinger (1995). *Product design and development.* McGraw-Hill, New York, NY, US.

UNEP/SETAC (2000). *The Life Cycle Initiative—Letter of intent*, signed May 21, 2000. (http://www.uneptie.org/pc/sustain/lca/lcini.htm)

US Federal Register (1998). "Executive order 13101. Greening the government through waste prevention, recycling and federal acquisition." *Federal register*, vol 63, no 179, pp 49643–49651.

US-EPA (1993). Life-Cycle *Assessment: Inventory Guidelines and Principles.* US Environmental Protection Agency, USA.

Van Hemel, GG (1995). "The LiDS wheel". In Brezet, H & C van Hemel (1997), *Ecodesign—a promising approach to sustainable production and consumption.* United Nations Environment Programme, Industry and Environment, Paris, France.

van Eijk, J, JW Nieuwenhuis, CW Post & JH de Zeeuw (1991*). Reusable vs. Disposable—a comparison of the environmental impact of polystyrene, paper/cardboard and porcelain crockery.* Materials and risk assessment no 1991:2, Ministry of housing, physical planning and environment (VROM), Deventer, the Netherlands.

Vanek, Francis M & Edward K Morlok (2000). "Improving the energy efficiency of freight in the United States through commodity-based analysis: justification and implementation." *Transportation Research part D: Transport and Environment*, vol 5, no 1, pp 11–29.

VCNI (1991). *Integrated substance chain management.* Verniging Nederlandse Chemische Industrie, Leidschendam, NL.

Verschor, AH & L Reijnders (1999). "Notes from the field. The use of life cycle methods by seven major companies." *Journal of Cleaner Production*, vol 7, pp 375–382.

Viotti, Paulo, Silvio Di Cesare & Luciano Cavalli (1997). "Application of LCI: Environmental profile of LAB and detergent alcohols". *International Journal of LCA*, vol 2, no 2, pp 116–120.

Volkswagen (2001/2002). *Environmental report 2001/2002. Mobility and Sustainability.* Volkswagen AG, Wolfsburg, Germany.

Wackernagel M & W Rees (1996). *Our Ecological Footprint. Reducing human impact on the Earth.* New Society Publishers, Gabriola Island, Canada.

Wandén, Stig (1993). *Ideologiska kontroverser i miljövården.* (Ideological controversies in the care of the environment.) SNV report 4196, Swedish Environmental Protection Agency, Stockholm.

Weidema, B P (1998). "Application typologies for life cycle assessment—A Review." *International Journal of LCA*, vol 3, no 4, pp 237–240.

Weidema, Bo P (1997). *Environmental assessment of products. A textbook on life cycle assessment.* The Finnish Association of Graduate Engineers (TEK), Helsinki, Finland.

Weitz, Keith, Morton Barlaz, Ranji Ranjithan, Downey Brill, Susan Thorneloe & Robert Ham (1999). "Life cycle assessment of municipal solid waste." *International Journal of LCA*, vol 4, no 4, pp 195–201.

Wenzel, Henrik & Michael Hauschild (1998*). Environmental assessment of products (vol 2). Scientific background.* Chapman & Hall, London.

Wenzel, Henrik, Michael Hauschild & Leo Alting (1997). *Environmental assessment of products. Volume 1: Methodology, tools and case studies in product development.* Chapman & Hall, London, UK.

Westkämper, E, L Alting & G Arndt (2001). "Life cycle management and assessment: approaches and visions towards sustainable manufacturing." *Proceedings of the Institution of Mechanical Engineers*, vol 215 (part B), pp 599–626.

Wheelwright, Steven C & Kim B Clark (1992). *Revolutionizing product development. Quantum leaps in speed, efficiency and quality.* The Free Press, New York, NY, USA.

WICE (1994). *Life cycle assessment.* World Industry Council for the Environment, the International Chamber of Commerce, Paris, France.

Wilson, B & B Jones (1994). *The Phosphate report.* Landbank Environmental Research & Consulting, London, UK.

White, PR, M Franke & P Hindle (1995). *Integrated Solid Waste Management: A Lifecycle Inventory.* Blackie Academic and Professional, London, UK.

Wrisberg, Nicoline, Helias A Udo de Haes, Ursula Triebswetter, Peter Eder & Roland Clift (2000). *Analytical tools for environmental design and management in a systems perspective. The combined use of analytical tools.* Report from the EU Concerted Action CHAINET. Kluwer Academic Publishers, Dordrecht, the Netherlands.

Young, Alex & Aleksandra Kielkiewicz-Young (2001). "Sustainable supply network management." *Corporate Environmental Strategy,* vol 8, no 3, pp 260–268.

Exercises

Here follow a number of exercises, both smaller and larger ones.

You should start with the smaller ones (exercises A to G) since they prepare you for the larger ones, ten complete LCA exercise projects (H1 to H10). The smaller ones (exercises A to G) train different aspects of LCA methodology and follow up on the different chapters in the methodology part of the book.

The smaller exercises consist of the following:

Exercise A on functional unit definition and exercise B on goal and scope definition can be carried out after having read chapter 3 (Goal and scope definition). Exercise C, Beginner's LCA, and exercise E on allocation follow up on chapter 4 (Inventory analysis). Exercise D on data documentation builds both on chapter 4 and chapter 8 (Data management). Exercise F is an exercise in classification, which is a part of life cycle impact assessment, the topic of chapter 5 (Life cycle impact assessment). Chapter 7 (Critical review) prepares you for exercise G on critical review, which requires finding and reading an LCA report.

There are solutions to some of the smaller exercises towards the end of the book.

The larger exercises consist of exercise projects. These are complete LCA projects, based on real LCA studies, with all the necessary data provided, but small enough so that they can be calculated by hand and with the help of simple spreadsheet software. The purpose is for students to be able to have full control over modelling, methodological choices and data. Data is somewhat dated but this has little importance for learning to execute LCA. Some general LCA data is provided in the data appendix.

There are 10 exercise projects, hopefully enough for a class. It is not necessary for a student to carry out all of them! Two to four students can work together on an exercise project.

Exercise A
Functional units

The functional unit is a central concept in LCA. It is a measure of the performance that the systems under study have in common. In addition to that, it is also a basis for the calculations. For this reason, the functional unit needs to be (quantitatively) measurable (see chapters 1 and 3).

A careful definition of the functional unit is important for all LCA applications, particularly where comparisons are involved. Think for example of LCA-based eco-labelling. The definition of the functional unit also defines what products can be included in the particular product group. Furthermore, thinking about what the function really is can be a starting point in a new product development process – what other product concepts can deliver the same type of function?

1 Define the functional unit for the following products/services. It may help to list different versions of the studied product (for example, buses, bicycles, etc in the case of people transportation). In some cases, you may come up with more than one functional unit depending on the number of properties/qualities of the product you want to specify.

- Soft drink packaging
- Light bulbs
- Waste management options for discarded cardboard boxes from a large furniture store
- Wall paper/paint
- Newspapers
- People transportation
- Goods transportation

- Clothes washing
- Shoes
- Bread

2 Given the function of the products listed above, can you think of other ways of providing those functions? Will the functional unit have to be modified?

Exercise B
Goal and scope definition

This exercise takes you through the different steps of a goal and scope definition. It will require you to make all sorts of methodological choices, both those relating to modelling and those relating to procedure. The goal and the context, however, will largely be given to you. The exercise places you in the role of an LCA analyst, working out the goal definition of an LCA study on newsprint.

The exercise comes in two versions, B1 and B2. Both versions are based on the same technical systems (newsprint production, use and disposal). They differ with respect to the perspective from which the product is being studied. B1 takes a national perspective, whereas B2 takes a producer's perspective. When doing the exercise on your own, you may choose either of the two. When doing the exercise with a full class it is useful if half the class does B1 and the other half B2. In a following discussion the results and reasoning can be contrasted.

First, a technical background on newsprint production is presented. The two versions of the exercise, B1 and B2, are presented next.

Technical background on newsprint production

Newsprint is produced from mechanical pulp and/or recycled newsprint. Mineral fillers are also added. The main raw materials are the following:

- Groundwood, which is produced by grinding logs at atmospheric pressure and under wet conditions. The pulp yield is high but so is electricity consumption.
- Thermo-mechanical pulp (TMP), which is produced by grinding wood chips in refiners. Also this process gives a high pulp yield. The electricity consumption is high, but as the refining takes place under pressure part of the energy can be recovered as steam.
- Recycled fibres produced through de-inking collected newspapers. Fibres are separated from ink and mineral fillers, which, together with some lost fibres, are removed as a sludge. The sludge is incinerated and the energy used to supply steam.

Newsprint is usually produced in integrated mills, which means that pulp production and paper production takes place in the same mill without the pulp being dried before being converted to paper. The main energy inputs are the following:

- Electricity for production of mechanical pulp.
- Energy for drying the newsprint. The energy is supplied as steam, often originating from refiners or from burning bark and/or de-inking sludge. Such by-product energy is, however, not enough. Additional energy is needed and usually supplied by fossil fuels.

The main environmental impacts associated with newsprint production are emissions to water and energy use (steam for drying and electricity). Air emissions originate from the energy production.

There are mills producing newsprint from virgin raw materials only, and there are mills that use recycled paper as their main raw material. There are also mills using a mixture of the two. It should be noted that a certain input of virgin fibres is needed when looking at the market as a whole, since fibres are inevitably degraded and lost.

B1. Newsprint recycling

Goal definition and context

National authorities are working to prepare regulation on waste management and recycling for a number of different products. For newsprint, two waste management options have been identified as environmentally better than others, recycling and incineration with energy recovery. Different actors such as waste management companies, newsprint producers and environmentalists argue for either of the options, largely with environmental arguments. So now the authority comes to you, the LCA analyst, to get an "objective" and quantitative environmental assessment of the two options.

Choose for yourself in which country to place the study.

1 Formulate the *question* of the commissioner as precisely as possible.

Scope and modelling requirements

2 Express clearly which *alternatives* are to be compared.

3 Draw a *flowchart* showing what processes and transportation activities need be modelled in order to answer the question. Try not to make the flowchart too full of detail at this stage. You can fill in details later during the inventory analysis. Think about whether there are parts of the life cycle that can be omitted.

4 Decide on a *functional unit*. Think not only about the fact that the functional unit must be expressed in quantitative metrics but also about relating it to a specific flow in the flowchart (i.e. *which* flow is the reference flow). Since you are comparing different options, think also about whether there are qualitative differences between how well the alternative technical systems fulfil their functions. If yes, how do you suggest dealing with such differences?

5 Impact categories and impact assessment

a) Decide on which *impact categories* are to be considered. Will your strategy be to make the study "as complete as possible" or can you concentrate on certain types of environmental impact and leave the rest out?

b) Suggest, on a general level, how to *present and interpret* the results. Do you think inventory results will be enough and the most meaningful to draw conclusions from, or do you think that it will be a better option to present characterisation results of even weighted one-dimensional results?

6 What *type of LCA* is this? Is it a change-oriented study, designed to describe the consequences of alternative ways of action or is it mainly concerned with accounting for the environmental impact related to newsprint?

7 Geographical system boundaries.

a) Should environmental impact caused by newsprint being exported from the studied country be included?

b) Some of the chemicals used are imported. Should the environmental impact of producing them be included?

c) Emissions from processes in the studied country cause environmental impacts in other countries. Should such impacts be included?

8 What is the *time horizon* of the study, with respect to the technical system being modelled? Years, decades or centuries? Are you looking forward or backwards in time?

9 Should environmental impact from forestry be included in the study? This question concerns *system boundaries between technical and natural systems*. Are there more such boundaries to be drawn that may be critical for the outcome of the study? Which ones?

10 Increased recycling or increased incineration would probably require that additional recycling or incineration capacity be installed. Will you include the environmental impact of producing this *capital goods?* Why or why not? Are there other capital investments the production of which need be included?

11 One of the *allocation problems* in this study concerns incineration. Energy from incineration can be used for heat or electricity production, or combined heat and power production. For simplicity, assume that it will be used for electricity production only. Make decisions on the following, and motivate your choices:

   a) Should the environmental impact from incineration be split between its two functions waste treatment and power production, or should the system be enlarged in such a way that the newsprint system is credited with avoided power production elsewhere?

   b) If you have chosen to split the impact of incineration between waste treatment and power production, decide on what basis the allocation will be made.

   c) If you have chosen system enlargement, decide in greater detail how to model the avoided electricity production, average production mix or marginal production?

12 What *type of data* will you preferably use in the study? Choose between international sector averages or national averages or site specific data for the following processes:

   a) Virgin newsprint production
   b) Incineration
   c) Recycling process

13 You have now made the main methodological choices related to the modelling ahead of you. You have made them in order to answer the question posed under 1. Now, summarise what will be the main *limitations* of your study. In other words, try to be specific about what answers the study will *not* provide.

Procedural aspects

14 What type of review process, if any, will be required for your study? Would you prefer to have reviewers follow the project as it proceeds or would it be better to have the report reviewed afterwards? What kind of people need be involved, LCA experts or experts on the technologies at stake? Or rather people representing the different stakeholders?

15 How do you plan to find the data for your study?

16 What kind of reporting do you suggest? A detailed, fully transparent LCA report or only a summary? Do you think the report should be made public? If so, in what form should it be published, as a full report or only a summary?

17 Depending on your suggestion for reporting, what kind of confidentially issues can you foresee and how do you suggest dealing with them?

B2. Newsprint production

Goal definition and context

A newsprint producer is planning its very first LCA and has turned to you, the LCA analyst, to carry out the study. The producer is a big international producer, with several production units for newsprint located in different countries. It has mills producing newsprint from virgin fibres as well as mills producing from recycled fibres.

Being a large company in a sector often exposed to environmental pressures of varying kinds, the company is of course well aware that LCA is available, but they have not used it before. They have quite clear ideas about the main applications of LCA, and if this first pilot project goes well they have a plan for how they want to use LCA in a longer time perspective. In this first LCA they want to test the instrument, and confirm that LCA can supply information for a variety of purposes, among which are the following:

• Building up their own knowledge about the product's life cycle, its environmental strengths and weaknesses.
• Internal process and product development needs. There are a large number of possible changes to the production that may be undertaken and with an LCA model at hand the commissioner hopes to be able to assess their environmental performance in a structured cost-efficient way. Examples of such possible developments are changed raw material composition, recycling not only of fibres but also of mineral fillers, and a variety of ways to reduce energy use in production.

380

- Market communication. There are already customers asking very specific questions about the environmental performance of the newsprint and the company must be prepared to answer them. Some of the questions asked can only be answered through applying a life cycle perspective. For the future, they want to be prepared to publish an environmental product declaration.

Since this is a pilot project there are strict budget constraints. It will not be possible to assemble data for all the different newsprint mills of the company. Instead the idea is to make a strategic selection of a few mills on which to base the study. The commissioner has already decided that they want to include their largest and most modern mill in Finland, which uses only virgin fibres and exports most of its produce, and a large unit in France, which bases its production entirely on recycled paper.

1 As you have seen, the commissioner has many different questions at once. As there are budget constraints, you as an analyst must suggest a limited study. Try to formulate a specific *question* that will answer as many of the commissioner's needs as possible. At the same time, the question must not lead to a too comprehensive LCA study.

Scope and modelling requirements

2 Draw a *flowchart* showing what processes and transportation activities need be modelled in order to answer the question. Try not to make the flowchart too full of detail at this stage. You can fill in details later during the inventory analysis. Think about whether there are parts of the life cycle that may be omitted.

3 Decide on a *functional unit*. Think not only about the fact that the functional unit must be expressed in quantitative metrics but also about relating it to a specific flow in the flowchart (i.e. *which* flow is the reference flow). If you are comparing different options, think about whether there are qualitative differences between how well the alternatives fulfil the function. If there are, how do you suggest dealing with them?

4 Impact categories and impact assessment

   a) Decide on which impact categories are to be considered. Will your strategy be to make the study "as complete as possible" or can you concentrate on certain types of environmental impact and leave the rest out?

   b) On a general level decide on how to present and interpret the results. Do you think inventory results will be enough and the most meaningful to draw conclusions from, or do you think that it will be a better option to present characterisation results of even weighted one-dimensional results?

5 What *type of LCA* is this? Is it a change-oriented study, designed to describe the consequences of alternative ways of action or is it mainly concerned with accounting for the environmental impact related to newsprint?

6 Geographical system boundaries.

   a) Should environmental impact caused by newsprint being exported from Finland and France be included?

   b) Some of the chemicals used are imported. Should the environmental impact of producing them be included?

   c) Emissions from the mills in Finland and France cause environmental impacts in other countries. Should such impacts be included?

7 What is the *time horizon* of the study with respect to the technical system being modelled? Years, decades or centuries? Are you looking forward or backwards in time?

8 Should environmental impact from forestry be included in the study? This question concerns *system boundaries between technical and natural systems*. Are there more such boundaries to be drawn that may be critical for the outcome of the study? Which ones?

9 Will you include the environmental impact of producing the *capital goods* (production units, vehicles for transportation, etc) necessary for the life cycle of the newsprint? Why or why not?

10 Some of the newsprint will end up in incineration, while other portions will be dumped in landfill sites or recycled. One of the

allocation problems in this study concerns incineration. Energy from incineration can be used for heat or electricity production, or combined heat and power production. For simplicity, assume that it will be used for electricity production only. Make decisions on the following and motivate your choices:

a) Should the environmental impact of incineration be split between its two functions waste treatment and power production, or should the system be enlarged in such a way that the newsprint is credited with avoided power production elsewhere?

b) If you have chosen to split the impact of incineration between waste treatment and power production, decide on what basis the allocation will be made.

c) If you have chosen system enlargement, decide in greater detail how to model the avoided electricity production, average production mix or marginal production?

11 What *type of data* will you preferably use in the study? Choose between international sector averages or national averages or site specific data for the following processes:

a) Virgin newsprint production.
b) Incineration.
c) Recycling process.

12 You have now made the main methodological choices related to the modelling ahead of you. You have made them in order to answer the question posed under 1. Now, summarise what will be the main *limitations* of your study. In other words, try to be specific about what answers the study will *not* provide.

Procedural aspects

13 What type of review process, if any, will be required for your study? Would you prefer to have reviewers follow the projects as it proceeds or would it be better to have the report reviewed afterwards? What kind of people need be involved, LCA experts or experts on the technologies at stake? Or rather people representing different stakeholders?

14 How do you plan to find the data for your study?

15 What kind of reporting do you suggest? A detailed, fully transparent LCA-report or only a summary? Do you think the report should be made public? If so, in what form should it be published, as a full report or only a summary?

16 Depending on your suggestion for reporting, what kind of confidentially issues can you foresee and how do you suggest dealing with them?

Exercise C
A beginner's introduction to LCA

This exercise is a very simple LCA. Its purpose is to take you through all the important steps of carrying out an LCA.

The example in the exercise represents a simplified industrial system producing a product made of metal. Production data have been invented for hypothetical plants for the sake of the exercise. Furthermore, the industrial system in the exercise does not represent a full LCA from cradle-to-grave. Only parts of from cradle-to-gate are included.

Often an LCA is a comparison between two alternative products or scenarios. Here only one product/scenario is investigated. However, the calculations can be seen as part of a larger investigation for which the goal is to study the environmental impacts of different recycling rates.

In order to carry out the exercise it is necessary to start with step 1 and then work your way through the following steps since answers from earlier parts of the exercise are needed further on in the exercise. Tables with environmental data needed in the exercise are given towards the end of the exercise.

1. Drawing a flowchart

Consider the following industrial system:

The metal product P is produced in plant C, where metal sheets are cut and pressed to form the product P. Plant B delivers the metal sheets to plant C. In plant B, ingots are melted and rolled into sheets. The ingots come from plant A where mineral is extracted, turned into metal and cast into ingots. Plan A is situated 1 000 km from plant B and the metal is transported to B by truck. Plant B and plant C are neighbouring plants. Since the distance between them is small the transportation is negligible. In the production of P in plant C there is also some process scrap (pieces of metal clippings from the cutting of the metal sheets). The process scrap is sent back to plant B where it is melted together with the "new" metal and then rolled into sheets.

Draw a flowchart that includes all the activities in the system. Each plant is to be considered as an activity of its own. Also transportation is to be considered as an activity. It is not necessary to make a detailed description of all the process steps inside the plants. Represent the flow of material from plant to plant by arrows. Indicate what goes in (raw material) and what comes out (product) from each plant.

2. Data normalisation

Data normalisation means that inputs to and outputs from a plant are described in proportion to the main output of the plant, i.e. the product. In other words, how much resources (raw material and energy) are needed in order to produce one kg of the main product of the plant and how large are the emissions?

Normalise the data for plants A, B and C. The annual environmental report of each plant is given in the data section (towards the end of this exercise).

3. Calculating the flows linking the activities

Calculate the amount of raw materials and products for each plant (A, B and C) needed for producing 1 000 pieces of product P. Present the results in a table, listing the amount of input and output for each activity.

Calculating the material flows is the most important step when carrying out an LCA. Comparing different products (i.e. industrial systems) requires some careful consideration in order to make comparison possible. The definition of the functional unit and how the sizes of the material flows are calculated are important issues here.

'1 000 pieces of ...' is our functional unit. The functional unit is a computational unit of reference and it should "describe" the purpose of the industrial system (here, to produce P). The solution to the material balance shows how much material is needed from each step (i.e. plant) in order to produce one functional unit (= 1 000 pieces of P). The functional unit is also the basis for comparison – when comparing two industrial systems producing similar products both systems must have the same functional unit.

To calculate the flows linking the processes you need to set up an equation system which describes the relations between different flows. One of the equations is the one defining the functional unit. Here, with 4 activities in the flowchart there will be at least 4 equations. Solving the material balance means that you can answer questions such as "How much process scrap (in kg) is produced?", "How much metal needs to be rolled in plant B?", "How much metal is transported from A to B?", "How much raw material (the mineral) is needed in plant A?". Please note that the material balance for a plant as such (as given in the environmental report) is not necessarily the same as the material balance of an activity in relation to the functional unit. A plant usually has many customers and therefore some of the material is used to produce products other than the product under study (here P).

Each product P weighs 40 g. To produce 1 000 pieces of P, 6 m^2 of metal sheet is needed in plant C. The thickness of the metal sheet is 1.0 mm. The density of the metal is 8 000 kg/m^3.

4. Energy calculations

Calculate the amount of energy needed in order to produce one functional unit.

Different sorts of energy are added up separately. One can make a distinction between electricity and thermal energy, and between renewable and non-renewable energy resources or other categories. If electrical energy and thermal energy are to be summed, electrical energy has to be recalculated as primary energy, taking into consideration the efficiency of the electricity production. If this is not possible, then electricity and thermal energy are added up separately. In Sweden, electricity is mainly derived from hydroelectric (49 %)

and nuclear (45 %) sources. A small proportion (6 %) is obtained from incineration of fossil fuels. Thermal energy includes fossil fuels, biofuels and energy inherent in the material.

For transportation, energy requirements are treated in a standard way by multiplying energy requirements per tonne of load per kilometre for various kinds of transport by the distance involved.

Total energy requirement / functional unit =

$$= \sum_{\text{all plants}} \frac{\text{product flow from the plant}}{\text{functional unit}} \times \text{normalised energy requirement of the plant} +$$

$$+ \sum_{\text{all transports}} \text{standard transportation energy} \times \frac{\text{load}}{\text{functional unit}} \times \text{distance}$$

5. Emission factors

Sometimes the actual emissions from a process are not measured. This is the case for transportation and heat production in industry. Although emissions are not measured, when the fuel consumption is known the amount of pollutants can be calculated approximately using emission factors.

Identify the activities where emissions have not been measured. Calculate the amount of pollutants from these activities per functional unit. (Emission factors are listed in the data section towards the end of this exercise.)

6. Process emissions

By now energy requirements and non-measured emissions have been calculated and added up. Only process emissions remain. For each plant, the normalised process emissions are multiplied by the material flow required in proportion to the functional unit. Each pollutant, both measured and calculated, is then added up.

Present the total sum of emissions connected with the production of 1 functional unit in a table.

388

7. Impact assessment

It is often very difficult to compare two products, especially when their production gives rise to different emissions. For instance production of paper bags mainly give rise to emissions to water, while production of plastic bags mainly give rise to emission to air. In order to compare such alternatives, the emissions may be translated using environmental impact weighting indices. Each pollutant has an index with a certain number of environmental points. The indices are additive.

Make an impact assessment by calculating the total impact. The index list is in the data section towards the end of this exercise.

the total impact = Σ index × total emission
                   all emitted
                   pollutants

Environmental data for exercise C

Annual environmental report on Plant A

Products from Plant A:	Metal ingots (product A)
Raw material to Plant A:	Mineral (raw A)
Total annual production:	1 200 tonnes of A/year
Use of raw material:	4 800 tonnes raw A/year
Use of energy in the process:	12×10^6 MJ/year, from oil combustion
Emissions to air:	600 kg HCl/year (hydrochloric acid)
Emissions to water:	600 kg Cu/year (copper)
Non-hazardous solid waste:	3 800 tonne solid waste/year

Annual environmental report on Plant B

Product from Plant B: Metal sheets (product B)
Raw material to Plant B: Metal ingots and process scrap
Total annual production: 1 600 tonnes/year
Raw material – ingots: 900 tonnes/year
Raw material – scrap: 700 tonnes/year
Use of energy – smelting: 3.04×10^6 MJ electricity/year
Use of energy – rolling process: 1.76×10^6 MJ electricity/year
Emissions to air: 480 kg HC/year (hydrocarbons)

Emissions do not change with changes in the input-output ratio of metal ingots and process scrap.

Annual environmental report on Plant C

Product from Plant C: Consumer product P
Raw material to Plant C: Metal sheets
Total annual production: 400 tonnes P/year
Raw material, sheets: 480 tonnes/year
Use of energy: 0.3×10^6 MJ from oil/year
                                               1.2×10^6 MJ electricity/year
Emissions to air: 250 kg HC/year
Process scrap, metal for recycling: 80 tonnes/year

Transportation

Long distance transportation by truck requires 1.0 MJ/tonne-km (driving in city traffic requires 2.7 MJ/tonne-km). The fuel is diesel.

Energy Production

The energy production describes the amount of the different pollutants emitted due to combustion of a fuel. In this exercise, use the emission factors in the simplified table below.

390

Table C.1 Energy production (gram pollutant/MJ of fuel consumed)

Substance	Oil	Diesel
HC	0.018	0.208
NO_x	0.15	1.3
CO_2	79.8	78.6

Index list

Table C.2 Environmental impact indices according to the ecoscarcity method

Emission	Index (ecopoints/gram)
NO_x (NO_2)	6.31
CO_x (CO_2)	0.0248
HCl	6.31
HC (except CH_4)	9.751
Copper, Cu	5 917
Solid waste	0.167

Exercise D
Data collection and documentation

Environmental and technical data provide the basis upon which all LCA calculations are made. Data can be of many types, e.g. measured emission data from an industrial plant, estimates, industrial sector averages, calculated data, theoretical data, approximations based on similar technologies, worst case data, best case data and aggregated data. There are also many types of sources of data, e.g. process and emission reports of industrial processes, technical specifications, experts providing estimates, technical handbooks, LCA reports and LCA databases. The documentation of data needs to record all this and a little more … The advantages of well-documented data are that it allows a report that is transparent and possible to review by a third party and that the data can be used again in the future by other LCA analysts for other LCA studies.

In this exercise, you are to collect a data set and document it according to the ISO/TS 14048 data documentation format. It can be a set of data that fills a data gap or updates data in the exercise projects (H1-H10). For your help, data collection is described in chapter 4 and data documentation in chapter 8. Also, the empty ISO/TS 14048-based data form on the next three pages can be used. Please note that certain data fields are used several times, e.g. an identification number, direction, etc is given for *each* emission. For this reason, you may want to make several copies of that part of the data form.

Process description

Process	Name:	
Class	Name:	
	Reference:	
Quantitative reference	Type:	
	Name:	
	Unit:	
	Amount:	
Technical scope:		
Aggregation type:		
Technology	Short technology description:	
	Technical content & functionality:	
	Technology picture:	

	Process contents
	  Included processes:
	  Intermediate product flows
	  – Source process:
	  – Input & output source:
	  – Input & output destination:
	  – Destination process:	

	Operating conditions:	

	Mathematical model
	  Formulae:
	  Name of variable:
	  Value of variable:	

Valid time span	Start date:	
	End date:	
	Time-span description:	
Valid geography	Area name:	
	Area description:	
	Sites:	
	GIS:	
Data acquisition	Sampling procedure:	
	Sampling site:	
	No of sites:	
	Sample volume Absolute: Relative:	

Flows – inputs and outputs

Identification number:	
Direction (of flow):	
Group:	
Receiving environment:	
Receiving environment specification:	
Environment condition:	
Geographical location:	

Related external systems
    Origin of destination:
    Transport type:
    Information refer-
    ence:	

Internal location	

Name
    Substance name:
    Reference to nomen-
    clature:
    Name specification:	

Property
    Name of property:
    Unit of property
    Amount of property:	

Amount
    Name:
    Unit
    – Symbol:
    – Explanation:
    Parameter
    – Name:
    – Value:	

Mathematical relations
    Formulae:
    Name of variable:
    Value of variable:	

Documentation
    Data collection
    (methods):
    Collection date:
    Data treatment:
    Reference to data
    source:	

Modelling & validation

Intended application:	
Information sources:	

Modelling principles
    Data selection principles:
    Adaptation principles:
    Modelling constants
    – Name:
    – Value:	

Modelling choices
    Criteria for excluding
    elementary flows:
    Criteria for excluding inter-
    mediate product flows:
    Criteria for externalizing
    processes:
Allocations performed
    – Allocated co-products:
    – Allocation explanation:
Process expansion
    – Process included in
    expansion:
    – Process expansion
    explanation:	

Data quality statement:	

Validation
    Method:
    Procedure:
    Result:
    Validator:	

Other information:	

Administrative information

Identification number:	
Registration authority:	
Version number:	
Data commissioner:	
Data generator:	
Data documentor:	
Date completed:	
Publication:	
Copyright:	
Access restrictions:	

Exercise E
Allocation

Calculate the environmental load of 1 kg polyhypothene produced according to the flowsheet below. Use the allocation method based on economic value. The different products are sold at the following prices:

- Polyhypothene 7 €/kg
- Polyimaginene 25 €/kg
- Polyassumptene 15 €/kg

Process data

Extraction of resources and refinery

- Resources   1 kg crude oil (The energy content of the crude oil is 40 MJ/kg. Part of the crude oil is the raw material for the product. The remainder of the crude oil is used as an energy source in the process.)
- Product   0.5 kg polymer raw material
- Emissions   1.5 kg CO_2

Polymer production

Resources	5 kg polymer raw material
Products	3 kg polyhypothene
	1 kg polyimaginene
	1 kg polyassumptene
Emissions	3 g hydrocarbons (HC)

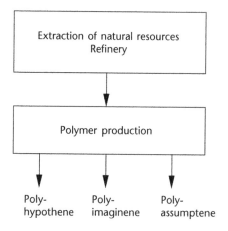

Exercise F
Impact assessment: classification

In table F.1 below, inventory results from an LCA study on flooring materials are presented (Jönsson 1995). The results presented were calculated for one square meter of linoleum flooring material used in Sweden. The estimated lifetime of the linoleum floor was 25 years. Wastes from laying it were incinerated with heat recovery. At the end of its life-time the linoleum flooring was also incinerated with heat recovery. Cleaning, care and maintenance were excluded from the study, which is why there are no data from these activities. The chief cause of each type of load is indicated in the table after the inventory data.

Classify the inventory result parameters in table F.1 according to the impact categories of the Nordic Guidelines (see table 5.1 in chapter 5 on impact assessment).

Table F.1 Total environmental load for 1 m^2 linoleum (2.556 kg, including waste from laying it) (Jönsson 1995).

Parameter	Amount	Source
Use of resources		
Acrylate	2.5 g	Raw material
Titanium oxide	102 g	Raw material
Limestone	460 g	Raw material
Resin	204 g	Raw material
Wood	767 g	Raw material
Cork	128 g	Raw material
Jute fibre	280 g	Raw material
Linseed	588 g	Raw material
K_2O	13.5 g	Raw material
P_2O_5	16.5 g	Raw material
Forest land	4.52 m^2 year	Fertiliser
Arable land	9.82 m^2 year	Fertiliser
Use of energy		
Electricity	16.3 MJ	Linoleum production (44 %), titanium oxide (30 %)
Fossil fuel	25 MJ	Linoleum production
Calorific value	45.2 MJ	
Recovered energy	−28.8 MJ	Incineration
Emissions to air		
CO_2	1 600 g	Linoleum production (58 %)
CO	1 060 mg	Transportation (80 %)
SO_2	4 300 mg	Transportation (62 %)
NO_x	12.8 g	Incineration (40 %), transportation (31 %), linoleum production (20 %)
VOC	5 870 mg	Linoleum production (87 %)
Solvents	3.12 g	Linoleum production
Terpenes	34.5 mg	Powdered wood
Dust	34.5	Powdered limestone (96 %)
Emissions to water		
Oil	2.38 mg	Fossil fuel refining
Phenol	0.034 mg	Fossil fuel refining
COD	6.96 mg	Fossil fuel refining
Tot-N	1.14 mg	Fossil fuel refining
Waste		
Ash	555 g	Incineration
Sector-specific waste	17.2 g	Jute fibre production
Hazardous waste	238 g	Titanium dioxide production

Exercise G
Critical review

This exercise puts you in the position of a critical reviewer of an LCA. The type of review is one where an external expert (you, in this exercise) reviews the final report of an LCA study. The commissioner has asked you to review the study with respect to the items marked in table G.1 and write a review statement on the study.

For the sake of the exercise, you will have to do the following. Find a report from an LCA study. It needs to be a "full" LCA report with methodological considerations and underlying data included. Review the report according to the items marked under "What" in table G.1 and write a review statement with your assessment on how the study stands up with respect to those aspects. Please observe that you are not asked to check the calculations and the validity of the data and that the commissioner is not concerned with whether or not the report conforms with the detailed ISO requirements on LCA reports. In more general terms the transparency of the report is of interest, however.

When doing the review, think especially about the following:

- Is the used methodology (functional unit, system boundaries and allocation procedures, impact assessment, type of data used, etc) relevant with respect to the purpose of the study? What assumptions are there with implications for the methodology?
- Are the conclusions valid, considering the numerical results, the limitations of the study, the uncertainty, etc? Are there any assumptions that limit what kind of conclusion may be drawn? What kinds of uncertainty and sensitivity analyses have been made?

Table G.1 Issues to be considered in the external critical review in this exercise.

		When	Mandatory ISO review	EPD review	Internal expert review	External expert review

What	Methods:
	– in line with norma-
	  tiva documents
	– relevant with respect
	  to goal definition
	– scientifically and
	  technically valid
						X
						
						X
						
						X

	Data – relevant – valid – documented					X – X
	Calculations correct					–

	Conclusions:
	– supported by study
	  results
	– within study limita-
	  tions
						X
						
						X

	Report:
	– transparent
	– in line with detailed
	  requirements in
	  standards
						X
						
						–

How	Interactive critical review					–
	Review of final report only					X

- Does the report contain all the information that would make it possible for someone else to repeat the study and come to the same results? Are the data and data sources reported? Are all assumptions in the report? Are all the methodological considerations in the report? Does it say anything about the computational procedures? When assessing transparency, remember that transparency does not necessarily mean that everything has to be in the actual report. It may also mean that the report refers to other documents that are transparent and available, for instance a report on how characterisation indicators were produced.

Exercise H
General introduction to LCA projects

Exercise H is an exercise in the skills to carry out LCA projects. It consists of several exercises exploring different kinds of material and waste management issues. In this introduction some general guidelines as to how the project should be conducted and reported are given. The objective of each exercise in this section is to conduct a "full" LCA. There are several different LCA projects to choose from:

Exercise H1   Roofing. Comparison of concrete tiles with clay tiles.
Exercise H2   Clay tiles. Comparison of single use with reuse.
Exercise H3   Concrete tiles. Comparison of single use with reuse.
Exercise H4   Polyethylene. Comparison of incineration and recycling.
Exercise H5   Polyethylene. Comparison of landfilling and recycling.
Exercise H6   Glass. Comparison of single use with material recycling.
Exercise H7   Glass. Comparison of single use with refilling.
Exercise H8   Linoleum. Choice of linseed oil supplier.
Exercise H9   Linoleum. Choice of waste management.
Exercise H10 Apples. Development of type III eco-labelling.

To make the LCA projects as realistic as possible, you are given the role of an LCA consultant working on behalf of various commissioners (national authorities, private companies and municipal authorities). As an LCA consultant you will have to make a number of methodological choices and assumptions to adapt your LCA to the given situation. You are expected to deliver a written report on the project to the commissioner. The overall requirement on the report is that it should be transparent and credible so that it can be reviewed by an external third party and so that the commissioner can use it when communicating with various stakeholders.

For educational reasons, the exercise is performed without special LCA software. Therefore, the exercises have been chosen and designed to involve a limited amount of data. The data may seem old, but it is useful for the sake of the exercise since the objective is to *carry out an LCA*.

Practical instructions

General inventory data (i.e. transportation data, energy data and waste management data) is presented in appendix 1. More specific data is presented in each exercise. Impact assessment data is presented in appendix 2 (characterisation indicators) and appendix 3 (weighting indices). References are listed towards the end of exercise H and in the appendices.

Exercise H1
Roofing. Comparison of concrete tiles with clay tiles

Context

A housing management company, owning and managing a number of apartment buildings, is in the process of introducing environmental issues into its operations in order to undergo environmental certification according to EMAS, to live up to commitments stated in the company environmental policy and to improve its environmental image. In the course of this process, the housing management company is considering what roofing material to use on its buildings.

404

Corrugated tin roofing was laid on all of the company's buildings, which were built between 1965–1970. The buildings are situated in suburban areas and the company is considering whether or not a style-changing refurbishment is an effective way to improve the popularity of the housing areas. Tile roofs are seen as a way to make the buildings more attractive. In any case, the tin roofing has corroded over the years and is in need of changing.

Task

Compare the two types of tiles, concrete ones and clay ones in order to determine which kind of tile is environmentally preferable.

Calculate the inventory tables for the two cases and evaluate with the different methods for impact assessment.

Discuss how stakeholders, i.e. other actors in the "roofing system" might react or be affected by your conclusions and recommendations concerning the choice of tiles. Examples of stakeholders are raw material producers, architects, building contractors, municipal waste companies and residents, to name a few.

Technical description

Tiles are used mainly to protect the house from rain. They need to be of a certain weight in order to withstand the wind. At the same time they should not be too heavy, the extra weight causing a need for a stronger construction. A concrete tile has an average weight of 4 kg per tile, while a clay tile weighs about 3 kg. In both cases, 10 tiles are needed for one m^2 roof. The two types of tiles can be said to have the same function and generally (but not always) one of the types can be replaced by the other type without altering the roof construction in other ways.

Concrete tiles

Concrete has three major components: aggregates, water and cement. The aggregates are usually a mixture of coarse and fine materials such as gravel, crushed stone and sand. The cement binds these aggregates together by combining chemically with water during a curing process.

After mixing cement, water and aggregates, the mixture is poured into forms to get its final shape. The tiles are then left for curing. This is done without adding extra heat.

Clay tiles

Baked clay and loam has been used as building material for at least 5000 years. The raw material is extracted from natural stores, which originate from aquatic deposits. The clay is shaped, dried and then baked at a temperature of 950–1 100 °C.

Production

Some of the data and descriptions given in the following text have been generalised and simplified in order not to complicate this exercise too much.

Concrete tiles

All data for production of concrete tiles are taken from one of the production units of Zanda (Rydell 1992), the most important producer of concrete tiles in Sweden. The tiles have the following composition per unit weight: sand 75 %, cement 20 % and iron oxide 5 %.

- Sand
  The sand comes from a local pit situated 12 km from the factory in Borensberg. It is taken from there by lorry. Such pits may sometimes affect groundwater. Extraction of sand consumes electrical energy at the rate of 18–20 kWh/tonne (Sundström 1990).

- Cement
  The cement is produced by the company Cementa in Skövde, 150 km from Borensberg. It is transported to Borensberg by truck. The main raw material used is limestone, taken from a limestone quarry close to the production unit. Explosives are used once or twice per week for quarrying (Björklund et al. 1996).

406

Raw materials

Explosives	0.27 g/kg
Gypsum	45.8 g/kg
Limestone	1361 g/kg
Quartzite	46 g/kg
Iron sulfate	9.2 g/kg

Energy

Oil	0.73 MJ/kg
Diesel	0.06 MJ/kg
Coal and petcoke	3.3 MJ/kg
Electricity	0.5 MJ/kg

Emissions to air

CO_2	806 g/kg
CO	0.8 g/kg
CH_4	0.3 g/kg
VOC	0.15 g/kg
NO_x	1.94 g/kg
SO_2	0.45 g/kg
Particulates	0.16 g/kg
Cr	1.7×10^{-5} g/kg

- Iron oxide
  Iron oxide is used for pigmentation. It is produced in Germany and is taken to Borensberg by truck (950 km) and ferry (230 km).

- Tile production at Zanda, Borensberg
  The annual production is around 10 million tiles. A production of this size has an energy use of 95 m^3 of oil and 4.2 million kWh of electricity. 2 % of the production is lost as waste. This is mainly landfilled but recycling within the tile production is under consideration. In addition, 50 m^3 of special oil is used as lubricant or loosening agent in moulding. This oil evaporates during the process. The moulds are made of aluminium and have a lifetime of 10–12 years. After that they are recycled. Each mould weighs 2.4 kg.

Clay tiles

Clay tiles consist of 100 % clay. The clay pit is about 5 km away from the manufacturing plant in Vittinge (Stålmalm 1992). The clay, which from the beginning has a water content of 40 % by weight, is excavated and transported to Vittinge by road. There the raw material is put in stock and mixed, to get an equal quality of the products. The electricity consumption of the process is 0.3 MJ/kg. Any remaining stones are crushed.

The clay is squeezed mechanically to its final shape, dried and finally baked in a tunnel oven for 3 days and nights. Before the baking, the density of the clay tile is approximately 2 500 kg/m^3 and after the baking it is approximately 1 800–2 000 kg/m^3. Oil is used as fuel for the oven as well as for the drying process. Approximately 2.4 MJ of oil is needed for producing 1 kg of tile.

Other data

The average time interval in Sweden today for exchanging concrete tiles and clay tiles is about 40 years (REPAB 1992). This lifetime is based on economics and maintenance intervals for roof constructions. The technical lifetime of the tiles is longer, approximately 80 years depending on quality and weathering.

Material losses caused by the transport and the building process are around 5 % for both kinds of tiles. According to the producers, waste from the production process could be re-entered in the tile production, but it is usually deposited in landfills.

- The average distance from tile producer to user is 150 km (by road).
- The average distance from user to final disposal is 30 km (by road). Tiles are generally disposed of in landfills.

Exercise H2
Clay tiles. Comparison of single use with reuse

Context

A city council is setting up a programme for "greening the city and its buildings". Part of this programme is to obtain environmental information on building materials and to formulate guidelines on what to do with various building wastes. The only waste management facility in the area is a landfill site. The idea of organising a second-hand market for building materials has been discussed in the city council. This requires new demolition procedures and the set-up of "pools" for various building materials and components. A building component has been selected for a pilot project. It is the clay tile. It is valuable as well as plentiful.

Task

The question asked by the commissioner was:

- What is the environmental impact of clay tiles?
- Is it environmentally preferable to reuse clay tiles, as compared to production from virgin raw materials? Compare the following alternatives:

  a) No reuse
  b) Build-up of a central storage facility and reuse of 50 % of the tiles once
  c) Build-up of a central storage facility and reuse of 80 % of the tiles once

Calculate inventory tables for the three cases and evaluate with the different methods for impact assessment. Calculate also the recycling rate with losses considered for alternative b and c. Discuss how stakeholders i.e. other actors in the "roofing system", might react or be affected by your conclusions and recommendations concerning the choice of tiles. Example of stakeholders are raw material producers, architects, building contractors, municipal waste companies and residents, to name a few.

Technical description

Tiles are utilised mainly to protect the house from rain. They need to be of a certain weight in order to withstand the wind. At the same time they should not be too heavy, the extra weight causing a need for a stronger construction. A clay tile has an average weight of 3 kg per tile and 10 tiles are needed for 1 m^2 roof.

Baked clay and loam have been used as building material for at least 5000 years. The raw material is extracted from natural stores, which originate from aquatic deposits. The clay is shaped, dried and then baked at a temperature of 950–1 100 °C.

The average time interval in Sweden today for exchanging concrete tiles and clay tiles is about 40 years (REPAB 1992). This lifetime is based on economics and maintenance intervals for roof constructions. The technical lifetime of the tiles is longer, approximately 80 years depending on quality and weathering. It is thus technically possible to reuse a considerable part of the tiles instead of depositing all of them, although this is not common.

Production

Some of the data and descriptions given in the following text have been generalised and simplified in order not to complicate this exercise too much.

Clay tiles consists of 100 % clay. The clay pit is about 5 km away from the manufacturing plant in Vittinge (Stålmalm 1992). The clay, which from the beginning has a water content of 40 % by weight, is excavated and transported to Vittinge by road. There the raw material is put in stock and mixed to get an equal quality of the products. The electricity consumption of the process is 0.3 MJ/kg. Any remaining stones are crushed.

The clay is squeezed mechanically to its final shape, dried and finally baked in a tunnel oven for 3 days and nights. Before the baking, the density of the clay tile is approximately 2 500 kg/m^3 and after the baking is approximately 1 800–2 000 kg/m^3. Oil is used as fuel for the oven as well as for the drying process. Approximately 2.4 MJ of oil is needed for producing 1 kg of tile.

Other data

- Material losses caused by the transports and the building process is 5 %.
- The average distance from tile producer to user is 150 km (by road).
- The distance to a storage facility for reused building materials is assumed to be 150 km by road, as well as the distance from the storage facility to the new user.
- The average distance from user to final disposal is 30 km (by road). Tiles are generally disposed of in landfills.

Exercise H3
Concrete tiles. Comparison of single use with reuse

Context

A housing management company, owning and managing a number of apartment buildings, is in the process of introducing environmental issues in its operations in order to undergo environmental certification according to EMAS, to live up to commitments stated in the company environmental policy and to improve its environmental image. In the course of this process, the housing management company is considering reuse of roofing material to use on its buildings.

Task

Is it environmentally preferable to reuse concrete tiles, as compared to buying new tiles? Compare the following alternatives:

a) No reuse
b) 50 % of the tiles are reused on the same site once
c) 80 % of the tiles are reused on the same site once

Calculate inventory tables for the three cases and evaluate with the different methods for impact assessment. Calculate also the recycling rate with losses considered for alternatives b and c. Discuss how stakeholders i.e. other actors in the "roofing system", might react or be affected by your conclusions and recommendations concerning the choice of tiles. Example of stakeholders are raw material producers, architects, building contractors, municipal waste companies and residents, to name a few.

Technical description

Tiles are utilised mainly to protect the house from rain. They need to be of a certain weight in order to withstand the wind. At the same time they should not be too heavy, the extra weight causing a need for a stronger construction. A concrete tile has an average weight of 4 kg per tile, while a clay tile weighs about 3 kg. In both cases, 10 tiles are needed for one m^2 roof.

Concrete has three major components: aggregates, water and cement. The aggregates are usually a mixture of coarse and fine materials such as gravel, crushed stone and sand. The cement binds these aggregates together by combining chemically with water during a curing process.

After mixing cement, water and aggregates, the mixture is poured into forms to get its final shape. The tiles are then left for curing. This is done without adding extra heat.

The average time interval in Sweden today for exchanging concrete tiles and clay tiles is about 40 years (REPAB 1992). This lifetime is based on economics and maintenance intervals for roof constructions. The technical lifetime of the tiles is longer, approximately 80 years depending on quality and weathering. It is thus technically possible to reuse a considerable part of the tiles instead of depositing all of them, although this is not common.

Production

Concrete tiles

All data for production of concrete tiles are taken from one of the production units of Zanda (Rydell 1992), the most important producer of concrete tiles in Sweden. The tiles have the following composition by weight: sand 75 %, cement 20 % and iron oxide 5 %.

- Sand
  The sand comes from a local pit situated 12 km from the factory in Borensberg. It is taken from there by truck. Such pits may sometimes affect groundwater. Extraction of sand consumes electrical energy at a rate of 18–20 kWh/tonne (Sundström 1990).

- Cement
  The cement is produced by the company Cementa in Skövde, 150 km from Borensberg in Sweden. It is transported to Borensberg by truck. The main raw material used is limestone, taken from a limestone quarry close to the production unit. Explosives are used once or twice a week for quarrying. Cradle-to-gate data are given in the table below (Björklund et al. 1996).

Raw materials

Explosives	0.27 g/kg
Gypsum	45.8 g/kg
Limestone	1 361 g/kg
Quartzite	46 g/kg
Iron sulfate	9.2 g/kg

Energy

Oil	0.73 MJ/kg
Diesel	0.06 MJ/kg
Coal and petcoke	3.3 MJ/kg
Electricity	0.5 MJ/kg

Emissions to air

CO_2	806 g/kg
CO	0.8 g/kg
VOC	0.15 g/kg
NO_x	1.94 g/kg
SO_2	0.45 g/kg
Particulates	0.16 g/kg
Cr	1.7×10^{-5} g/kg

- Iron oxide
  Iron oxide is used for pigmentation. It is produced in Germany and is taken to Borensberg by truck (950 km) and ferry (230 km).

- Tile production at Zanda, Borensberg
  The annual production is around 10 million tiles. A production of this size has an energy use of 95 m^3 of oil and 4.2 million kWh of electricity. 2 % of the production is lost as waste. This is mainly landfilled but recycling within the tile production is under consideration. In addition, 50 m^3 of special oil is used as lubricant or loosening agent in moulding. This oil evaporates during the process. The moulds are made of aluminium and have a lifetime of 10–12 years. After that they are recycled. Each mould weighs 2.4 kg.

Other data

Material losses caused by the transport and the building process are 5 %.

- The average distance from tile producer to user is 150 km (by road).
- The average distance from user to final disposal is 30 km (by road). Tiles are generally disposed of in landfills.

Exercise H4
Polyethylene. Comparison of incineration and recycling

Context

The context of your LCA study is that it is a part of a national investigation into the environmental impacts related to the use of packaging and packaging waste. It is conducted on the behalf of the Ministry of Environment that wishes to underpin regulatory measures on recycling and producer take-back schemes in the packaging sector.

Public policy aims at reducing the amount of packaging waste in society. Statistics in this area are unreliable. When it comes to household waste, packaging waste makes up approximately 25 % of the weight, corresponding to approximately 50 % of the volume.

Concerning waste management facilities, landfills are well distributed in the country, whereas incineration plants are fewer but have larger treatment capacity. The incineration plants, which operate with heat recovery, are located close to larger urban areas making use of the recovered energy in their district heating systems. Recycling facilities are still relatively few.

Task

Compare two waste management options for dealing with polyethylene as a packaging waste. Questions asked by the commissioner of the LCA study are:

- Which type of waste management is environmentally preferable for polyethylene in household wastes, incineration or recycling? Is it appropriate to recommend the same type of waste management for HDPE as for LDPE?
- What improvements are desirable for further reducing environmental impacts stemming from the use of polyethylene packaging?

415

Discuss how stakeholders, i.e. other actors in the "polyethylene system" might react or might be affected by your conclusions and recommendations concerning the use of polyethylene as a packaging material and as a waste. Example of stakeholders are raw material producers, packaging industry, retailers, municipal waste companies and consumers, to name a few.

General information

Polyethylene is a thermoplastic, used for bags, sacks, bottles, drums and other containers. There are two kinds of polyethylene: LDPE (low-density polyethylene) and HDPE (high-density polyethylene). The primary use of LDPE is for plastic film, while HDPE is used for containers. The total national consumption of polyethylene in packaging is in the region of 300 000 tonnes/year. Its consumption in terms of packaging is described in table H4.1.

Table H4.1 Consumption of polyethylene in the packaging industry.

Type of packaging	Volume of LDPE (kilotonnes/year)	Volume of HDPE (kilotonnes/year)
Packaging film	115.0	2.0
Carrier bags	15.0	6.0
Injection-moulded products	1.0	101.0
Blow-moulded products	10.0	–
Paper board for liquids, coatings	50.0	–
Total	191.0	109.0

Overall technical description

The raw material consists of crude oil, which is refined to make naphtha and propane among other compounds. The next step is to break these down by heating them in the steam cracking process. Steam is added in this form of cracking, hence its name. The main products are ethylene and propylene. Others are burning gas, which is used internally as fuel, cracked gasoline and heavy unsaturated hydrocarbons. The various products are separated after the cracking furnaces by distillation, compression and cooling.

416

Refining oil starts with distillation, where light fractions are separated from the heavier ones. Examples of light fractions are gas, naphtha, gasoline and paraffin. Heavier fractions are diesel, followed by heavy fuel oils and residues. Cracking then enables the proportion of light fractions to be increased. Some of the crude oil that arrives at the refinery is used internally as process fuel, i.e. for distillation and cracking, while some of it is lost via process emissions into the air and water. This means that for 1 kg of refinery products more than 1 kg of crude oil is required. The yield is the ratio of the outgoing amount of product to the incoming amount of raw material, i.e. output/input. It varies with the product range. The yield for a refinery with a fairly normal product range is 0.9573 kg product/kg raw material (or 1.0446:1) (Scanraff 1990).

Petrochemical industries are often co-located. In such cases, the ethylene is piped from the steam cracker to the plastics manufacturer who can use the ethylene directly in the polymerisation process. Production of LDPE and HDPE takes place in two different processes. LDPE is manufactured in a high-pressure process, while HDPE is made in a low-pressure process. For steam cracking the yield is 0.8190 kg product/kg raw material (Neste Polyeten AB 1990), while for polymerisation it is 0.9932 for LDPE and 0.99746 for HDPE (Statoil Petrokemi AB 1990).

LDPE is polymerised at approximately 230 MPa (2 300 bar) and 300 °C. Since the reaction occurs at such high pressures there are relatively large, diffuse emissions of hydrocarbons. The pressure is maintained by electrically powered pumps. The resulting polyethylene base resin is transferred to an extruder where pelletisation of the base resin takes place. The base resin is then modified by admixture of additives in an intensive mixer. The melted plastic material from the intensive mixer is converted to a pelletised product in subsequent extrusion and pelletising equipment.

HDPE is polymerised in a fluidised bed of catalytic sand at a maximum of 2.1 MPa (21 bar) and 110 °C. The polymerisation catalyst (Ziegler-Natta catalyst) consists of metal compounds precipitated in extremely fine quartz sand. The base resin is removed from the reactor in the form of a powder and processed in the same way as LDPE.

Polyethylene granulate is transported from the plastics manufacturer to the varous packaging manufacturers for production of finished packaging (film, containers, etc.). The conversion of granulates to LDPE film and other types of packaging also results in waste, which is recycled. The waste flow is approximately 12 % based on the output from the machine (Chalmers Industriteknik 1990). The same value can be assumed to apply to HDPE containers.

The collected plastic is ground in a mill at the recycling plant. It is washed and dried before being extruded and regranulated. In view of the varying quality and colour mixing of the collected material the recovered plastic is used mainly for 'black' products, e.g. garbage sacks and road noise barriers. The amount of waste during recovery is 15 % (Karlsson 1991). This waste is usually disposed of in landfill sites.

Stepwise technical description

Extraction of crude oil

The extraction of crude oil may follow one of three basic technologies. In primary extraction, pumping is sufficient to draw up the oil; in secondary extraction, water has to be pumped into the oil reservoir in order to draw up the oil, and in tertiary extraction, steam or carbon dioxide is injected. The data presented here come from the Norwegian Oil Directorate (Röstein 1991) in Stavanger. The figures describe tertiary extraction in the Norwegian sector.

Energy consumption for extracting crude oil:	$0.760\ MJ_{th}$/kg oil equivalents (oe)
Production in the Norwegian sector:	107.3 Mt oe (79 Mt oil + 25.4 Mt gas) (Röstein 1991)

The emissions to air consist predominantly of carbon dioxide and derive mostly from energy production on the platforms (75 %). The energy is used for operations such as transporting the oil ashore by pipeline and injecting water and gas into the reservoirs. The rest of the air emissions come from flaring (5 %) and diffuse emissions (20 %). The emissions correspond to 55.92 g CO_2/kg oil equivalent, totalling approximately 6 Mt CO_2/year.

Discharges of oil into water come from four sources. The total figure for oil emissions into water is 1,611 tonnes, which is 15.67 mg/kg oil (Röstein 1991). These sources are the following:

The largest oil emission is from the drilling mud during the actual drilling process. This may be water or oil-based and is added to increase the drilling range. The trend towards increasing use of water-based drilling mud is bringing about a steady reduction in oil emissions from this source. In 1988 emissions from drilling mud totalled 1,700 tonnes while in 1989 this figure fell to 954 tonnes, which corresponds to 8.89 mg oil/kg oe.

From the reservoir comes a mixture of oil, gas and water. These are separated, the water is cleaned and then discharged into the sea. This water contains small amounts of oil. In 1989 about 221 tonnes of oil were discharged in this way. This corresponds to 2.06 mg oil/kg oe.

Emptying tankers is done by piping in water in order to get the oil out. When the water (ballast water) is later discharged, it contains a small amount of oil. The emission of oil from the ballast water was 159 tonnes in 1989, which corresponds to 1.48 mg oil/kg oe.

The last source consists of unforeseen oil emissions, 277 tonnes, which have remained at a constant level in recent years. They are the equivalent of 2.58 mg oil/kg oe.

The refinery

Of crucial importance for energy consumption at the refinery is the extent to which the crude oil is processed. The more processing, the larger the proportion of light fractions and the higher the energy consumption. Emission and energy data for refining crude oil presented in the following come from a large refinery with a fairly normal product range (Scanraff 1990).

Incoming raw material: 8 652 kt crude oil

Energy requirements

Internal fuel: 319 468 tonnes, i.e. 16 620 TJ_{th} per 8 282 245 tonnes product or 2.0055 MJ_{th}/kg

Electricity: 0.12 MJ_e/kg

Table H4.2 Emissions into the air (Scanraff 1990).

Emissions to air	SO_2	NO_x	HC	CO_2	Particulates
g/kg product	0.5423	0.149	0.3545	108.11	0.0167
Annual total (tonnes)	4 491	1 237	2 936	895 000	138

The crude oil contains sulphur and is desulphurised in order to obtain products with a lower sulphur content. Sulphur emissions at the refinery come largely from burning internal fuel (713 tonnes S) and from the desulphurisation plant (1 442 tonnes S) (Scanraff 1990).

The NO_x emissions come from burning internal fuel (1 237 tonnes NO_x) (Scanraff 1990).

Hydrocarbon emissions derive mainly from diffuse emissions (2 750 tonnes) and also to a small extent from what is not burnt off in the flares (186 tonnes) (Scanraff 1990).

Carbon dioxide emissions occur while burning internal fuel (870 600 tonnes) and during flaring (24 800 tonnes) (Scanraff 1990).

Particulate emissions arise from catalytic cracking and in the burning of internal fuel (69 tonnes and 69 tonnes each) (Scanraff 1990).

Heavy metals such as nickel and vanadium are present in the oil (45 mg Ni/kg oil and 145 mg V/kg) and emissions occur in combustion (Scanraff 1990):

Ni: 829 kg/year
V: 2 640 kg/year

Emissions into water

Emissions into water arise from the waste water process and surface water and also to some extent from the ballast water. Below follows a summary of emissions into water (Scanraff 1990).

420

Table H4.3 Emissions into water (Scanraff 1990).

Emissions to water	Annual total	Per kg refinery product
Oil	10.3 tonnes	1.255 mg/kg
Aromatics	<2 tonnes	0.241 mg/kg
Phenol	0.2 tonnes	0.0241 mg/kg
Susp.	59.9 tonnes	7.232 mg/kg
COD	412 tonnes	49.7 mg/kg
BOD-7	52.9 tonnes	6.387 mg/kg
Cyanide	0.1 tonnes	0.0121 mg/kg
Tot-N	68 tonnes	8.210 mg/kg
Tot-P	2.86 tonnes	0.133 mg/kg
Nickel	205 kg	24.75 µg/kg
Vanadium	140 kg	16.9 µg/kg
Cadmium	55 kg	6.64 µg/kg
Lead	95 kg	11.47 µg/kg
Mercury	0.2 kg	24.15 µg/kg

Steam cracking

Environmental data from steam cracking is based on the environmental report of Statoil Petrokemi AB (1990).

Energy requirements:

1.270 MJ_e/kg crack product, in this case ethylene
11.603 MJ_{th}/kg crack product

Emissions into air

NO_x: 0.847 g/kg ethylene
HC: 1.632 g/kg ethylene
CO_2:   634 g/kg ethylene

Emissions into water

Oil: 3.83 mg/kg ethylene
Phenol: 75.36 mg/kg ethylene
Tot-N: 5.98 mg/kg ethylene

Polymerisation

LDPE is polymerised at high pressure and high temperature (approximately 230 MPa (2 300 bar) and 300 °C), while the polymerisation of HDPE takes place at maximally 2.1 MPa (21 bar) and 110 °C.

Only some of the emissions at the polymerisation plant are measured. The process emissions measured are presented in table H4.4. Other emissions, such as CO_2, can be calculated based on the amount of oil burnt in the process.

Table H4.4 Energy requirements and emissions from LDPE and HDPE polymerisation processes (Neste Polyeten AB 1990; Holmgren 1991).

	LDPE	HDPE
Energy requirements		
Electricity	6.578 MJ$_e$/kg	2.101 MJ$_e$/kg
Fossil fuels (oil)	2.190 MJ$_{th}$/kg	0.113 MJ$_{th}$/kg
Emissions into air		
Ethylene (diffuse emissions, rejects)	8.0 g/kg	0.97 g/kg
Propylene	1.01 g/kg	–
Flaring, CO_2	8.0 g/kg	49 g/kg
Freons, R22	0.86 mg/kg	0.40 mg/kg
Hydrogen, H_2	–	0.176 g/kg
SO_2	117 mg/kg	6.03 mg/kg
NO_x	275 mg/kg	14.16 mg/kg
Emissions into water		
TOC	25.5 mg/kg	11.83 mg/kg
Wastes		
Oils to SAKAB (hazardous waste)	0.40 g/kg	0.40 g/kg

Packaging manufacture

The energy requirement for manufacturing blow-moulded products can be assumed to be at the same level as that for film manufacture. In both cases, electric extruders are used (Chalmers Industriteknik 1990).

Film manufacturing of LDPE:
Energy requirements:	3.10 MJ$_e$/kg
To air: BHT (hydrocarbon anti-oxidant)	0.30 g/kg
Injection moulding of HDPE:	3.10 MJ$_e$/kg

Recovery, recycling plant

The material characteristics for HDPE and LDPE differ. One is used predominantly for containers, the other for plastic film. This affects the way and the extent to which these materials are collected. Moreover, HDPE and LDPE are recycled separately. Approximately 15 % of the material is lost as waste.

Grinding, washing, drying, extrusion and granulation: 2.98 MJ$_e$/kg

Data on transportation

- Oil is assumed to be transported by tankers from the North Sea to West Sweden, about 350 km at 0.11 MJ/tonne-km giving an energy consumption of 38.5 MJ$_{th}$/tonne crude oil.
- Transportation of naphtha from refinery to steam cracker is by ship from Lysekil to Stenungsund approximately 100 km.
- Mean transportation distance of PE granulate from producer to packaging manufacturer: 400 km by long-distance road transport (Holmgren 1991).
- Transportation of waste plastic, from consumer to recycling plant: 300 km by long-distance road transport (Karlsson 1991).
- Transportation of recovered polyethylene granulate, from recycler to packaging manufacturer. Estimated at 300 km by long-distance road transport.

Exercise H5
Polyethylene. Comparison of landfilling and recycling

Context

The context of your LCA study is that it is a part of a national investigation into the environmental impacts related to the use of packaging and packaging waste. It is conducted on the behalf of the Ministry of Environment that wishes to underpin regulatory measures on recycling and producer take-back schemes in the packaging sector.

Public policy aims at reducing the amount of packaging waste in society. Statistics in this area are unreliable. When is comes to household waste, packaging waste makes up approximately 25 % of the weight, corresponding to approximately 50 % of the volume.

Concerning waste management facilities, landfills are well distributed in the country, whereas incineration plants are fewer but have larger treatment capacity. The incineration plants, which operate with heat recovery, are located close to larger urban areas making use of the recovered energy in their district heating systems. Recycling facilities are still relatively few.

Task

Compare two waste management options for dealing with polyethylene as a packaging waste. Questions asked by the commissioner of the LCA study are:

• Which type of waste management is environmentally preferable for polyethylene in household wastes, landfilling or recycling? Is it appropriate to recommend the same type of waste management for HDPE as for LDPE?
• What improvements are desirable for further reducing environmental impacts stemming from the use of polyethylene packaging?

Discuss how stakeholders, i.e. other actors in the "polyethylene system" might react or might be affected by your conclusions and recommendations concerning the use of polyethylene as a packaging material and as a waste. Example of stakeholders are raw material producers, packaging industry, retailers, municipal waste companies, consumers, to name a few.

General information

Polyethylene is a thermoplastic used for bags, sacks, bottles, drums and other containers. There are two kinds of polyethylene: LDPE (low-density polyethylene) and HDPE (high-density polyethylene). The primary use of LDPE is for plastic film, while HDPE is used for containers. The total national consumption of polyethylene in packaging is in the region of 300 000 tonnes/year. Its consumption in terms of packaging is described in table H4.1.

Table H5.1 Consumption of polyethylene in the packaging industry.

Type of packaging	Volume of LDPE (kilotonnes/year)	Volume of HDPE (kilotonnes/year)
Packaging film	115.0	2.0
Carrier bags	15.0	6.0
Injection-moulded products	1.0	101.0
Blow-moulded products	10.0	–
Paper board for liquids, coatings	50.0	–
Total	191.0	109.0

Overall technical description

The raw material consists of crude oil, which is refined to make naphtha and propane among other compounds. The next step is to break these down by heating them in the steam cracking process. Steam is added in this form of cracking, hence its name. The main products are ethylene and propylene. Others are burning gas, which is used internally as fuel, cracked gasoline and heavy unsaturated hydrocarbons. The various products are separated after the cracking furnaces by distillation, compression and cooling.

Refining oil starts with distillation, where light fractions are separated from the heavier ones. Examples of light fractions are gas, naphtha, gasoline and paraffin. Heavier fractions are diesel, followed by heavy fuel oils and residues. Cracking then enables the proportion of light fractions to be increased. Some of the crude oil that arrives at the refinery is used internally as process fuel, i.e. for distillation and cracking, while some of it is lost via process emissions into the air and water. This means that for 1 kg of refinery products more than 1 kg of crude oil is required. The yield is the ratio of the outgoing amount of product to the incoming amount of raw material, i.e. output/input. It varies with the product range. The yield for a refinery with a fairly normal product range is 0.9573 kg product/kg raw material (or 1.0446:1) (Scanraff 1990).

Petrochemical industries are often co-located. In such cases, the ethylene is piped from the steam cracker to the plastics manufacturer who can use the ethylene directly in the polymerisation process. Production of LDPE and HDPE takes place in two different processes. LDPE is manufactured in a high-pressure process, while HDPE is made in a low-pressure process. For steam cracking the yield is 0.8190 kg product/kg raw material (Neste Polyeten AB 1990), while for polymerisation it is 0.9932 for LDPE and 0.99746 for HDPE (Statoil Petrokemi AB 1990).

LDPE is polymerised at approximately 230 MPa (2300 bar) and 300 °C. Since the reaction occurs at such high pressures there are relatively large, diffuse emissions of hydrocarbons. The pressure is maintained by electrically powered pumps. The resulting polyethylene base resin is transferred to an extruder where pelletisation of the base resin takes place. The base resin is then modified by admixture of additives in an intensive mixer. The melted plastic material from the intensive mixer is converted to a pelletised product in subsequent extrusion and pelletising equipment.

HDPE is polymerised in a fluidised bed of catalytic sand at a maximum of 2.1 MPa (21 bar) and 110 °C. The polymerisation catalyst (Ziegler-Natta catalyst) consists of metal compounds precipitated in extremely fine quartz sand. The base resin is removed from the reactor in the form of a powder and is processed in the same way as LDPE.

Polyethylene granulate is transported from the plastics manufacturer to the varous packaging manufacturers for production of finished packaging (film, containers, etc.). The conversion of granulates to LDPE film and other types of packaging also results in waste, which is recycled. The waste flow is approximately 12 % based on the output from the machine (Chalmers Industriteknik 1990). The same value can be assumed to apply to HDPE containers.

The collected plastic is ground in a mill at the recycling plant. It is washed and dried before being extruded and regranulated. In view of the varying quality and colour mixing of the collected material the recovered plastic is used mainly for 'black' products, e.g. garbage sacks and road noise barriers. The amount of waste during recovery is 15 % (Karlsson 1991). This waste is usually disposed of in landfill sites.

Stepwise technical description

Extraction of crude oil

The extraction of crude oil may follow one of three basic technologies. In primary extraction, pumping is sufficient to draw up the oil; in secondary extraction, water has to be pumped into the oil reservoir in order to draw up the oil, and in tertiary extraction, steam or carbon dioxide is injected. The data here presented come from the Norwegian Oil Directorate (Röstein 1991) in Stavanger. The figures describe tertiary extraction in the Norwegian sector.

Energy consumption for extracting crude oil:	$0.760 \ MJ_{th}$/kg oil equivalents (oe)
Production in the Norwegian sector:	107.3 Mt oe (79 Mt oil + 25.4 Mt gas) (Röstein 1991)

The emissions into the air consist predominantly of carbon dioxide and derive mostly from energy production on the platforms (75 %). The energy is used for operations such as transporting the oil ashore by pipeline and injecting water and gas into the reservoirs. The rest of the air emissions come from flaring (5 %) and diffuse emissions (20 %). The emissions correspond to 55.92 g CO_2/kg oil equivalent, totalling approximately 6 Mt CO_2/year.

Discharges of oil into water come from four sources. The total figure for oil emissions into water is 1 611 tonnes, which is 15.67 mg/kg oil (Röstein 1991). These sources are the following:

The largest oil emission is from the drilling mud during the actual drilling process. This may be water or oil-based and is added to increase the drilling range. The trend towards increasing use of water-based drilling mud is bringing about a steady reduction in oil emissions from this source. In 1988 emissions from drilling mud totalled 1 700 tonnes, while in 1989 this figure fell to 954 tonnes, which corresponds to 8.89 mg oil/kg oe.

From the reservoir comes a mixture of oil, gas and water. These are separated, the water is cleaned and then discharged into the sea. This water contains small amounts of oil. In 1989 about 221 tonnes of oil were discharged in this way. This corresponds to 2.06 mg oil/kg oe.

Emptying tankers is done by piping in water in order to get the oil out. When the water (ballast water) is later discharged, it contains a small amount of oil. The emission of oil from the ballast water was 159 tonnes in 1989, which corresponds to 1.48 mg oil/kg oe.

The last source consists of unforeseen oil emissions, 277 tonnes, which have remained at a constant level in recent years. They are the equivalent of 2.58 mg oil/kg oe.

The refinery

Of crucial importance for energy consumption at the refinery is the extent to which the crude oil is processed. The more processing, the larger the proportion of light fractions and the higher the energy consumption. Emission and energy data for refining crude oil presented in the following come from a large refinery with a fairly normal product range (Scanraff 1990).

Incoming raw material: 8 652 kt crude oil

Energy requirements

Internal fuel: 319 468 tonnes, i.e. 16 620 TJ_{th} per 8 282 245 tonnes product or 2.0055 MJ_{th}/kg

Electricity: 0.12 MJ_e/kg

Table H5.2 Emissions into the air (Scanraff 1990).

Emissions to air	SO_2	NO_x	HC	CO_2	Particulates
g/kg product	0.5423	0.149	0.3545	108.11	0.0167
Annual total (tonnes)	4 491	1 237	2 936	895 000	138

The crude oil contains sulphur and is desulphurised in order to obtain products with a lower sulphur content. Sulphur emissions at the refinery come largely from burning internal fuel (713 tonnes S) and from the desulphurisation plant (1 442 tonnes S) (Scanraff 1990).

The NO_x emissions come from burning internal fuel (1 237 tonnes NO_x) (Scanraff 1990).

428

Hydrocarbon emissions derive mainly from diffuse emissions (2 750 tonnes) and also to a small extent from what is not burnt off in the flares (186 tonnes) (Scanraff 1990).

Carbon dioxide emissions occur when burning internal fuel (870 600 tonnes) and during flaring (24 800 tonnes) (Scanraff 1990).

Particulate emissions arise from catalytic cracking and in the burning of internal fuel (69 tonnes and 69 tonnes each) (Scanraff 1990).

Heavy metals, such as nickel and vanadium are present in the oil (45 mg Ni/kg oil and 145 mg V/kg) and emissions occur in combustion (Scanraff 1990):

Ni: 829 kg/year
V: 2 640 kg/year

Emissions into water

Emissions into water arise from the waste water process and surface water and also to some extent the ballast water. Below follows a summary of emissions into water (Scanraff 1990).

Table H5.3 Emissions into water (Scanraff 1990).

Emissions to water	Annual total	Per kg refinery product
Oil	10.3 tonnes	1.255 mg/kg
Aromatics	<2 tonnes	0.241 mg/kg
Phenol	0.2 tonnes	0.0241 mg/kg
Susp.	59.9 tonnes	7.232 mg/kg
COD	412 tonnes	49.7 mg/kg
BOD-7	52.9 tonnes	6.387 mg/kg
Cyanide	0.1 tonnes	0.0121 mg/kg
Tot-N	68 tonnes	8.210 mg/kg
Tot-P	2.86 tonnes	0.133 mg/kg
Nickel	205 kg	24.75 µg/kg
Vanadium	140 kg	16.9 µg/kg
Cadmium	55 kg	6.64 µg/kg
Lead	95 kg	11.47 µg/kg
Mercury	0.2 kg	24.15 µg/kg

Steam cracking

Environmental data from steam cracking are based on the environmental report of Statoil Petrokemi AB (1990).

Energy requirements:

1.270 MJ_e/kg crack product, in this case ethylene
11.603 MJ_{th}/kg crack product

Emissions into air:

NO_x: 0.847 g/kg ethylene
HC: 1.632 g/kg ethylene
CO_2:   634 g/kg ethylene

Emissions into water:

Oil: 3.83 mg/kg ethylene
Phenol: 75.36 mg/kg ethylene
Tot-N: 5.98 mg/kg ethylene

Polymerisation

LDPE is polymerised at high pressure and high temperature (approximately 230 MPa (2 300 bar) and 300 °C), while the polymerisation of HDPE takes place at maximally 21 bar and 110 °C.

Only some of the emissions at the polymerisation plant are measured. The process emissions measured are presented in table H5.4. Other emissions, such as CO_2, can be calculated based on the amount oil burnt in the process.

Table H5.4 Energy requirements and emissions from LDPE and HDPE polymerisation process (Neste Polyeten AB 1990; Holmgren 1991).

	LDPE	HDPE
Energy requirements		
Electricity	6.578 MJ_e/kg	2.101 MJ_e/kg
Fossil fuels (oil)	2.190 MJ_{th}/kg	0.113 MJ_{th}/kg
Emissions into air		
Ethylene (diffuse emissions, rejects)	8.0 g/kg	0.97 g/kg
Propylene	1.01 g/kg	–
Flaring, CO_2	8.0 g/kg	49 g/kg
Freons, R22	0.86 mg/kg	0.40 mg/kg
Hydrogen, H_2	–	0.176 g/kg
SO_2	117 mg/kg	6.03 mg/kg
NO_x	275 mg/kg	14.16 mg/kg
Emissions into water		
TOC	25.5 mg/kg	11.83 mg/kg
Wastes		
Oils to SAKAB (hazardous waste)	0.40 g/kg	0.40 g/kg

Packaging manufacture

The energy requirement for the manufacture of blow-moulded products can be assumed to be at the same level as that for film manufacture. In both cases, electric extruders are used (Chalmers Industriteknik 1990).

Film manufacturing of LDPE:
Energy requirements:	$3.10 \text{ MJ}_e/\text{kg}$
To air: BHT (hydrocarbon anti-oxidant)	0.30 g/kg
Injection moulding of HDPE:	$3.10 \text{ MJ}_e/\text{kg}$

Recovery, recycling plant

The material characteristics for HDPE and LDPE differ. One is used predominantly for containers, the other for plastic film. This affects the way and the extent to which these materials are collected. Moreover, HDPE and LDPE are recycled separately.

Grinding, washing, drying, extrusion and granulation: $2.98 \text{ MJ}_e/\text{kg}$

Data on transportation

- Oil is assumed to be transported by tankers from the North Sea to West Sweden, about 350 km at 0.11 MJ/tonne-km giving an energy consumption of $38.5 \text{ MJ}_{th}/\text{tonne}$ crude oil.
- Transportation of naphtha from refinery to steam cracker by ship from Lysekil to Stenungsund approximately 100 km.
- Mean transportation distance of PE granulate from producer to packaging manufacturer: 400 km by long-distance road transport (Holmgren 1991).
- Transportation of waste plastic, from consumer to recycling plant: 300 km by long-distance road (Karlsson 1991).
- Transportation of recovered polyethylene granulate, from recycler to packaging manufacturer. Estimated at 300 km by long-distance road transport.

Exercise H6
Glass. Comparison of single use with material recycling

Context

The context of your LCA study is that it is a part of a national investigation into the environmental impacts related to the use of packaging and packaging waste. It is conducted on the behalf of the Ministry of Environment that wishes to underpin regulatory measures on recycling and producer take-back schemes in the packaging sector.

Public policy aims at reducing the amount of packaging waste in society. Statistics in this area are unreliable. Concerning household waste, packaging waste makes up approximately 25 % of the weight, corresponding to approximately 50 % of the volume.

Concerning waste management facilities, landfills are well distributed in the country, whereas incineration plants are fewer but have larger treatment capacity. The incineration plants, which operate with heat recovery, are located close to larger urban areas making use of the recovered energy in their district heating systems.

Task

Compare two waste management options for dealing with glass as a packaging waste. Questions asked by the commissioner of the LCA study are:

- Is it environmentally preferable to recycle broken glass, as compared to production from virgin raw materials?
- If so, how far may broken glass be transported before possible environmental gains from recycling are lost due to the extra environmental loads caused by transportation?

Discuss how stakeholders, i.e. other actors in the "glass system" might react or might be affected by your conclusions and recommendations concerning the use of glass as a packaging material and

432

as a waste. Example of stakeholders are raw material producers, packaging industry, retailers, municipal waste companies and consumers, to name a few.

Technical description

Glass is mainly made from the raw materials sand, lime and soda, which are fused at 1 500–1 600 °C. The process is a continuous one and the raw materials are added constantly while the finished glass is continuously taken out and cut into pieces suitable for the product that is shaped in the glass machine.

Glass containers can be refilled. This is done on a large scale in the case of beverage containers for beer and soft drinks. Glass can also be recovered from broken glass, which is remelted. Uncoloured glass can only be made from uncoloured broken glass while coloured glass can be produced from unsorted raw materials.

Glass production

The raw material composition for a plant producing packaging glass is presented in table H6.1. The fraction of broken glass may vary, while the relative composition of virgin ingredients is kept constant. The data in tables H6.1 and H6.2 applies to a plant that makes both uncoloured and coloured glass (PLM 1991).

Table H6.1 Raw material composition for packaging glass.

Compounds	Amount (kg/tonne molten glass)
Sand	476
Soda	136
Lime	83
Dolomite	58
Feldspar	43
Sodium sulphate	4
Broken glass	366
Total	1 166

There are weight losses during melting. Losses comprise carbon dioxide from lime and soda together with loss of water from sand and broken glass (5 % moisture content in sand, 1–2 % moisture content in broken glass) (Eriksson 1991). Consequently, melting losses vary with raw material composition.

Soda may be supplied by both natural soda from the US and Solvay soda. Here it is assumed that equal parts of Solvay and natural soda are used.

For the melting process, oil and electricity are needed in an amount of 1050–1150 kcal/kg molten glass, depending on capacity utilisation. 7–8 % of this is electrical energy. The energy consumption is valid for a raw material composition with approximately 50 % broken glass (Eriksson 1991). A 2 % energy savings is achieved per 10 % broken glass added (Nyström 1991).

Irrespective of the amount of broken glass added, liquid petroleum gas (LPG) is also used at a rate of 0.564 MJ/kg glass (Sundström 1990), plus electricity in general for fans, conveyor belts, etc. This general electricity consumption is estimated at 0.4 MJ/kg glass.

Table H6.2 Emissions from glassworks (PLM 1991).

Receiving body	Emission	Amount (g/kg glass)
Into air	SO_2	1.01
	NO_x	2.69
	Particulates	0.26
Into water	Oil + fat	0.009
	Suspended matter	0.018

In addition to the emissions listed in table H6.2, carbon dioxide emissions are caused by burning oil and gas and by the release of gas from the melt. The CO_2 emissions in the form of melting losses amount to approximately 170 g CO_2/kg virgin raw materials. CO_2 emission levels are thus linked to the proportion of broken glass added through:

- variations in fuel consumptions
- variations in melting losses

434

Other data

- Extraction of sand (Sundström 1990)
  Electrical energy 18–20 kWh/tonne = 0.684 MJ/kg

- Transport of sand (Sundström 1990)
  Rail 200 km to the glass plant in Limmared

- Extraction of lime (Sundström 1990)
  Fossil fuel 132 MJ/tonne = 0.132 MJ/kg (diesel assumed)
  Electrical energy 22 kWh/tonne = 0.0792 MJ/kg

- Transport of lime (Sundström 1990)
  Rail 110 km
  Sea 240 km

- Extraction of feldspar (estimate)
  Fossil fuel 132 MJ/tonne = 0.132 MJ/kg (diesel assumed)
  Electrical energy 22 kWh/tonne = 0.0792 MJ/kg

- Transportation of feldspar (Sundström 1990)
  Rail 110 km
  Sea 280 km
  Road 10 km

- Production of Solvay soda (Sundström 1990)
  Electrical energy 1 671 kWh/tonne soda = 6.02 MJ/kg soda
  Oil 106 l/tonne soda = 4,060 MJ/kg soda

- Transportation of Solvay soda (Sundström 1990)
  Rail 110 km
  Sea 1 090 km
  Road 40 km

- Extraction of Portland soda (Sundström 1990)
  Estimated at 5 kWh/tonne = 0.018 MJ/kg (diesel assumed)

- Transportation of Portland soda (Sundström 1990)
  Rail 110 km
  Sea 15 740 km
  Transport prior to shipping 1 617 km (road assumed)

- Extraction of dolomite (Sundström 1990)
  Fossil fuel 634 MJ/tonne = 0.634 MJ/kg (diesel assumed)
  Electrical energy 27 kWh/tonne = 0.0972 MJ/kg

- Transportation of dolomite (Sundström 1990)
  Estimated at 200 km by rail

- Production of sodium sulphate (Sundström 1990)
  Electrical energy 80 kWh/tonne = 0.288 MJ/kg
  Fossil fuel 395 MJ/tonne = 0.395 MJ/kg (oil assumed)

- Transportation of sodium sulphate
  Estimated at 200 km by rail

- Transport of finished glass packaging to customer (Sundström 1990)
  Road 300 km

- Transport of broken glass to glassworks (Sundström 1990)
  Road 252 km

- Crushing and cleaning of broken glass (Sundström 1990)
  Electrical energy 3 kWh/tonne = 0.011 MJ/kg

Exercise H7
Glass. Comparison of single use with refilling

Context

The context of your LCA study is that it is a part of a national investigation into the environmental impacts related to the use of packaging and packaging waste. It is conducted on the behalf of the Ministry of Environment that wishes to underpin regulatory measures on recycling and producer take-back schemes in the packaging sector.

Public policy aims at reducing the amount of packaging waste in society. Statistics in this area are unreliable. Concerning household waste, packaging waste makes up approximately 25 % of the weight, corresponding to approximately 50 % of the volume.

Containers of glass can be used several times if collected, cleaned and refilled. Return systems are already in place for some high-volume products, such as milk and beer, whereas other glass containers, e.g. jars are mainly single-use containers. Logistics are relatively simple in the case of returnable bottles. In such systems, deliveries to retailers do not pass a wholesaler. Returned bottles are picked up at the collection point at the retailer and transported back to the beverage producer (e.g. brewery) by the same vehicle that delivered the filled bottles. The development of a return system for other types of products would require different logistical solutions.

Concerning waste management facilities, landfills are well distributed in the country, whereas incineration plants are fewer but have larger treatment capacity. The incineration plants, which operate with heat recovery, are located close to larger urban areas making use of the recovered energy in their district heating systems.

Task

Compare two waste management options for dealing with glass as a packaging waste. Questions asked by the commissioner of the LCA study are:

- Is it environmentally preferable to refill glass, as compared to single use of glass?
- If so, how much heavier may a refillable glass container be than its disposable alternative before possible environmental gains from refilling are lost due to the extra environmental loads caused by production and transportation of the heavier refillable container?
- Assess the environmental implications of introducing a refill system for low-volume products (as compared to beer or milk) that would require separate collection systems.

Discuss how stakeholders, i.e. other actors in the "glass system" might react or might be affected by your conclusions and recommendations concerning the use of glass as a packaging material and as a waste. Example of stakeholders are raw material producers, packaging industry, retailers, municipal waste companies and consumers, to name a few.

Technical description

Glass is mainly made from the raw materials sand, lime and soda, which are fused at 1 500–1 600 °C. The process is a continuous one and the raw materials are added constantly while the finished glass is continuously taken out and cut into pieces suitable for the product that is shaped in the glass machine.

Glass containers can be refilled. This is done on a large scale in the case of beverage containers for beer and soft drinks. A standard refillable bottle weighs 300 grams; a single-use bottle weighs approximately half of that. Glass bottles in refill system are typically used 20–30 times. Glass can also be recovered from broken glass, which is remelted. Uncoloured glass can only be made from uncoloured broken glass while coloured glass can be produced from unsorted raw materials.

Glass production

The raw material composition for a plant producing packaging glass is presented in table H6.1. The fraction of broken glass may vary, while the relative composition of virgin ingredients is kept constant. The data in tables H7.1 and H7.2 applies to a plant that makes both uncoloured and coloured glass (PLM 1991).

Table H7.1 Raw material composition for packaging glass.

Compounds	Amount (kg/tonne molten glass)
Sand	476
Soda	136
Lime	83
Dolomite	58
Feldspar	43
Sodium sulphate	4
Broken glass	366
Total	1 166

There are weight losses during melting. Losses comprise carbon dioxide from lime and soda together with loss of water from sand and broken glass (5 % moisture content in sand, 1–2 % moisture

438

content in broken glass) (Eriksson 1991). Consequently, melting losses vary with raw material composition.

Soda may be supplied by both natural soda from the US and Solvay soda. Here it is assumed that equal parts of Solvay and natural soda are used.

For the melting process, oil and electricity are needed in an amount of 1 050–1 150 kcal/kg molten glass, depending on capacity utilisation. 7–8 % of this is electrical energy. The energy consumption is valid for a raw material composition with approximately 50 % broken glass (Eriksson 1991). A 2 % energy savings is achieved per 10 % broken glass added (Nyström 1991).

Irrespective of the amount of broken glass added, liquid petroleum gas (LPG) is also used at a rate of 0.564 MJ/kg glass (Sundström 1990), plus electricity in general for fans, conveyor belts, etc. This general electricity consumption is estimated at 0.4 MJ/kg glass.

Table H7.2 Emissions from glassworks (PLM 1991).

Receiving body	Emission	Amount (g/kg glass)
Into air	SO_2	1.01
	NO_x	2.69
	Particulates	0.26
Into water	Oil + fat	0.009
	Suspended matter	0.018

In addition to emissions listed in table H7.2, carbon dioxide emissions are caused by burning oil and gas and by the release of gas from the melt. The CO_2 emissions in the form of melting losses amount to approximately 170 g CO_2/kg virgin raw materials. CO_2 emission levels are thus linked to the proportion of broken glass added through:

• variations in fuel consumption
• variation in melting losses

Other data

- Extraction of sand (Sundström 1990)
  Electrical energy 18–20 kWh/tonne = 0.684 MJ/kg

- Transport of sand (Sundström 1990)
  Rail 200 km to Limmared

- Extraction of lime (Sundström 1990)
  Fossil fuel 132 MJ/tonne = 0.132 MJ/kg (diesel assumed)
  Electrical energy 22 kWh/tonne = 0.0792 MJ/kg

- Transport of lime (Sundström 1990)
  Rail 110 km
  Sea 240 km

- Extraction of feldspar (estimate)
  Fossil fuel 132 MJ/tonne = 0.132 MJ/kg (diesel assumed)
  Electrical energy 22 kWh/tonne = 0.0792 MJ/kg

- Transportation of feldspar (Sundström 1990)
  Rail 110 km
  Sea 280 km
  Road 10 km

- Production of Solvay soda (Sundström 1990)
  Electrical energy 1 671 kWh/tonne soda = 6.02 MJ/kg soda
  Oil 106 l/tonne soda = 4060 MJ/kg soda

- Transportation of Solvay soda (Sundström 1990)
  Rail 110 km
  Sea 1 090 km
  Road 40 km

- Extraction of Portland soda (Sundström, 1990)
  Estimated at 5 kWh/tonne = 0.018 MJ/kg (diesel assumed)

- Transportation of Portland soda (Sundström 1990)
  Rail 110 km
  Sea 15 740 km
  Transport prior to shipping 1 617 km (road assumed)

- Extraction of dolomite (Sundström 1990)
  Fossil fuel 634 MJ/tonne = 0.634 MJ/kg (diesel assumed)
  Electrical energy 27 kWh/tonne = 0.0972 MJ/kg

- Transportation of dolomite (Sundström 1990)
  Estimated at 200 km by rail

- Production of sodium sulphate (Sundström 1990)
  Electrical energy 80 kWh/tonne = 0.288 MJ/kg
  Fossil fuel 395 MJ/tonne = 0.395 MJ/kg (oil assumed)

- Transportation of sodium sulphate
  Estimated at 200 km by rail

- Transport of finished glass packaging to customer, e.g. brewery (Sundström 1990)
  Road 300 km

- Transport of broken glass to glassworks (Sundström 1990)
  Road 252 km

- Crushing and cleaning of broken glass (Sundström 1990)
  Electrical energy 3 kWh/tonne = 0.011 MJ/kg

- Transport between brewery and retailer (Sundström 1990)
  Road 300 km

- Cleaning of returned bottles at the beverage producer (Sundström 1990)
  Soda (50 % solution) 7 l/1000 bottles
  Fossil fuel 0.11 kWh/l beverage
  Electricity 0.06 kWh/l beverage

Exercise H8
Linoleum. Choice of linseed oil supplier

Context

The flooring market is a very competitive market. One of the world's largest manufacturer of flooring is considering whether an environmental adaptation of their production of one of their main products, linoleum flooring, is an effective way of gaining advantages by positioning themselves on the market as a "green" company. In the course of this process, the company is reviewing its suppliers, in particular, linseed oil suppliers since linseed oil is a major raw material.

Task

Assess the overall environmental impact of linoleum flooring. In addition, answer the following questions:

- What are the possibilities for reducing the environmental impact of linoleum flooring?
- Is it environmentally favourable to use European linseed oil in the production of linoleum instead of the linseed oil used today?

Discuss how stakeholders, i.e. other actors in the "linoleum system" might react or might be affected by your conclusions and recommendations concerning environmental improvements of linoleum flooring. Examples of stakeholders are flooring producers, architects, housing management companies and citizens to name a few.

Technical description

The name linoleum comes from the Latin "linioleum" which means linseed oil. The name comes about because linseed oil is one of the main ingredients of linoleum. One of the world's largest production plants of linoleum at present is located at Krommenie, just outside Amsterdam in the Netherlands. 75 % of its production is exported throughout the world. The company operating the plant is the world's largest producer of linoleum.

Linoleum flooring for domestic use generally has a thickness of 2 mm and is estimated to have an average weight of 2.3 kg/m². The average lifetime is estimated at 25 years. The composition of the flooring material is presented in table H8.1.

442

Table H8.1 Raw material composition of linoleum (Jönsson et al. 1994).

Material	Weight %
Linseed oil	24
Resin	8
Powdered wood	30
Powdered cork	5
Powdered limestone	18
Pigment	4
Jute	11
Total	100

Raw material production

Linseed oil

Linseed oil, which is the most important raw material in the actual linoleum paste, acts as a binder. Linseed oil is bought from Argentina, Canada and the USA (Potting & Blok 1993). All the oils travel by ship to the Netherlands. The average transport distance from Argentina, Canada and the USA to the Netherlands is estimated at 1 500 km by train and 4 350 km by ship.

Cultivation in the Americas produces about 0.6 tonnes of seed per hectare and year. On average 35 kg nitrogen, 17 kg P_2O_5 and 14 kg K_2O per hectare are added as fertiliser during cultivation. Energy use in the production of fertilisers is 34.9 MJ/kg nitrogen, 15.5 MJ/kg P_2O_5 and 8.6 MJ/kg K_2O (Potting & Blok 1993). Linseed cultivation requires relatively little fertiliser input compared with other common crops and any leakage of nutrients to water is negligible. The stalk is generally burnt or left in the field and is therefore not considered as waste. Energy use for threshing linseed amounts to 0.65 MJ/kg linseed oil.

The linseed is crushed and the oil is extracted either by pressing or by using naphta as a solvent. The oil can be extracted with or without supply of heat, resulting in hot-pressed or cold-pressed linseed oil. Hot-pressed oil is normally used in linoleum manufacturing. Electrical energy usage in the extraction process amounts to 0.54 MJ/kg linseed. Linseed extraction produces approximately 34 % oil, 64 %

linseed shells and 2 % losses. The linseed shells are pressed into linseed cake, which is used as cattle feed. Linseed cake has an economic value that periodically approaches that of linseed oil (Kuling 1993).

Resin

Resin from coniferous trees, which is used in linoleum, is known as colophonium. The principal function of resin is to hold the material together and to make it stick to the hessian. Resin is purchased chiefly from Portugal (van Oosterbosch 1993–1994). No data are available on cultivation, but the manufacturers assess the environmental impact of cultivation as negligible. The resin is transported in bulk by ship. The length of the voyage from Portugal to the Netherlands is estimated at 2 000 km.

Powdered wood

Powdered wood is used to give the sheeting resilience. The wood dust comes from southern Germany, mainly from the Schwarzwald and surrounding area. Coniferous trees are the most suitable type of wood. No data is available for the cultivation of wood in Germany, but it may be assumed that the powdered wood in linoleum is equivalent to that from Swedish pine. Powdered wood is usually transported in bulk by truck. The distance transported from southern Germany to the Netherlands is estimated at 600 km.

Table H8.2 Cradle-to-gate data for powdered wood production in Sweden (Jönsson et al. 1994).

Parameter	Amount	Source
Forest land	5.9 m^2, year/kg	–
Electricity	3.2 MJ/kg	Cultivation, grinding
Fossil fuel	0.2 MJ/kg	Felling, drying

Powdered limestone

Powdered limestone is used as mineral filler in linoleum for increasing the wear resistance of the flooring and giving it dimensional stability. The powdered limestone (calcium carbonate) comes from

444

southern Germany and southern France. It is transported in bulk on large trucks. At the time of the quarrying process the calcium carbonate is so solid that the stone has to be crushed. Mining and crushing give rise to an environmental load of 72 g dust/kg and 0.08 MJ electricity per kg powdered limestone. The distance transported is estimated at 800 km by truck. Half of the limestone is assumed to come from each place.

Pigment

Titanium dioxide is one of the most important pigments for linoleum flooring. For simplicity, it can be assumed that all pigment consists of titanium dioxide. Titanium dioxide is produced from ilmenite ore through the chloride process. The ore is transported approximately 500 km by road to the Netherlands and Belgium where the pigment is produced.

Table H8.3 Cradle-to-gate data for the production of 1 kg titanium dioxide from ilmenite ore (50 %) by the chloride process (Potting & Blok 1993).

Parameter	Amount
Electricity	47 MJ/kg
Coal	23 MJ/kg
Hazardous waste	2.3 kg/kg

Jute

Jute is an annual, 2–3 m tall plant in the lime family. It is native to north-eastern India, where it is cultivated on a large scale. Hessian from jute has long been used as a backing in linoleum flooring. For the studied product, jute is imported from plantations in India and Bangladesh (van Oosterbosch 1993–1994). It is harvested manually and the fibres are then separated from the rest of the trunk by a fermentation process. The fibres are dried, rolled through cylinders to soften them and then beaten and spun to a thread. These stages of the process take place locally. No data are available for the environmental impact of cultivation and extraction. Jute fibre is transported by ship. The distance transported from India to the Netherlands is estimated at 12 900 km by ship.

Linoleum production

Linseed oil is catalytically oxidised and polymerised in air in large tanks. This produces linoxyn, which is then mixed with resin. This cement is then mixed with powdered cork, powdered wood, powdered limestone and pigment. After the mixing process, a homogenous linoleum mass is obtained that is then converted into granules. The granules are fused to backing made from jute under pressure and with heat. The still soft sheeting is hung up in long loops in drying rooms to mature further. It is left there for two to three weeks. The sheets are coated, and the sheeting is trimmed and rolled. After packaging it is ready for sale. The production chain takes four to six weeks.

The data below applies to the production plant at Krommenie outside Amsterdam (van Oosterbosch 1993–1994). Linoleum wastage (from trimming and similar processes) is to more than 99 % recovered in the production process. The sheets go by truck from the factory to docks near Amsterdam, from where they are exported to customers around the world.

Table H8.4 Plant data for the production of 1 m^2 linoleum (density 2.3 t/m^3), simplified (van Oosterbosch 1993–1994).

Parameter	Amount
Electricity	6.5 MJ/m^2
Natural gas	15 MJ/m^2
VOC	4.6 g/m^2
Dust	0.7 g/m^2

Laying/use

According to floor-layers and material manufacturers, the wastage of material in laying is estimated at 10 %. The effective calorific value of linoleum prior to oxidation is estimated to be 17.7 MJ/kg. It is assumed that the material is removed by hand after use, and the actual removal process therefore does not have any major environmental impact.

446

European production of linseed oil

When the production plant in Krommenie buys linseed oil for lino-leum, the choice is governed by the price and quality of the prod-uct. European linseed oil could become a future alternative. There is a surplus of arable land in many European countries and farmers mainly in Northern Europe have started to grow linseed. European linseed cultivation can be found in France, Germany, Britain, the Netherlands, Scandinvia and the Baltic countries. The data pre-sented in the following concern linseed oil production in Sweden. Cultivation presently takes place on a small scale and the data would probably look different for large-scale cultivation.

Swedish linseed cultivation is mainly concentrated to the middle of the country, the Örebro region. A normal yield is around 1500 kg seed/hectare and the land use is 6.67 m^2/kg seed. Under favourable conditions the yield can rise to 3 000 kg seed/hectare. 60–70 kg of nitrogen fertiliser is recommended and a suitable fertiliser is NPK 16-6-17 (Larsson 1993). Energy use in the production of fertiliser is 47 MJ/kg nitrogen, 32 MJ/kg P and 10 MJ/kg K (Bertilsson 1990). Methods of cultivation and machinery (e.g. tractors) are conven-tional with an energy consumption of 80–100 l diesel oil/hectare during the whole of the cultivation. The linseed stem is chopped and ploughed back into the ground.

A screw press is used to extract the linseed oil. It produces 10–20 l of oil per hour and draws at least 2 kW. Around 25 % of the quan-tity of seed is oil and the remaining 75 % is turned into linseed cake and sold as animal feed. The density of the oil is 800 kg/m^3.

Exercise H9
Linoleum. Choice of waste management

Context

A city council is setting up a programme for "greening the city and its buildings". Part of this programme is to obtain environmental information on building materials and to formulate guidelines on what to do with various building wastes. In the area, there is only a landfill site used for waste management. The city is considering alternatives to landfilling, especially the possibility of sending the wastes to the waste incineration plant in another city located 75 km away.

Generally concerning waste management facilities, landfills are well distributed in the country, whereas incineration plants are fewer but have larger treatment capacity. The incineration plants, which operate with heat recovery, are located close to larger urban areas making use of the recovered energy in their district heating systems.

Task

Assess the overall environmental impact of linoleum flooring. In addition, answer the following question:

• From an environmental point of view, is it preferable to landfill linoleum after use or to incinerate it with heat recovery?

Discuss how stakeholders, i.e. other actors in the "linoleum system" might react or might be affected by your conclusions and recommendations concerning waste management of linoleum flooring. Examples of stakeholders are flooring producers, architects, housing management companies and citizens to name a few.

Technical description

The name linoleum comes from the Latin "linioleum" which means linseed oil. The name comes about because linseed oil is one of the main ingredients of linoleum. One of the world's largest production plants of linoleum at present is located at Krommenie, just outside Amsterdam in the Netherlands. 75 % of its production is exported throughout the world. The company operating the plant is the world's largest producer of linoleum.

Linoleum flooring for domestic use generally has a thickness of 2 mm and is estimated to have an average weight of 2.3 kg/m^2. The average lifetime is estimated at 25 years. The composition of the flooring material is presented in table H9.1.

448

Table H9.1 Material composition of linoleum (Jönsson et al. 1994).

Material	Weight %
Linseed oil	24
Resin	8
Powdered wood	30
Powdered cork	5
Powdered limestone	18
Pigment	4
Jute	11
Total	100

Raw material production

Linseed oil

Linseed oil, which is the most important raw material in the actual linoleum paste, acts as a binder. Linseed oil is bought from Argentina, Canada and the USA (Potting & Blok 1993). All the oils are transported by ship to the Netherlands. The average transport distance from Argentina, Canada and the USA to the Netherlands is estimated at 1 500 km by train and 4 350 km by ship.

Cultivation in the Americas produces about 0.6 tonnes of seed per hectare and year. On average 35 kg nitrogen, 17 kg P_2O_5 and 14 kg K_2O per hectare are added as fertiliser during cultivation. Energy use in the production of fertilisers is 34.9 MJ/kg nitrogen, 15.5 MJ/kg P_2O_5 and 8.6 MJ/kg K_2O (Potting & Blok 1993). Linseed cultivation requires relatively little fertiliser input compared with other common crops and any leakage of nutrients to water is negligible. The stalk is generally burnt or left in the field and is therefore not considered as waste. Energy use for threshing linseed amounts to 0.65 MJ/kg linseed oil.

The linseed is crushed and the oil is extracted either by pressing or by using naphta as a solvent. The oil can be extracted with or without supply of heat, resulting in hot-pressed or cold-pressed linseed oil. Hot-pressed oil is normally used in linoleum manufacturing. Electrical energy usage in the extraction process amounts to 0.54 MJ/kg linseed. Linseed extraction produces approximately 34 % oil, 64 % linseed shells and 2 % losses. The linseed shells are pressed into linseed cake, which is used as cattle feed. Linseed cake has an economic value that periodically approaches that of linseed oil (Kuling 1993).

Resin

Resin from coniferous trees, which is used in linoleum, is known as colophonium. The principal function of resin is to hold the material together and to make it stick to the hessian. Resin is purchased chiefly from Portugal (van Oosterbosch 1993–1994). No data is available on cultivation, but the manufacturers assess the environmental impact of cultivation as negligible. The resin is transported in bulk by ship. The length of the voyage from Portugal to the Netherlands is estimated at 2 000 km.

Powdered wood

Powdered wood is used to give the sheeting resilience. The wood dust comes from southern Germany, mainly from the Schwarzwald and surrounding area. Coniferous trees are the most suitable type of wood. No data is available for the cultivation of wood in Germany, but it may be assumed that the powdered wood in linoleum is equivalent to that from Swedish pine. Powdered wood is usually transported in bulk by truck. The distance transported from southern Germany to the Netherlands is estimated at 600 km.

Table H9.2 Cradle-to-gate data for powdered wood production in Sweden (Jönsson et al. 1994).

Parameter	Amount	Source
Forest land	5.9 m², year/kg	–
Electricity	3.2 MJ/kg	Cultivation, grinding
Fossil fuel	0.2 MJ/kg	Felling, drying

Powdered limestone

Powdered limestone is used as mineral filler in linoleum for increasing the wear resistance of the flooring and giving it dimensional stability. The powdered limestone (calcium carbonate) comes from

450

southern Germany and southern France. It is transported in bulk on large lorries. At the time of the quarrying process the calcium carbonate is so solid that the stone has to be crushed. Mining and crushing gives rise to an environmental load of 72 g dust/kg and 0.08 MJ electricity per kg powdered limestone. The distance transported is estimated at 800 km by truck. Half of the limestone is assumed to come from each place.

Pigment

Titanium dioxide is one of the most important pigments for linoleum flooring. For simplicity, it can be assumed that all pigment consists of titanium dioxide. Titanium dioxide is produced from ilmenite ore through the chloride process. The ore is transported approximately 500 km by road to the Netherlands and Belgium where the pigment is produced.

Table H9.3 Cradle-to-gate data for the production of 1 kg titanium dioxide from ilmenite ore (50 %) by the chloride process (Potting & Blok 1993).

Parameter	Amount
Electricity	47 MJ/kg
Coal	23 MJ/kg
Hazardous waste	2.3 kg/kg

Jute

Jute is an annual, 2–3 m tall plant in the lime family. It is native to north-eastern India, where it is cultivated on a large scale. Hessian from jute has long been used as a backing in linoleum flooring. For the studied product, jute is imported from plantations in India and Bangladesh (van Oosterbosch 1993–1994). It is harvested manually, and the fibres are then separated from the rest of the trunk by a fermentation process. The fibres are dried, rolled through cylinders to soften them and then beaten and spun to a thread. These stages of the process take place locally. No data is available for the environmental impact of cultivation and extraction. Jute fibre is transported by ship. The distance transported from India to the Netherlands is estimated at 12 900 km by ship.

Linoleum production

Linseed oil is catalytically oxidised and polymerised in air in large tanks. This produces linoxyn, which is then mixed with resin. This cement is then mixed with powdered cork, powdered wood, powdered limestone and pigment. After the mixing process a homogenous linoleum mass is obtained, which is then converted into granules. The granules are fused to backing, made from jute, under pressure and with heat. The still soft sheeting is hung up in long loops in drying rooms to mature further, and is left there for two to three weeks. The sheets are coated and the sheeting is trimmed and rolled. After packaging it is ready for sale. The production chain takes four to six weeks.

The data below applies to the production plant at Krommenie outside Amsterdam (van Oosterbosch 1993–1994). Linoleum wastage (from trimming and similar processes) is to more than 99 % recovered in the production process. The sheets go by truck from the factory to docks near Amsterdam, from where they are exported to customers around the world. The transportation distance between Amsterdam and the city undertaking the LCA study is 900 km by ship and 400 km by truck from the port.

Table H9.4 Plant data for the production of 1 m^2 linoleum (density 2.3 t/m^3), simplified (van Oosterbosch 1993–1994).

Parameter	Amount
Electricity	6.5 MJ/m^2
Natural gas	15 MJ/m^2
VOC	4.6 g/m^2
Dust	0.7 g/m^2

Laying/use

Following consultation with floor-layers and material manufacturers, the wastage of material in floor laying is estimated at 10 %. The effective calorific value of linoleum prior to oxidation is estimated at to 17.7 MJ/kg. It is assumed that the material is removed by hand after use, and the actual removal process therefore does not have any major environmental impact.

Final disposal

Landfill

It is assumed that after use the flooring is generally disposed of in landfills. The average distance from user to final disposal is estimated as 30 km by road (Audelius 1993).

Incineration

As an alternative to landfilling, linoleum may be incinerated with heat recovery after use. The calorific value of linoleum is 12.5 MJ/kg.

Exercise H10
Apples. Development of type III eco-labelling

Context

The "International Fruit Growers' Association" (IFGA) wants to introduce a type III ecolabel (ISO 14025) for apples, i.e. an environmental product declaration (EPD). Such a declaration would be applicable to all apples, not just ecologically produced apples. An EPD presents the environmental profile of a product. According to the ISO 14025 standard, certain information is required in the EPD. In addition, product-specific information can be added.

To help the LCA consultant, IFGA has sent out a questionnaire to apple growers in three different geographic regions. The information collected via the questionnaire has been compiled and handed over to the LCA consultant.

Task

The assignment from IFGA consists of preparing for an EPD for apples. Questions asked by the commissioner are:

1 Should the EPD be aimed at end-consumers or food retailers or another actor in the product chain?

2 Are the general information criteria sufficient to ensure fair comparisons between different apples? What additional, product-specific parameters should be included in the product specific requirements (PSR)?

In the report, IFGA wants a presentation of the most important aspects of the EPD and the PSR for apples (recommended audience, information criteria, other aspects to be included in the product specific rules, etc). The recommendations should be explained and motivated. In addition, IFGA wants examples of what the EPD would look like for three types of apples.

Technical description

Apple production consists roughly of the following steps: orchard preparation, apple cultivation, sorting/packing/storing, transportation and distribution, selling, and finally, consumption.

The objective of the orchard preparation phase is to prepare the soil for new apple cultivation. Before trees are planted, the soil must be drained, limed and fertilised properly. In addition, different measures for plant protection are needed to prevent insect and fungus attacks. Apple trees are productive for 15 to 25 years, depending on the type, and it takes up to 2 years before the first crop can be harvested.

Apple cultivation includes all the activities necessary to harvest the apple at the end of the season. Weed control, plant protection, fertilisation and irrigation are carried out repeatedly during the growth season. Pruning, which influences harvest quality and quantity, is done some time after the harvest. Normally it is done manually.

After the harvest, the apples are usually transported to a packing house where apples are quality sorted, packaged and put in cool storage. Apples are often stored in controlled atmosphere (low oxygen concentration, high CO_2 concentration). Storage time varies a lot since apples are sold all year round. Some fruit can be stored until the next season. Sometimes pest and fungus control is needed during storage.

454

Apples are distributed to apple grocers all over the world from the packing house. Long-distance transportation requires special cooling facilities. The apple grocers, in turn, deliver the apples to retailers and supermarkets, where they eventually are sold to end-consumers.

French apple production

Fruit and vegetable cultivation play a very important role in French agriculture. There is a wide range of cultivation thanks to the varying climatic conditions between the north and south, west and east regions. Apple cultivators in France are careful in maintaining high quality fruit and many intend to change to more environmentally friendly production methods. Different regions have their specific problems. Fungus attacks are a problem in the northwest due to the humidity, while insect attacks are a problem in the dry climate in the south. French cultivators prefer trees with longer lifetimes. Mas du Mourges, the most common tree, brings a crop 2 years after planting and has a 25-year cultivation period before it is exchanged. Data presented below come from orchards producing approximately 72 400 kg of apples per year and hectare in the Rhône valley.

Orchard preparation

Draining: Not needed since the soil is quite loose and the climate is dry.

Liming: Not needed since the soil is rich in lime.

Fertilising: A total of 1 000 kg granular fertiliser is spread 4 times per season. The total amount of nutritive substance is 179 kg N/ha, 212 kg P/ha and 152 kg K/ha. Tractor total diesel consumption is 7.68 MJ/ha.

Soil cultivation: Ploughing and harrowing consumes 1296 MJ diesel/ha.

Planting: 1426 plants are planted per hectare. Planting is manual and tractors are used for transport, ploughing, digging and filling back the soil after planting. Tractors consume 232 MJ diesel/ha.

Irrigation: The orchard is irrigated every 12 days between June 2 and August 15. Water is pumped from the river. Total water consumption during this period is 2 887 m^3/ha. Electrical pumps consume 641.7 kWh/ha.

Plant protection: Chemicals used for preparing the orchard are listed in table H10.1. The orchard preparation needs less chemical control for plant protection than during apple cultivation (compare tables H10.1 and H10.3). Tractors consume 1 368 MJ/ha.

Table H10.1 Chemicals used for orchard preparation (f: fungicide; i: insecticide).

Pesticide	Manu-facturer	Cate-gory	Active substance	Total amount (kg/ha)	Total active substance (kg/ha)
Manzate	DuPont	f	Mancozeb 80 %	9.6	7.68
Bayleton	Bayer SA	f	Triadimethon 5 %	2.4	0.12
Enduro	Bayer SA	i	Betacyfluthryne Oxydemethon-methyl	0.96	7.68×10^{-3} 0.24
Golclair S	DuPont	–	Sulphur 58.3 % Oil element 1.8 %	63	36.7 1.134
Sépicap	DuPont	f	Captan 83 %	9.6	7.97
Insegar	La Qui-noléine	i	Fenoxycarbe 25 %	0.6	0.15
Score	Ciba-Geigy	f	Difenoconazole	0.36	0.09
Gusathion XL	Bayer SA	i	Azinphosmethyl 25 %	4.2	1.05
Omite 30 WP	Schering	i	Propargite 30 %	4.8	0.147

Apple cultivation

Pruning: Done manually with scissors and saws. Remains are put in a crusher consuming 53.4 MJ diesel/ha. Chemical thinning is done in addition to manual pruning. 0.9 l liquid trifocide is sprayed per hectare. The active substance is DNOC (562.2 g/ha). The spraying tractor uses 83 MJ diesel/ha.

456

Fertilising: 150 kg granulated ammonium nitrate/ha is spread in March. Tractor uses 82.9 MJ diesel/ha.

Irrigation: The orchard is irrigated every 12 days between June 2 and August 15. Water is pumped from the river. A total of 3850 m^3/ha is used each season. The electrical pumps use a total of 855.6 kWh/ha.

Weed control: Control of weed is done once per season (in March) and only under the trees and not on the pathway. The type and amount of herbicides used are shown in table H10.2. The tractor uses 60.5 MJ diesel/ha.

Table H10.2 Herbicides for weed control during apple cultivation.

Herbicide	Manu-facturer	Active substance	Total amount (l/ha)	Total amount (g/kg) apple	Total active substance (g/kg) apple
Azural AT	Monsanto	Glyphosat 120 g/l	10	0.138	0.0166
Compliss	Sipcam-Phyteurop	Diuron 250 g/l Terbuthylazine 250 g/l	6	0.0414 0.0414	0.02072 0.02072
Actiprom AM		Petroleum oil 850 g/l	2	0.0235	0.0235

Plant protection: Chemical plant protection plays an important role mainly against insect attacks but also for tree growth (see table H10.3). Spraying can be done up to 22 times in a season. The chemicals are dissolved in water (1 200 l water/ha and spraying). The spraying tractor uses 124 MJ diesel/ha and spraying. In addition to the chemical control, the orchard also has a sophisticated protection system against hail. A radar detects hail in a 30 km radius around the plantation. When hail is detected, 6 carbide canons are fired into the clouds to break the hail.

Table H10.3 Chemicals used for plant protection during apple cultivation (f: fungicide; i: insecticide).

Pesticide	Manu-facturer	Cate-gory	Active substance	Total amount (g/kg) apple	Total active substance (g/kg) apple
Manzate	DuPont	f	Mancozeb 80 %	0.133	0.106
Bayleton	Bayer SA	f	Triadimethon 5 %	0.0331	1.657×10^{-3}
Enduro	Bayer SA	i	Betacyfluthryne 8g/l Oxydemethonme-thyl 250 g/l	0.0133	1.06×10^{-4} 3.31×10^{-3}
Golclair S	DuPont	–	Sulphur Oil element	0.870	0.50 0.0157
Sépicap	DuPont	f	Captan 83 %	0.199	0.165
Insegar	La Qui-noléine	I	Fenoxycarbe 25 %	8.29×10^{-3}	2.072×10^{-3}
Score	Ciba-Geigy	f	Difenoconazole 250g/l	4.97×10^{-3}	1.24×10^{-3}
Klartan	Sandoz Agro	i	Tau Fluvalinate 240 g/l	9.94×10^{-3}	2.39×10^{-3}
Masai	Syanada-mid Agro	i	Tebufenpyrad 20 %	8.29×10^{-3}	1.66×10^{-3}
Gusa-thion XL	Bayer SA	i	Azinphosmethyl 25 %	0.116	0.029
Decis Micro	Procida	i	Deltamethrine 6.25 %	3.31×10^{-3}	2.072×10^{-3}
Omite 30 WP	Schering	i	Propargite 30 %	0.0663	0.0203
Methyle-uparene	Bayer SA	f	Tolylfluanide 50 %	0.0497	0.0249

Harvesting: The 24 picking teams use ladders and picking baskets. One picking team can harvest 60 tonnes of apples in 20 hours. Two tractors are used to transport the apples from the field to the farm-yard. The tractors use 0.1836 MJ/kg apple. At the farmyard apples are sprayed with fungicides before being sent to the packing house (see table H10.4). Each day 180 tonnes of apples pass the farmyard.

Table H10.4 Fungicides used on harvested apples. The amount of apples daily treated with fungicides is 180 tonnes.

Fungicide	Manu-facturer	Active substance	Total amount (kg/day)	Total active substance (g/ kg apple)
Xédamine	Xéda	Diphenylamine 200 g/l	2	2.22×10^{-3}
Xédaquine	Xéda	Ethoxyquine 500 g/l	2	5.56×10^{-3}

Sorting/packing/storage of apples

Transportation: The packing house in Marsillargues is close to the farmyard, only 4 km away. Trucks with a capacity of 14 tonnes of apples are used for the transport.

Sorting and packaging: The packing house has a modern handling system to sort, store and pack the fruit. Around 19 200 tonnes of apples are packed in a year. The apples are sorted according to size, form, colour and other quality properties as soon as they arrive. Sorting is done using picture analysis in a water container system. After sorting the fruit is put in boxes in the cool storage. Natural gas is used to dry apples and to run the trucks in the packing house. Annual gas consumption is 36 037 (normal) m^3 (energy content: 11.525 kWh/(normal) m^3). The annual electricity usage for packing and sorting is 693 361 kWh.

Storage: Apples are stored in a modern store with controlled atmosphere (low oxygen concentration, high CO_2 concentration). Storing time varies a lot. Some fruit leaves the storage after a short time while some is stored until the next harvest in June. Average storage time is 5 months. Electricity consumption is 751 143 kWh/year. Apples are taken out of storage and packed in cartons when they are sold. Apples leave the packing house in trucks with cooling facilities. Each truck can carry up to 23 tonnes.

Swedish apple production

The most famous Swedish apple is Ingrid Marie followed by Cox Orange. Traditionally, only thin layer soil is utilised for apple cultivation because more fertile soil is used to grow other crops (corn, grain or wheat). Probably the biggest problem in apple cultivation is scurf (a fungus attack due to humid climate), which is controlled chemically. 15 years is considered to be the normal cultivation duration in Sweden. The time before the first harvest depends on the type of plant material. For plants of B-AAA quality from Holland the first harvest is on the second season, i.e. one or one and a half years after planting. The amount of the first harvest is up to 4.55 tonnes/ha. It increases to full harvest (40 tonnes) after 5 years. Around 90 % of the Swedish apples are grown in the south-east.

Orchard preparation

Draining: The soil in the area needs draining. It is done by laying PVC draining pipes in the ground (388 g/m; 660 m/ha). This system is assumed to last for 30 years. Pipes are laid using either a plough or a chain digger. Additional machines for digging, coupling pipes and filling in the ditches are also used. Diesel consumption for laying pipes is 0.1 litre/m pipe. Diesel consumption for digging and filling is 5.5 l/ha.

Liming: It is not necessary to lime the soil due to the natural availability of lime in the soil.

Fertilising: Granular monoammonphosphate (MAP) is added when new seeds are planted. Another fertiliser, N28, is applied four weeks later. Each fertiliser is added at 32.7 kg/ha.

Soil cultivation: A diesel tractor is used for ploughing (31.7 l/ha) and harrowing (5.37 l/ha).

Planting: 1 633 seed plants are planted per hectare. Part of the planting is done manually, but much of it is done with machines (digging and soil covering). An old gasoline-driven Massey Ferguson is used (29.9 l/ha). Trees are trimmed once before harvest. Trimming is done manually with a pneumatic trimmer. A diesel tractor powers the compressor (27.8 l/ha). The remains are crushed mechanically (1.5 l diesel/ha).

Irrigation: Drip irrigation takes place during the whole growth season (3 250 litres per day and hectare; 120 days per year). The drip irrigation system consists of pipes, which run along the tree rows. The water drips through a small hole near each tree. This construction is meant to make it possible to add fertiliser for the plants. An electrical pump (4 kW, 200 l/min) is used. During the first season 12 kg N/ha, 3 kg P/ha, 16 kg K/ha and 4 kg Mg/ha are added to the irrigation water.

Plant protection: The trees are sprayed up to 9 times/season with one or more pesticides (see table H10.5) to avoid fungus and insect attacks. Benlate is used against scurf, Topas C against fungus, Pirimor G against loess and Gusathion for apple quality improvement. A diesel tractor is used for spraying (3 l/ha × spraying).

Table H10.5 Chemicals for plant protection during orchard preparation (f: fungicide; i: insecticide).

Pesticide	Manu-facturer	Cate-gory	Active substance	Total amount (kg/ha)	Total active substance (kg/ha)
Benlate	Bayer AG	f	Benomyl 50 %	6.3	3.15
Topas C	Bayer AG	f	Penconazole 2,5 % Captan 48 %	4.5	0.1125 2.16
Pirimor	Zeneca Agro	i	Pirimicarb 50 %	0.4	0.2
Gusathion 50WP	Bayer AG	i	Azinphosmethyl 25 %	1	0.25

Apple cultivation

The activities listed below are carried out every apple season in order to be able to harvest at the end of the season. Weed control and irrigation are done repeatedly during the whole season, but the total sums per season are given below. The average crop is 40 tonnes of apples/ha.

Pruning: This is done in the late winter to influence harvest quality and quantity. A pneumatic trimmer is used for the manual trimming. A diesel tractor powers the compressor (55.6 l/ha). The remains are put in a crusher (3 l diesel/ha).

Fertilising: Fertilisers are applied via the drip irrigation system: 0.9725 g N/kg apple; 0.215 g P/kg apple; 0.1525 g K/kg apple; 0.299 g Mg/kg apple; 0.545 g S/kg apple.

Irrigation: Irrigation starts in mid-May and continues until mid-October (120 days). Daily water consumption is 6500 litre/hectare. The electrical pump (4 kW) has a capacity of 200 litres/minute.

Weed control: Herbicides are applied four times per season. They are spread between the apple rows, which means that only half of the orchard area is sprayed. Roundup (total amount 10.53 kg/ha; total amount of active substance Glyphosate 4.42 kg/ha) and Hormotex 750 (total amount 3 l/ha; total amount of active substance MCPA 2.25 kg/ha) are used. Spraying is done with a single ramp-spray box on a gasoline-driven tractor (9.24 l/ha).

Plant protection: Spraying is done 13 times per season. Mostly chemical control is used (see table H10.6), although biological control is also possible. The chemicals are dissolved in water (200 l/ha per spraying). The spraying equipment is mounted on a diesel tractor (3 l/ha per spraying).

Table H10.6 Chemicals used for plant protection during apple cultivation (f: fungicide; i: insecticide).

Pesticide	Manu-facturer	Cate-gory	Active substance	Total amount (g/kg) apple	Total active substance (g/kg) apple
Topas C	Bayer AG	f	Penconazole 2.5 % Captan 48 %	0.1875	0.004688 0.09
Europaren M	Bayer AG	f	Tolylfluanid 25 %	0.1875	0.0938
Roxion 40 EC	Bayer AG	i	Dimethoate 38 %	0.0389	0.01478
Pirimor	Zeneca Agro	i	Pirimicarb 50 %	0.1875	0.00938
Gusathion WP	Bayer AG	i	Azinphosmethyl	0.05625	0.01406

Harvesting: Apple picking is manual with 2 gasoline driven tractors transporting the fruit within the plantation (6 l/ha). The crop amounts to 40 ton/ha and the harvest capacity is 2 ha/day.

Sorting/packing/storage of apples

Transportation: The packing house is located 7 km away from the orchard. Apples are loaded in boxes (260 kg apples/box). A tractor is used for the transport. Each trip takes 35 boxes. Empty boxes are returned on the way back to the orchard. For a return trip the tractor consumes 2.8 l of diesel fuel.

Storage: Apples not immediately sold are stored in cool storage (3 °C). Storage starts in mid-October and continues until January. The cool storage has room for 600 tonnes of apples. Electricity consumption varies with outdoor temperature (from 282 kWh/day to 382 kWh/day).

Sorting and packaging: Apples are taken out from the cool storage when there is a purchase order. Apples are sorted and packed before they are transported to the client. Sorting machines, pneumatic carton folders and packing equipment have a capacity of approximately 1750 kg/hr. The whole sorting and packing line is electrically powered (3.46 kWh/tonne of apples). Most transportation is by truck.

New Zealand apple production

Apple cultivation is an important industry in New Zealand. The country exports cover around 20 % of the world's market. The climate in New Zealand is very favourable for fruit cultivation with a long season with suitable temperatures and high precipitation. The most popular products are Gala and Royal Gala. Development of apple species is important and a lot of money has been invested in it. Previously big trees with rapidly growing stems were common. Now slower growing stem trees with a shorter cultivation period are preferred. An apple tree can last for 17 years before it is replaced by a new one. Data are given for Hawkes Bay with a 15-year cultivation period.

Orchard preparation

Draining: Draining is not necessary since the soil is self-draining.

Liming: Analysis establishes whether liming is needed. Liming is usually conducted every 7 years. Agricultural lime is used (1 t/ha; 12.82 g/kg apple) and spread using the fertiliser spray and a diesel tractor (3.65 l/ha; 1.658×10^{-3} MJ/kg apple).

Fertilising: The soil in Hawkes Bay is rich in nutrient, since it consists of old sea bottom and flood sediment, which is why only a small amount of is fertiliser is needed. Granulated nitrogen fertiliser (250 N-rich urea kg/ha; 3.205 g/kg apple) is used. It is spread by a centrifuge spreader on a Honda mini-tractor (1.5 litre gasoline/ha; 2.04×10^{-4} MJ/kg apple).

Soil cultivation: The soil is cultivated in four steps (soil mill, deep cultivation and 2 laps of harrowing the soil surface) using a diesel tractor (7.6 l/ha; 0.0242 MJ/kg apple).

Planting: Relatively large trees are used, for which reason fewer seed plants are planted per unit area (888 plants/ha; 11.4 g/kg apple). Planting is mostly manual with the help of a furrow dragged by a diesel tractor (33.2 l/ha; 0.0150 MJ/kg apple).

Irrigation: A low angle spreader is used and there are 5 sprayings during each season (total water used: 2 500 m³/ha and season; 32.050 g/kg apple). The pump system uses 0.0425 MJ electricity/kg apple.

Plant protection: Plants are protected chemically with insecticides and fungicides (see table H10.7). A breeze sprayer on a diesel tractor is used (19.49 l/ha; 8.841×10^{-3} MJ/kg apple).

Table H10.7 Chemicals for plant protection during orchard preparation (f: fungicide; i: insecticide).

Pesticide	Manu-facturer	Cate-gory	Active substance	Total amount (kg/ha)	Total active substance (kg/ha)
Dodine 400	NuFarm Ltd.	f	Dodine 50 %	3.84	1.92
Lorsban WP	Dow Elanco	i	Chlorpyrifos 25 %	2.4	0.6
Pallitop	BASF	f	Nitrothalisopro-pyl 48 %	2.4	1.152
			Metiram 3.2 %		0.0768

Apple cultivation

The cultivation period is 15 years. There are variations from year to year, but some data represent the mean value collected for several years. Otherwise, data are from 1995–1996.

Pruning: This is done manually with saws and scissors. The waste is crushed using a machine powered by a diesel tractor (7.34×10^{-3} MJ/kg apple).

Fertilising: Although the soil is nutrient rich, some fertiliser is added every year. Granulated fertiliser (300 kg calcium ammonium nitrate/ha; 3.846 g/kg apple) is spread with a centrifuge spreader on a diesel tractor (7.3 litre/ha; 8.83×10^{-4} MJ/kg apple).

Irrigation: A low angle spreader is used, and there are 5 sprayings during each season (total water used: 2 500 m³/ha and season; 32.050 g/kg apple). The pump system uses 0.0425 MJ electricity/kg apple.

Weed control: This is done five times per season with chemicals and spraying tractors (15 l diesel/ha; 6.81×10^{-3} MJ/kg apple). The pesticide used is "Roundup" (active substance: glyphosate 42 %). The total amount of pesticide is 0.075 g/kg apple (5.85 kg/ha) and the total amount of active substance is 0.0315 g/kg apple.

Plant protection: Chemicals are used against disease, fungus and insect attacks (see table H10.8). 15 rounds of spraying take place in a season. The chemicals are dissolved in water. The total water consumption is 15 326 l/ha (0.1965 l/kg apple). The spraying tractor uses 0.02160 MJ diesel/kg apple.

Table H10.8 Chemicals used for plant protection during apple cultivation (f: fungicide; i: insecticide).

Pesticide	Manu-facturer	Cate-gory	Active substance	Total amount (g/kg apple)	Total active substance (g/kg apple)
Syllit Plus	Rhône-Poulenc	f	Dodine 50 %	0.0640	0.0326
Nustar	DuPont	f	Flusilazole 39 %	3.384×10^{-3}	1.31×10^{-3}
Manzate	DuPont	f	Mancozeb 80 %	0.05128	0.041
Orthocide	Chevron Chemicals	f	Captan 50 %	0.03846	0.01923
Pallitop	BASF	f	Nitrothal isopropyl 48 %	0.02308	0.01108
			Metiram 3.2 %		7.39×10^{-4}
Diazinon 50WP	Ciba Geigy	i	Diazinon 50 %	0.01646	8.23×10^{-3}
Lorsban WP	Dow Elanco	i	Chlorpyrifos 25 %	0.03846	9.615×10^{-3}
Gusathion 50WP	Bayer AG	i	Azinphosmethyl 25 %	0.05	0.0125
Applaud	Dow Elanco	i	Buprofezin 25 %	0.02564	6.41×10^{-3}
D-C-Tron			Mineral oil	0.44	0.44

Harvesting: 78 000 kg apples/ha are harvested manually. Picking bags and ladders are mostly used. A diesel tractor is used for transportation around the field (306.6 litres/ha; 0.1382 MJ/kg apple).

Sorting/packing/storage of apples

Transportation: After the harvest boxes full of apple are transported by lorry to the Horticulture Packing House in Whakatu around 15 km from the cultivation field. Each truck has a capacity of 21 tonnes of apples.

Sorting and packaging: the fruit is sorted according to 3 categories (79 % export quality, 10 % local quality and 11 % industrial quality). Each package weighs 20 kg (18.3 kg apple and 1.7 kg paper material). Electricity is used for packing and sorting (0.0041 MJ/kg apple).

Storage: ENZA's cool storage is located 1 km away from the packing house and 20 km from the harbour in Napier. The fruit is stored here while waiting to be exported by boat. Storage time varies but is normally 3 weeks. The cool storage requires electricity (0.02814 MJ/kg apple and month).

General information – fertiliser production

In addition to water, sunshine and carbon dioxide, plants need small amounts of inorganic nutrients for growth. The major elements required by most plants are nitrogen, potassium, phosphorus, calcium, magnesium, and sulphur. Calcium is usually plentiful in soil, but nitrogen (N), potassium (K) and phosphorus (P) availability often limit plant growth and are added through fertilisers. The different nutrients can be added individually, but there are fertiliser products that include two or more nutrients, e.g. ammonium nitrate. An NPK fertiliser is a fertiliser product that contains N, P and K. The amount of N, P and K is given in the fertiliser name, for example in NPK 18.46.0 the content of N is 18 % (by weight), P 46 % and K 0 %. The following data are based on Patyk's work on fertiliser production (Patyk 1996).

Nitrogen-based fertilisers: Industrial fertiliser production is very energy intensive (see table H10.9). Although there are several types

466

of N-based fertilisers, the chemical process for producing them is similar. It extracts nitrogen (N_2) from the air and transforms it into a nitrate (NO_3^-).

Table H10.9 Cradle-to-gate data on the production of nitrogen based fertilisers (Patyk 1996).

Fertilisers	HNO_3	Urea	CAN*	KNO_3
N-content (%)	22.2 %	46.7 %	25.8 %	13.8 %
K-content (%)	0	0	0	38.6 %
Total (MJ/kg)	35.0	49.3	40.5	35.0
Oil (MJ/kg)	5.82	5.64	6.02	5.82
Natural gas (MJ/kg)	34.4	33.3	35.6	34.4
Coal (MJ/kg)	4.27	4.14	4.42	4.27
Heat (MJ/kg)	−9.6	5.4	−5.9	−9.6
Electricity (MJ/kg)	0.1	0.8	0.4	0.1

* CAN: calcium ammonium nitrate

Phosphorus-based fertilisers: These are based on phosphate mineral, which is mined. The energy consumption is therefore lower than for nitrogen-based fertilisers (see table H10.10). Phosphate is a common ingredient in several fertilisers such as NPK and ammonium nitrate.

Table H10.10 Cradle-to-gate data on the production of phosphorous-based fertilisers (Patyk 1996).

Fertilisers	MAP (monoammon-phosphate)	H_3PO_4
P_2O_5-content (%)	50 %	54 %
Total (MJ/kg P_2O_5)	8.39	5.76
Oil (MJ/kg P_2O_5)	0.69	0.51
Natural gas (MJ/kg P_2O_5)	0.52	0.39
Heat (MJ/kg P_2O_5)	5.33	3.65
Electricity (MJ/kg P_2O_5)	1.84	1.21

References

Audelius, B (1993). RVF, the Swedish Association of Solid Waste Management, Malmö, Sweden. Personal communication.

Bertilsson, Göte (1990). *Hydro Supra*, Sweden. Personal communication.

Björklund, Thomas, Åsa Jönsson & Anne-Marie Tillman (1996). *LCA of building frame structures. Environmental impact over the life cycle of concrete and steel frames.* TEP report 1996:8, Technical Environmental Planning, Chalmers University of Technology, Göteborg, Sweden.

Chalmers Industriteknik (1990). *Resurs- och avfallssnåla förpackningar (Resource and waste saving packaging).* Electrolux-PADD. Göteborg, Sweden.

Eriksson, Karl Johan. Personal communication, 1991. PLM AB, Limmared, Sweden.

Holmgren, Bo. Personal communication 1991. Neste Polyeten AB. Stenungsund, Sweden.

Jönsson, Åsa, Anne-Marie Tillman & Torbjörn Svensson (1994). *Livscykelanalys av golvmaterial.* (Life cycle assessment of flooring materials.) R30:1994, Swedish council for building researchers, Stockholm, Sweden.

Karlsson, Lars. Personal communication 1991. Rosenlew Emballage AB.

Kuling, M (1993). *Örebro county agricultural society.* Personal communication.

Larsson, S-E (1993). *National linseed advisor,* Örebro, Sweden. Personal communication.

Neste Polyeten AB (1990). *Environmental Report 1990.* Stenungsund, Sweden.

Nyström, Ebbe. Personal communication, 1991. Svensk glasåtervinning AB.

van Oosterbosch, J (1993–1994). *Linoleum production plant,* Krommenie, the Netherlands. Personal communication and visits to the factory.

Patyk, Andreas (1996). "Balance of Energy Consumption and Emissions of Fertiliser Production and Supply". In: *Pre-prints from the International Conference on Application of Life Cycle Assessment in*

Agriculture, Food and Non-Food Agroindustry and Forestry. Brussels. 4–5 April 1996.

Potting, J & K Blok (1993). *De milieugerichte levensyklusanlyse van vier typen vloerbedekking.* (The environmental life cycle assessment of four types of floor covering). P-UB-93-4, Coordination point science shops, Utrecht, the Netherlands.

REPAB (1992). *Underhållskostnader 1992, utvändigt och invändigt bygg.* (Maintenance costs 1992, for exterior and interior of buildings.) REPAB Program AB, Mölndal Sweden.

Rydell, Ewa. Personal communication 1992. Zanda AB. Borensberg, Sweden.

Röstein. Personal communication 1991. Norska Oljedirektoratet (The Norwegian Oil Directorate). Stavanger, Norway.

Scanraff (1990). *Environmental Report 1990.* Lysekil, Sweden.

Statoil Petrokemi AB (1990). *Environmental Report 1990.* Stenungsund, Sweden.

Stålmalm, O. Personal communication 1992. Vittinge AB. Vittinge, Sweden.

Sundström, G (1990). *Energiförbrukning och miljöbelastning för distributionssystem för öl och läsk i Sverige (Energy consumption and environmental load of beer and soft drink distribution system in Sweden).* Miljöbalans Gustav Sundström AB, Malmö, Sweden.

Solutions to some exercises

Here you will find the solutions to exercise A on functional unit definition, exercise C, the Beginner's LCA and exercise E on allocation.

Exercise A
Problem solution

Solution 1

- Soft drink packaging
  Compared alternatives are for example glass bottles, PET bottles, aluminium cans, steel cans. The functional unit is *litre in a particular size of packaging*, for example 33/50 cl servings or for 1.5 l servings.

- Light bulbs
  Compared alternatives are for example normal light bulbs, energy saving ones, etc. The functional unit is *year (use time) for a specified lux*.

- Waste management options for discarded cardboard boxes.
  Compared alternatives are for example landfilling, incineration, recycling. The functional unit is *kg cardboard*.

- Wall cover
  Compared alternatives are for example wall paper, paint, etc. The functional unit is *m^2 and year* owing to different life times of wall covers.

- Newspaper
  The functional unit is *journal and day*.

- Passenger transportation
  Compared alternatives are for example cars, buses, bicycles, etc. The functional unit is *person and km*.

- Goods transportation
  Compared alternatives are for example goods transportation by air, ship, rail or road. The functional unit is *tonne and km* (weight limited transport) or *tonne and m^3* (volume limited transport).

- Clothes washing
  The functional unit is *kg wash specified as either white/coloured and at a particular temperature*. How white is white is a qualitative aspect – it is, however, possible to refer to a standard.

- Bread
  Compared alternatives are for example industrial factory bread, local bakery bread, home baked bread. The functional unit is *loaf* or *kcal* or *normal daily serving*. Qualitative aspects such as taste, smell, etc have to be considered in parallel.

Solution 2

- Soft drink distribution. Alternative product concepts: soda fountains? Soda streams? Powders to mix with water?
- Lighting. Alternative concepts: windows, candles, solar cell operated lights.
- Waste management. Alternative concepts: not easily found.
- Wall covers. Alternative concepts: decoration and wall cover in one (e.g. recycled music sheets), spray paint, wall and furniture in one (bookcase, cupboards).
- Newspaper. Alternative concepts: news on-line in various ways? Personalised news-papers (without the sections you are not interested in).
- Person transportation. Alternative concepts: personal mobility, accessibility => video conferencing.
- Goods transportation. Alternative concepts: not easily found.
- Clothes washing. Alternative concepts: dry cleaning, laundromat (large scale centralised clothes washing).
- Bread. Alternative concepts: more müsli? Other carbohydrates?

Exercise C
Problem solution

1. Flowchart

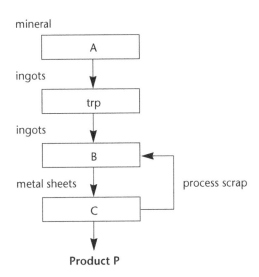

2. Normalisation for each activity

Plant A

Main product (ingots):	1 200 tonnes A/year
Resource use:	
Mineral 4 800 tonnes/yr	4 kg mineral/kg A
Energy (oil) 12×10^6 MJ/year	10 MJ_{th}/kg A
Emissions:	
HCl 600 kg/year	0.5 g HCl/kg A (to air)
Cu 600 kg/year	0.5 g Cu/kg A (to water)
Solid waste:	3.17 kg waste/kg A

Plant B

Main product (metal sheets):	1 600 tonnes B/year
Resource use:	
Ingots 900 tonnes/year	0.565 2 kg A/kg B
Metal scrap 700 tonnes/year	0.437 5 kg scrap/kg B
Energy (electricity) 3.04×10^6 MJ/year	1.9 MJ_e/kg B
Energy (electricity) 1.76×10^6 MJ/year	1.1 MJ_e/kg B
Emissions:	
HC 480 kg/year	0.3 g HC/kg B (to air)

Plant C

Main product:	400 tonnes P/year
Resource use:	
Metal sheets 480 tonnes/year	1.2 kg B/kg P
Energy (oil) 0.3×10^6 MJ/year	0.75 MJ_{th}/kg P
Energy (electricity) 1.2×10^6 MJ/year	3 MJ_e/kg P
Emissions:	
HC 250 kg/year	0.625 g/kg P
Scrap: 80 tonnes/year	0.20 kg scrap/kg P

3. Input-output balance

Input-output balance for each activity:

A: $r = 4a$ (1)
Trp: $a = a'$ (2)
B: $a' + s = b$ (3)
C: $b = p + s_c$ (4)
     $s_c = 0.2p$ (5)

Functional unit:

f.u. p = 1 000 pieces × 40 g/piece = 40 kg metal (6)

The equation system contains 7 variables and 6 equations, 1 more equation is needed:

Solution 1:

B: $s = s_c$ (7a) => $s = s_c = 0.2p = 8$ kg metal scrap/f.u.

  $b = 1.2p = 48$ kg metal sheet/f.u.

  $a = a' = b - s = p = 40$ kg metal ingot/f.u.

  $r = 4a = 4p = 160$ kg mineral/f.u.

Solution 2:

B: $s = 0.4375b$ (7b) => $s_c = 0.2p = 8$ kg metal scrap/f.u.

  $b = 1.2p = 48$ kg metal sheet/f.u.

  $s = 0.525p = 21$ kg metal scrap/f.u.

  $a = a' = b - s = p = 27$ kg metal ingot/f.u.

  $r = 4a = 4p = 108$ kg mineral/f.u.

  $s^* = s - s_c = 13$ kg metal scrap/f.u.

4. Energy calculation

Σ energy requirement = Σ normalised energy requirement × mass flow/f.u.

A   10 MJ oil/kg A × 40 kg A/f.u. = 400 MJ oil/f.u.

Trp 0.001 MJ diesel/tonne-km × 1000 km × 40 kg A/f.u.

B   3.0 MJ electricity/kg B × 48 kg B/f.u. = 144 MJ_e/f.u.

C   0.75 MJ oil/kg P × 40 kg P/f.u. = 30 MJ oil/f.u.

  3.0 MJ electricity/kg P × 40 kg P/f.u. = 120 MJ_e/f.u.

Σ 400 MJ oil + 40 MJ diesel + 30 MJ oil = 470 MJ fossil

Σ 144 MJ_e + 120 MJ_e = 264 MJ electricity

5. Emission factors

Σ emission = Σ energy requirement × emission factor

A   400 MJ oil × 0.018 g HC/MJ oil = 7.2 g HC

  400 MJ oil × 0.15 g NO_x/MJ oil = 60 g NO_x

  400 MJ oil × 79.8 g CO_2/MJ oil = 31920 g CO_2

Trp 40 MJ diesel × 0.208 g HC/MJ diesel = 8.32 g HC

  40 MJ diesel × 1.3 g NO_x/MJ diesel = 52 g NO_x

  40 MJ diesel × 78.6 g CO_2/MJ diesel = 3144 g CO_2

B   – (electricity)

C   30 MJ oil × 0.018 g HC/MJ oil = 0.54 g HC
30 MJ oil × 0.15 g NO_x/MJ oil = 4.5 g NO_x
30 MJ oil × 79.8 g CO_2/MJ oil = 2394 g CO_2
– (electricity)

6. Process emissions

Σ emission = Σ normalised emission × mass flow/f.u.

A   0.5 g HCl/kg A × 40 kg A/f.u. = 20 g HCl/f.u.
0.5 g Cu/kg A × 40 kg A/f.u. = 20 g Cu/f.u.
Trp. –
B   0.3 g HC/kg B × 48 kg B/f.u. = 14.4 g HC/f.u.
C   0.625 g HC/kg P × 40 kg P/f.u. = 25 g HC/f.u.

(see table)

7. Impact assessment

Total impact = Σ load × index

Table ExC.1

Environmental load		Index ecopoints/g	Impact ecopoints/f.u.
Oil	470 MJ	–	–
Electrical energy	264 MJ	–	–
Mineral	160 kg	–	–
HC	55.46 g	9.751	541
NO_x	116.5 g	6.31	735
CO_2	37458 g	0.0248	929
HCl	20 g	6.31	126
Cu	20 g	5917	118 340
Solid waste	126.7 kg	0.167	211 59
Total impact			**141 830**

Table ExC.2   The spreadsheet illustrates how data and calculations can be structured.

		Reference mass flow	Transportation distance	Energy — normalised energy requirements			Emissions — normalised measured emissions			
		kg/kg f.u.	km	oil	diesel	electr.	HCl	Cu	solid waste	HC
A	in: 160 kg raw A	40		10			0.5	0.5	3.1667	
	out: 40 kg A									
trp	in=out: 40 kg A	40	1000		0.001					
B	in: 40 kg A + 8 kg C									
	out: 48 kg B	48				3				0.3
C	in: 48 kg B									
	out: 40 kg P + 8 kg C	40		0.75		3				0.625

RESULTS

Energy usage			Emissions					
oil	diesel	electr.	HCl (g)	Cu (g)	solid waste (kg)	HC (g)	NOx (g)	CO2 (g)
400	0	0	20	20	20	126.668	0	0
0	40	0	0	0	0	0	14.4	
0	0	144	0	0	0	0	25	
30	0	120	20	20	20	126.668	39.4	116.5
430	40	264	20	20	20	126.668	16.06	116.5
—	—		6.31	6.31	5917	0.167	55.46	6.31
0	0	0	126.2	126.2	118340	21153.556	9.751	735.115

					sum	0		
					em. calc. w.	37458		
					TOTAL LOADING	37458		
					index	0.0248		
					TOTAL IMPACT	928.958	1401160.5465	

EMISSION FACTORS

	oil	diesel	electr.
HC	0.018	0.208	
NOx	0.15	1.3	
CO2	79.8	78.6	

For figure ExC.1

	A	trp	B	C
fossil	400	40	40	30
electr.				144 / 120

For figure ExC.2

HC	541
NOx	735
CO2	929
HCl	126.2
Cu	118340
solid waste	21154

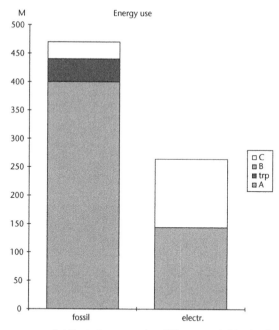

Figure ExC.1 Energy use distributed among the different activities in the life cycle.

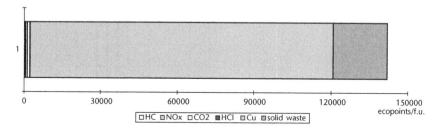

Figure ExC.2 Weighted results. Emissions of copper and solid waste contribute most to overall environmental impact.

Exercise E
Problem solution

Two important conditions for obtaining the correct answer must be met:

- Both processes must be allocated (polyhypothene is partly "responsible" for the emissions from polymer production and partly for those from the natural resource extraction and the refinery).
- It is necessary to multiply the material flows by the prices.

Correct answer:

1.15 kg crude oil/kg polyhypothene

46 MJ/kg polyhypothene (of which half is the inherent energy of the product, polyhypothene)

1.72 kg CO_2/kg polyhypothene

0.34 g HC/kg polyhypothene

A typical mistake is not to take the allocation upstream, i.e. condition 1 is not met. In a way this means that the calculation started from the "top", i.e. from the raw material end, instead of from the functional unit, i.e. from the end of the studied product calculation. The way the economic allocation factor is calculated is as follows. First the value of the total output is calculated. Then the product's share can be calculated.

3 kg polyhypothene × 7 €/kg polyhypothene + 1 kg polyimaginene × 25 €/kg polyimaginene + 1 kg polyassumptene × 15 €/kg polyassumptene = 21 + 25 + 15 = 61 €/total output

1 kg polyhypothene represents the following share of the total output: 7 €/kg output / 61 €/total output = 0.115 or 11.5 %

Appendices

Here, you will find general LCA data of various kinds. Appendix 1 contains general inventory data on for example energy production, transportation and waste management. Appendices 2 and 3 contain data useful for life cycle impact assessment. Appendix 2 lists characterisation indicators and appendix 3 lists weighting indices.

Appendix 1
General inventory data

Inventory data useful for exercises H1-H10 is presented in this appendix. There is data on electricity production, transportation data, emission factors for combustion in stationary installations and data concerning waste management. The data presented is for exercise purposes only. The data on electricity production and transportation is based on extensive data compilations performed by experts in the respective fields, but only a selection of the data is presented here. The emissions factors for combustion in stationary installations are quite old. Also, they are valid only for Swedish conditions. The waste management data is based on modelling calculations performed for LCA purposes specifically. Generally, the data is given as presented in the different sources, usually with more digits than represent their accuracy.

For "real" LCAs the original data sources should be consulted as well as data more specifically representing the technologies and geographical regions modelled in the case study in question.

App 1.1 Electricity production

The data for electricity production presented in this section consists of inventory tables for electricity produced from a number of energy resources and statistics on electricity production mixes. The types of electricity production technologies included are those based on fossil fuels (hard coal, oil, fuel gas and lignite), nuclear energy and electricity based on renewable resources (biofuel, hydro energy and wind).

The data is a selection from a larger data set, kindly provided by Vattenfall. Vattenfall's data, in turn, is based on an extensive LCI study performed at ETH, Zurich and the Paul Sherrer Institute, Villingen (Frischknecht et al. 1996). For electricity produced from biofuel, the ETH data was combined with data from a study performed at Vattenfall (Brännström-Norberg et al. 1996). For wind electricity the ETH data was modified to fit UCPTE[1] conditions. Vattenfall's purpose in interpreting and compiling the data was to supply EPD practitioners with general LCI data for electricity generation to be used in the absence of specific data in accordance with the Swedish EPD guidelines (MSR 1999). Three digit results are reported, but in the original source it is stated that this does not mean that the accuracy is that high.

In spite of Vattenfall's aggregating and selecting from the information in the original ETH study, the inventory tables in the data set consist of more than 160 parameters. For exercise purposes such a long list of inventory parameters is not necessary. Here only a selection of parameters is presented.

Electricity production mix

Electricity production mixes, for a selection of regions and countries, are presented in table App 1.1. The data is valid for 1998 and based on IEA statistics (IEA 2000).

Inventory table

Life cycle data for various production systems for electricity is shown in tables App 1.2a and App 1.2b. Together with the production mixes in table App 1.1, these may be used to calculate the environmental loads of the electricity production in different geographical regions.

---

1   UCPTE Union pour la co-ordination de la production et du transport de l'électricité. The following countries were members of the union in 1994: Belgium, Germany, France, Greece, Italy, Ex-Yugoslavia (Bosnia/Herzegovina, Croatia, Slovenia, and Rest-Yugoslavia), Luxembourg, Netherlands, Austria, Portugal, Switzerland, Spain.

Table App 1.1 Electricity production based on different energy sources, in different countries and regions, during 1998 (IEA 2000).

Geographic region	Quantity (GWh) – Percentage %					
	Hard coal, coke oven & blast furnace	Lignite sub bituminous coal, peat	Liquid fuels (e.g. oil), refinery gas	Natural gas, gas works gas	Nuclear energy	Geother-mal
OECD total[1]	2971253	537062	660661	1280305	2124071	32047
Percentage	32.81	5.93	7.29	14.14	23.45	0.35
OECD Europe[2]	590653	330258	207542	104740	907139	5012
Percentage	19.65	10.99	6.90	3.48	30.18	0.17
OECD North America[3]	1976125	155452	266609	607797	794900	21026
Percentage	43.45	3.42	5.86	13.36	17.48	0.46
OECD Pacific[4]	404475	51352	186510	270768	422032	6009
Percentage	26.90	3.42	12.41	18.01	28.07	0.40
Australia	108763	46781	2233	17423	0	0
Percentage	55.97	24.07	1.15	8.97	0.00	0.00
Denmark[5]	23648	0	4968	8166	0	0
Percentage	57.56	0.00	12.09	19.88	0.00	0.00
European Union[6]	476575	191713	190762	366002	854182	4272
Percentage	19.31	7.77	7.73	14.83	34.61	0.17
Finland	8595	4936	1153	8823	21853	0
Percentage	12.25	7.03	1.64	12.57	31.14	0.00
France[7]	35550	1762	11651	4975	387990	0
Percentage	7.01	0.35	2.30	0.98	76.54	0.00
Germany	160124	139402	6376	54312	161644	0
Percentage	28.99	25.24	1.15	9.83	29.26	0.00
Italy[8]	27503	324	107305	70883	0	4214
Percentage	10.84	0.13	42.31	27.95	0.00	1.66
Japan[9]	198035	0	169955	218343	332343	3531
Percentage	19.11	0.00	16.40	21.07	32.07	0.34
Norway	192	0	7	222	0	0
Percentage	0.17	0.00	0.01	0.19	0.00	0.00
Spain[10]	17499	16212	58993	0	15	2284
Percentage	9.04	8.38	30.48	0.00	0.01	1.18
Sweden	3155	60	3264	431	73583	0
Percentage	1.99	0.04	2.06	0.27	46.50	0.00
Switzerland[11]	0	0	376	846	25830	0
Percentage	0.00	0.00	0.61	1.37	41.86	0.00
United Kingdom	123040	0	5715	115975	100140	0
Percentage	34.50	0.00	1.60	32.52	28.08	0.00
United States	1929428	76900	147173	557772	714124	15369
Percentage	50.72	2.02	3.87	14.66	18.77	0.40

[1] OECD: Organisation for Economic Co-operation Development. It includes Australia, Austria, Belgium, Canada, Czech Republic, Denmark, Finland, France, Germany, Greece, Hungary, Iceland, Ireland, Italy, Japan, Korea, Luxembourg, Mexico, Netherlands, New Zealand, Norway, Poland, Portugal, Spain, Sweden, Switzerland, Turkey, United Kingdom and United States.

[2] OECD Europe includes Austria, Belgium, Czech Republic, Denmark, Finland, France, Germany, Greece, Hungary, Iceland, Ireland, Italy, Luxembourg, Netherlands, Norway, Poland, Portugal, Spain, Sweden, Switzerland, Turkey and United Kingdom.

[3] OECD North America includes Canada, Mexico and United States.

[4] OECD Pacific includes Australia, Japan, Korea and New Zealand.

[5] Denmark includes Greenland and the Danish Faroes

Table App 1.1 (continued)

Geographic region	Quantity (GWh) – Percentage %						
	Solar	Combustible renewable wastes	Hydro energy, pumped storage excluded	Tide, wave, ocean	Wind	Other fuel sources	Total electricity production, pumped storage hydro electricity excluded
OECD total[1]	1034	142536	1291618	622	14288	1480	9056977
Percentage	0.01	1.57	14.26	0.01	0.16	0.02	100.00
OECD Europe[2]	70	45015	505074	590	11228	1468	3005789
Percentage	0.00	1.50	16.80	0.02	0.37	0.05	100.00
OECD North America[3]	893	72210	649713	32	2993	0	4547750
Percentage	0.02	1.59	14.29	0.00	0.07	0.00	100.00
OECD Pacific[4]	71	25311	136831	0	67	12	1503438
Percentage	0.00	1.68	9.10	0.00	0.00	0.00	100.00
Australia	30	3320	15766	0	8	0	194324
Percentage	0.02	1.71	8.11	0.00	0.00	0.00	100.00
Denmark[5]	0	1456	27	0	2780	38	41083
Percentage	0.00	3.54	0.07	0.00	6.77	0.09	100.00
European Union[6]	62	42098	304583	5.9	112.09	9.77	2468109
Percentage	0.00	1.71	12.34	0.00	0.00	0.00	100.00
Finland	0	9753	15051	0	23	0	70169
Percentage	0.00	13.90	21.45	0.00	0.03	0.00	100.00
France[7]	0	2308	62070	590	36	0	506932
Percentage	0.00	0.46	12.24	0.12	0.01	0.00	100.00
Germany	35	8673	17216	0	4600	0	552382
Percentage	0.01	1.57	3.12	0.00	0.83	0.00	100.00
Italy[8]	6	1228	41220	0	231	727	253641
Percentage	0.00	0.48	16.25	0.00	0.09	0.29	100.00
Japan[9]	0	21482	92513	0	6	12	1036220
Percentage	0.00	2.07	8.93	0.00	0.00	0.00	100.00
Norway	0	296	115359	0	7	0	116083
Percentage	0.00	0.25	99.38	0.00	0.01	0.00	100.00
Spain[10]	34005	0	1352	0	58866	10300	193526
Percentage	17.57	0.00	0.70	0.00	30.42	5.32	100.00
Sweden	0	3088	74328	0	317	0	158226
Percentage	0.00	1.95	46.98	0.00	0.20	0.00	100.00
Switzerland[11]	8	1177	33471	0	3	0	61711
Percentage	0.01	1.91	54.24	0.00	0.00	0.00	100.00
United Kingdom	0	5640	5226	0	886	0	356622
Percentage	0.00	1.58	1.47	0.00	0.25	0.00	100.00
United States	890	65920	293208	0	2926	0	3803710
Percentage	0.02	1.73	7.71	0.00	0.08	0.00	100.00

[6] European Union countries include Austria, Belgium, Denmark, France, Finland, Germany, Greece, Ireland, Italy, Luxembourg, Netherlands, Portugal, Spain, Sweden and United Kingdom.

[7] France includes Monaco and excludes overseas departments such as Martinique, Guadeloupe, French Polynesia and Réunion.

[8] Italy includes San Marino and the Vatican.

[9] Japan includes Okinawa.

[10] Spain includes the Canary Island.

[11] Switzerland includes Liechtenstein.

488

Table App 1.2a Inventory table for electricity production systems based on fossil fuels, selected parameters. The data relate to a functional unit of 1 TJ net electricity delivered from the power plant. Based on Frischknecht et al. (1996).

Direc-tion	Flow type	Substance	Quantity				Unit	Environ-ment
			Hard coal	Oil	Fuel gas	Lignite		
Input	Natural resource	Copper in ore	4.28	4.18	4.39	5.46	kg	Ground
Input	Natural resource	Crude oil	2580	73100	1260	478	kg	Ground
Input	Natural resource	Lignite	1950	1230	265	41400	kg	Ground
Input	Natural resource	Limestone	2210	431	200	1880	kg	Ground
Input	Natural resource	Natural gas	1898	6058	59112	392	Nm^3	Ground
Input	Natural resource	Hard coal	183000	1490	12100	1400	kg	Ground
Input	Natural resource	Uranium in ore	0.133	0.0839	0.0183	0.0947	kg	Ground
Input	Natural resource	Water	1.07×10^7	1.93×10^7	6.08×10^5	1.35×10^7	kg	Ground
Input	Natural resource	Wood	1320	28.6	104	27.5	kg	Ground
Output	Emission	Cd	1.79×10^{-3}	0.0158	2.87×10^{-4}	9.28×10^{-3}	kg	Air
Output	Emission	CH_4	1003.5	307.0	373.7	31.49	kg	Air
Output	Emission	CO	56.60	75.15	81.97	45.1	kg	Air
Output	Emission	CO_2	275833	229380	245831	370979	kg	Air
Output	Emission	Cs-134	0.0388	0.0245	5.35×10^{-3}	0.0277	kBq	Air
Output	Emission	Hg	0.0325	1.01×10^{-3}	7.48×10^{-4}	0.0194	kg	Air
Output	Emission	Kr-85	5.03×10^6	3.18×10^6	6.93×10^5	3.59×10^6	kBq	Air
Output	Emission	N_2O	1.79	5.53	1.50	1.80	kg	Air
Output	Emission	NH_3	1.497	0.224	0.0601	1.800	kg	Air
Output	Emission	NMVOC	33.9	588	62.0	12.6	kg	Air
Output	Emission	NO_x	451.7	504.6	408.44	558.0	kg	Air
Output	Emission	PAH	3.52×10^{-3}	5.34×10^{-3}	0.0216	3.58×10^{-3}	kg	Air
Output	Emission	Particles	321.59	96.87	16.13	257.66	kg	Air
Output	Emission	Pb	0.0659	0.136	4.05×10^{-3}	0.0292	kg	Air
Output	Emission	Rn-222	7.30×10^6	4.62×10^6	1.01×10^6	5.21×10^6	kBq	Air
Output	Emission	SO_2	1062.07	2359.4	58.29	3623.53	kg	Air
Output	Emission	Sr-90	0.0536	0.0338	0.00738	0.0382	kBq	Air
Output	Emission	U-238	12.184	0.317	0.0778	5.024	kBq	Air
Output	Emission	COD	1.180	6.140	0.8	0.098	kg	Water
Output	Emission	Cs-134	6.888	4.359	0.9	4.915	kBq	Water
Output	Emission	N total	0.714	7.423	0.270	0.098	kg	Water
Output	Emission	Oil	2.55	69.8	2.96	0.474	kg	Water
Output	Emission	PO_4^{3-}	17.5	0.193	1.19	0.138	kg	Water
Output	Emission	Sr-90	6.49	4.10	0.894	4.63	kBq	Water
Output	Emission	U-238	25.7	1.82	0.281	1.45	kBq	Water
Output	Product	Electricity	1	1	1	1	TJ	Techno-sphere
Output	Residue	Highly radio-active waste	2.27×10^{-5}	1.44×10^{-5}	3.13×10^{-6}	1.62×10^{-5}	M3	Techno-sphere
Output	Residue	Medium and low radioactive waste	2.78×10^{-4}	1.76×10^{-4}	3.83×10^{-5}	1.98×10^{-4}	M3	Techno-sphere
Output	Residue	Waste in deposit	6.58×10^4	2.00×10^3	5.02×10^3	4.83×10^4	kg	Techno-sphere

Table App 1.2b Inventory table for electricity production systems based on nuclear and renewable resources, selected parameters. The data relate to a functional unit of 1 TJ net electricity delivered from the power plant. Based on Frischknecht et al. (1996) and for biofuel data on Brännström-Norberg et al. (1996).

Direc-tion	Flow type	Substance	Quantity				Unit	Environ-ment
			Nuclear	Biofuel	Hydro electricity	Wind		
Input	Natural resource	Copper in ore	2.26	0.444	0.0578	41.4	kg	Ground
Input	Natural resource	Crude oil	246	2777	74.8	670	kg	Ground
Input	Natural resource	Lignite	238	126	65.4	233.5	kg	Ground
Input	Natural resource	Limestone	163	85.7	655	755	kg	Ground
Input	Natural resource	Natural gas	415	285	23.6	378	Nm^3	Ground
Input	Natural resource	Hard coal	1260	293	294	1530	kg	Ground
Input	Natural resource	Uranium in ore	7.85	0.00866	0.00449	0.0166	kg	Ground
Input	Natural resource	Water	2.53×10^6	6.58×10^4	1.17×104	46450	kg	Ground
Input	Natural resource	Wood	21.4	1.74×10^5	2.95	15.7	kg	Ground
Output	Emission	Cd	1.30×10^{-4}	2.49×10^{-4}	6.71×10^{-5}	0.00132	kg	Air
Output	Emission	CH_4	10.26	13.69	2.39	15.28	kg	Air
Output	Emission	CO	6.01	187.89	5.79	34.61	kg	Air
Output	Emission	CO_2	3605	8964	1045	4578	kg	Air
Output	Emission	Cs-134	2.30	2.54×10^{-3}	1.31×10^{-3}	0.00487	kBq	Air
Output	Emission	Hg	2.28×10^{-4}	0.0128	4.01×10^{-5}	0.00023	kg	Air
Output	Emission	Kr-85	2.97×10^8	3.28×10^5	1.70×10^5	630000	kBq	Air
Output	Emission	N_2O	0.80	13.6	0.015	0.0755	kg	Air
Output	Emission	NH_3	0.051	0.00322	0.00560	0.02146	kg	Air
Output	Emission	NMVOC	3.93	45.8	0.947	10.54	kg	Air
Output	Emission	NO_x	9.599	252	3.196	9.845	kg	Air
Output	Emission	PAH	4.50×10^{-4}	2.97×10^{-4}	9.92×10^{-5}	8.49×10^{-4}	kg	Air
Output	Emission	Particles	7.08	29.40	2.09	12.16	kg	Air
Output	Emission	Pb	1.73×10^{-3}	9.38×10^{-3}	1.27×10^{-3}	0.02671	kg	Air
Output	Emission	Rn-222	4.32×10^8	4.78×10^5	2.47×10^5	905000	kBq	Air
Output	Emission	SO_2	25.1	42.7	2.86	19.04	kg	Air
Output	Emission	Sr-90	3.17	0.00349	0.00181	0.0067	kBq	Air
Output	Emission	U-238	22.776	0.0337	0.01766	0.0692	kBq	Air
Output	Emission	COD	0.090	0.554	0.0263	0.305	kg	Water
Output	Emission	Cs-134	407.62	0.450	0.233	0.865	kBq	Water
Output	Emission	N total	1.491	0.603	0.019	0.15	kg	Water
Output	Emission	Oil	0.252	10.0	0.0745	0.685	kg	Water
Output	Emission	PO_4^{3-}	0.128	0.0563	0.0290	0.149	kg	Water
Output	Emission	Sr-90	384	0.424	0.220	0.815	kBq	Water
Output	Emission	U-238	109	0.133	0.069	0.256	kBq	Water
Output	Product	Electricity	1	1	1	1	TJ	Techno-sphere
Output	Residue	Highly radio-active waste	1.34×10^{-3}	1.48×10^{-6}	7.69×10^{-7}	2.85×10^{-6}	M3	Techno-sphere
Output	Residue	Medium and low radioactive waste	0.0164	1.81×10^{-5}	9.41×10^{-6}	3.4×10^{-5}	M3	Techno-sphere
Output	Residue	Waste in deposit	1.52×10^3	3.84×10^3	5.67×10^3	986.5	kg	Techno-sphere

About the electricity data

The electricity data provided by Vattenfall was extensively documented. A compilation is given in the following. The full documentation is available at www.globalspine.com (2002).

Representativity

For hard coal, oil, fuel gas, lignite and nuclear power based electricity generation the data is intended to be representative for the UCPTE countries in 1994.

For biofuel based electricity, the data is intended to be an approximation of biofuelled (wood chips from light thinning) electricity generation in CFB plants in Europe.

For wind power, the ETH data, representative of Swiss conditions, was adapted to UCPTE conditions. The production volume per installed kW was doubled since operation time in Switzerland is much shorter than the average in the UCPTE.

The LCI data for hydro power is valid for hydro power in Switzerland and is thought to be a rather good approximation for hydro power in UCPTE. The ETH study includes three types of plants. Data for two of the types, with and without storage, were summarised to one set of data "Hydro Power in UCPTE" in accordance with existing percentages of those types of plants in the UCPTE region. Only this aggregated set of data is reported here.

Data for the cokery included in the study are representative of Germany. Other European cokeries probably have higher emissions.

The main phases inventoried in ETH's life cycle study of electrical generation are described in table App 1.3.

Table App 1.3 Summary of main life cycle phases included in the LCA studies underlying the electricity data (Frischknecht et al. 1996).

Energy system	Description
Hard coal	Mining of coal (open pit and underground), processing I, processing II, transports, storage, power plant operation.
Oil	Exploration, extraction (onshore and offshore), transports, refinery, regional distribution and power plant operation. The average situation in the UCPTE region in 1994 concerning the origin of the oil, transports of different kinds (Swiss conditions), refinery processes, distribution, power plant operation etc. is described.
Fuel gas	The average situation in the UCPTE region in 1994 concerning the origin of the gas, compression and transport, processing (of gas with more or less sulphur content), distribution, power plant operation etc. is described. The fuel gas mixture described is: 74.5 % natural gas with 36 MJ/m^3, 6.9 % coke oven gas with 18 MJ/m^3, 18.6 % blast furnace gas with 3.3 MJ/m^3. About 15 % of the natural gas is extracted together with crude oil and 20 % of natural gas used in the UCPTE is extracted offshore. Included life cycle phases are: exploration of natural gas, extraction (onshore and offshore), processing, long distance transport and storage, regional distribution and power plant operation
	Coke oven gas is produced in a cokery out of hard coal. Blast furnace gas is seen as a by-product in steel production and is not charged with any environmental impact for its supply in this study.
Lignite	Mining, transports and power plant operation.
Nuclear energy	Uranium mine, uranium ore processing, conversion, enrichment, fuel fabrication, nuclear power plant, reprocessing of spent fuel, interim and final storage for conditioned low, medium and high level radioactive waste.
Biofuel	Data about the fuel chain i.e. fuel production and transports of fuel has been acquired from ETH and data about power plant operation has been provided by Vattenfall's study. The main phases inventoried in ETH's fir wood chips chain are: wood growth, forest care, light thinning of young forests and gathering of forest residues, transport by tractor to a nearby forest road, wood chipper, interim storage in containers, transport to combustion plant.
Hydro-power	The main emphasis in ETH's study has been in the description of hydro power plants typical for Switzerland and the alpine region, with power outputs between about 0.1 MW and 350 MW. Three types of power plants are distinguished, namely, run of river (without storage), water storage and pumped storage power plants.
Wind electricity	One wind power plant with an output of 30 kW has been inventoried in detail and two other plants (30 kW and 150 kW) also have been analysed with the help of the detailed study together with specific data for those plants. Construction, demolition and operation of the plants have been studied. The yield of studied plants is about 50 % lower than the yield of plants at more windy locations at for instance the seashore.

Functional unit

The functional unit was defined as 1 TJ net electricity delivered from the power plant, i.e. after the electricity need in the power plant has been supplied by the plant itself. Electricity distribution and distribution losses were not accounted for.

System boundaries

All subsystems are described on a cradle-to-grave basis. Fuel chains and the life cycles of equipment were included. The materials used and energy carriers were followed from extraction and processing of natural resources. Emissions from energy conversion in manufacturing processes and transports (infrastructure and vehicle construction included) were considered as well as emissions from landfills (infrastructure included) where waste material is disposed of. Manufacturing processes for the use of recycled material were accounted for. Waste material supposed to be recycled are reported as outputs from the system (i.e. in those cases where recycling processes were not included). In other words, the cut-off method has been used for *allocation in open loop* recycling.

Other *allocations* concern the cokery. Allocation between the products according to energy content, weight and price resulted in allocation of 76–83 % of the environmental impact to the coke. In the ETH study 80 % was allocated to coke. For oil, allocations were made with respect to lower heating value or weight. In the refinery, allocation was done in accordance with the weight of the oil products in the different sub-processes. Allocation between natural gas and crude oil when extracted together was done according to the lower heating value. Allocation between electricity and heat in fuel gas power plants was done according to exergy.

Time was considered in the study in several different respects. Electricity used during the life cycle was assumed to be a mix based on the average generation in the UCPTE countries between 1990–94. All processes, also those conducted in the past, were assumed to use the average technology of the early nineties. For capital goods and infrastructure, technical lifetimes ranging from 15 year for wood chip containers to 200 years for concrete constructions in hydropower dams were used. However, most equipment was assumed to have a technical lifetime of 30–40 years.

As for *geography*, processes conducted outside the UCPTE region were assumed to be supplied with UCPTE electricity. Data concerning resource use, emissions and waste in connection with manufacturing processes mainly originate from sources in Switzerland, Germany and other western European countries.

For *hard coal* the data is based on average hard coal power plants in Austria, Belgium, Spain, Italy, Ex-Yugoslavia, France, Netherlands, Portugal, and Germany. The emphasis concerning the inventory of coal mining was the UCPTE but also North and South America, South Africa, Australia and the Far East and Eastern Europe were considered since those regions export hard coal to the UCPTE. About 45 % of the hard coal used in UCPTE power plants is imported from those other regions.

The world was divided into 7 supply regions for *oil*: The Middle East, Latin America (including Mexico), North and Central Africa, Europe, the former Soviet Union and North America (excluding Mexico). The European harbours were grouped into two regions, the North Sea Region and the Mediterranean Region. Crude oil from the Middle East, discharged in Mediterranean harbours, was assumed to pass through the Suez Channel while Middle East oil, discharged in the North Sea Region was supposed to pass Cape Hope. Refinery locations were divided into three categories: Switzerland, Western Europe the former Soviet Union. Refineries in North America and Africa were assumed to keep the same standard as refineries in Europe.

For *fuel gas* the most important supply countries for natural gas in the UCPTE are the Netherlands (39 %), the states of the former Soviet Union (22 %), Algeria (11 %), Norway (9 %) and Germany (7 %). Only the Swiss regional distribution net for natural gas was inventoried as a whole. The resulting data was adapted to UCPTE conditions.

The *lignite* data is based on average lignite power plants in Austria, Germany, Spain, Ex-Yugoslavia, France and Greece. Lignite mining was studied in the UCPTE since less than 1 % is imported. 67 % of the lignite used in UCPTE is mined in Germany.

The following countries in the UCPTE have *nuclear electricity production*: Germany, Belgium, France, The Netherlands, Switzerland, Slovenia and Spain.

Data from one open-pit mine in Canada and two underground mines in the USA was used as well as general literature data. Data for the uranium ore processing phase comes from the literature, one plant in Canada and two plants in the USA. Literature data describing American conversion plants has been used. Examined enrichment plants (literature data) were: EURODIF in France and USEC in the USA (gaseous diffusion); URENCO in Germany, the UK and the Netherlands and TENEX in Russia (gas centrifugation).

Two Swiss nuclear power plants were studied in detail concerning their actual fuel chain and their operation. Data received from the Swiss plants was adapted to the average situation in the UCPTE region in 1994 with the help of certain specific data from France and Germany. Data about radioactive emissions of nuclear power plants was taken from statistics in Switzerland, France and Germany. Data from the most modern reprocessing plant in Sellafield, UK (THORP) and a planned plant in Germany for spent uranium fuel was used in the study together with other literature data.

The concepts studied for storage of radioactive waste (interim and final) are Swiss.

For *hydroelectricity,* no geographical boundaries were drawn except concerning the location of the studied plants in Switzerland. Processes conducted outside the UCPTE region were assumed to be supplied with UCPTE electricity.

Also for *wind electricity,* no geographical boundaries were drawn, except concerning the location of the studied plants in Switzerland.

Other assumptions and limitations

The environmental load from material production is based on literature data on energy use for material production. The energy used was assumed to be a mix of 10 % UCPTE electricity, 45 % oil and 45 % natural gas. Further manufacturing processes of components and machines were approximated by 50 % of the energy used to produce the materials.

Big accidents that seldom occur are not included. The threshold was fixed at 10 accidents per year provided one energy carrier/system (e.g. oil) would cover the entire primary energy demand of the world.

Selection of inventory parameters

ETH's LCI results comprise all parameters received during inventory and calculation. A selection among these parameters was made by Vattenfall for the data set intended for EPD purposes, resulting in a list including more than 160 parameters. Since the data presented here are only for exercise purposes, a further selection was made down to a more manageable number of parameters.

Vattenfall's criterion in selecting and aggregating ETH's LCI results for electricity generation in the UCPTE region was to make the figures usable as general electricity LCI data in EPDs according to the Swedish EPD guidelines (MSR 1999). Reports on waste were added, in spite of all waste handling processes being included in the ETH study. The latter was an adaptation to other LCI data for electricity generation where waste amounts are reported.

The ETH study comprises data concerning use of land based on an advanced approach including eight different categories of land use. No land use data is reported here. Also data on usable content in water storage and amount of turbine water was excluded.

ETH specifies about 160 radioactive isotopes emitted to air and water. Radioactive emissions in the Vattenfall data set were selected in accordance with SETAC guidelines, resulting in more than 60 parameters describing emissions of radioactive substances.

The parameters list in the Vattenfall data was shortened considerably in the data presented here, as follows:

All energy resources were included. As for other resources, copper was selected as an indicator for all the different metals and other raw materials used in constructing the power production plants. All other metal raw materials were excluded.

Among the emissions to air only the major emissions were selected. In addition emission of a few heavy metals is reported.

496

Among the emissions to water only two indicators for organic substances were selected, namely COD and oil. Also nitrogen and phosphorous emissions are reported.

Emissions to ground were excluded, and some of the waste parameters selected instead.

Highly and medium/low radioactive waste was included. Two categories for waste to deposit were aggregated into one.

Only a few parameters describing radioactive emissions were selected. U 238 and Rn 222 are indicators of emissions during fuel production, Kr 85 is an indicator for emissions during operation. Cs 134 and Sr 90 are fission products. Plutonium and other actinides, mainly present in the waste, are not reported. The amount of highly radioactive waste is instead taken as an indicator for these.

App 1.2 Transportation

Inventory data for transportation is given in the following section. The data is a selection of the data compiled and presented by the Network for Transport and the Environment (NTM, Nätverket för Transporter och Miljön). Members of the network are Swedish experts and actors in the sector. The data represent Swedish conditions. The purpose of the work was to create a common platform for calculation of the environmental impact of different modes of transportation. NTM stresses that their data is not intended for direct comparisons between different modes of transportation.

The NTM transportation data (NTM 2002) are quite extensive regarding the types of transportation modes covered. Only a selection is presented here. The original data is presented with a high, low and average estimate, but only the averages are given here. For a thorough documentation of the data, see NTM (2002).

Road transport

Table App 1.4 gives some key characteristics of different types of road transports and vehicles and the actual data is presented in table App 1.5.

Table App 1.4 Types of vehicles and their characteristics.

Type of vehicle	Total weight (tonnes)	Pay load capacity (tonnes)	Approximate length (m)
Light distribution truck, short distance distribution	3.5–14	1.5–8.5	9
Medium sized distribution truck, regional distribution	14–24	8.5–14	10
Truck with semi-trailer, long distance transport	40	26	18
Truck with draw bar trailer, long distance transport	60	40	24

Table App 1.5 Energy requirements and emissions for road transport. Fuel supply chain included (NTM 2002).

Energy requirement and emissions MJ/tkm or g/tkm	Light distribution truck, short distance distribution		Medium sized distribution truck, regional distribution		Truck with semi-trailer, long distance transport		Truck with draw bar trailer, long distance transport	
	Euro 2	Euro 3	Euro 2	Euro 3	Euro 2	Euro 3	Euro 2	Euro 3
Energy	2.41	2.41	1.87	1.87	0.72	0.72	0.65	0.65
CO_2	176	176	136	136	52	52	48	48
NO_x	1.6	1.1	1.2	0.9	0.46	0.33	0.42	0.30
HC	0.16	0.16	0.12	0.12	0.047	0.047	0.043	0.043
Particulate matter, PM	0.025	0.019	0.019	0.015	0.0074	0.0057	0.0067	0.0052
CO	0.17	0.15	0.13	0.12	0.049	0.046	0.045	0.041
SO_2	0.043	0.043	0.034	0.034	0.013	0.013	0.01	0.01

Data for the two most recent age categories for trucks reported by NTM are given here. They correspond to emission regulations for new vehicles, e.g. manufactured during 1996–2000 (Euro 2) and later than 2000 (Euro 3).

The data includes the fuel consumption in and emissions from the vehicles and also energy requirements and emissions from production and distribution of the fuel. The environmental impact of construction of vehicles, roads or other infrastructure is not included. The data is based on fuel of environmental class 1 (more

498

than 90 % of the fuel sold in Sweden is of this type). This fuel gives significantly lower emissions than standard fuel (environmental class 3).

The data is given as MJ/tonne kilometer (MJ/tkm) or grammes/ tonne kilometer (g/tkm). It is based on the assumption that on the average 70 % of the load capacity is used in long distance transports and 50 % in medium and short distribution. (This implies that for LCA purposes, empty return transports are already accounted for in the transportation data).

The load capacity of a vehicle is limited by weight for dense loads but by volume for less dense loads (<250–300 kg/m^3). NTM recommends that for goods with a density below 275 kg/m^3 the load to be used together with the data in table App 1.5 be calculated as load volume (m^3) × 275 kg/m^3.

Railroad transport

The data presented in tables App 1.6 and App 1.7 represents the following types of trains:

- Rail car goods train: the "traditional" goods transport train. Railroad cars of differing size and model are pulled in the same train. Cars are connected and disconnected along the road.
- System train: a train always going the same route between two addresses, containing the same cars. System trains are usually fully loaded in one direction and empty in the other.
- Diesel trains.

For electrically driven trains the data are based on RC-locomotives, whereas the diesel driven train is based on a T44 locomotive fuelled with diesel of environmental class 3. (In Sweden, only a minor portion of the rail transportation is diesel driven).

Table App1.6 Electricity use for rail transport (NTM 2002). Electricity supply chain not included.

Type of train	Electricity consumption (MJ/t km)
Rail car goods train	0.151
System train	0.180

Table App 1.7 Energy requirements and emissions for diesel train transport (NTM 2002). Fuel supply chain included.

Energy use and emissions MJ/t km and g/t km	Amount
Energy	0.245
CO_2	18
NO_x	0.36
HC	0.023
Particulate matter, PM	0.008
CO	0.019
SO_2	0.00014

The electricity production chain is not included in the data given for electrically driven trains. Neither are losses in the distribution grid (approximately 4 %), but losses in the railroad grid are. However, the fuel supply chain is included in the diesel train data. This means that the data are not on a comparable basis.

Sea transport

For sea transport it is much more difficult to classify different types of ships into homogenous classes. Essentially every ship is designed for its unique purpose, which causes large variations. Never the less, the goods transport ships were grouped into classes as presented in table App 1.8. The data given in table App 1.9 is based on capacity use rates of 50 %–60 %, for RoRo ships 80 %. The capacity use rate is based on the payload, which includes load carriers, for example containers or in the case of ferries even trucks. The data may be seen as a best estimate of Swedish shipping, as described in general terms. However, the variability is large.

Table App 1.8 Classes of ships and some characteristics.

Type of ship	Size (dwtonne)	Approximate speed (knots)
RoRo	2000–30 000	10–20
Small ship	< 2000	11
Medium sized ship	2000–8000	13
Large ship	> 8000 (max 280 000)	14

Table App 1.9 Energy requirements and emissions for sea transport (NTM 2002).
Fuel supply chain included.

Energy requirement and emissions MJ/t km or g/t km	RoRo ship	Small ship	Medium sized ship	Large ship
Energy	0.349	0.432	0.299	0.216
CO_2	24.9	30.8	22	15.4
NO_x	0.67	0.729	0.54	0.429
HC	0.032	0.020	0.018	0.020
Particulate matter, PM	0.0335	0.0246	0.020	0.0204
CO	0.0134	0.0420	0.025	0.0087
SO_2	0.424	0.515	0.36	0.262

App 1.3 Emission factors for combustion in stationary installations

When collecting data for an LCA, sometimes only energy data are received for some of the processes. In such cases an estimate of the emissions may be done using emissions factors. A set of such emission factors is given in table App 1.10. The data estimates the emissions from the combustion of various types of fuels on an industrial scale.

Use of emissions factors is only a second best choice. When measured data from specific processes are available, these should of course be used. The emission factors may also be used to fill in certain data gaps, for example when data for a certain parameter is missing from a data set known to involve combustion.

The data given in table App 1.10 is quite old. For NO_x and SO_2 it is based on Swedish legislation and guidelines current in 1991.

Table App 1.10 Emission factors for combustion in stationary installations (Tillman et al. 1992).

Emissions	Fuel			
g/MJ fuel	Oil	Coal	Biofuel	Natural gas
SO_2	0.38	0.38	0.03	0.002
NO_x	0.15	0.15	0.15	0.15
CO	0.013	0.017	1.00	0.001
HC	0.010	0.010	0.10	15×10^{-6}
CO_2	75.8	91.6	0	55.2
Particulates	0.03	0.013	0.03	–
Ash	0.007	0.30	0.10	–

App 1.4 Waste management

In this section we present data for treatment of solid (municipal) waste on landfills and in incinerators. The data is based on model calculations. They are representative of Swedish conditions and were presented in the mid-1990s (Sundqvist et al. 1997; Finnveden et al. 1995). Swedish incinerators are equipped with advanced flue gas cleaning. They produce heat for the district heating systems and electricity. In countries without district heating, electricity is usually the main output from incinerators.

Waste management processes constitute a multi-input allocation problem. In LCA we want to associate emissions and resource consumption with a specific product. In waste treatment processes many different products are treated together, but there is only one flue gas stack from the incinerator and only one flow of leachate from the landfill. So how do we know which amount of emission is related to the product in question? Physical causality was used as the guiding allocation principle behind the data presented here. For details, see the original data sources.

Incineration

Emissions, resource consumption and energy production, as allocated to specific types of waste, are given in table App 1.11.

502

Table App 1.11 Allocated emissions, resource consumption and energy production from incineration of municipal waste (Sundqvist et al. 1997). [1), 2), 3)]

Emissions / Resource consumption / Energy production g/kg waste component MJ/kg waste component	Waste component									
	Wood	Paper	PVC plastic	Polyethylene plastic	Plastic mixture	Textiles	Iron waste	Glass	Rubber and leather	Organic municipal waste
Emissions and waste products										
CO_2	1110	1190	1410	2440	2750	1350	0	0	1460	913
SO_2	0.15	0.15	0	0	0.20	0.749	0	0	1.50	0.24
HCl	0.154	0.077	58.4	0	4.52	0.386	0	0	1.54	0.247
Hg	3.75×10^{-5}	3.75×10^{-5}	1.50×10^{-4}	5.0×10^{-5}	5.0×10^{-5}	3.75×10^{-5}	0	0	5.63×10^{-5}	3.0×10^{-5}
CO	1.45	1.55	1.83	3.17	3.58	1.75	0	0	1.90	1.19
PAH	9.47×10^{-6}	1.01×10^{-5}	1.20×10^{-5}	2.07×10^{-5}	2.34×10^{-5}	1.15×10^{-5}	0	0	1.24×10^{-5}	7.77×10^{-6}
Dioxins (heating value allocation)	6.41×10^{-9}	6.41×10^{-9}	1.01×10^{-8}	2.11×10^{-8}	1.78×10^{-8}	7.33×10^{-9}	0	0	9.16×10^{-9}	4.12×10^{-9}
Dioxins (Cl allocation)	4.21×10^{-10}	2.10×10^{-10}	1.59×10^{-7}	0	1.23×10^{-8}	1.05×10^{-9}	0	0	4.21×10^{-9}	6.73×10^{-10}
NO_x	0.817	1.16	0.183	0.317	0.806	17.0	0	0	2.88	5.49
Dust	1.13	0.75	0.20	0.20	0.50	0.375	10.0	10.0	1.88	0.90
Fly ash	32.6	21.8	5.80	5.80	14.5	10.9	290	290	54.4	26.1
Slag	78.8	52.5	14.0	14.0	35.0	26.3	700	700	131	63.0
Resource consumption [4)]										
$CaCO_3$	4.63	3.53	833	0	67.8	17.7	0	0	46.3	7.41
NH_3	0.32	0.456	0.0719	0.124	0.316	6.66	0	0	1.13	2.15
Energy production										
Thermal energy	7.7	7.7	12.1	25.3	21.4	8.8	0	0	11.0	4.95
Electrical energy	3.5	3.5	5.5	11.5	9.72	4.0	0	0	5.0	2.25

1) As modelled for a specific waste composition
2) No difference made between CO_2 with fossil and biological origin.
3) Dioxins emissions given according to two different allocation methods
4) Used for flue gas cleaning

Landfill disposal

Waste disposal in landfill sites presents the same allocation problems as does incineration. In addition, for landfills the time perspective needs to be considered. Studies of LCA and waste management have concluded that there are two time frames that are relevant when describing landfills in LCA terms. The surveyable time period is approximately a century. During this period methane formation diminishes and afterwards the landfill goes into a pseudo steady state during which all changes occur much more slowly. The other time perspective of relevance is infinity during which time all the material in the landfill is degraded and dispersed.

Organic materials

In a landfill, biodegradable organic materials are biologically degraded, predominantly under anaerobic (oxygen-free) conditions. Anaerobic degradation of organic matter leads to formation of methane and carbon dioxide. Methane is a potent greenhouse gas, for which reason these emissions are of concern in LCA. The conditions in the landfill are largely governed by the biodegradation of organic matter. When methane formation starts to decrease other conditions also change and the landfill goes into a pseudo steady state, where all changes occur much more slowly.

Finnveden et al. (1995) calculated the amounts of CO_2 and CH_4 produced from different materials during the surveyable period. They based their calculations on formula 1, which describes anaerobic degradation of organic matter in general.

$$C_aH_bO_cN_dS_e + (a - b/4 - c/2 + 3d/4 - e/2)H_2O ->$$
$$(a/2 + b/8 - c/4 - 3d/8 - e/4)CH_4 + (a/2 - b/8 + c/4 + 3d/8 + e/4)CO_2 + dNH_3 + eH_2S \quad (1)$$

In addition, cellulose was estimated to be 70 % degradable during the surveyable time period, whereas lignin is fairly stable. They also assumed that 15 % of the methane formed is oxidised to CO_2 before it reaches the atmosphere and that 50 % of the methane formed is caught by landfill gas recovery systems. The results for a hypothetical material consisting of pure cellulose and for corrugated cardboard are shown in table App 1.12.

504

Table App 1.12 Estimated methane emissions from landfilled cellulose and corrugated cardboard during the surveyable time period (Finnveden et al. 1995).

Material	CH_4 emissions, no landfill gas extraction g/kg landfilled material	CH_4 emissions, landfill gas extraction g/kg landfilled material
Cellulose	158	79
Corrugated cardboard	130	67

Finnveden et al. (1995) also proposed that plastics such as PE, PS, PET and PVC are degraded 1 % to 5 % during the surveyable time period.

Metals

Sundqvist et al. (1997) presented a compilation of best available data for leaching of metals from landfills during the surveyable time period. For the hypothetical, infinite time period all landfilled metal is dispersed, by definition.

Table App 1.13 Best available data for emission of landfilled metals during the surveyable time period (Sundqvist et al. 1997).

Element	Amount emitted kg emitted/kg landfilled
Fe	1×10^{-4}
Cu	7×10^{-5}
Zn	2×10^{-4}
Cd[1]	5×10^{-4}
Hg[2]	1×10^{-4}
Pb	6×10^{-5}
Ni	5×10^{-3}
Cr	7×10^{-4}
As	2×10^{-3}

[1] Approximately 10 % by gas, the rest by leachate
[2] Approximately 50 % by gas and 50 % by leachate

Operation energy

At landfills, the waste is compacted from about 150–200 kg/m³ to 700–800 kg/m³. The energy consumption for this is around 40 kJ/ tonne, as diesel (Sundqvist et al. 1995).

Collection and transport of municipal waste

Swedish weighted mean distance for the transportation of household waste to an incinerator was 18 km in 1986, while the mean distance to a landfill site was 15 km (Tillman et al. 1991).

References

Brännström-Norberg, Britt-Marie, Ulrika Dethlefsen, Roland Johansson, Caroline Setterwall & Sofie Tunbrant (1996). *Life-cycle Assessment for Vattenfall's Electricity Generation, Summary Report 1996*. Vattenfall AB, Sweden.

Frischknecht R, U Bollens, S Bosshart, M Ciot, L Ciseri, G Doka, R Hischier, A Martin (Swiss Federal Institute of Technology – ETH Institutionen für Energieteknik Gruppe Energie, Stoffe, Umwelt (ESU), Zurich) and Dones R, U Ganther (Paul Scherrer Institute Sektion Ganzheitliche Systemanalysen – Villigen/Würenlingen) (1996). *Ökoinventare von Energiesystemen, Grundlagen für den ökologischen Vergleich von Energiesystemen und den Einbezug von Energiesystemen in Ökobilanzen für die Schweiz* (Environmental life cycle inventories of energy systems – An environmental database for the accounting of energy consumption in the product life cycle assessment and the comparative assessment of energy systems.) 3rd edition, Bundesamt für Energie, Bern, Sweitzerland. (http://www.energieforschung.ch)

IEA (2000). *IEA Statistics, Statistics of OECD countries 1997–1998*. 2000 edition, International Energy Agency, Paris. (http://www.iea.org)

MSR (1999). *Requirements for Environmental Product Declarations, EPD. An application of ISO TR 14025 Type III Environmental Declarations*. AB Svenska Miljöstyrningsrådet (Swedish Environmental Management Council), Stockholm, Sweden.

Tillman, Anne-Marie, Henrikke Baumann, Elin Eriksson & Tomas Rydberg (1991). *Miljön och förpackningarna. Livscykelanalyser av förpackningsmaterial.* SOU 1991:77, Statens offentliga utredningar, Allmänna Förlaget, Stockholm, Sweden. Also as *Life cycle analysis of selected packaging materials. Quantification of environmental loadings.* Translation of SOU 1991:77. Chalmers Industriteknik, Göteborg, Sweden 1992.

NTM (2002). NTM Nätverket för transporter och miljö (The Network for Transport and the Environment), www.ntm.a.se, accessed March 2002.

Sundqvist, Jan-Olof, Göran Finnveden, Håkan Stripple, Ann-Christine Albertsson, Sigbritt Karlsson, Jaak Berendson & Lars-Olof Höglund (1997). *Life Cycle Assessment and Solid Waste – Stage 2.* AFR report 173, AFN, Swedish Environmental Protection Agency, Stockholm, Sweden.

Finnveden et al. (1995). "Solid waste treatment within the framework of life-cycle assessment". *Journal of Cleaner Production*, vol 3, no 4, pp 189–199.

www.globalspine.com (2002), accessed March 2002.

Appendix 2
Characterisation indicators

Depletion of abiotic resources

Table App 2.1 Depletion equivalents for abiotic resources, expressed relative to antimony (Sb) and based on ultimate reserves (Guinée 1995; in CML 2002).

Substance	Static reserve life (years)
Aluminium (Al)	1×10^{-8} kg Sb_{eqv}/kg
Iron (Fe)	8.43×10^{-8} kg Sb_{eqv}/kg
Silicon (Si)	2.99×10^{-11} kg Sb_{eqv}/kg
Uranium	0.00287 kg Sb_{eqv}/kg
Crude oil	0.0201 kg Sb_{eqv}/kg
Natural gas	0.0187 kg Sb_{eqv}/m^3
Hard coal	0.0134 kg Sb_{eqv}/kg
Soft coal	0.00671 kg Sb_{eqv}/kg
Fossil energy	4.81×10^{-4} kg Sb_{eqv}/MJ

Land use

The equation for characterising land use resources with regard to increasing competition of land use is (CML 2002):

$$\text{Increase of land competition} = \sum_{\substack{\text{All} \\ \text{land} \\ \text{types}}} \text{area used} \times \text{occupation time} \quad (m^2 \text{ year})$$

Global warming

Table App 2.2 Global warming potentials for different time horizons expressed relative to CO_2 (IPCC 1994 & 1996; in CML 2002).

Trace Gas	GWP 20 years (kg $CO_{2\,eqv}$/kg)	GWP 100 years (kg $CO_{2\,eqv}$/kg)	GWP 500 years (kg $CO_{2\,eqv}$/kg)
CO_2	1	1	1
CH_4	56	21	6.5
1,1,1-trichloroethylene	360	110	35
CCl_4	2 000	1 400	500
N_2O	280	310	170
SF_6	16 300	23 900	34 900
CF_4	4 400	6 500	10 000
CFC-11	5 000	4 000	1 400
CFC-12	7 900	8 500	4 200
CFC-13	8 100	11 700	13 600
CFC-113	5 000	5 000	2 300
CFC-114	6 900	9 300	8 300
HCFC-22	4 300	1 700	520
HCFC-123	300	93	29
HCFC-124	1 500	480	150

Ozone depletion potential

Table App 2.3 Steady-state ozone depletion potentials expressed relative to CFC-11 (WMO 1992 & 1999; in CML 2002). Some time-dependent ODPs expressed relative to CFC-11 (Solomon & Albritton 1992; in CML 2002).

Substances	ODP_∞ (kg CFC-11/kg)	ODP 10 years (kg CFC-11/kg)	ODP 25 years (kg CFC-11/kg)
CFC-11	1	1	1
CFC-12	0.82	–	–
CFC-113	0.90	0.56	0.59
CFC-114	0.85	–	–
HCFC-22	0.034	0.17	0.13
HCFC-123	0.012	0.19	0.07
HCFC-124	0.026	0.12	0.07
Halon 1201	1.4	–	–
Halon 1202	1.25	–	–
Halon 1301	12	10.4	10.6
Halon 2401	0.25	–	–
CCl_4	1.2	1.25	1.22
1,1,1-trichloroethylene	0.11	0.75	0.38
CH_3Br	0.37	5.4	1.8
CH_3Cl	0.02	–	–

Human toxicity

Table App 2.4 Human toxicity potentials, HTP_{inf} for infinite time horizon and global scale. The indicators are expressed relative to 1,4-dichlorobenzene (Huijbregts 2000; Huijbregts et al. 2000; in CML 2002).

Substance	HTP for emissions to air	HTP for emissions to (fresh)water	HTP for emissions to (agri.) soil
As	3.5×10^5	950	3.2×10^4
Cd	1.5×10^5	23	2.0×10^4
Cr III	650	2.1	5 100
Cr VI	3.4×10^6	3.4	8 500
Co	1.7×10^4	97	2 400
Cu	4 300	1.3	94
Pb	470	12	3 300
Hg	6 000	1 400	5 900
Ni	3.5×10^4	330	2 700
V	6 200	3 200	1.9×10^4
Zn	100	0.58	64
NO_2	1.2	–	–
SO_2	0.096	–	–
HCl	0.5	–	–
PAH, carcinogenic	5.7×10^5	2.8×10^5	7.1×10^4
Dust (PM10)	0.82	–	–
Benzene	1 900	1 800	1.5×10^4
Ethylene	0.64	0.65	0.78
Toluene	0.33	0.30	0.35
Azinphosmethyl	14	2.5	39
Benomyl	0.021	0.14	0.43
Captan	0.59	0.0053	0.097
Chlorpyriphos	21	44	14
DDT	110	37	270
Deltamethrine	1.6	2.8	0.16
Diazinon	59	66	120
Dimethoate	44	18	320
Diuron	210	53	1 300
Glyphosate	0.0031	0.066	0.015
MCPA	15	15	100
Oxydemethonmethyl	120	74	610
Pirimicarb	3.4	1.7	26

Ecotoxicity

Table App 2.5 Ecotoxicity indicators for infinite time horizon and global scale for freshwater aquatic ecotoxicity (FAETP), marine aquatic ecotoxicity (MAETP) and terrestrial ecotoxicity (TETP). The indicators are expressed relative to 1,4-dichlorobenzene (Huijbregts 2000; Huijbregts et al. 2000; in CML 2002).

Substance	FAETP (kg 1,4-DCB/kg)	MAETP (kg 1,4-DCB/kg)	TETP (kg 1,4-DCB/kg)
Emissions to air			
As	50	2.3×10^5	1 600
Cd	290	1.1×10^6	81
Cr III	1.9	5 200	3 000
Cr VI	7.7	2.1×10^4	3 000
Co	640	5.4×10^6	110
Cu	220	8.9×10^5	7
Pb	2.4	7 000	16
Hg	320	1.2×10^6	2.8×10^4
Ni	630	3.8×10^6	120
V	1 700	1.2×10^7	670
Zn	18	6.7×10^4	12
PAH, carcinogenic	170	4 300	1
Benzene	8.4×10^{-5}	2.8×10^{-3}	1.6×10^{-5}
Ethylene	1.4×10^{-11}	7.9×10^{-11}	1.3×10^{-12}
Toluene	7×10^{-5}	7×10^{-4}	1.6×10^{-5}
Azinphosmethyl	420	200	0.19
Benomyl	30	21	0.47
Captan	16	10	0.024
Chlorpyriphos	520	62	0.13
Deltamethrine	1 800	3 500	0.76
DDT	320	8.6×10^4	19
Diazinon	230	120	0.29
Dimethoate	13	1.6	0.3
Diuron	530	110	8.7
Glyphosate	22	17	0.047
MCPA	1.1	0.28	0.043
Oxydemethonmethyl	2 400	500	41
Pirimicarb	2 400	410	46
Emissions to (fresh)water			
As	210	1.2×10^5	1×10^{-17}
Cd	1 500	2.2×10^5	1.4×10^{-20}
Cr III	6.9	860	2.3×10^{-19}
Cr VI	28	3 400	2.3×10^{-19}
Co	3 400	4.4×10^6	2.7×10^{-18}
Cu	1 200	2.3×10^5	4.1×10^{-21}
Pb	9.6	1 100	4.8×10^{-22}
Hg	1 700	2.1×10^5	930
Ni	3 200	2.2×10^6	1.0×10^{-18}

512

Substance	FAETP (kg 1,4-DCB/kg)	MAETP (kg 1,4-DCB/kg)	TETP (kg 1,4-DCB/kg)
V	9 000	8.6×10^6	1×10^{-17}
Zn	92	1.4×10^4	2.5×10^{-21}
PAH, carcinogenic	2.8×10^4	5.5×10^3	2.1×10^{-3}
Benzene	0.091	0.0027	1.4×10^{-5}
Ethylene	0.022	2.8×10^{-5}	1.1×10^{-12}
Toluene	0.29	0.0012	1.4×10^{-5}
Azinphosmethyl	5.2×10^4	35	3.3×10^{-6}
Benomyl	6 800	8.6	8.2×10^{-8}
Captan	2 100	0.1	6.2×10^{-8}
Chlorpyriphos	6.4×10^5	240	0.021
DDT	2.9×10^4	4 400	0.31
Deltamethrine	6.5×10^5	980	0.032
Diazinon	1.1×10^5	640	0.0041
Dimethoate	170	0.75	1.2×10^{-5}
Diuron	9 400	55	0.0017
Glyphosate	1 400	4.2	2.2×10^{-11}
MCPA	27	0.036	1.4×10^{-11}
Oxydemethonmethyl	7×10^4	140	4.6×10^{-4}
Pirimicarb	3.6×10^4	160	9.3×10^{-4}
Emissions to (agri.) soil			
As	130	7.7×10^4	3 300
Cd	780	1.1×10^5	170
Cr III	5.3	650	6 300
Cr VI	21	2 600	6 300
Co	1 700	2.2×10^6	220
Cu	590	1.2×10^5	14
Pb	6.5	750	33
Hg	850	1.7×10^5	5.6×10^4
Ni	1 700	1.2×10^6	240
V	4 700	4.5×10^6	1 400
Zn	48	7 200	25
PAH, carcinogenic	58	12	6.3
Benzene	7.2×10^{-4}	0.0024	0.0034
Ethylene	1.1×10^{-9}	7.8×10^{-11}	2.3×10^{-9}
Toluene	5.7×10^5	2.8×10^5	7.1×10^4
Azinphosmethyl	190	0.14	0.97
Benomyl	4.6	0.0058	3.5
Captan	0.40	6.9×10^{-5}	0.041
Chlorpyriphos	360	0.14	17
DDT	87	43	60
Deltamethrine	240	0.06	8.5
Diazinon	1 300	7.8	12
Dimethoate	8.9	0.039	0.8
Diuron	350	2.1	23
Glyphosate	0.92	0.0028	0.096
MCPA	0.46	6.2×10^{-4}	0.094
Oxydemethonmethyl	970	2	92
Pirimicarb	1 700	7.3	120

Photochemical ozone creation potential

Table App 2.6   Photochemical ozone creation potentials (POCPs) for high NO_x and low NO_x background concentrations expressed relative to ethylene (CML 2002 and Finnveden et al. 1992, respectively). Also Maximum Ozone Incremental Reactivities (MOIRs) (Carter et al. 1997; in CML 2002).

Substance	High NO_x POCPs (kg ethylene/kg)	Low NO_x POCPs (kg ethylene/kg)	MOIRs (kg formed ozone/kg)
CO	0.027	0.04	0.029
NO_2	0.028	–	–
NO	– 0.427	–	–
SO_2	0.048	–	–
Methane	0.006	0.007	0.007
Ethane	0.123	0.126	0.15
Propane	0.176	0.503	0.27
n-butane	0.352	0.467	0.55
n-pentane	0.395	0.298	0.65
Ethylene	1	1	2.31
Propylene	1.12	0.599	2.9
Benzene	0.218	0.402	0.17
Toluene	0.637	0.470	0.87
Methanol	0.14	0.213	0.2
Ethanol	0.399	0.225	0.66
Acetone	0.094	0.124	0.13
Formaldehyde	0.519	0.261	1.16

Acidification

Table App 2.7   Generic acidification equivalents expressed relative to SO_2 (CML/ NOH 1992; Wenzel & Hauschild 1998; in CML 2002).

Substance	AP (g $SO_{2\,eqv}$/g)
SO_2	1
HCl	0.88
HF	1.60
NO_x	0.7
NH_3	1.88

Eutrophication

Table App 2.8 Generic eutrophication equivalents for emissions to air, water and soil. Indicators are expressed relative to PO_4^{3-} (CML/NOH 1992; CML 2002).

Substance	$(g\ PO_{4\ eqv}^{3-}/g)$
PO_4^{3-}	1
H_3PO_4	0.97
P	3.06
NO_x	0.13
NO_2	0.13
NH_3	0.35
NH_4^+	0.33
NO_3^-	0.1
HNO_3	0.1
N	0.42
COD	0.022

References

Carter, WPL, D Luo & IL Makina (1997). *Environmental chamber studies for development of an updated photochemical mechanism for VOC relativity assessment.* Draft, final report to CARB, CRC, NREL, Los Angeles, Cal, USA.

CML/NOH (1992). *Environmental life cycle assessments of products. Guide and Backgrounds.* Contributing authors: R Heijungs, J Guinée, G Huppes, RM Lankreijer, HA Udo de Haes, A Wegener Sleeswijk, AMM Ansems, PG Eggels, R van Duin & HP de Goede. NOH reports 9266 and 9267. The National Reuse of Waste Programme (NOH), the Netherlands.

CML (2002). *Life cycle assessment. An operational guide to the ISO standards.* Editor: Jeroen Guinée, Centrum Milieukunde Leiden (CML), Leiden University, NL. Kluwer, Dordrecht, the Netherlands.

Finnveden, Göran, Yvonne Andersson-Sköld, Mats-Ola Samuelsson, Lars Zetterberg & Lars-Gunnar Lindfors (1992). "Classification (Impact Analysis) in Connection with Life Cycle Assessment – A Preliminary Study". In *Product Life Cycle Assessment – Principles and Methodology.* Nord 1992:2. Nordic Council of Ministers, Copenhagen, Denmark.

Guinée , Jeroen B (1995). *Development of a methodology for the environmental life-cycle assessment of products; with a case study of margarines.* PhD thesis, Leiden University, Leiden, NL.

Huijbregts, Mark (2000). *Priority assessment of toxic substances in the frame of LCA. Time horizon dependency of toxicity potentials calculated with the multi-media fate, exposure and effects model USES-LCA.* Institute for Biodiversity and Ecosystem Dynamics, University of Amsterdam, Amsterdam, the Netherlands. (Available at http://www.leidenuniv.nl/interfac/cml/lca2.)

Huijbregts, M, U Thissen, J Guinée, T Jager, D van de Meent, AMJ Ragas, A Wegener-Sleeswijk & L Reijnders (2000). "Priority assessment of toxic substances in the frame of LCA, I: Calculation of toxicity potentials for 181 substances with the nested multi-media fate, exposure and effects model USES-LCA". *Chemosphere,* vol 41, no 4, pp 541–573.

IPCC (1994). *Climate change 1992. The supplementary report to the IPCC scientific assessment.* Editors: JT Houghton, LG Meira Filho, BA Callander & SK Varney. Cambridge University Press, Cambridge, UK.

IPCC (1996). *Climate change 1995. The science of climate change.* Authors: JT Houghton, LG Meira Filho, BA Callander, N Harris, A Kattenberg & K Maskell. Cambridge University Press, Cambridge, UK.

Solomon, S & DL Albritton (1992). "Time-dependent ozone depletion potentials for short- and long-term forecast". *Nature,* vol 357, pp 33–37.

Wenzel, Henrik & Michael Hauschild (1998*). Environmental assessment of products. Volume 2: Scientific background.* Chapman & Hall, London, UK.

WMO (1992). *Scientific assessments of ozone depletion: 1991.* Global ozone research and monitoring project report 25. World Meteorological Organisation, Geneva, Switzerland.

WMO (1999). *Scientific assessments of ozone depletion: 1994.* Global ozone research and monitoring project report 37. World Meteorological Organisation, Geneva, Switzerland.

Appendix 3
Weighting indices

Weighting indices for the following LCIA methods are presented:

- Ecoindicator'99 (Goedkoop & Spriensma 1999)
- Environmental Themes (Eriksson et al. 1995)
- EPS2000 (Steen 1999)
- EDIP (Wenzel et al. 1998)

Ecoindicator'99

- Weighting based on distance-to-target principle.
- Target defined as environmental critical loads 5% ecosystem impairment, or corresponding.
- As seen from three different cultural perspectives: hierarchist, egalitarian and individualist.

Table App 3.1 Ecoindicator'99, based on Goedkoop and Spriensma (1999).

Substance	Damage category	Hierarchist weights	Egalitarian weights	Individualist weights
Resources (/kg)				
Coal (29.3 MJ/kg)		0.00599	0.0687	0
Crude oil (41 MJ/kg)		0.140	0.114	0
Natural gas (30.3 MJ/kg)		0.108	0.0909	0
Bauxite (Al ore)		0.0119	0.0168	0.667
Copper ore		9.87×10^{-3}	0.0140	0.553
Iron ore		6.90×10^{-4}	9.76×10^{-4}	0.0387
Zinc ore		1.78×10^{-3}	2.53×10^{-3}	0.10

Substance	Damage category	Hierarchist weights	Egalitarian weights	Individualist weights
Land use (/m² year or /m²)				
Industrial area	Occupation (/m² year)	0.0655	0.0819	0.0466
Industrial area	Conversion (/m²)	1.96	2.45	1.39
Forest land	Occupation (/m² year)	8.58×10^{-3}	0.0107	6.10×10^{-3}
Farm land	Occupation (/m² year)	0.0897	0.112	0.0637
Farm land	Conversion (/m²)	2.68	3.35	1.91
Road & rail area	Occupation (/m² year)	0.0655	0.0819	0.0466
Road & rail area	Conversion (/m²)	1.96	2.45	1.39
Urban area	Occupation (/m² year)	0.0897	0.112	0.0637
Urban area	Conversion (/m²)	2.69	3.37	1.91
Green urban area	Occupation (/m² year)	0.0655	0.0819	0.0466
Green urban area	Conversion (/m²)	1.96	2.45	1.39
Emissions to air (/kg)				
CO	Human health, respiratory	0	0.00579	0
CO_2	Human health, climate	0.0297	0.0222	0.0497
NH_3	Human health, respiratory	0.0902	0.673	0.938
	Ecosystem quality, acidification and eutrophication	1.21	1.52	0.863
	Sum, NH_3 to air	2.112	2.193	1.801
NO	Human health, respiratory	1.45	1.08	0.0337
	Ecosystem quality, acidification and eutrophication	0.685	0.857	0.487
	Sum, NO to air	2.135	1.937	0.5207
NO_x, NO_2	Human health, respiratory	0.941	0.705	0.0219
	Ecosystem quality, acidification and eutrophication	0.445	0.557	0.317
	Sum, NO_x to air	1.386	0.262	0.3319
N_2O	Human health, climate	0.732	0.546	1.23

Substance	Damage category	Hierarchist weights	Egalitarian weights	Individualist weights
SO_2	Human health, respiratory	0.579	0.432	0.717
	Ecosystem quality, acidification and eutrophication	0.0812	0.101	0.0577
	Sum, SO_2 to air	0.660	0.533	0.775
Azinphosmethyl	Ecosystem quality, ecotoxic (agricult.)	858	1070	1070
Benzene	Human health, carcinogenic	0.0265	0.0198	0.0291
	Human health, respiratory	0.00497	0.00371	0.0080
	Ecosystem quality, acidification and eutrophication	2.14×10^{-4}	2.64×10^{-4}	1.52×10^{-4}
	Sum, benzene to air	0.0317	0.0238	0.0373
Diuron	Ecosystem quality, ecotoxic (agricult.)	345	432	432
Ethylene	Human health, respiratory	0.0226	0.0169	0.0364
Ethene oxide	Human health, carcinogenic	1.94	1.45	0
Methane, CH_4	Human health, respiratory	1.36×10^{-4}	1.01×10^{-4}	2.19×10^{-4}
	Human health, climate	0.0467	0.0348	0.0809
	Sum, CH_4 to air	0.0468	0.0349	0.0811
Methylene chloride	Human health, carcinogenic	0	0.145	0
	Human health, respiratory	1.18×10^{-4}	8.79×10^{-5}	1.84×10^{-4}
	Human health, climate	0.0202	0.0150	0.0349
	Human health, ozone	0.224	0.167	0.313
	Sum, methylene chloride	0.2443	0.3271	0.3481

Substance	Damage category	Hierarchist weights	Egalitarian weights	Individualist weights
PAH	Human health, carcinogenic	1.80	1.35	0
	Ecosystem quality, ecotoxic	6.08×10^{-5}	7.60×10^{-5}	4.32×10^{-5}
	Sum, PAH to air	1.80	1.35	4.32×10^{-5}
Toluene	Human health, respiratory	0.0144	0.0108	0.0234
	Ecosystem quality, ecotoxic	1.87×10^{-5}	2.34×10^{-5}	1.33×10^{-5}
	Sum, toluene to air	0.01442	0.01082	0.02341
Vinyl chloride	Human health, carcinogenic	0.00222	0.00135	0.00246
VOC	Human health, respiratory	0.00685	0.00511	0.0110
NMVOC	Human health, respiratory	0.0136	0.0101	0.0219
Particulates diesel soot	Human health, carcinogenic	0.104	0.0774	0
Particulates PM10	Human health, respiratory	3.98	2.97	5.04
CFC-11	Human health, climate	30.8	23	53.3
	Human health, ozone	11.1	8.31	15.6
	Sum, CFC-11 to air	41.9	31.3	68.9
CFC-12	Human health, climate	191	142	331
	Human health, ozone	9.16	6.83	12.8
	Sum, CFC-12 to air	200.16	148.83	343.8
Metals	Human health, carcinogenic	55.2	41.2	4.05
	Ecosystem quality, ecotoxic	20.3	25.3	1.88
	Sum, metals to air	75.5	66.5	5.93

Substance	Damage category	Hierarchist weights	Egalitarian weights	Individualist weights
As	Human health, carcinogenic	261	195	18.4
	Ecosystem quality, ecotoxic	46.2	57.7	2.77
	Sum, As to air	307.2	152.7	21.17
Cd	Human health, carcinogenic	1 430	1 070	189
	Ecosystem quality, ecotoxic	752	941	147
	Sum, Cd to air	2 182	2 011	336
Hg	Ecosystem quality, ecotoxic	64.6	80.4	2.51
Ni	Human health, carcinogenic	249	186	125
	Ecosystem quality, ecotoxic	554	692	50.2
	Sum, Ni to air	803	878	175.2
Zn	Ecosystem quality, ecotoxic	225	282	36.6
Emissions to water (/kg)				
As	Human health, carcinogenic	697	520	629
	Ecosystem quality, ecotoxic	0.889	1.11	0.507
	Sum, As to water	697.9	521.1	629.5
Cd	Human health, carcinogenic	755	564	686
	Ecosystem quality, ecotoxic	37.4	46.8	21.4
	Sum, Cd to water	792.4	610.8	707.4
Hg	Ecosystem quality, ecotoxic	15.4	19.2	1.07
Ni	Human health, carcinogenic	330	246	300
	Ecosystem quality, ecotoxic	11.2	13.9	6.43
	Sum, Ni to water	341.2	259.9	306.4

Substance	Damage category	Hierarchist weights	Egalitarian weights	Individualist weights
Zn	Ecosystem quality, ecotoxic	1.27	13.9	6.43
Benzene	Human health, carcinogenic	0.0437	0.0326	0.0451
	Ecosystem quality, ecotoxic	0.00374	0.00468	0.00266
	Sum, benzene to water	0.0474	0.0373	0.0478
Ethene oxide	Human health, carcinogenic	1.47	1.10	0
PAH	Human health, carcinogenic	27.6	20.6	0
	Ecosystem quality, ecotoxic	1.64×10^{-4}	2.05×10^{-4}	1.16×10^{-4}
	Sum, PAH to water	27.3	20.6	1.16×10^{-4}
Toluene	Ecosystem quality, ecotoxic	0.0135	0.0169	0.00959
Emissions to soil (/kg)				
Azinphosmethyl	Ecosystem quality, ecotoxic (agricult.)	0.0277	0.0346	0.0346
Cd	Ecosystem quality, ecotoxic (agricult.)	2.25	2.93	0.13
2,4-D	Ecosystem quality, ecotoxic (agricult.)	9.9×10^{-5}	1.24×10^{-5}	7.04×10^{-6}
Diuron	Ecosystem quality, ecotoxic (agricult.)	0.00317	0.00397	0.00397

Environmental Themes

- Weighting based on distance-to-target principle.
- Targets defined by reduction targets in Swedish environmental public policy.

Table App 3.2 Indices with a 20–100 year perspective according to the Environmental Themes method (ET-long), based on Eriksson et al. (1995).

Parameter	ET-long	Parameter	ET-long	Parameter	ET-long
Resources (/MJ or kg)		*Halogenated organic substance*		Trihloroethylene	2.69
Electricity (/MJ)	2.45	ODP equivalent	4.88×10^3	Perchloroethylene	26.9
Oil (/kg)	5.72	CFC-11	4.92×10^3	Vinylchloride	6.38
Oil (/MJ)	1.34	CFC-12	4.96×10^3		
Coal (/kg)	4.38	CFC-113	5.27×10^3	*Persistent halog.orgamic substance*	
Coal (/MJ)	0.161	CFC-114	3.98×10^3	Chlorinated benzenes	148
Fossil gas (/kg)	41.7	CFC-115	2.52×10^3	Chlorinated phenols	9.48
Gas (/MJ)	0.804	HCFC-22	262	Dioxines	7.09×10^8
Renewable fuel	See land use	HCFC-123	98.6		
		HCFC-124	112	*Non halog. organic substance*	
Land use (/m² year)		HCFC-125	37.8	Acetone	1
Forest land	4.06	HCFC-134a	13.3	Acrolein	10.8
Road area	1.86×10^{-5}	HCFC-141b	543	Acrylonitrile	9.2
Emissions to air (/g)		HCFC-142b	337	Benzene	5.8
CO_2	0.0111	HCFC-143a	42.2	Ethene	8.07
NO_x (as NO_2)	3.95	HCFC-152a	1.67	Etheneoxide	11.5
N_2O	3	HCFC-225ca	122	Formaldehyde	4.66
SO_x (as SO_2)	2.42	HCFC-225cb	161	Isopropanol	1.64
Acids (as H^+)	77.5	Halon 1201	6.83×10^3	Isobutane	3.32
CH_4	0.289	Halon 1202	6.10×10^3	Pentane	2.42
H_xC_y (non CH_4)	3.23	Halon 1211	1.95×10^4	Phenolics	17.9
POCP equiv.	7.76	Halon 1301	7.81×10^4	PAH	1.97×10^3
CO	0.334	Halon 2311	683	Propene	4.83
HCl	2.12	Halon 2401	1.22×10^3	Propeneoxide	3.48
H_2SO_4	1.58	Halon 2402	3.41×10^4	Styrene	3.26
H_2S	4.84	CH_3Br	2.93×10^3	Toluene	3.8
NH_3	10.5	1-chloro-methane	117		
SF_6	211	Dichloro-methane	21.1		
Particulates	0.0357	Trichloro-methane	2.66		
		CCl_4	5.38×10^3		
		1,2-dichloro-ethane	27.3		
		1,1,1-trichloroethane	586		

Parameter	ET-long	Parameter	ET-long	Parameter	ET-long
Emissions to air (/g)		**Emissions to water (/g)**		**Emissions to water (/g)**	
Metals & semi metals		*Halogenated organic substances*		*Aggregated parameters*	
As	144	HCl	2.12	Halogen VOC	0.689
Cd	7.28×10^3	CCl_4	5.37×10^3	Per.halog. VOC	512
Cr	74.8	Dichloromethane	21.1	VOC non-halo-genated	2.56
Co	74.8	Trichloromethane	27.6	Non-volatile HC, non-halogenated	98.4
Cu	472	1,2 dichloro-ethane	27.3	Toxic metals	5.12×10^3
Ga	768	1,1,1 trichloro-ethane	586		
Hg	4.72×10^4	Trichloroethylene	2.66	**Emissions to soil (/g)**	
Mn	768	Vinylchloride	6.23	Persistent halog. organic substance	0.14
Ni	144	Perchloro-ethylene	26.9	Chlorinated ben-zenes	1.87×10^{-3}
Pb	57.1			Dioxines	2.95×10^5
Sb	472	*Persistent halog. organic substances*			
Zn	144	Chlorinated phenols	65	*Non-halogenated organic sub-stance*	
		Chlorinated benzenes	984		
Aggregated parameters		Dioxines	4.72×10^9	Phenolics	0.187
Halogenated VOC	0.689			PAH	0.0945
Persistent halo-gen. VOC	78.7	*Non halog. organic substances*			
VOC, non halo-genated	2.56	Acrolein	4.13	*Metals & semi metals*	
Non volatile HC, non-halogen	14.8	Acrylonitrile	2.56	As	0.63
Toxic metals	768	Benzene	2.56	Cd	17.3
		Ethene oxide	8.27	Cr	0.0906
Emissions to water (/g)		Formaldehyde	2.56	Co	0.0906
Phenol	98.4	PAH	1.34×10^4	Cu	0.965
N tot	7.18	Propeneoxide	0.256	Hg	68.9
P tot	71.8	Styrene	0.0315	Ni	0.984
BOD	0.4	Toluene	8.27×10^{-3}	Pb	0.065
COD	0.4			Sb	0.236
TOC	1.2	*Metals & semi metals*		Zn	0.236
Dissolved solids	0.0357	As	965		
		Cd	4.72×10^4	*Aggregated parameters*	
Oil	2.56	Cr	472	Persistent halog. VOC	0.0709
		Co	472	Non-volatile HC, non-halogenated	1.87×10^{-3}
		Cu	3.15×10^3	Toxic metals	1.91
		Ga	5.12×10^3		
		Hg	3.15×10^3	*Landfilled waste*	
		Mn	5.12×10^3	Ashes	0.0357
		Ni	965	Waste	0.0357
		Pb	374	Hazardous waste	2.02
		Sb	3.15×10^3		
		Zn	965		

EPS2000

Weighting based on willingness-to-pay for avoiding damages on environmental safeguard subjects. The table below presents selected EPS indices. For more indices, especially on mineral ores, CFCs and particular VOCs, see in complete list in Steen (1999).

Table App 3.3 EPS2000, from Steen (1999).

Parameter	EPS	Parameter	EPS	Parameter	EPS
Energy resources		**Emissions to air (ELU/ kg)**		**Emissions to air (ELU/kg)**	
Oil (/kg)	0.507	As	95.3	NO_x (as NO_2)	2.13
Coal (/kg)	0.0483	Benzene	3.65	PAC (PAH)	64300
Natural gas (/kg)	1.1	Butadiene	10.7	Particulates (PM10)	36.0
Renewable fuel	See land use	Cd	10.2	Pb	2910
Nuclear power	See uranium ore	CF_4	697	Propylene	2.64
		CFC-11	541	SF_6	2760
Land use		CFC-12	1040	SO_2	3.27
Arable land use	$1.56 \times 10^{-3}/m^2$ year	CH_2O	6.47	Zn	0
Hardmaking of forestland	$4.55 \times 10^{-3}/m^2$ year	CH_4	2.72	Noise (/vehicle km)	2.53×10^{-3}
Forestry	$6.25/m^3$ wood			**Emissions to water (ELU/kg)**	
Forestry	$5.5 \times 10^{-4}/m^2$ year	CO	0.331	N tot	-0.381
Littering	$13.9/m^2$	CO_2	0.108	P tot	0.055
		Cr	20.0	BOD	2.01×10^{-3}
Material resources (ELU/kg)		Cu	0	COD	1.01×10^{-3}
Crop	0.15	Ethylene	3.45	Hg	180
Wood	0.04	H_2S	6.89		
Meat/fish	1	HCFC-22	194	**Emissions to soil (ELU/kg)**	
Irrigation water	0.003	HCFC-123	12.3	Benomyl	7.13×10^{-3}
Drinking water	0.03	HCl	2.13	Captan	2.74×10^{-2}
Bauxite (Al ore)	0.449	HF	2.07	Cd	5
Cu ore	208	Hg	61.4	Chlorpyrifos	1.19
Iron ore	1.23	N_2O	38.3	Dimethoate	8.92
Phosphorous minerals	4.47	NH_3	2.90	Glyphosate	3.57×10^{-2}
		Ni	0	Hg	180
Uranium ore	1190	NMVOC average	2.14		

EDIP

EDIP indices based on Wenzel and Hauschild (1998) kindly provided by Chalmers Industriteknik (Eriksson 2000).

Table App 3.4 EDIP indices (based on Wenzel & Hauschild 1998).

Parameter	EDIP	Parameter	EDIP	Parameter	EDIP
Energy resource (/kg)		**Emissions to air (/kg)**		**Emissions to air (/kg)**	
Coal	0.00001	Ozone	1.53×10^{-5}	Ethene	0.000060
Crude oil	0.000039	Phenol	0.000426	Ethyl acetate	5.89×10^{-5}
Natural gas	0.000052	SF_6	3.72×10^{-6}	Fluoride	2.89×10^{-5}
		SO_2	1.09×10^{-5}	Formaldehyde	0.016823
Material resources (/kg)		SO_3	8.29×10^{-6}	Hexane	0.001038
Al	0.0015	VOC coal combustion	0.000030	Iso-Propanol	6.22×10^{-5}
Cu	0.016			Ketones	0.000024
Fe	0.000085	VOC diesel engines	0.000036	Methanol	1.48×10^{-5}
Mn	0.0067			n-butyl acetate	0.000456
Ni	0.11	VOC nat gas combustion	0.000012	Pentane	0.000024
Pb	0.075			Propane	0.000024
Sn	0.93			Propene	0.000060
Zn	0.036	*Halogenated organic substances*		Propylene	0.000060
		CFC-11	0.113861	Styrene	3.04×10^{-7}
Emissions to air (/kg)		CFC-113	0.088812	Toluene	0.000128
CH_4	4.16×10^{-6}	HCFC-22	0.007970	Xylenes	0.000104
Cl_2	1.03×10^{-5}	HCFC-123	0.003416		
CO	2.36×10^{-6}	HCFC-124	0.003416	*Metal & semi metals*	
CO_2	1.49×10^{-7}	HCFC-141b	0.014802	Ag	0.031255
F^-	2.89×10^{-5}	HCFC-142b	0.009109	As	0.747335
H_2S	0.002284	Halon 1211	0.557921	Cd	0.229169
HC	3.64×10^{-5}	Halon 1301	1.309406	Co	0.004053
HCl	9.23×10^{-6}	Halon 2402	0.79703	Cr, Cr^{3+}	0.009375
HCN	0.491091	CH_3Br	0.0078564	Cu	0.014040
HF	1.68×10^{-5}	CCl_4	0.129802	Fe	0.005869
N_2O	4.84×10^{-5}	CH_3CCl_3	0.017079	Hg	6.405131
NH_3	3.44×10^{-5}	Dioxines	14770.65	Mn	0.004390
NMVOC	0.000024			Mo	0.013622
NMVOC diesel engine	0.03949	*Non halogenated organic subst.*		Ni	0.001633
		Acetaldehyde	3.11×10^{-5}	Pb	0.036049
NMVOC el-coal	0.006055	Acetic acid	6.54×10^{-5}	Sb	0.0129498
NMVOC el-eur baseload	0.006668	Acetone	2.428846	Se	0.031095
		Acetylene	0.000012	Sr	0.014420
NMVOC el-nat gas	0.014644	Alcohols	0.000018	Tl	0.762224
		Aldehydes	0.000030	V	0.007410
NMVOC nat gas combust	0.000024	Alkanes	0.000024	Zn	0.00107
NMVOC oil combustion	0.000018	Alkenes	0.000054		
		Aromates (C_{9-10})	0.000048		
NMVOC petrol eng.	0.000036	Aromatics	0.000048		
		Benz(a)pyrene	0.015217		
NMVOC power plant	0.000030	Benzene	0.107297		
NO	2.22×10^{-5}	Butanol	0.001072		
NO_2, NO_x	1.54×10^{-5}	Ethane	0.000006		
		Ethanol	1.89×10^{-5}		

526

Parameter	EDIP	Parameter	EDIP	Parameter	EDIP
Emissions to water (/g)		**Emissions to water**		**Emissions to water**	
Acid as H^+	0.000335	*Halogenated organic substance*		*Metals & semi metals*	
Cl_2	1.03×10^{-5}	HCl	9.23×10^{-6}	Ag	1.42×10^{-5}
CN^-	9.58×10^{-6}	Dioxines	88452.64	As	0.022746
CO	2.53×10^{-7}			Cd	1.460948
F^-	6.31×10^{-7}	*Non halogenated organic substance*		Cr, Cr^{3+}	0.008281
H_2S	0.215934	Acetaldehyde	1.3×10^{-5}	Co	0.021898
H_2SO_4	6.81×10^{-6}	Acetic acid	0.111180	Cu	0.143225
H_3PO_4	1.03×10^{-5}	Acetone	0.016814	Fe	0.001097
HCN	0.599424	Benz(a)pyrene	0.107820	Hg	6.513465
Hexane	0.005022	Benzene	1.36×10^{-7}	Mn	0.003943
HF	1.68×10^{-5}	Ethanol	1.36×10^{-5}	Mo	0.021911
HNO_3	5.35×10^{-6}	Ethyl acetate	6.31×10^{-7}	Ni	0.007337
N_2O	6.09×10^{-7}	Fluoride	0.003914	Pb	0.035558
NH_3	3.44×10^{-5}	Formaldehyd	2.25×10^{-6}	Sb	0.016814
NH_4^+	5.12×10^{-5}	Methanol	4.77×10^{-5}	Se	0.193828
NH_4-N	6.58×10^{-5}	n-butyl acetate	0.002167	Sr	0.109486
Nitrates	4.03×10^{-6}	Styrene	0.00634	V	0.002200
NO	8.34×10^{-6}	Toluene	0.00592	Zn	0.0109499
NO_2^-	5.44×10^{-6}				
NO_2	1.28×10^{-5}				
NO_3^-	4.03×10^{-6}				
NO_3-N	1.78×10^{-5}				
NO_x	1.28×10^{-5}				
Ozone	1.53×10^{-5}				
$P_2O_7^{2-}$	4.59×10^{-5}				
Sr	0.014420				
Phenol	0.001437				
Phosphate	0.000129				
PO_4^{3-}	4.21×10^{-5}				
SO_2	1.09×10^{-5}				
Tot-N	1.78×10^{-5}				
Tot-P	0.000129				

References

Eriksson, Elin, Viveca Johanisson, Thomas Rydberg (1995). *Comparison of four valuation methods.* Chalmers Industriteknik, Göteborg, Sweden.

Eriksson, Elin (2000). EDIP indices, personal communication. Chalmers Industriteknik, Göteborg, Sweden.

Goedkoop, Mark & Renilde Spriensma (1999). *The Ecoindicator'99. A damage oriented method for Life Cycle Impact Assessment.* PRé Consultant. 17 April 2000. Amersfort. The Netherlands.

Steen, Bengt (1999). *A Systematic Approach to Environmental Priority Strategies in Product Development (EPS). Version 2000 – Models and Data of the Default Method.* Göteborg, Sweden, CPM (Centre for Environmental Assessment of Products and Material Systems) & Technical Environmental Planning, Chalmers University of Technology, Göteborg, Sweden.

Wenzel, Henrik & Mikael Hauschild (1998). *Environmental assessment of products. Volume 2: Scientific Background.* Chapman & Hall, London, UK.

Glossary

Accounting LCA Type of LCA study in which the environmental impact that can be associated with a product or service is described. Can be used in comparative LCA studies. Accounting LCA in a regulated form is used for type III eco-labelling (environmental product declarations). See also Stand-alone LCA and Change-oriented LCA.

Actual effect Environmental impact which takes into account different sensitivities to pollution in different geographical areas. See also Potential effect.

Allocation problem An allocation problem occurs when several products share the same industrial process and the environmental load of the process is to be expressed in relation to only one of the products. Allocation problems can be dealt with Allocation through partitioning and System Expansion.

Allocation through partitioning Way of dealing with an allocation problem through dividing the emissions and resource use among the different products of an industrial process. The partitioning can be made on for example weight basis, energy content or economic value of the process' products. See also System Expansion.

Background system Part of the LCA model, which consists of those processes which are not under the direct influence of the decision maker. See also Foreground system.

Change-oriented LCA Type of LCA study in which environmental consequences of alternative courses of action are compared, e.g. the existing situation is compared with a new one involving for example more recycling or new process technology. See also Accounting LCA and Stand-alone LCA.

Characterisation indicators Scientifically based indicators that are quantitative measures of environmental impact. Characterisation indicators may also be called equivalents, potentials, category indicators or characterisation factors.

Characterisation methods Scientific methods and models used for the development of characterisation indicators.

Classification Part of the life cycle impact assessment. Sorting of the inventory results according to the type of environmental impact they contribute to, e.g. global warming and acidification.

Commissioner Person or organisation initiating and paying for an LCA study.

Comparative assertion Term used in marketing applications of LCA to denote an environmental claim regarding the superiority of equivalence of a product versus a competing product. An LCA study used to make comparative assertions requires critical review.

Comparative LCA LCA study in which two or more alternative product / service systems are compared. Comparative studies may use Accounting LCA or Change-oriented LCA methodology; can be used for comparisons (see these terms); methodological choices should enable a fair comparison. See also Stand-alone LCA.

Cradle-to-grave LCA model which includes the whole product life cycle, i.e. all steps from raw material extraction to waste disposal.

Cradle-to-gate LCA model which includes upstream part of the product life cycle, i.e. all steps from raw material extraction to product at factory gate.

Critical review Process for the quality assurance of an LCA study, involves for example evaluation of the validity of the results and the transparency of the report. There are several types of critical review. See also Comparative assertion.

Cut-off criteria Criteria for simplifying the LCA model, includes possibility to leave out negligible environmental impacts and upstream production minor components.

Data collection Process of searching, collecting and documenting data in an LCA study.

Data documentation format Specifications on how to document LCI data; is described in ISO/TS 14048.

Data supplier Person or organisation that has environmental data of interest for an LCA study.

Ecobalance Old term for LCA used in Europe (Ökobilanz in Geman, Ecobilan in French and Miljöbalans in Swedish).

Environmental impact Consequences of pollution, e.g. eutrophication and depletion of stratospheric ozone.

Environmental load Emissions of pollutants, sometimes also called environmental burden or intervention.

Equivalents See Characterisation indicators.

Flowchart Visual representation of the LCA model.

Foreground system Part of the LCA model, which consists of those processes on which measures may be taken as a result of decisions based on the LCA study. See also Background system.

Functional unit The functional unit expresses the function of studied product or service in quantitative terms and serves as basis of calculations. It is the reference flow to which all other flows in the LCA model are related. It also serves as unit of comparison in comparative studies.

Goal and scope definition Phase during which the purpose of an LCA study is defined and specifications on the LCA model and procedure are determined. The goal and scope of an LCA study is usually determined by the commissioner and the practitioner in collaboration.

Interpretation Phase of an LCA study, in which the results from the inventory analysis and/or the impact assessment are evaluated in order to draw conclusions and make recommendations.

Inventory analysis Phase during which the LCA model is build according to the specifications determined in the goal and scope definition, data are collected and calculations indicating the environmental load of the product are made.

Impact assessment See Life cycle impact assessment.

Impact category Category of environmental impact, e.g. global warming, acidification and resource use.

LCA analyst See Practitioner.

LCA model The LCA model of a product or service describes the material flows from its "cradle" where raw materials are extracted from natural resources through production and use to its "grave", the disposal. See also LCA procedure.

LCA procedure The step-wise process of conducting an LCA study. The LCA procedure consists of the goal and scope definition, the inventory analysis, the impact assessment and the interpretation. It is described in ISO 14040-14043. See also LCA model.

LCI Life Cycle Inventory, LCA study that goes as far as an inventory analysis, but does not include impact assessment. See Inventory analysis.

Life cycle assessment Method for the environmental assessment of products and services, covering their life cycle from raw material extraction to waste treatment. The method includes a step-wise work description (see LCA procedure) and principles for modelling the product life cycle (see LCA model).

Life cycle impact assessment Phase of an LCA study during which the environmental impacts of the product are assessed and evaluated. The impact assessment consists of several steps, among others classification, characterisation and weighting.

Life cycle management Managerial practices and organisational arrangements in a company or a product chain that are expressions of life cycle thinking.

Life cycle model See LCA model.

Life cycle thinking A way of thinking that considers cradle-to-grave implications of different activities and products without going into the details of an LCA study.

Methodological choices Each LCA study involves a number of methodological choices, e.g. definition of functional unit, choice of system boundaries in relation to natural systems, type of data, how to deal with allocation problems, among others. Since different methodological alternatives lead to different results it is important that methodological choices are made in line with the defined goal and scope of the LCA study.

Modelling specification See Methodological choices.

Normalisation Term used both in the context of the inventory analysis and the impact assessment to indicate relation to a reference value. Normalisation in the context of the inventory analysis means to relate collected production data, which are often given on a yearly basis, to the amount of production during the same period so that the environmental loads are given relative to the amount of production. In the context of impact assessment, normalisation means that the impact of a studied product is related to the total environmental impact in a region so the relative contribution of the product can be determined.

Open loop recycling When a product is recycled into a different product, e.g. recycling of food packaging into other types of packaging and recycling of energy from waste incineration.

Potential effect Possible, usually meaning maximum environmental impact of a pollutant. See also Actual effects.

Potentials See Characterisation indicators.

Practitioner Person conducting an LCA study and in charge of the practical work (life cycle modelling, data collection, calculations, etc).

Qualitative LCA LCA study in which the environmental load and impact of a product / service are described in words, rather than calculated. See also Quantitative LCA.

Quantitative LCA LCA study in which the environmental load and impact of a product / service are described with numbers and calculated.

Red flag characterisation Qualitative impact assessment method used for indicating and evaluating environmental loads for which no characterisation indicators exist.

Resource and Environmental Profile Analysis Old term for LCA, coined by LCA consultants in the US in the early 1970s.

Stand-alone LCA Type of LCA study in which a single product or service is studied. See also Accounting LCA and Change-oriented LCA.

Simplified LCA Type of LCA, which has a simplified methodology. Simplifications are often based on experience from previous LCA studies. Sometimes calles Streamlined LCA.

System expansion Way of dealing with an allocation problem. System expansion means that surrounding industrial systems affected by changes in the studied product system are included in the LCA model. See also Allocation through partitioning.

Weighting method Method that indicate the environmental harm of pollutant or a resource relative to other pollutants and resource. Weighting methods evaluate all kinds of environmental loads or problems on a single scale and can be used to express the overall environmental impact as a single number.

Index

540